LI TA-CHAO AND THE ORIGINS

OF CHINESE MARXISM

Li Ta-chao
in the 1920's

LI TA-CHAO AND THE ORIGINS

OF CHINESE MARXISM

BY MAURICE MEISNER

originally published by Harvard University Press

ATHENEUM   New York   1977

Preparation of this volume was aided by a grant from
the Ford Foundation. The Foundation is not, however,
the author, owner, publisher or proprietor of this publication
and is not to be understood as approving by virtue of its grant
any of the statements made or views expressed therein.

Published by Atheneum
Reprinted by arrangement with Harvard University Press
Copyright © 1967 by the President and Fellows of Harvard College
All rights reserved
Library of Congress catalog card number 67-10904
ISBN *0-689-70221-3*
Manufactured in the United States of America by
The Murray Printing Company,
Forge Village, Massachusetts
Published in Canada by McClelland and Stewart Ltd.
First Atheneum Printing January 1970
Second Printing February 1973
Third Printing September 1974
Fourth Printing February 1977

To Earl Pritchard and Leopold Haimson

ACKNOWLEDGMENTS

THE RITUAL of writing an Acknowledgments page is a very inadequate means of thanking friends and teachers who have been so generous with their time and ideas. Intellectual debts cannot be discharged, and the kindness of friends cannot be returned, by perfunctory expressions of gratitude such as those that follow.

This study originated as a doctoral dissertation prepared for the Department of History at the University of Chicago. To my teachers there I am grateful for providing me with many years of intellectual stimulation as well as for indulging me with more fellowships than I deserved. I owe special debts to Professors Earl H. Pritchard and Leopold H. Haimson, to whom this book is dedicated.

The writing of the book was accomplished mainly at the East Asian Research Center of Harvard University, where I spent a year as a post-doctoral research fellow. Were it not for that excellent year, this book would never have appeared. I am profoundly grateful to Professors John K. Fairbank and Benjamin Schwartz for their patient reading and incisive criticism of various versions of the manuscript and for their many other kindnesses.

I apologize to many friends and colleagues upon whom I inflicted, at one time or another, parts or all of the manuscript. I appreciate especially the criticism and advice provided by Dr. Conrad Brandt, Mr. Edward Friedman, Professor Sylvia Glagov, Professor Stephen Hay, Mr. Winston Hsieh, Dr. Ellis Joffe, Professor Lin Yü-sheng, Professor Mark Mancall, Dr. Stuart Schram, Professor Franz Schurmann, and Professor Ezra Vogel.

I should also like to express my appreciation to the Ford Foundation, who granted me a Foreign Area Training Fellowship to undertake the research for this study, and to the Social Science Research

Council, whose grant enabled me to complete the manuscript in the summer of 1964. Thanks are also due to Professors Julian Bishko and Robert Langbaum of the Research Committee of the University of Virginia for financing the typing of the final version of the manuscript and to Mrs. Margaret Pertzoff for actually performing the task.

Throughout the preparation of this study, my wife, Dr. Lorraine Faxon Meisner, served nobly as typist, critic, and proofreader. For this, but also for other and more important things, I wish to express to her my very deepest affection.

Needless to say, neither the organizations nor individuals mentioned above are responsible for the views, interpretations, and misinterpretations that appear in the following pages. All errors of fact and judgment are my own, but there would have been many more of them were it not for those whose generous assistance is acknowledged here.

CONTENTS

CONTENTS

INTRODUCTION

THE YEAR 1927 ended the first phase of the history of the Chinese Communist movement. The tiny Communist groups that had been organized seven years before by Ch'en Tu-hsiu and Li Ta-chao from among a handful of their more devoted student followers had grown with a speed unparalleled in the history of Communist parties. In the appearance of militant labor and student organizations, in the peasant risings, and in the seething anti-imperialist crusade that marked China's great revolutionary upsurge of the mid-1920's, the Chinese Communist party was centrally involved and frequently exercised a dominant influence.

The early successes of the Chinese Communists were all the more remarkable in that they occurred in a country which lacked a Marxist Social-Democratic tradition and in which the material prerequisites for the realization of the Marxist program were almost totally absent. Although such deficiencies have since been converted into positive advantages by Chinese Communist ideologists, those of less "dialectical" persuasions may be inclined to attribute the early Communist successes, in part, to the political vacuum left by the collapse of the Ch'ing dynasty in 1911 and the chaotic years of separatist warlord rule and civil war that followed. In part, the early triumphs of the Chinese Communists in what was then called the "national revolution" were dependent upon the same tactical factor that soon led to their near destruction — the Comintern-sponsored alliance with the Kuomintang. The united front with the party of Sun Yat-sen helped to provide the Communists with access to the popular movement, but the military power of the alliance remained firmly in the hands of the Nationalists. In the spring of 1927 Chiang Kai-shek chose to exercise that power against his Communist allies. On April 12 in Shanghai Chiang abruptly shattered the united front and began the bloody reign of terror that destroyed the Communist and labor movements in the major urban centers of China and very nearly extinguished the party itself.

Six days before Chiang Kai-shek struck in Shanghai, a grim prelude to the disasters that were to befall the Chinese Communist party began in Peking, then under the control of warlord forces hostile to both the Communists and the Nationalists. On April 6, Li Ta-chao, the leader of the party in North China, was arrested in the Soviet embassy compound in Peking by soldiers of the Manchurian warlord Chang Tso-lin. Three weeks later, still in his thirty-ninth year, Li was secretly executed by strangulation.

Li is now honored by the Chinese Communist party as its first true leader and its greatest martyr. He is not the Lenin of China, for that honor is reserved for Mao Tse-tung. But Li represents the link between the older generation of democratically oriented and Western-educated intellectuals of the early phase of the New Culture movement (ca. 1915–1919), from whom the first Chinese Marxists emerged, and the new generation of young Communist intellectuals who inherited party leadership after 1927. In the unbroken chain of continuity that the Chinese Communists are attempting to forge with the Chinese past, Li is the link just preceding Mao Tse-tung.

A professor of history and the chief librarian at Peking University, Li Ta-chao was the first important Chinese intellectual to declare his support for the Russian October Revolution. He is also known as one of the two principal founders of the Chinese Communist party and a leading architect of the ill-fated Communist alliance with the Kuomintang. Yet Li was perhaps less important as a Communist political leader than as a Chinese interpreter of Marxist theory. He was the first to undertake the task of adapting Marxism to the Chinese environment. He not only introduced Marxist-Leninist ideas but was the harbinger of changes that were to come, for his writings foreshadowed the most explosive revolutionary ideology of our time — the combination of a voluntaristic interpretation of Marxism and a militant nationalism. Li's interpretation of Marxist doctrine profoundly influenced both the thought and the actions of a whole generation of future Chinese Communist leaders. Not the least of these was his young assistant at the Peking University Library in the crucial winter months of 1918–1919, Mao Tse-tung.

This book is in part a study of the intellectual evolution of China's first Marxist, Li Ta-chao. It is also a study of the early reception and transformation of Marxist ideas in China. The chapters which follow are concerned with Marxist theory as a philosophic world view, as an interpretation of history and social change, and as a theory of revolution. Although some attention is paid to the manner in which Li Ta-chao's interpretation of Marxist doctrine was reflected in his political practice, no attempt is made to investigate in any detail the fluctuating "party line" and the polemical writings that were linked directly with the political strategy and internal disputes of the Chinese Communist party in the 1920's. The study begins with the assumption that Marxist theory qua theory has been (and still is) an historical force in its own right which has molded as well as reflected Chinese reality. It is further assumed that the various political strategies employed by the Chinese Communist party were at least partially the product of the way in which Chinese Communist leaders understood and interpreted the inherited body of Marxist ideas.

Some justification of this approach should be given since the validity of studying the Chinese Communist movement from the point of view of its Marxist ideas has frequently been brought into question. For orthodox Marxists, or for those whose view of Marxism is orthodox, the significance of the changes that Marxist doctrine has undergone in the Chinese environment has seemed to lie in the distortions and deformities that have been inflicted upon the original theory; from this perspective it has been argued that there has never been a serious Marxist tradition in China worth considering. Others have treated Chinese Marxist ideology as no more than an elaborate rationalization designed to justify the power interests of a new ruling group. It has also been asserted that the history of Chinese Communism is a history of the triumph of pragmatic methods of organization and strategy over ideology, and that the inherited body of Marxist theory was thus largely irrelevant in the Chinese situation.

Yet these and similar assertions, all of which would tend to deny that the study of the Chinese Communist movement is the proper concern of the intellectual historian, ignore the truism that men make history and that men act, at least partially, on the basis of what they think. In the infinitely complex interrelationships between the consciousness of men and the historic situations in which they live, the study of ideas is one of several ways to approach historical experience as a whole. This proposition is no less valid for the history of China than elsewhere. Unless one chooses to believe that the modern history of China was predestined, Marxist theory must be granted an important role in setting the goals and conditioning the responses of men to objective situations that permitted a variety of subjective choices.

In the confrontation of Marxist theory with the Chinese environment, three general areas of interrelationship are evident. In each area Marxist theory merged imperceptibly into the historic situation, and the sharp distinction between theory and "objective" reality tended to break down. First, both the explicit and the implicit changes in Marxist doctrine can be seen as reflections of the Chinese historic situation of the 1920's and after. However, these changes were never reflections of objective Chinese reality; they were reflections of the images of reality held by Chinese Communists — images that were themselves conditioned by Marxist categories of thought.

Second, Chinese Marxism can be understood as an attempt to rationalize Communist political practice, to obscure historical realities, and to conceal the implications of Chinese Communist practice for Marxist theory. Yet ideologies are not necessarily conscious deceptions. Myths are often taken for truths, which are converted into norms and profoundly influence thought and action.

Finally, Marxism in China can be seen as a form of utopian mentality — a radically new interpretation of history and society and a vision of the future — which has tended to transcend and transform the existing historic situation. This new body of ideas has served as a spur to political action to change China in accordance with Marxist ideals. In the process the ideas and goals have themselves been conditioned by a variety of pre-existing cultural and intellectual factors, as well as by the practical possibilities for revolutionary action. Just as the influence of Marxism changed the Chinese intellectual's goals and his image of Chinese reality, so the impact of that reality modified the content of the doctrines he employed and the ends to which they were put.

The history of Marxist theory in China must be studied not only in terms of the complex interaction between the Chinese historic situation and the inherited body of Marxist ideas but in terms of the individual Marxist and his particular intellectual and emotional predispositions. The early Chinese Marxists were not formed in the same mold. They came to Communism for different reasons and by different roads, and their interpretations of Marxism were influenced profoundly by their differing pre-Marxian intellectual experiences and orientations. When they looked at the Chinese situation through the prism of the same doctrine, they saw different pictures.

The pages that follow are concerned only with the way in which one Chinese Communist received, interpreted, and applied Marxist theory. But the problems that Li Ta-chao dealt with were confronted by all the members of the early Chinese Marxist intelligentsia. Those problems, and Li Ta-chao's response to them, are especially relevant to the manner in which Marxist theory has been treated by Li's one-time assistant librarian, Mao Tse-tung.

Maurice Meisner

Center for Advanced Study in the Behavioral Sciences
Stanford, California
September 1966

CHRONOLOGY

1888   October 6: Birth of Li Ta-chao in a village in Hopei.

1905   Li enters Yung-p'ing prefectural middle school.

1907–   Li becomes a student at the Peiyang College of Law and Political
1913   Science in Tientsin.

1911–   Revolution of 1911 overthrows Ch'ing dynasty and establishes Chi-
1912   nese republic.

1913   March: Assassination of Sung Chiao-jen and usurpation of power
        by Yüan Shih-k'ai. Summer: Li edits the newspaper *Fa-yen pao* in
        Peking. Autumn: Li leaves China to study at Waseda University
        in Tokyo.

1915   Ch'en Tu-hsiu founds the periodical *Hsin ch'ing-nien* (New
        youth); beginning of the New Culture movement.

1916   April: Li returns to China and becomes associated with T'ang Hua-
        lung and the Chinputang (Progressive party) in Shanghai. June:
        Death of Yüan Shih-k'ai. Summer: Li appointed editor of Chinpu-
        tang newspaper *Ch'en-chung pao* in Peking. September: Publication
        of Li's essay "Spring" in *Hsin ch'ing-nien*. October: Li breaks with
        T'ang Hua-lung and the Chinputang.

1917   January: Li appointed editor of the liberal newspaper *Chia-yin
        jih-k'an* in Peking. June: Li flees to Shanghai; becomes associated
        with the New Youth group.

1918   January: Li appointed to editorial board of *Hsin ch'ing-nien*.
        February: Li appointed chief librarian of Peking University. July:
        Li is first important Chinese intellectual to announce his support
        for the Russian October Revolution. September: Mao Tse-tung be-
        comes Li's assistant at the Peking University Library; Li organizes
        the Marxist Research Society. November: Publication of Li's article
        "The Victory of Bolshevism" in *Hsin ch'ing-nien*.

1919   February: Li calls upon young Chinese intellectuals to "go to the
        villages." May: Publication of Li's "My Marxist Views"; beginning
        of May Fourth movement. Summer: "Problems and Isms" contro-
        versy (Li Ta-chao versus Hu Shih); beginning of breakup of the
        New Youth group. Li begins a reinterpretation of Marxist theory.

1920   Ch'en Tu-hsiu's conversion to Marxism and Communism. March:
        Li organizes Peking Society for the Study of Marxist Theory;
        Comintern agent Voitinsky arrives in Peking. May–December: Or-
        ganization of local Communist groups in various cities in China.

1921   Debate on "industrialization and socialism" between Marxists and
        non-Marxian socialists. July: First Congress of Chinese Communist
        party held at Shanghai; official establishment of the CCP on a
        national basis.

1922   August: Li attends special plenary session of CCP central committee
        at Hangchow; Comintern representative Maring proposes CCP al-

liance with Kuomintang. Autumn: Li is first Communist to join Kuomintang.

1923   February 7: Suppression of Peking-Hankow railroad worker's strike destroys main proletarian base of CCP in North China. June: Third Congress of Chinese Communist party meets at Canton and officially approves alliance with Kuomintang, of which Li Ta-chao is principal Communist advocate.

1924   January: Li selected by Sun Yat-sen as the only Communist on the five-man presidium at the First National Congress of Kuomintang in Canton. June: Li goes to Moscow as head of the Chinese delegation to the Fifth Comintern Congress and remains six months.

1925   January: Sun Yat-sen discusses the unification of China with the Peking government. March: Death of Sun Yat-sen in Peking. December: Rise of the right-wing "Western Hills" faction of the Kuomintang in Peking; de facto collapse of the Kuomintang-Communist alliance in North China; appearance of first part of Li's article "Land and the Peasants," signifying revival of his interest in the revolutionary potentialities of the peasantry.

1926   January: Feng Yü-hsiang forced to retire from Peking; government under Tuan Ch'i-jui becomes increasingly anti-Communist. March: The March Eighteenth Massacre; suppression of Communist and left-wing Kuomintang organizations in Peking; Li takes sanctuary in the Soviet embassy in Peking. Summer: Publication of Li's article on the Red Spear Societies advocating armed peasant revolt.

1927   April 6: Li arrested by troops of the warlord Chang Tso-lin in raid on Soviet embassy. April 12: Chiang K'ai-shek launches anti-Communist campaign in Shanghai. April 28: Li Ta-chao executed in Peking.

PART ONE

THE ORIGINS OF A CHINESE MARXIST

CHAPTER I THE EARLY YEARS

THE PROVINCE of Hopei in Northeast China is one of the oldest centers of Chinese civilization — an area rich in historical tradition. During the fourth and fifth centuries B. C. the state of Yen, one of the seven contestants in the famous "Era of the Warring States," had its capital at the site of present-day Peking and covered roughly the area of modern Hopei. It was in the northeastern part of the former state of Yen, in the plains near the Yellow Sea, that Li Ta-chao was born on October 6, 1888.

During Li's youth the traditional Chinese order was in an advanced stage of disintegration. The moribund Ch'ing dynasty, beaten into submission by the imperialist powers, was lingering ingloriously into its final two decades. New economic forces from abroad were undermining the old rural economic structure and intensifying the crisis of the traditional economy while preventing the employment of traditional methods for its solution. In the late 1890's reformers and then revolutionaries began preparing the final assaults that would soon bring about the complete collapse of the old order. With the end of the Manchu emperors went a more than two-thousand-year-old bureaucratic system, which left a vacuum of power and ideology that only the Communists proved capable of filling.

Even conservative Hopei province, the last stronghold of the archaic Ch'ing court, could not escape the onrush of the new forces. In 1878 the T'ang-shan coal mines in eastern Hopei became the first in China to introduce Western mining techniques. From the treaty port of Tientsin the influences of Western commerce, religion, and education radiated to the countryside. Especially after the suppression of the Boxer Rebellion in 1900 the Western "new learning" became increasingly popular in the schools of Hopei province.

Yet the ancient traditions persisted. The Chinese environment was still permeated by the Confucian belief that there were eternal human values, which were to be found in the corpus of classical literature and in the records of Chinese history. Young Li Ta-chao was influenced profoundly by the Chinese historical tradition and especially by the romantic tales of the legendary heroes of the Era of the Warring States. In his writings appear many allusions to the history of this turbulent age. Several of his early essays were written in the style of Ch'ü Yüan's *Li Sao* (The lament), the famous poem of the third century b. c. in which the ill-fated statesman passionately revealed his deep sorrow over the fate of his land and his profound loyalty to the prince who had exiled him.[1] The Confucian concepts of loyalty and public service, as symbolized in the heroic figure of Ch'ü Yüan, nurtured in Li a highly romantic temperament, a fierce Chinese patriotism, and a burning desire to serve his country and people. Li's later life illustrated how easily elements of this Chinese historical tradition could be used for radical and antitraditionalist ends.

Li Ta-chao was born in the village of Ta-hei-t'o in Lo-ting county. His father, a young farmer only nineteen years old when Li was born, died before his only child had reached his second birthday. A few months later Li Ta-chao's mother died.[2] More than two decades later, in a composition entitled "My Autobiography" prepared for an English language class in Tokyo, Li wrote, in imperfect English, of the tragic events of his childhood: "When I was just two years old my father died and next year my mother died also, leaving a baby who needed her very sadly, as I was without a brother and sister. Then I lived with my grandfather and grandmother and they left me lonely in the world until [when?] I was fifteen years old. How poor I was."[3]

Despite the tragic tones of this recollection, the orphaned child appears to have been well treated by his grandparents, and his grandfather provided as best he could for his education. The experience of living with an elderly and apparently indulgent guardian undoubtedly contributed much to the formation of Li Ta-chao's personality. In China, as in many other societies, the relationship of a grandparent to a grandchild is often particularly close and warm.

This is especially true in situations where parental authority is absent.[4] One may suppose that there were affectionate ties between the young Li and his grandparents, and that these ties were at least partly responsible both for the sympathy that Li later showed for older people and their traditions and for his generally warm and open temperament. In his adult years he was known by his fellow intellectuals as "a friend of everyone" and was regarded as a benevolent and fatherly adviser by his student followers at Peking University.[5] Even as a Communist, Li maintained close personal relationships with many non-Communist intellectuals, avoided personal disputes, and within the party played the role of a conciliator rather than an authoritarian leader. However one may interpret the influences of Li's early upbringing on the development of his personality, it seems clear that the sources of Li's political radicalism must be sought in factors other than those suggested by the peculiarly simplistic theory that men become revolutionaries because they are in revolt against parental authority.

Li Ta-chao's early years were spent in a village though not in a wholly peasant environment. Like Mao Tse-tung, Li came from China's rural middle classes. His grandfather had in his younger days been engaged in commerce. With the capital he had managed to accumulate in trade he purchased land and became a small village landlord.[6] Since there were few for whom he had to provide, the grandfather was able to promote the education of his young ward. At the age of four Li began to attend a private village school, where he embarked upon the study of the Four Books, the Five Classics, and the traditional histories. In 1904 Li's grandfather died, but he left a portion of his modest estate to provide for his grandson's further education. The following year the sixteen-year old Li left his village home and enrolled in a prefectural middle school, where the traditional pattern of learning was combined with Western studies. In his English composition "My Autobiography" Li noted: "Next year [1905] I went to Yung Ping Fu to study the primer sciences in the middle school. It was the beginning of my English lesson and I spent two years time there."[7]

Li Ta-chao's private life, like his education, was cast in a traditional mold. When Li was eleven years old, his grandfather, in accordance with village custom, married him to a young girl with bound feet, named Ch'ao Chi-lan, the daughter of a neighboring peasant.[8] Unlike most of the arranged marriages among the future members of the Western-educated intelligentsia — marriages that sometimes ended in divorce or more often in desertion — Li grew devoted to Chi-lan, who bore him six children.[9] It was characteristic of Li to adapt himself to the traditional way of things unless the most compelling reasons dictated otherwise.

Despite the traditional pattern of Li Ta-chao's early life, it was no longer possible in the last decade of the nineteenth century to be educated in Confucian values without being aware of the challenge to those values posed by the intrusion of outside forces. During the period that young Li was being trained in the ancient classics, the battered Chinese Empire suffered its greatest humiliation — the disastrous defeat of 1895 at the hands of a modernized Japanese army. This shock was followed by the near partition of China among the foreign powers, by the abortive reform movement of Western-influenced politicians in 1898, and by the Boxer Rebellion of 1899–1900, bringing the intervention of foreign armies to suppress the Boxers. By the end of the nineteenth century the pressures had become too great to ignore. Even a young boy being trained in the belief that "the ways of Heaven do not change" could hardly fail to notice that the "ways of Heaven" were indeed profoundly altered.

Because of the dramatic events of these formative years, Li's response to the Confucian value system was of a different character from that of the intellectuals of the previous generation. Those who were born before the 1880's and who reached maturity before the disasters of 1895 and afterward, were still, as youths, largely insulated from the direct impact of the foreign impingement while they were being trained in the Confucian classics and being innoculated with the old aspirations for official careers. Only after they had reached maturity did many of them become fully aware of the challenge posed to the traditional order. Whether their response was to defend doggedly the tradition against the menace from abroad, to attempt to reconcile traditional values with "Western learning," or to advocate all-out Westernization, they all remained preoccupied with the fate of traditional values and institutions. Even the future Marxist Ch'en Tu-hsiu, who was born in 1879 — nine years before Li Ta-chao — was continually concerned with the role of traditional ethics and ideas in modern Chinese life. Ch'en's response was entirely negative. He looked upon the persistence of old ideas and

4

habits as the main obstacle to the reformation of Chinese society and to the survival of the Chinese nation. Yet the very intensity of his assault on traditional values and his strident calls for Westernization reflected the influence that those values once exerted on him.

For Li the confrontation between the traditional world view and the modern West did not appear in so sharp a form because the events of 1895 and after had made that confrontation apparent before he could become so deeply immersed in the traditional culture. Because his original attachment to traditional values was not as deep-rooted, his reaction against them was not as severe. Li's intellectual development was indeed influenced by traditional modes of thought and language, but they never became a burden upon him. He was concerned but never obsessed with the question of the relevance of the Chinese tradition to the modern world, and thus he felt relatively free to dissect the tradition, to accept or reject its various parts, and to use what he accepted as he saw fit.

Nor could Li have ever seriously aspired to an official career. In 1905, the very year that Li entered the middle school in Yung-p'ing-fu, the Empress Dowager abolished the antiquated civil service examination system, without providing for any other regular means of bureaucratic recruitment. It was no longer possible for Chinese students to study the Confucian canon with the expectation that such studies might lead to an official career. This development accelerated the formation of a new, nontechnical intelligentsia that was politically oriented like the older scholar class but, unlike its predecessor, alienated from the existing organs of political power. Whereas the members of the earlier generation had usually looked upon attendance at a school of Western learning as a painful alternative to a traditional education and an official career, Li must have considered the acquisition of a Western education as the preferred alternative.

One event of Li's youth that influenced his intellectual development in a quite different way was the Boxer Rebellion, which originated in neighboring Shantung province and reached its climax in his native province of Hopei. The mass antiforeignism that the Boxer movement reflected, and the even stronger antiforeign sentiments that were aroused when the Boxers were suppressed with the intervention of foreign armies, did not escape the attention of young Li. Powerful antiforeign strains appeared prominently in his early

5

essays and never disappeared completely from his world view. Unlike his future Communist colleague Ch'en Tu-hsiu, who saw in the Boxers only the most backward and reactionary elements in the Chinese environment,[10] Li later interpreted the Boxer Rebellion as one of the glorious chapters in the history of the Chinese people's struggle against imperialism.

In 1907 after two years in middle school Li determined to use what remained of the money left him by his grandfather to pursue Western studies in the treaty port of Tientsin. Rejecting the possibilities of entering military, medical, or banking schools, Li took examinations for the Peiyang College of Law and Political Science (Pei-yang fa-cheng chuan-men hsüeh-hsiao), a school modeled on modern Japanese educational methods. It is said that his wife, who remained in her village home while Li pursued his education, encouraged him in his plans to go to Tientsin.[11]

Li spent the six years from 1907 to 1913 in Tientsin. He majored in political economy and studied Japanese and English. By choosing not to pursue a technical or scientific education, he deliberately cut himself off from the professional opportunities afforded by the newly developing economic forces. Instead, he cast his lot with the emerging group of young intellectuals who rejected practical professional pursuits and who, like their Confucian predecessors, were predisposed to public life and service.

While Li was studying in Tientsin, there occurred the stirring events of 1911–12 that finally destroyed the traditional monarchy. Li was profoundly inspired by the hope for a new and powerful China that the republic promised. This hope soon turned to despair, however, as the republican constitution was perverted by the tyranny and chaos of warlordism.

After the fall of the Ch'ing dynasty the problem facing young intellectuals concerned with the fate of China was no longer the old dilemma of whether the interests of the state could be reconciled with the preservation of Confucian values, for one could no longer seriously seek a solution for China's problems within the framework of the traditional value system. It soon became equally clear that one could no longer offer one's loyalties to the Chinese state, for in the confusion of warlordism responsible political authority had virtually ceased to exist. The first need was to create out of the chaos left by the Manchus a new social and political order that would be worthy of loyalty and service. Whereas many leading intellectuals of Li's generation felt that the first task in building a new order was the introduction of new social and cultural values, Li's instincts were basically political. He was committed to the ideal that the duty of the intellectual is to serve his country and people, and he could conceive of no other way of doing so except through political activity.

Li not only committed himself to political participation at an early point in his intellectual development, but also clearly thought of living for politics rather than off of it. For Li politics was a passion rather than a career. Throughout his life his major concern was the salvation of China, and his image of his own role in political life was one of national service and individual sacrifice. The ideal of service was romantically associated in Li's mind with the heroes of the Chinese past, particularly Ch'ü Yüan, whom Li often contrasted with his contemporaries who "hanker after wealth and power." In his famous essay "Spring," written early in 1916,[12] Li described "seekers after profit and position" as "ants grubbing for grease or moths fluttering around a flame; they devote most of their lives to the search for these things. Straining forward under the incubus of wealth and power, they are bound to stagger and fall. The greater their wealth and power, the less able they are to retain their youth." [13] In 1919, shortly after he had announced his conversion to Communism, Li once more defined the goals of political participation in tones that invoked the heroic image of the martyr Ch'ü Yüan: "The aim of human life is to develop one's own life, but there are times when the development of life necessitates the sacrifices of life. This is because there are times when ardent sacrifice can extend the beauty of life further than normal development . . . Tragic melodies usually make the most exciting music. The life of superior attainment always lies in ardent sacrifice." [14]

In the years 1912–13 Li's political interests drew him into journalistic activities. He took a leading part in the organization of the Peiyang Legal and Political Study Society, an organization of students in Tientsin whose purpose was to investigate political and social problems. Yü I, Li's close friend during his years in Tientsin, wrote of Li that when the members of the organization proposed the creation of Yen-chih tsa-chih (Statesman magazine) "in order to express the ideas that have accumulated in us over the years, you [Li] rose up from among the group to plan and manage this magazine with me." Through *Yen-chih tsa-chih* Li first began to make his mark upon the new intellectual and political scene. Several of his articles were reprinted in popular newspapers and journals early in 1913. In the summer of that year, following his graduation from the Peiyang school, he went to Peking to edit the newspaper *Fa-yen pao*.[15] In addition to his journalistic ventures, Li was engaged in translating Japanese books and articles during his last two years in Tientsin. These included a long treatise on Chinese international law and an interpretation of the principles of Tolstoy,[16] whose writings influenced Li's early intellectual development.

Li's political ideas during the first years of the republic consisted of a rather uncertain mixture of Confucian moral precepts and Western liberal constitutional theory. He expressed a faith in the efficacy of good rulers and a belief that China needed a political system that would express the "will of the people." Like many other Chinese intellectuals of the early republican era, Li was totally unprepared for the realities of political power. The monarchy was gone, but he had only the dimmest idea of how the new China was to be reorganized politically. While in Tientsin, Li read widely in nineteenth-century European constitutional and democratic theory. He spoke vaguely of the sovereignty of the people and the desirability of representative government. He debated the question of whether China should have a unicameral or bicameral legislature,[17] and he deplored the fact that the bureaucratic patterns of the Ch'ing had carried over into the republic.[18] But he had few firm ideas about what the new order in China should look like, and even less to offer in the way of specific proposals to bring it about. In 1913 he could say little more than that political party activity should be based upon the principle of "making our country stronger and the people prosperous." In many respects his political thought was still tied to the traditional concept that a good social order consisted of prosperous peasants and virtuous rulers: "The basis of wealth and strength lies in the support of the peasants, the conduct of commerce, and the granting of benefits to the workers. What is produced by the peasants is completed by the workers and circulated by the traders . . . If we had a good government, then in less than ten years there would be abundance."[19]

The advocacy of "wealth and strength" or *fu-ch'iang*, which appeared frequently in Li's essays of this period, was a common theme in the writings of Chinese reformers of the late nineteenth and early twentieth centuries. The term *fu-ch'iang* was traditionally used by those who were primarily concerned with the necessity of strengthening the power of the state. Li was also very much concerned with the strength of the Chinese nation and its ability to withstand the onslaught of the "evil foreigners." However, he expressed equal concern for the welfare of the people, which he did not identify solely with the interests of the state. Li expressed the idea of *fu-ch'iang* in an almost Populist context, in which "the people" were conceived as a single, indivisible entity and the state as a continual threat to the "natural" social life of the people. His essay "The Great Grief," written early in 1913, was subtitled "Grief for that which has been lost by the people." What had been lost was their "natural freedom of social relationships" (*t'ien-chih tzu-yu*), which had been usurped by "those who rule the state." This usurpation, Li argued, was a millenial process that began with the Ch'in dynasty in the third century B. C., was intensified under the "dictatorship of foreign tribes" (i.e., the Manchus), and was further aggravated by the tyranny of the provincial viceroys and local warlords who seized power after 1911.[20]

This argument was no doubt partly inspired by the orthodox Confucian view that the state should not interfere with the productive activities of the people. Li was not interested, however, in the resurrection of the traditional Confucian order, and this particular traditional conception led him to very nontraditional ideas — first to the notion of popular sovereignty as a means of protecting the people from the state, and then to a full-blown Populist strain.

The year 1913 inaugurated a half-decade of deep disappointment and profound pessimism among the members of China's newly emerging Westernized intelligentsia. During this period they withdrew from or refused to enter public life, often went abroad as students or exiles, and devoted themselves to study and writing. The fragile structure of the republic, born with such high hopes the year before, had collapsed within a matter of months, and free rein was given to what Ch'en Tu-hsiu later described as China's "three evils" — politicians, bureaucrats, and warlords. Among the latter, the most ominous was Yüan Shih-k'ai, who had replaced Sun Yat-sen as president of the republic in March 1912. A year later, on March 20, 1913, Yüan's henchmen assassinated Sung Chiao-jen, a leader of the newly organized Kuomintang. By the summer of 1913 the increasingly dictatorial and terroristic character of the Yüan regime provoked Sun himself into an abortive revolt and subsequent exile.

The spectacle of the cynicism and corruption that characterized Chinese political life under the Yüan regime filled Li with such despair that he expressed the fear that "our country will be destroyed and our people will not produce another generation." [21] The Revolution of 1911, he wrote, had been the work of martyrs who died for their country in order to "achieve good and save the people":

If one asks why they struggled and sacrificed their lives, it can be said that it was for the benefit of the people and to obtain the blessings of a republic. Our people appreciate the righteousness of these martyrs and their deeds are deeply imbedded in our hearts. We understand the virtuousness of their wills . . . But arrogant and evil rascals have taken the flesh and blood of the martyrs to adorn their faces . . . and they dare to say to the people that 'we strongly support you people who are creating the benefits of the republic.' Alas! Our martyrs are dead and the rascals are boasting . . . The republic is the republic, yet how can it be said that blessings have come to the people? [22]

Not only had the republic failed to mitigate the evils of the old system, but it seemed to have intensified these evils:

Before the revolution [our people] owed their loyalty to a single dictatorial monarch; now, after the revolution, they owe their loyalty to dozens of dictatorial viceroys . . . The former excessive authority of the single dictatorial monarch, whose power was spread throughout the various provinces, did not equal that of today's viceroy and therefore the suffering of the people was comparatively light. Today the excessive authority of a single dictatorial viceroy is double that of the former monarchs, their power is concentrated in one province, and thus the suffering of the people is even heavier than before.[23]

Although Li held resolutely to the belief that China could be saved through the political participation of dedicated men willing to serve their country unselfishly, his search for firm political loyalties was beset with endless frustrations. He was torn by the conflict between the need for a strong government to bring order out of the chaos in the republic and the fear that a strong state would suppress the "natural freedom" of the people. The need for order prompted Li to support the government of Yüan Shih-k'ai during the first year of his presidency. The Peiyang Legal and Political Study Society was, in fact, closely associated with Yüan. It received the financial support of the government and served as a political training ground for young intellectuals who later joined the entourages of Yüan and other northern warlords.[24] Although Li did not follow this particular bureaucratic path, he later indirectly acknowledged his early support for Yüan when he wrote Yüan "rose to power when he followed the peoples will and was destroyed when he betrayed the peoples will." [25] It is not exactly clear when Li came to the conclusion that Yüan was betraying the will of the people, but the assassination of Sung Chiao-jen seems to have finally destroyed whatever hopes he had in the existing regime.

Li's early support for Yüan Shih-k'ai did not seem to him inconsistent with a sympathy for the principles of Sun Yat-sen. Although it is highly unlikely that at the time of the Revolution of 1911 Li was a member of Sun's revolutionary organization, the T'ung-meng hui (Alliance society), as some Communist accounts have claimed,[26] his earliest writings of 1912 and 1913 suggest that he admired Sun and particularly Sun's close associate Sung Chiao-jen. His early essays stressed the need for *min-sheng* or "peoples livelihood," a traditional term that Sun had appropriated for one of his "Three Principles of the People." Li wrote of the evils wrought by the departed Manchu rulers in the same racialistic tones that characterized Sun's writings. The assassination of Sung Chiao-jen inspired a bitter essay in which Li passionately mourned Sung's death. He described Sung as one of the "most virtuous and heroic men of our age" and attributed his death not simply to the hand of the assassin but to the moral corruption of Chinese society.[27]

Li's admiration for Sun Yat-sen and Sung Chiao-jen in 1912–13 did not extend to the Kuomintang as a whole, however. A major theme in his writings of these early years was the accusation that the political factionalism and opportunism of "party politicians" was responsible for the disorderly and corrupt character of Chinese life under the republic. Most prominent among "party politicians" were the members of the Kuomintang, many of whom had compromised with, and some of whom had been corrupted by, the increasingly repressive regime of Yüan Shih-k'ai.

Li's antipathy to "party politicians" and his disillusionment with the republic under Yüan did not draw him to the most radical Chinese political current of this period — the anarchist movement. He clearly made known his opposition to both the methods and the philosophy of anarchism in two essays written in the spring and summer of 1913. In "Assassination and Social Morality" Li dealt with the question of terrorism. His basic argument against the anarchists (at least those who advocated terrorism) was that assassination was justified as a weapon against tyrants only when the level of social morality was high, such as he assumed it had been during the Era of the Warring States or even during the years when Chinese patriots were struggling to throw off the Manchu yoke. But when social morality disintegrated, terrorism became a purely destructive, unprincipled, and irrational phenomenon. "Since the Celestial Empire has regained independence," Li repeatedly emphasized, "the decline of our public morality has been [as rapid as] the descent of a river into the sea." Terrorism then expressed the worst aspects of Chinese society and inspired the most evil instincts of men; the former revolutionary terrorist heroes had become murderers. "How could it have been known," Li cried, "that the very people who earlier tried to destroy the enemies of the people would now be killing our patriots, that those who formerly brought merit to the republic would now be the scourge of the republic?" [28]

Li's basic antipathy to the anarchist point of view became further evident in his "Essay on Right and Wrong." There he took a rather conservative, almost Confucian, approach to the problem of freedom and order. He argued that the post-1911 reaction against the restraints imposed by the Manchu regime had gone to extremes. As a result, standards of right and wrong had become confused, and a multitude of political factions had arisen to engage in a partisan struggle that threatened the nation with fragmentation. "I am saddened," Li wrote, "that from the bloody waves of the revolution there have hardly come forth even a few men who are capable of managing the affairs of the nation . . . amidst the disorders of China there is not even one perfect man [*wan jen*]." [29]

These views point to the second of the two contradictory strands that marked Li's approach to the problem of political authority. On the one hand, he tended to view with suspicion the intrusion of political power upon the "natural" condition of man's social life. On the other hand, as the "Essay on Right and Wrong" suggested, he was concerned as much with the search for order and national unity as with the revolt against authoritarian social and political restraints. Li seemed to be arguing that there were times when freedom must be subordinated to maintaining the fabric of the nation, particularly when the nation was threatened from without (it was doubtless this latter view that lay behind Li's early support for Yüan Shih-k'ai). Although these conflicting strands could to some extent be reconciled in the idea of popular sovereignty towards which Li was groping at this time, both remained prominent and contradictory features of his attitude toward political authority.

The point to be emphasized is that Li found terrorism and the anarchist impulse inconsistent with the needs of China in the chaotic conditions of the post-Manchu period. When the Ch'ing dynasty still exercised despotic authority, anarchism appeared as a reasonable response to the political situation. Indeed, in the early years of the century the influences of anarchist thought had been widespread among the members of the Chinese revolutionary intelligentsia. But the fall of the Ch'ing dynasty transformed the environment and created the new milieu from which the first Chinese Marxists emerged. The Chinese intellectuals of the second decade of the twentieth century were faced not with the power of an authoritarian bureaucratic state but with overwhelming political chaos and social disintegration. Although many were in revolt against the remaining restraints of the Confucian past, they were also motivated by a quest for order and unity. After 1911 anarchism was no longer a dynamic force in radical intellectual circles. In a society searching for order amidst chaos the anarchist impulse had become anachronistic. The birth of Marxism in China, in fact, owed more to the Western liberal and democratic tradition (more precisely, to disillusionment with that tradition) than to the earlier anarchist movement.[30]

Nevertheless, anarchists and their intellectual influences were still present after 1911, and many future Chinese Communists, including Mao Tse-tung, were influenced by anarchist theories at one time or another.[31] Yet the nature of many of these influences illustrates a characteristic phenomenon in the history of the modern Chinese intelligentsia: the selective borrowing of particular ideas from many different Western ideologies for purposes that were often far removed from the premises upon which they were based. Li Ta-chao, for example, looked with great favor upon Kropotkin's theory of "mutual aid"; but the influence of Kropotkin was most strongly evident only after Li had already declared himself a Marxist in

1919, and he then used the idea of "mutual aid" for the explicit purpose of reinterpreting the Marxist theory of class struggle.

Insofar as Li had developed political ties by mid-1913, they were with the newly formed constitutionalist group, the Chinputang (Progressive party), which was then in an uneasy alliance with the Yüan Shih-k'ai regime. His association with this rather conservative group was in part the product of an intellectual affinity, for Li was then genuinely attracted to the liberal constitutional philosophy propagated by the leaders of the Chinputang; in part it was based on the more mundane bond of the financial patronage of T'ang Hua-lung, a well-known constitutional monarchist who after the Revolution of 1911 had become a principal founder (along with Liang Ch'i-ch'ao) of the Chinputang. Li's early political inclinations had attracted the attention of T'ang Hua-lung when Li was still a student in Tientsin. T'ang had helped to support Li during his last two years at college in Tientsin, and T'ang's financial aid enabled him to go to Japan to study in the autumn of 1913.[32]

However, while Li had rejected the anarchists and the Kuomintang, he was also unwilling to commit himself fully to the Chinputang. Since the Chinputang was less a political party than a loose grouping of parliamentary politicians, it could hardly have seemed to Li the most suitable instrument to express the long suppressed "will of the people" that he so ardently championed. By the spring of 1913 the prospects for constructive political participation seemed utterly hopeless. Recurrent in his essays of this period is the theme of rapacious politicians plundering the republic and cynically sacrificing the interests of the nation to their selfish ends. Radical and conservative politicians seemed equally guilty. Li described the conservatives as "hypocritical and evil bureaucrats" and the radicals as "barbarian and ill-behaved insurrectionists," while the moderates were only "waiting for a place between the two to feed like chickens."[33]

Li's despair grew so great that at one point he appears to have considered retreating into the Buddhist "Pure Land" sect, a popular monastic sect with a simple doctrine of salvation that had traditionally appealed to Chinese during times of trouble. In his brief autobiographical sketch he noted: "During my stay in Peking [in the summer of 1913] I envied the life of a pure society in a fit of misanthropic thought. In the nick of time, my friend[s] wanted me to come to Tokyo to continue our studying with them."[34] Li was rescued from the Buddhists not only by his classmates but also by T'ang Hua-lung, who provided the money for him to pursue his education abroad. But although Li accepted T'ang's financial assistance, he did not accept T'ang's political philosophy. Filled with the deepest intellectual and political doubts, and impelled by the hopelessness of the internal political situation, Li embarked for Japan in September 1913. In a farewell letter Li's friend Yü I described his motivations: "you looked at yourself and felt inadequate, and thus you want to go to Japan to study social and economic problems, investigate the sources of the poverty of the people, and how to suppress the powerful and help the weak, thereupon to return to serve virtue and help the people . . . Your aims are high . . . How can I hinder your departure?"[35]

Politics in Japan

In the autumn of 1913 Li enrolled in the department of political economy at Waseda University. He lived in the YMCA Chinese students' dormitory at Waseda and enrolled in an English language class taught by Arthur G. Robinson, an American YMCA worker.[36] During the nearly three years he studied in Japan, he became fully exposed to the ideas of the West. His interests, however, were more political than academic, and he regarded himself as an exile as much as a student. As he wrote in 1914, "Today in China our plans and methods cannot be victorious; all we can do is study."[37] When the political situation seemed ripe, he was to hurry back to China without waiting to receive his degree.

In Tokyo he worked closely with the Chung-hua ko-ming-tang (Chinese revolutionary party), the secret organization established by Sun Yat-sen after he fled to Japan following the failure of his revolt against Yüan Shih-k'ai in July 1913. With the support of members of the revolutionary party, Li organized the Shen-chou hsüeh-hui (China study society), which attempted to mobilize Chinese students in Japan against the Yüan dictatorship.[38]

During Li's years in Tokyo the nationalist and antiforeign sentiments that had been nurtured by the experiences of his youth burst fully forth. The environment of Japan was no doubt an important factor in stimulating the development of nationalist feelings. Despite China's humiliating defeat in the War of 1894–95, Chinese intellectuals still widely admired Japan as an Asian nation that had successfully resisted the political and economic impingement of the West and which had, in fact, inflicted a decisive military defeat upon a great European power (Russia) in 1905. When in 1915 Japan finally revealed herself as the most ruthless and aggressive of the imperialist powers threatening China, this admiration was transformed into a fiery anger, which was expressed in violently nationalistic outbursts.

Even before 1915, however, Li was unable to resist the temptation to put his nationalist views in print. The immediate occasion was the expression in 1914 of the views of Yüan Shih-k'ai's "constitutional adviser," Dr. Frank Goodnow, an American professor of political science, who argued that because of political traditions and social customs the Chinese were ill-adapted to participate in representative government and that for the present, at least, a monarchical form of government was more in tune with China's needs. Li responded with an angry article in *Chia-yin tsa-chih* (Tiger magazine), in which he accused all foreigners of being incapable of understanding China. However sincere foreigners might be, he declared, they were unable to escape their own national limitations, and their views on China were superficial at best and frequently harmful:

Today our people feel that they are able to discuss the national condition [of China] with the Japanese Ariga Nagao and the American Goodnow. I do not presume to judge the scholastic abilities of these two gentlemen. But I do know that Mr. Goodnow's discussion of the condition of the nation necessarily follows [the interests of] America . . . and the national condition of China ·in the eyes of an American is not our own simple and true view of the condition of the nation. Mr. Ariga's discussion of the condition of the nation necessarily is in accord with [the interests of] Japan . . . Fortunately there is only an American and a Japanese discussing the national condition and thus there are only two different views about the new provisional constitution. If we had a great deal of money we could open houses and build buildings to invite the doctors of philosophy of the various nations to come to engage in skilful debate with each other, write articles . . . and applaud each other while they discussed the condition of our nation . . . Then China could be divided up according to the plans of the [foreign] scholars.[39]

Li continued, "The relations between nations are antagonistic, and this causes foreigners to be prejudiced and filled with hate; if they are loyal to their own [countries] they cannot be loyal to other [countries]." Thus, he proclaimed, "the national condition cannot be discussed with foreigners." Especially galling was the assumption that China was inferior to Japan: "If the Japanese have the ability to participate in government, why is it that we alone do not?" [40]

Li buttressed his argument against Goodnow with a lengthy interpretation of Chinese history and the nature of the traditional Chinese state. Traditional Chinese society, he argued, was based upon clan ties and village organization. As a result, the power and organization of the state was very limited; except for the collection of taxes and the administration of justice, the state did not interfere in the lives of the people. Under these conditions there was little reason for people to develop an interest in political affairs. As long as China remained insulated from outside forces, the clan-based society and the traditional political system were able to persist. But with the intrusion of the West, the military, financial, and administrative responsibilities of the state became increasingly heavy. "Previously the people had little interest in politics, and the utilization of the power of the state in regard to the individual was light; now the duties and responsibilities have become momentous . . . and the activities of the people are entirely linked up with the state." Li regarded this intrusion of the state as a major cause of the Revolution of 1911; having been forced to submit to the control of various governmental organs, the people had risen up to demand political power and representative government.[41]

In Li's discussion there was a curious nostalgia for the stability of the old system, an almost Rousseauist aversion to the intrusion of the state upon the natural condition of society. This attitude was still within the bounds of the Confucian world-view. But Li's overall response was hardly a Confucian response. He called not for the elimination of the expanded role of the state and a return to the past but rather for popular control of the new state power. Although in responding to what he regarded as an attack by a foreigner upon the national traditions of China, Li felt compelled to defend tradition, he knew that there was no turning back. "Unfortunately," he observed, "there is now no power in the world that can resist the tendency of the times." [42] For better or worse, the old society had been destroyed by the forces of the modern world, the power of the state had expanded to meet the new conditions, and a representative republic was necessary both to defend the rights of the people against the power of the state and to ensure China's security in a hostile world.

One important stimulus in the development of modern Chinese nationalism was Japan's presentation of the infamous "Twenty-One Demands" to the government of Yüan Shih-k'ai. Taking advantage of the involvement of the Western powers in the First World War, the Okuma government in a secret memorandum, delivered in January 1915, demanded what amounted to a political and economic protectorate over all China. When the contents of the note became known early in the spring, anti-Japanese feeling among Chinese students and intellectuals reached fever pitch. Nowhere was the indignation more intense than among Chinese students in Japan. Four thousand students immediately laid down their books and returned to China en masse as a sign of protest.[43] Those who remained were no less eager to demonstrate their resentment. Li Ta-chao, who at the time was a member of the editorial committee of the Association of Chinese Students in Japan (Liu-Jih hsüeh-sheng tsung-hui) was asked to write a letter of protest on behalf of the association. Li's long manifesto, entitled "A Letter of Admonition to the Elders of the Nation," was sent to the central government in Peking. Shortly before, he had also written a historical survey of Sino-Japanese relations, whose purpose was revealed in its title, "To Rouse the Courage of the Citizens. A Record to Commemorate the Humiliation of the Nation."

In these essays Li's nationalist emotions culminated in a chauvinistic outburst that exalted the traditional superiority of China and deplored all foreign influences. "For more than four thousand years," Li cried, "our people have stood in a superior position, the ways of heaven did not change and the race continued to flourish . . . How brilliant is the past and how withered the present." Whereas Japanese imperialism was the immediate object of attack, the plight of China was attributed to all foreigners. "Even in our sleep we cannot forget that the misfortunes which have befallen our lost nation have come with the guns of the Europeans." [44]

The two essays were replete with references to the "traditional glorious history of our ancestors," the need to seek national revenge, and the desire to be able "to face without guilt our ancestors since the time of Huang Ti" — all of which were suggestive of the old conservative rallying cry to "expel the barbarians." But these melodramatic visions of the glories of the past and the perfidy of foreigners were curiously mingled with a sense of national shame — "a shame so large that it covers the heavens" — suggesting that the deficiencies of the Chinese themselves were also responsible for the plight of China. As to what these deficiencies were, Li could say very little. He had previously lamented the moral decline of China after the Revolution of 1911; now he could only repeat his charges about the shameful behavior of the republican politicians and observe that the people of China had not yet experienced "a self-awakening." He was fearful, moreover, that the coming generation of young Chinese would "look at us as we today look at the past generation." [45]

One thought that frequently troubled Li at this time was the notion of *wang-kuo* (literally, loss of state or nation). In classical literature *wang-kuo* usually referred to the downfall of a dynasty. Li employed the term in an entirely nationalistic fashion to express both his fear of foreign conquest and his apprehension that China stood on the brink of losing its very nationhood. As contemporary examples of *wang-kuo*, he pointed to not only the colonization of India, Vietnam, and Korea but also the dilemma of the Jews. "The Jews are a lost people who dream about recovering their country; intellectuals and well-to-do businessmen write ardent articles and spend vast sums of money to seek a land where they can collect and settle their people . . . [but] to no avail." [46] The example of the Jews may not have been relevant to the condition of China but it did suggest the extent of Li's despair.

The bitterly antiforeign passions that marked Li's reactions to the Twenty-One Demands should be distinguished from the older Chinese antiforeignism that was intimately tied to the defense of traditional Chinese cultural and intellectual values. The antiforeign element in Li's thought did not necessarily demand a defense of old traditions. The painful transition from "culturalism" to nationalism, which had wracked the earlier generation of the Chinese intelligentsia,[47] had not disturbed Li's intellectual development. From the very beginning of his mature intellectual life his basic loyalties had been to China as a nation and a people rather than to the particular values and beliefs of the past. Thus, the antiforeign strain in his thought merged with and reinforced his modern nationalist commitment to the survival and power of the Chinese nation in a world of contending nation-states; it never came into conflict with that commitment.

The more chauvinistic passions that were inspired in Li by the events of 1914 and 1915 shortly gave way to a more restrained view of the relationship between China and the foreign powers and a growing realization that the real problem was not so much foreign intrusion as China's response to it. Li never again expressed his nationalist feelings in as extreme a manner, even though nationalism. with a strongly antiforeign strain remained central to his thought — the prism through which he looked at all the ideas and ideologies of the West, including Marxism.

As a nationalist whose overriding concern was the survival and resurrection of the Chinese nation, Li found it possible to be both antiforeign and yet eager to learn from the foreigners the secrets of national success. Thus, despite the dominance of a still conservative and tradition-oriented nationalism, his mind was by no means closed to the ideas of the West. In Japan the new ideas came with such dizzying rapidity that it is almost impossible to follow accurately the process of their reception or to weigh their real impact. A characteristic feature of modern Chinese intellectual history is that the members of the intelligentsia felt impelled to assimilate within a few years alien ideas based upon centuries of intellectual evolution. Driven by their overriding concern with the problem of China's survival, as well as by their own unsatisfied intellectual and emotional needs, the young intellectuals were disposed to seek out and consider as many new ideas and ideologies as possible. In their eagerness to absorb all that the West had to offer, they picked up almost simultaneously bits and pieces of various, often contradictory ideologies. The intellectual life of this period was not so much a process of shifting from one all-embracing philosophy to another as of experimenting with and selecting particular aspects of sometimes heterogeneous systems of thought that fitted immediate intellectual, emotional, and political needs.

It would be fruitless to catalog here the many Western philosophers and political thinkers that Li Ta-chao encountered during his three years in Japan. They ranged from Aristotle and Plato to Francis Bacon and Hegel. They included English utilitarian and

THE EARLY YEARS

constitutional theorists as well as French and Japanese exponents of utopian socialism. However, the philosophies of Henri Bergson and Ralph Waldo Emerson had the most immediate and profound impact upon Li's intellectual development — an impact that was apparent in an exchange of views on the problem of "self-consciousness" between Li and his future Communist colleague Ch'en Tu-hsiu (1879–1942) in the summer of 1915.

Patriotism, Pessimism, and Self-Consciousness

Shortly before Ch'en Tu-hsiu returned to China from semi-exile in Japan in the autumn of 1915 to establish the periodical *Hsin ch'ing-nien* (New youth), he set forth his views on the value of patriotism in contemporary Chinese life. His essay, "Patriotism and Self-Consciousness," appeared in the April 1915 issue of *Chia-yin tsa-chih*, which was published in Tokyo by the liberal constitutionalist Chang Shih-chao.[48] This essay foreshadowed some of the basic assumptions that were held by the influential group of intellectuals associated with Ch'en and *Hsin ch'ing-nien* in the period 1915–19.

In "Patriotism and Self-Consciousness" Ch'en argued that there were two radically different forces contending for control of the minds of men — emotion and knowledge. Men who were mainly inspired by emotions tended to think in general terms rather than about specific problems. They were usually self-sacrificing people who were inclined to martyrdom. The defect in emotional thinking was that it led to irrational actions, which flowed from inadequate study and understanding. As an example of a man ruled by emotions, Ch'en pointed to Ch'ü Yüan, who took his own life out of a misguided sense of loyalty. Ch'en identified the spirit of patriotism with emotional thinking. Knowledge, on the other hand, was reasoning and the understanding of particular things; it was the basis of true self-consciousness. Its virtues and defects were epitomized by Lao Tzu, the most eminent example of a man of pure knowledge, who perceived the meaning of life but withdrew from the world of men. As for contemporary China, Ch'en drew a bleak picture. Its people lacked both genuine emotion and genuine knowledge, and thus China had neither true patriots nor self-conscious men. Under such conditions it was doubtful that China could be considered a real nation.[49]

21

Patriotism, Ch'en acknowledged, was an important factor in creating a nation, but in the Chinese context it had far different implications from those it had elsewhere. Whereas patriotic feelings in the Western countries were based upon the constitutional rights of the people, who viewed the state as an organization through which they planned for their own welfare, in China people still looked upon the state as the private possession of the imperial clan, to which they owed blind loyalty and to which they must sacrifice themselves. Patriotism in lieu of knowledge and self-consciousness, Ch'en declared, was both foolish and harmful and, in the Chinese situation in particular, implied the enslavement of the people to the state. What China required first was knowledge; it needed self-conscious men who were capable of clear thinking about specific problems rather than emotionally inspired patriots. Only after the development of self-consciousness, Ch'en argued, could patriotism become a positive force in Chinese life.[50]

Li Ta-chao's reply to Ch'en, which appeared in August, was significantly entitled "Pessimism and Self-Consciousness." By substituting "pessimism" for "patriotism," he suggested that the former was the real barrier to the achievement of self-consciousness. Li's criticism was couched in most polite terms — for Ch'en, almost ten years his senior, was already widely recognized as the leader of the new intelligentsia. The criticism took the form of deploring that Ch'en's essay had been misunderstood. This misunderstanding, he wrote, had the unfortunate effect of encouraging pessimistic attitudes among young Chinese intellectuals, who, upon reading Ch'en's essay, often distorted the significance of his call for self-consciousness. "We want to seek the crucial point of self-consciousness," Li stated, "but we have lost our way in a fog of pessimism." [51]

The main point at issue, however, was not pessimism or optimism but the relevance of patriotism in the contemporary Chinese social and political context. Li admitted that there were basic differences between East and West in the nature of state and politics, but he argued that this did not diminish the need for patriotism. On the contrary, however abhorrent the political life of China, patriotic sentiments were necessary to inspire men to reconstruct the nation on new foundations: "The meaning of self-consciousness lies in the spirit of changing the nation and in seeking to make the country lovable and loving it. We ought not to stop thinking about our country and refuse to love it because the country has deficiencies . . . and thus abandon it and become people without a country . . . A country is a creation of men, the individual exists within the universe and within the vastness of the universe the individual is his own master. Together with people of his own race the individual is able to build a nation. Why should we be any different?" [52] Since a country was a creation of men, and since the goal of Chinese intellectuals was to "change the nation," Li was prompted to ask, "How can this be done without the patriotism of the people?"

Whereas Li's plea for patriotism was an old theme, his emphasis upon the role of individual consciousness, with its implication of activism, was a new element in his thought. He soon disclosed that the source of this new element was Bergson's *Creative Evolution*: "We cannot view theories in a kind of pessimistic and deterministic [manner] that weakens the spirit of struggling forward. It is necessary to employ the theory of free will, to exert efforts to move forward and develop, in order to change the situation to suit our will." [53]

Thus, not only was Li criticizing Ch'en Tu-hsiu for failing to encourage a sense of patriotism and optimism, but he was also presenting a radically different conception of the role of the intellectual in society and politics. The import of Ch'en's treatment of self-consciousness was that the intellectual should not, because of an emotionally motivated and misguided sense of patriotism, dissipate his energies in the quagmire of Chinese politics. He should first gain knowledge of "particular things"; that is, he should above all study and learn. In the contemporary Chinese situation this implied that the intellectual should withdraw from political life and devote himself to educational activities until social and political conditions offered opportunities for more fruitful activity. Li, on the other hand, by emphasizing the role of human activity in changing reality according to man's conscious will, was in effect calling for the active and immediate participation of the intellectual in politics. He found no contradiction between patriotism and self-consciousness and even regarded patriotism as an essential element in the development of man's self-consciousness — an element that was both good in itself and necessary to encourage human activity.

The disfavor with which Li looked upon the "fog of pessimism" that hung over the intelligentsia did not derive from an overly optimistic assessment of the condition of China, for he was no less aware than Ch'en of the corruption of Chinese politics and the inertia of the Chinese people. What disturbed him was that this mood of pessimism led to a retreat from society and political activity. The tragedies of Ch'ü Yüan and Lao Tzu, he suggested, lay in the fact that both in their different ways allowed pessimism to force them to reject society.[54]

In emphasizing the importance of the conscious will of the individual, Li stopped short of advocating individualism. His conception of individual consciousness demanded the participation of the individual in the common work of rebuilding the nation. He took "free will" to mean not freedom of individual action but the duty and ability of self-conscious men to change the conditions under which they live. In some respects Li's conception of "free will" parallels the use of the term "democracy" in present-day Chinese Communist ideology, in which "democracy" does not mean individual freedom but the obligation of individual participation.

Although Li did not come forth as an advocate of individualism, his stress on the ability of conscious, active men to shape events marked a fundamental departure for him from the traditional Chinese world view — a view that was predisposed to adapt human activities to nature and tradition rather than to change them. With his new emphasis on the role of human consciousness, Li's attitude towards the problems confronting China also began to undergo a crucial transformation. Whereas a few months before he had placed much of the blame for the plight of China upon the intrusion of foreigners, he now proclaimed that "the destruction of our country is not due to other people destroying us, but it is [because] we are destroying ourselves; the guilt for the destruction of the nation is not to be placed upon others but upon ourselves."[55] Spurred on by the idea that man, both individually and collectively, was responsible for his own situation and was capable of changing that situation through conscious action, Li now began to look inward to the defects of China and the Chinese. This did not make him any less ardent as a nationalist, but his nationalism began to throw off its cruder antiforeign overtones.

Li Ta-chao and Ch'en Tu-hsiu were the pioneers of Marxism and Communism in China. Yet when they are compared in mid-1915, important differences are already apparent in their intellectual orientations. Whereas Ch'en innately distrusted all overt manifestations of nationalism, Li extolled the virtues of patriotism. Although both had already rejected the traditional world view and turned to the West for new ideas, Ch'en's hostility to the Chinese tradition was more unyielding. Most important, Ch'en saw self-consciousness as essentially a process of education and the gaining of knowledge about specific problems, but Li took self-consciousness to mean a process in which purposeful men actively engaged in changing their political and social surroundings. Thus in 1915 Li was already psychologically and intellectually predisposed to a voluntaristic approach to the solution of the problems of China. These differences foreshadowed many of the later differences between Ch'en and Li as Marxists. Ch'en interpreted Marxism in a generally orthodox and deterministic fashion; Li was quick to abandon Marxist-Leninist orthodoxy when it conflicted with concrete opportunities for revolutionary practice and his own politically activistic needs. Yet the differences between Ch'en and Li in 1915 should not be exaggerated. More drew them together than pulled them apart. They were divided not by firm intellectual or ideological positions but by differences in temperament and emotional predilections.

Li's implicit criticism of Ch'en Tu-hsiu as a pessimist came rather unexpectedly, in view of his own doubts and fears about the future of China. Certainly he could have found little in the political events of 1915 to encourage his new-found optimism. If anything, China's crisis had grown more acute, and the prospects for representative government had never seemed darker. Only a few months before, in May 1915, the government of Yüan Shih-k'ai had capitulated to all but the most extreme Japanese demands; and at the very moment that Li was criticizing Ch'en for being unduly pessimistic, the movement to destroy what little remained of the republic and to establish Yüan as emperor of a new dynasty was approaching what seemed to be a successful climax. What, then, was the source of Li's new optimism?

It would seem that in the very depths of his despair Li consciously sought for elements in Western philosophy that could provide him with a more hopeful view of the future. The initial influence was Bergson's concept of free will, upon which Li had so passionately seized as proof that men could mold political and social reality. The optimism inherent in this view was reinforced by the buoyantly optimistic philosophy of Ralph Waldo Emerson, who was then very much in vogue in Japan. The influence of Emerson is especially evident in the poetic essay "Spring" (Ch'ing-ch'un), written early in 1916.

The Dialectic of Rebirth

The faith that man could shape objective reality according to his conscious desires was further cultivated by Li in the early months of 1916 and cast into the framework of a more elaborate and rather metaphysical world view. The influential essay "Spring," which Li wrote while he was still in Japan but which was not published until after his return to China, was a basic statement in the evolution of this world view. Since he elaborated upon these ideas in the following years, it is necessary here to consider only the themes of the essay that bear directly upon the points at issue between Li and Ch'en in 1915.

One of Li's aims in "Spring" was to find a firmer philosophic underpinning for his politically activistic, nationalistic, and optimistic proclivities. He therefore presented a dialectical view of progress in which the death of all things inevitably contained the seeds of rebirth. He used the analogy of the cycle of life — death and rebirth in nature, as manifested in the change of seasons — to explain the entire process of human life and history. At the core of this explanation was a transcendental belief in an eternal spirit of "Spring":

All the cycles of life and death, of prosperity and decline, of youth and old age are in fact but the progress of Spring. And this infinite, eternal whole without beginning or end is the infinite Spring. We who are young and hotblooded . . . can identify ourselves with the universe, our springtime with the springtime of the universe. Since the universe is eternal, Spring is also eternal and so are we ourselves. This is the spirit that restores youth and life, the spirit that moves mountains. Only those who love Spring can see eternal Spring in the universe; and only when this spirit is theirs can they enjoy it forever.[56]

Just as there was a cycle of life and death in nature and man, so too did a nation have a life cycle. There were young nations and old ones. Was China, Li asked, young or old?

Other nations often speak of China as an ancient country and the Chinese nation as moribund. Since the dawn of history countless nations have risen and fallen . . . It is clear from history that when a rising nation meets one in decline, the nation in decline will be defeated.

When a vigorous young life meets moribund life the moribund life will be defeated. When a young people meets an old, the old people will be defeated. This is an inevitable law of nature. For more than 4800 years, since the time of Huang Ti, China has stood as a mighty nation in East Asia. Its long, rich history is unique. We can consider the Chou dynasty as the time of China's youth when its culture was already splendid; after that, decline set in, but by such gradual degrees that some of the splendor has remained to this day. This is a glorious national tradition . . . At present, however, all we can see is corpses, while the whole of our splendor is gone. How can a nation in such a condition survive? [57]

But the "corpse" of China could be thrown off and China could be regenerated, for the corpse was merely the outer shell that had already produced within itself the seeds of rebirth. Just as the flower is followed by the fruit and the fruit by the seed, so "old China is the fruit from which young China is born, young China is the flower by means of which old China has a new birth. Old China is a fading flower; young China is a flower in bloom. Fading precedes fresh flowering; this was so in the past and will be so in the future." In this analogy the seeds of rebirth were the youth of China: "Our young people should pledge themselves to show the world not whether old China is going to live or die but that we are busily paving the way for the resurgence of a young China . . . Whether or not we can stand up in the world depends not on the survival of old China but on its resurrection as young China; for life is a cycle of birth and death and our problem is not one of national survival but of being born again and recovering the springtime of our nation." [58]

Li's transcendental philosophy of dialectical evolution and rebirth not only played a major role in his own intellectual evolution but was also an early expression of one of the dominant intellectual tendencies of the modern Chinese intelligentsia. The notion of the rebirth of a young China from within the very womb of the dying civilization stimulated the entire generation of young intellectuals and political leaders who burst into prominence with the May Fourth Incident of 1919. It became a deeply rooted emotional belief, which underlay much of both the form and the content of later Chinese Communist ideology.

This dialectical image of the universe and China's rebirth provided Li with a highly optimistic philosophy at a time when political developments in China offered very little cause for optimism. At the same time it helped satisfy his need to maintain a nationalistic attachment to traditional values when the influence of Western ideas was in fact increasingly alienating him from them — for from this dialectical point of view it could be denied that Chinese traditions were simply to be thrown onto the scrap heap of history and replaced with new ideas and an alien culture. Rather, it implied that however much might be new, the young China emerging in the present was somehow organically related to the old China of the past.

Precedents can be found in traditional Chinese thought for Li's philosophy, particularly in the dialectical thought of Chuang Tzu (whom Li referred to in "Spring"), the Buddhist doctrine of reincarnation, and the traditional Chinese cyclic view of history. But the immediate inspiration appears to have come from Emerson rather than from ancient Chinese philosophy. Li interpreted Emerson's transcendentalism and emphasis upon the role of the individual to reinforce his own very nontraditional conviction that man was capable of shaping his own environment and to express his growing desire for immediate political participation:

A young man's aim should be to advance from the present. Our life is an eternity within time, an eternity expressed in the present moment, not in the past or the future. A man who grasps the present grasps eternity. Emerson has said that one who loves eternity should make the best use of the present; yesterday is beyond recall and tomorrow is uncertain, the sole thing within our grasp is today. The present day is as good as two tomorrows. His words are well worth pondering, for the present is the springtime of our youth; with this eternal Spring we are capable of everything and should have no worries or fears.[59]

Armed with the Bergsonian theory of free will, the belief that "we are capable of everything," and Emerson's injunction to "grasp the present," Li Ta-chao, now in his twenty-eighth year, had become noticeably impatient with his exile in Japan and eager to return to the political struggles in China. He had not long to wait. In China the monarchical movement of Yüan Shih-k'ai collapsed early in 1916, and his dictatorship was tottering. The Chinputang was now in open opposition. In April Li received an urgent telegram from his patron, T'ang Hua-lung, with whom he had maintained close contact during his three years in Japan. The anti-Yüan movement, T'ang reported, was reaching a climax; Li should return to China as quickly as possible.[60] Without waiting to take his final examinations at Waseda, Li hurriedly embarked for Shanghai.

CHAPTER II   PRELUDE TO REVOLUTION

In view of the politically activistic implications of Li Ta-chao's views during his final years in Japan, it is hardly surprising that he should have immediately plunged into politics upon his return to China. For the first six months he was deeply involved in Chinputang activities, first in Shanghai and then in Peking. In order to participate in the movement against Yüan Shih-k'ai's crumbling dictatorship, he joined T'ang Hua-lung's faction of the Chinputang, the Hsien-fa t'ao-lun hui (Constitutional discussion association), and served as a personal secretary to T'ang.[1]

On June 6, 1916, less than two months after Li had arrived in Shanghai, Yüan died. With a great flurry the party politicians rushed to Peking to reconvene the parliament Yüan had dissolved in 1913. It soon became apparent, however, that the politicians were celebrating a victory that belonged to others. It was not the opposition of the political parties but rather a shift in the loyalties of the provincial warlords that had been responsible for the disintegration of Yüan's power, and it was the warlords who became the chief beneficiaries of the fall of his dictatorship. The process of disintegration had begun in December 1915, when Ts'ai Ao's "National Protection Army" had revolted in Yunnan. One by one the military leaders of the southern and central provinces had joined the revolt. By early spring eight provinces had declared their independence from the central government at Peking. The political parties had played a role in encouraging these defections, but instead of having used the warlords, as they imagined, they were in fact being used by them. By the time parliament convened on August 1, 1916, political power in China was more fragmented than ever among the provincial and subprovincial militarists. The power of the political parties, both within and outside parliament, extended no further than their ability to gain the favor of one or another of the rival militarists.

As China sank deeper into the dark age of warlordism, Li Ta-chao followed T'ang Hua-lung to Peking when the latter resumed his post as speaker of the House of Representatives. Upon T'ang's recommendation Li was selected chief editor of the Peking *Ch'en-chung pao* (Morning bell newspaper), which was established as the organ of the Chinputang elements.[2] Li also became a member of the Research Clique (Yen-chiu-hsi), the parliamentary grouping that through a series of inconsequential political maneuvers had succeeded the Chinputang and reunited the factions led by T'ang Hua-lung and Liang Ch'i-ch'ao.

In retrospect it seems astonishing that the young intellectual who was to be China's first Marxist should have chosen to associate himself with so conservative a group as the Chinputang just two years before he was to greet enthusiastically the Bolshevik Revolution. Of the antimonarchical political parties, the Chinputang was the most conservative. To its left stood the moderate wing of the Kuomintang; then came the more radical elements of the Kuomintang, which were still organized separately in Sun Yat-sen's Revolutionary party. Further to the left, on the outer fringes of Chinese politics, were various anarchist groups. Li's decision cannot be explained on grounds of political opportunism, for just at the moment that his personal political prospects appeared the brightest, he was abruptly to cut his conservative ties and temporarily retire from political life.

Li's gratitude to T'ang Hua-lung for his financial assistance and friendship was no doubt a factor in determining his association with the Chinputang, but more important was the character of his own political thought. At the time he returned to China the revolutionary implications of the dialectical and activistic philosophy that he had evolved in Japan had not yet expressed themselves in a radical political position, nor indeed was it inevitable that they should do so. Hegel had long before demonstrated that revolutionary politics do not necessarily follow from revolutionary philosophy. As both Hegel and Marx had shown in different ways, the dialectic has that remarkably convenient political quality of inevitably evolving toward whatever goal is arbitrarily set for it. In 1916 Li had not yet arrived at any firm political goals, much less a world view that was integrated with practical political ends; between his philosophy and his politics still lay a huge abyss. Insofar as he had developed concrete political goals, however, they centered upon the conviction that China required a constitutional system of government, and the main exponents of this proposition were the leaders of the Chinputang.

In Japan Li's early belief in the virtues of constitutional government had been reinforced by the writings of John Stuart Mill, Rousseau, Montesquieu, Voltaire, and even Tolstoy, as well as of numerous now obscure American and English writers on constitutional theory. Shortly before his return to China he wrote a long essay attempting to prove that a democratic constitutional system was appropriate to the needs and conditions of China. His argument was based upon the notion of *min-i*, literally "the rules of the people," a term that he apparently improvised and which he opposed to the principle of *tsung-i* or the "rules of the clan," the norms traditionally dominant in Chinese society. Li treated the "rules of the people" as an elemental expression of human nature. It was the inherent right of the people to decide all public matters and to measure the truth of all things. The "rules of the clan" could be changed, but the "rules of the people" were eternal. However much the "rules of the people" might be suppressed by the "unnatural" forces of history, they must inevitably come to the fore. "The rules of the people can create history, but history cannot restrain the rules of the people." [3]

Li defined *min-i* as a combination of the spirit of "only-peopleism" (*wei-min chu-i*) and a representative form of government. He pointed to the "advanced countries" of Europe and the United States as examples where the principle of *min-i* was flourishing. Since the principle of *min-i* was universal, he argued, China should follow the "advanced countries" in establishing a parliamentary form of government. [4]

Although Li's argument for representative government and parliamentary rule was clearly drawn from classical Western democratic theory (there were frequent references to Mill in particular), he was reluctant to admit that he was simply advocating a Western import, wholly alien to the Chinese tradition. While conceding that China was politically underdeveloped in comparison to the West, he maintained that "the flower of popular sovereignty and freedom is really already buried in the soil of our country."[5] In an earlier essay Li had found a precedent for the idea of republican government in China as early as the eleventh century B.C. when the people of Chou revolted against the tyrant Chou Hsin, the last of the Shang kings.[6] Although Li attributed the suppression of *min-i* in Chinese history to the oppressive nature of the Chinese tradition and the loss of the people's individuality owing to their blind veneration of the sages, he himself felt compelled to draw upon the sages for support. In passages reminiscent of Kang Yu-wei's reincarnation of Confucius as a modern constitutional democrat, Li argued that Mencius was an unappreciated advocate of individualism and that "the history of the past has been one in which the local gentry and the big officials have distorted and misinterpreted Yao and Shun [the mythical sage emperors] and Confucius."[7] Yet despite Li's need to seek roots in the Chinese past, the nature of the political reform that he advocated was clear: the constitutions of England and the United States were the models for China to follow. It was here that Li found a meeting of minds with the leaders of the Chinputang.

Throughout Li's discussion of constitutionalism there also ran a strong radical democratic and Populist current. The constitution and the parliament, he assumed, were only the means for the expression of a single, indivisible "will of the masses." The basis of the constitution must be the principle of "only peopleism." He negated the role of the individual hero in history and enthusiastically championed Tolstoy's emphasis upon the creative forces of the "collective mass."[8] Moreover, he was somewhat skeptical that even the most advanced constitutional systems of government in the West were truly able to reflect the will of the people. In an essay written in 1913 discussing the persistence of bureaucratic political patterns and habits in China, Li had found that a bureaucratic psychology was tending to vitiate French democracy and the English parliamentary system. Even America seemed to be succumbing to the evil practice of appointing officials.[9]

It was this side of Li's constitutionalism that set him apart from the Chinputang. He had assumed that the parliamentarism of the Chinputang leaders was consistent with his own Populist and democratic beliefs. He soon became aware of his mistake. Hardly had the ceremonies marking the reopening of parliament taken place than it became apparent that Liang Ch'i-ch'ao and T'ang Hua-lung, who were quick to appreciate where power really resided, were attempting to establish an alliance with the new prime minister, Tuan Ch'i-jui, the leader of the powerful Peiyang warlord coalition. In late October 1916, T'ang and Liang refused to allow Li to publish in *Ch'en-chung pao* an editorial that was implicitly critical of the Research Clique's support of Tuan Ch'i-jui. In protest, Li resigned his post as editor and terminated his association with T'ang.[10]

Left without the small salary he had received as editor, Li lived during the next few months in the house of a friend who was a minor official in the Peking government. He had lost faith in the parliamentary politicians but not yet in the idea of constitutional government. In January 1917 he was invited by Chang Shih-chao, his close friend and a leading Chinese advocate of constitutionalism who had remained aloof from party politics, to become editor of a newspaper that Chang proposed to publish in Peking. Li gladly accepted the new position. For the next four months *Chia-yin jih-k'an* (Tiger daily) provided Li an opportunity to comment upon current political developments.[11]

It has been suggested that friction developed between Li and Chang over the radical character of Li's articles, which Chang feared would provoke repressive measures by the warlord-controlled government.[12] Whatever disagreements there may have been, they were not allowed to come to a head. *Chia-yin jih-k'an* was suppressed and Chang was forced to flee Peking early in June when the Peiyang militarists chose to demonstrate their power by carrying out far-reaching measures of political repression, including the dissolution of parliament. Li also left Peking and took refuge in Shanghai, where he lived for the remainder of the year.

After his break with the Chinputang, Li's writings took on an increasingly radical tone. Removed from the compromising influences of direct political involvement, he began to look with a more critical eye at the Chinese tradition and grew increasingly doubtful over the prospects for constitutional government in China. His association with Chang Shih-chao and *Chia-yin jih-k'an* in the early months of 1917 marked the last phase of his belief that the plight of China could be resolved through the establishment of a parliamentary system of government.

Li's new radical orientation was first expressed in an attack upon

33

the Chinese tradition that was much more severe than any he had before been willing to make. Whereas he had previously been inclined to draw upon tradition to support social and political change, he now described the entire Confucian heritage as "the ethics of a dictatorial society that has been utilized to support a dictatorial monarchy." He dismissed Confucius himself as "the skeleton and dried bones of several thousand years ago" and the "screen that has sheltered imperial tyranny."[13] When the news of the Russian February Revolution reached China, Li welcomed it as foreshadowing a similar revolution in China.

The radical character of Li's thought became even more pronounced in an essay written shortly before the Bolshevik Revolution, in which he reluctantly came to the conclusion that political reform in China could not be accomplished without revolution. The essay, "Violence and Politics," published in the *T'ai-p'ing yang* (Pacific monthly) on October 15, 1917, marked the final abandonment of Li's faith in constitutionalism and attempted, with the assistance of Rousseau, to establish a theoretical justification for revolution.

"Violence and Politics" was written as a criticism of the political activities and philosophy of Liang Ch'i-ch'ao and thus served as a repudiation of Li's recent association with the Chinputang. Liang was attacked both for his practical political cooperation with warlords and for his theoretical opposition to revolution. Revolution might be undesirable, Li conceded, but it was inevitable in a situation where political authority was based upon violence. Political power in China, he maintained, was characterized by a degree of violence that exceeded even that of the sultans of Turkey or the czars of Russia at the height of their autocratic powers. In such a situation the "will of the people" must be realized by force if it cannot be realized by reason. It was thus inconsistent for Liang to oppose revolution when he supported the "unrestricted violence" of the warlords, for violence inevitably breeds revolution. In opposing revolution, Liang was like a man who does not wish the pot of water to boil but nevertheless adds more fuel to the fire. "Opposition to revolution has the result of promoting revolution. Reliance upon violence actually brings upon oneself the calamity of violence. Those who employ violence will themselves be destroyed by violence and be extinguished in a continuous revolution."[14]

In suggesting that Liang consider Rousseau's doctrine that authority dependent upon force and violence is evil and that a revolution that reacts against such authority is justified, Li revealed how much his own view of both Rousseau and the condition of China had changed. Two years before he had drawn from Rousseau the concept of popular sovereignty to support the argument that a constitutional system of government was just what China needed. Now he found the revolutionary side of Rousseau more relevant.

However, the growing radicalism in Li's thought and his increasing interest in revolution did not lead him to the revolutionary political movement of Sun Yat-sen or to the anarchist groups. Instead, he was drawn to the group of "nonpolitical" young intellectuals who were loosely associated with Ch'en Tu-hsiu and the periodical *Hsin ch'ing-nien* (New youth), the leading organ of China's emerging westernized intelligentsia. In January 1918, Li formally joined Ch'en as one of the six members of the editorial board of *Hsin ch'ing-nien*.[15]

The *Hsin ch'ing-nien* group in the period from late 1915 until the May Fourth Incident of 1919 was perhaps as close as China ever came to having an "alienated intelligentsia." Ch'en Tu-hsiu and his followers had proclaimed publicly their rejection of the entire Chinese intellectual and cultural tradition. In its place they had enshrined the Western concepts of "democracy" and "science" as the only worthy foundations for the erection of a new culture and a new society. They also rejected nationalism and proclaimed themselves "internationalists," who would bring to China what they regarded as the universally valid fruits of modern Western civilization; for as much as they were concerned with the problems of China's survival and the dangers of imperialist encroachment, they were also suspicious that any overt expression of Chinese nationalism would imply a defense of old Chinese values against the modern, Western forces of progress. They were a socially isolated group, since their intellectual values separated them as much from the business world of the cities in which they lived as their education and urban environment separated them from the peasant masses of the countryside and the gentry class from which most of them had sprung.

As Benjamin Schwartz has pointed out,[16] the alienation of the twentieth-century Chinese intelligentsia from the state was a less decisive sort of alienation than that of the nineteenth-century Russian intelligentsia. But if there was no powerful Chinese state to foster a sense of alienation, there was at least a self-imposed alienation from Chinese political life, for the members of the *Hsin ch'ing-nien* group attempted to avoid political commitments and at first refused even to discuss political issues.[17]

Li Ta-chao's own growing sense of isolation and alienation helped to draw him closer to the position of Ch'en Tu-hsiu and the *Hsin ch'ing-nien* group. His foray into parliamentary politics in 1916 had been a dismal failure. His suspicion that constitutionalism might not prove viable in the Chinese social and political environment, and the recognition that an antiforeign nationalism was in itself an insufficient response to the plight of China, left Li without the support of the two principles that had hitherto conditioned so much of his intellectual development and political orientation. Set adrift in a country to which he was deeply attached but in a society that offered few opportunities for participation and service, he now had less than ever to propose in the way of concrete measures to bring about the rebirth of China. His sense of alienation was no doubt intensified by his departure from the political arena in Peking and by the experience of living in foreign-dominated Shanghai.

At this time he became interested in a problem with which he had hitherto been little concerned — the problem of whether truth is to be determined by the individual or by society. In this case, at least, Li took his stand squarely in favor of the individual. "The highest ideal of human life," he stated, "is to seek the attainment of truth." As if to justify his own growing estrangement from Chinese society and politics, he wrote:

If what I say really corresponds to truth, then even though the society of any given time does not listen to what I say or even does not allow me to say it, then, because of my love for truth I dare not shrink back and refrain from speaking in order to accept this society. If what I say betrays truth, then even though society welcomes what I say and, moreover, showers me with esteem, still because of my love for truth I dare not play the sycophant and be subservient to society . . . In the former case it is difficult to avoid cheating oneself; in the latter one sinks [into the position of] cheating others.[18]

The notion that the individual himself must determine truth was very probably inspired by Li's reading of Emerson. Indeed, the major theme of Emerson's philosophy is intellectual and ethical individualism; for Emerson, the individual is the sole unit to judge and interpret all things. Although Li never repudiated the notion that the individual must interpret truth as he sees it, whatever the consequences, the individualist strain did not remain a prominent feature of his world view.

In 1917, however, his feeling that the individual in search of truth might be compelled to stand alone against society gave Li a certain spiritual identity with Ch'en Tu-hsiu and his followers. Li was in full accord with them on a variety of other matters as well. The influence of Western ideas had already led him to record publicly his opposition to traditional Chinese values. He shared the *Hsin ch'ing-nien* group's spirit of public service and their faith that the salvation of China lay with the youth, who would sweep away "the old and rotten" and create "the fresh and living." Although perhaps less enthusiastic about the benefits of science, Li's belief in democracy was no less strong than theirs — even though he had no more specific ideas about how a democratic system was to be established in China. Like the other intellectuals associated with *Hsin Ch'ing-nien*, moreover, Li now found himself without formal political commitments.

Despite these similarities, there were elements in Li's thought in the months prior to the Bolshevik Revolution that sharply distinguished him from Ch'en Tu-hsiu and his followers. Whereas Ch'en was deeply suspicious of any manifestation of patriotism or nationalism, Li continued to approach all political and intellectual issues with a strongly nationalistic predisposition. In his famous "Call to Youth," the manifesto in the first issue of *Hsin ch'ing-nien*, Ch'en had set the tone for the New Culture movement by raising the slogan: "Be cosmopolitan, not isolationist." No similar expressions of internationalist sentiment appeared in the writings of Li. Even after his acceptance of Marxism, Li never really abandoned Chinese nationalism for Marxist internationalism.

Although Li, like Ch'en, looked to the West for intellectual guidance, he never subjected the Confucian tradition to the thoroughgoing criticism and often sarcastic deprecation that marked the writings of Ch'en Tu-hsiu, Hu Shih, and other radical intellectual leaders of the New Culture era. To the latter, the Chinese past represented all that was stagnant and obscurantist, and they frankly called for the wholesale Westernization of China. Li's attack on traditional values stemmed more from his disgust with the reactionary uses of Confucianism in contemporary Chinese politics than from any deep-seated aversion to the tradition itself. Ch'en Tu-hsiu compensated for his almost total rejection of the Chinese cultural tradition by a passionate admiration for French culture as the crowning achievement of Western civilization, whereas Li could only display enthusiasm for particular Western ideas and particular Western thinkers, not for Western civilization as a whole.

Li's spirit of political activism further set him apart from Ch'en and other members of the new intelligentsia. In founding *Hsin ch'ing-nien* in the autumn of 1915, Ch'en Tu-hsiu had declared that the journal would avoid political involvements and would refuse even to discuss political issues. When in 1916 Ch'en was criticized for his opposition to political participation — an opposition which, his critic suggested, would only encourage bureaucratic tendencies in government and politics — Ch'en replied that in the absence of a "spirit of constitutional government" politics produced only tyranny and political parties inevitably became private cliques.[19] In 1917 he reaffirmed that "the purpose of this magazine does not lie in the criticism of current politics but in the cultivation of the youth," although he modified his position enough to admit that one cannot keep silent on "the great questions concerning the existence of the nation." While conceding that political matters were important, Ch'en stood firmly by his basic point of view that "the foundation of the progress of the masses is in education and industry and not in politics."[20] Ch'en adhered scrupulously to the principle of political nonparticipation until 1919, by which he fostered as well as reflected a tendency dominant among the acknowledged leaders of the advanced intelligentsia.

In contrast, Li Ta-chao's entire intellectual development had been conditioned by politically activistic instincts. Although in 1917 Li, like Ch'en, found himself separated from the political arena, it was a separation that had been forced by immediate political circumstances, whereas Ch'en's was a self-imposed separation demanded by his basic intellectual orientations. During this period of retreat Li did not abandon those assumptions that impelled him towards political activism but rather sought to develop them into a more comprehensive philosophic system.

The impulse for political action also prevented Li from sharing the enthusiasm of his fellow intellectuals of the *Hsin ch'ing-nien* group for Social Darwinism. In 1917 Li attacked both Social Darwinism and Malthusian theory for promoting war. He argued that the material resources of the world and man's ability to utilize them were sufficient to preclude the necessity of war among nations or a struggle for existence among men. Li attributed war not to the deterministic "laws of life" preached by the Malthusians and the Social Darwinists, but to weaknesses in human psychology, especially the "covetous and lazy nature" of men. "All the crimes and evils among men," he wrote, "flow from this evil psychology." Yet these psychological deficiencies were not innate; they could be overcome and all problems could be solved.[21] An optimistic belief in the ability of man to master his environment was a central assumption behind Li's faith in the efficacy of political activity. The essentially pessimistic and deterministic character of Social Darwinist theory seemed to him to challenge that faith.

There is, of course, nothing in Social Darwinism that necessarily precludes political action. The Darwinian emphasis on struggle may, indeed, encouraged a spirit of political activism. As Benjamin Schwartz has pointed out, many Chinese intellectuals drew from Social Darwinism not only an explanation of the determining forces of the universe but also a program of action to revitalize Chinese society.[22] Yet Ch'en Tu-hsiu and his followers employed Social Darwinism not as a program for political action but as a support for their argument that traditional Chinese values were outmoded and that the survival of China in the "struggle for existence" in the modern world depended upon the destruction of old values and the adoption of an entirely new culture. This preoccupation with cultural renovation was a major factor in Ch'en's opposition to political participation. For Li, however, the fear that men would draw fatalistic conclusions from the Social Darwinist message made him suspicious of the theory; such conclusions could only encourage human inertia, inhibit political participation, and cause men to "neglect to strive to recreate civilization."[23]

Although the intellectuals associated with *Hsin ch'ing-nien* were an alienated segment of the Chinese intelligentsia, Li was perhaps the least alienated among them. His nationalistic proclivities, his refusal to condemn completely the Chinese tradition, and his politically activistic impulses made his feelings of isolation from Chinese society less severe. They also lent a relatively conservative cast to his thought. In spite of the radical themes in his writings in the period following his break with the Chinputang, Li Ta-chao on the eve of the Bolshevik Revolution tended in many significant respects to think in less radical terms than did Ch'en Tu-hsiu. The conservative side of Li's thought was expressed in his essay "Youth and Old People," which appeared in *Hsin ch'ing-nien* in April 1917. This essay drew upon both John Stuart Mill and the traditional Chinese respect for old age to present a veiled criticism of the proclivity of contributors to *Hsin ching-nien* to exalt the virtues of youth and to condemn all generations preceding their own. "Contemporary civilization," Li stated, "is a cooperative civilization. Just as the nobility and the common people cooperate, the capitalists and the workers cooperate, and the landlords and the tenants cooperate, so the old people and the youth must also cooperate." [24]

This was the first time that Li explicitly distinguished between "capitalists and workers." It is noteworthy that he advocated class cooperation rather than class struggle. For one who little more than a year later was to become the leading Chinese supporter of the Bolshevik Revolution, his view of social relations is quite remarkable. Equally surprising is Li's interpretation of the nature of progress:

The road of social evolution lies in the strengthening of order, on the one hand, and in the promotion of progress, on the other. Without order it is difficult to expect progress. Without progress, order cannot be preserved. The person who explained this most clearly was Mill . . . The evolution of the world is controlled by two types of concepts and beliefs. A cart needs two wheels and a bird two wings, and if one is lacking progress will stop. In human nature these two concepts are progressivism and conservatism. In the generations of man it is youth and old age . . . Contemptuously looking down upon old age is an evil custom of a barbaric society. [25]

Social progress, Li concluded, was dependent upon both the vigor and strength of youth and the superior knowledge and experience of older people. Thus he enjoined youth to seek to cooperate with their elders and older people to use their knowledge to contribute to the progress of society rather than turning "to their sick beds." [26]

Li believed that the major responsibility for the reconstruction of China rested upon "new China's new youth," but his emphasis on the interdependence of progressivism and conservatism was a much more moderate view than was usually found in the pages of *Hsin ch'ing-nien.* In a brief note appended to Li's essay Ch'en Tu-hsiu politely wrote that he agreed with Li but then proceeded to strike a more radical note:

In this article, Mr. Li quotes from Mill and Christiansen to explain society's need for both the forces of progress and conservatism, and his interpretation is very correct. I also find reasonable his warning to youth that they cannot regard older people as worthless. But, with respect to Mr. Li's instruction, our youth must remember two things. One is that from ancient times the strength of conservatism in our society has greatly exceeded that of progress. Speaking from the point of view of the present, one must choose which is the more important. The other is that at the present time, age and the powers of knowledge of the people of the country are in inverse proportion. If we take knowledge as the criterion, then our country's old people ought to salute the young and vigorous.[27]

The theme of the interdependence of progressivism and conservatism was further cultivated by Li in the essay "The New and the Old" published in *Hsin ch'ing-nien* in May 1918. In it Li found contemporary Chinese society filled with contradictions that had given rise to a general feeling of insecurity and unhappiness. The root of these contradictions was the conflict between new and old patterns in every aspect of Chinese life. This conflict was not to be resolved by the suppression of the old and the ascendancy of the new but rather through their harmonization. Again employing the analogy of the cart and the bird, Li took as his main thesis the proposition that "the motive force of progress in the universe wholly revolves about the action of two kinds of spiritual forces . . . one is the new and the other is the old."[28] Although Li called for the destruction of the contradictions of contemporary Chinese society and the creation of a "new life" by China's "new youth," he assumed that this process would be based at least in part upon the reconciliation of the new and the old.

Li's essay immediately drew the fire of the liberal Ch'ien Hsüan-t'ung (1887–1939), who was then one of Li's colleagues on the editorial board of *Hsin ching-nien* and later a leading figure in Kuomintang intellectual circles. In a note appended to Li's essay

Ch'ien stated: "Shou-chang wants the new youth to create a new life and this certainly is quite correct. But I believe that there is no other way to destroy the contradictory life except through suppressing the old. It does not seem necessary to invite those decrepit old people to enjoy the blessings of the new civilization and taste the flavor of the new life, for, because of their psychology, they only know to hold onto the things that are dull and doltish." [29]

In these comments by Ch'en Tu-hsiu and Ch'ien Hsüan-t'ung the implied criticism of Li Ta-chao for holding excessively moderate views was indicative of the fact that during this period Li was not the pioneer of radicalism in the ranks of the Chinese intelligentsia that Communist writers now picture him to have been. In his call for progress within order, in his nationalist rather than internationalist inclinations, and in his reluctance to discard tradition, Li appeared more conservative than Ch'en and his followers and was indeed so regarded by his contemporaries. Why was it, then, that he, rather than Ch'en, became the first to respond to the revolutionary and internationalist message of the October Revolution? The answer seems to lie in certain unique features of Li's world view — features that cannot be conveniently placed in either radical or conservative categories.

Differences between East and West

When Chinese intellectuals first began seriously to consider the thought and culture of the West, it was inevitable that the question of the nature of the differences between Eastern and Western civilizations should arise. In Chinese intellectual history the question produced an endless series of controversies, which revolved about the respective merits and deficiencies of the modes of thought and cultural values of "the East" and "the West." At one time or another virtually every major figure in the Chinese intellectual world felt compelled to make known his views on the subject, and in the Chinese debate such foreign luminaries as Rabindranath Tagore and Bertrand Russell became direct participants. In spite of the impressive amount of intellectual power that was expended, the discussion of the question in China produced little more enlightenment than it has elsewhere. More often than not the discussions degenerated into vehicles for the expression of either cultural nihilism or cultural chauvinism, or else settled upon such cliché-ridden topics as whether the "spiritualism" of the East could be reconciled with the "materialism" of the West.

Although the question of the difference between East and West had been raised before in China, it was introduced into the rhetoric of the New Culture movement by Ch'en Tu-hsiu in 1915 and remained a major topic for polemical controversy in Chinese intellectual history for the following two decades. Those members of the intelligentsia who later accepted Marxism lost interest in the controversy after their conversion to the new creed with its universalistic assumptions, but in the pre-Marxian phases of their thought they stated their views on the subject. Despite the essential sterility of the topic, these views reflected certain fundamental intellectual and psychological predispositions with which they approached the more important problems confronting them.

Ch'en's article of 1915, "The Basic Differences in the Thought of the Eastern and Western Peoples," [30] found the West animated by a spirit of struggle while the East languished in an atmosphere of tranquillity and inertia; Western society was based upon the principle of individualism while Eastern life revolved about the family; the West was guided by the rational rule of law and the principle of utilitarianism while the East was ruled by emotions and convention. In this and his other writings Ch'en left no doubt about which set of values he favored. Not only must China adopt Western values for the purpose of sheer physical survival in the modern world, but the culture of the West was morally superior as well. Nor did Ch'en see any point in attempting to harmonize the two conflicting cultures: "Whether in politics, learning, morality or literature, Western methods and Chinese methods are absolutely different and they definitely cannot be reconciled or joined together." [31] For Ch'en the traditional culture of China had nothing to contribute to modern civilization. The West was young and growing; China was old and decadent. The only solution, he repeatedly emphasized, was to destroy the old culture completely and replace it with the modern democratic and scientific culture of the West.

However extreme Ch'en's view of the Chinese tradition was, it was shared by most of the leaders of the New Culture movement. In some cases their view was even more extreme, as in Hu Shih's often vehement denunciations of China's inferiority in every area of life. Yet more was involved than simply a rejection of a tradition that seemed unsuited to the modern conditions of life, for accompanying the rejection was a feeling that the traditional culture was fundamentally corrupt and even barbaric, and had probably always been so. This feeling was particularly evident in Lu Hsün's famous short story "Diary of a Madman," published in *Hsin ch'ing-nien* in April 1918.[32]

Lu Hsün's "madman" is a paranoid obsessed by the fear that he is the intended victim of a cannabalistic conspiracy. He is the product of an insane society, but through his very madness he is able to diagnose the fundamental disease of the society: "In ancient times, as I recollect, people often ate human beings, but I am rather hazy about it. I tried to look this up but my history book has no chronology, and scrawled all over each page are the words 'virtue' and 'morality.' Since I could not sleep anyway, I read hard half the night, until I began to see words between the lines, the whole book being filled with the two words — 'Eat People.'"

To his horror the "madman" soon discovers that cannibalism is not only a matter of ancient history: "The eater of human flesh is my elder brother! I am the younger brother of an eater of human flesh! I myself will be eaten by others, but nonetheless I am the younger brother of an eater of human flesh! . . . I have only just realized that I have been living all these years in a place where for four thousand years they have been eating human flesh." The disease seems almost incurable since it is passed down from father to son: "He was much younger than my elder brother, but even he was in it [the conspiracy to eat the madman]. He must have been taught by his parents. And I am afraid he has already taught his son: that is why even the children look at me so fiercely . . . Wanting to eat men, at the same time afraid of being eaten themselves, they all look at each other with the deepest suspicion." The affliction is so widespread that no one seems able to escape its corrupting influence: "How can a man like myself, after four thousand years of man-eating history — even though I knew nothing about it at first — ever hope to face real men?" There is only one glimmer of hope: "Perhaps there are still children who have not eaten men? Save the children."

The assumption shared by many of the leading figures of *Hsin ch'ing-nien* was that the real problem of China lay in basic deficiencies of Chinese culture and thus in the psychology of the Chinese people. If, as Ch'en and Hu believed, Chinese culture was so inferior and so completely without redeeming features, and if, as Lu Hsün felt, China was a place where human beings had been eaten for four thousand years, the disease of China could be cured only by the most radical and fundamental measures. Every vestige of the old culture and tradition had to be pulled up from its roots and destroyed, and the whole basis of thinking of the people had to be completely changed. Before the new could be introduced, the old had to be totally annihilated. Nothing short of a complete moral reformation could accomplish this. Thus, Lu Hsün's "madman" cries: "You should change, change from the bottom of your hearts. You must know that in the future there will be no place for man-eaters in the world. If you don't change, you may all be eaten by each other."

What were the political implications of these attitudes? If the crisis of China was seen as one that primarily grew out of the peculiarities of the Chinese way of thinking, if there were fundamental failings in the culture of the nation and the psychology of the people, then political methods offered little promise of reaching to the root of the problem. To change the thought of the people and erect a whole new culture presupposed methods that were primarily educational and efforts that were directed toward the youth, who might not yet be infected by the diseased culture. This would require decades, perhaps generations. Therefore, to participate in the politics of a society that was so diseased would at best be a complete waste of effort and might, indeed, result in one's own infection. Thus, it is hardly surprising that the radical intellectuals of the New Culture era generally rejected political participation.

These attitudes played an important role in conditioning responses to the Russian October Revolution. However sympathetic one might be to the socialist and internationalist goals of the Russian Revolution, those goals could not seem immediately relevant to one who was preoccupied with the sickness of the very soul and spirit of his country. Only after a cultural transformation could there be any real hope of reconstructing Chinese society — only then could one afford the luxury of thinking about politics. That Ch'en Tu-hsiu shared these assumptions partially explains his

45

relatively long delay in committing himself to Bolshevism and Marxism. Only after the stormy events of 1919 had forced him to become more concerned with the immediate problems confronting China than with the problem of her tradition, could he reconcile himself to the politically activist implications of the Bolshevik message.

On the question of the differences between East and West, Li Ta-chao was something of a deviationist in the ranks of the *Hsin ch'ing-nien* group. In his essay "The Basic Differences between Eastern and Western Civilizations," [33] Li began with a scheme that, although somewhat more elaborate, was similar to the distinctions made by Ch'en Tu-hsiu. Oriental civilization was characterized as natural, restful, passive, dependent, conformist, conservative, intuitive, abstract, artistic, and spiritual. Western civilization was described as artificial (i.e., "man-made"), motivated by the spirit of struggle, active, independent, creative, progressive, rational, concrete, scientific, and materialistic. Li attributed these alleged differences to the influences of geography; the Eastern peoples were favored by the benefits of nature and thus strove for harmony with nature, while the Westerners lived under less favorable geographical conditions and thus found themselves in conflict with nature. He placed particular emphasis upon the activistic impulses of Western civilization that grew out of these geographical differences: "In Oriental civilization man looked toward heaven and thus nature controlled man; in Western civilization man stood upon the earth and subdued nature."

In pointing to the deficiencies of Eastern civilization, Li also sounded very much like the radical antitraditionalists. Among the deficiencies he listed a pessimistic view of life, inertia, lack of individualism, disrespect for women, lack of sympathy, undue emphasis upon the powers of the gods, and autocratic government. Yet from a rather similar description of the differences between East and West Li drew strikingly different conclusions.

My own view is that the progress of the universe is entirely dependent upon these two kinds of world views . . . the peaceful and the active, the conservative and the progressive. Oriental and Occidental civilizations really are the two great pivots of world progress, and just as the cart must have two wheels and the bird two wings, it is impossible for one to be lacking. Moreover, these two great spirits will themselves gradually harmonize and fuse to create unlimited progress and a new life. Oriental civilization has become stagnant and Western civilization is weary under the burden of materialism; the crisis of the world cannot be overcome unless a new, third civilization emerges.[34]

Significantly, Li suggested Russia as a possible mediator between East and West. But the great harmony must eventually be based upon a "conscious awakening" of both East and West so that the "quiescent world view of the Orient" would be replaced by the "active world view of the West," and the material preoccupations of the West would be restrained by the "spiritual life of the Orient."[35]

Despite its defects Li felt that the cultural tradition was still basically sound and should be reformed rather than destroyed. Moreover, it was conforting to believe that the defects of Western civilization were no less serious than those that afflicted Chinese civilization. If China was to pay the price of surrendering part of her culture to accept modern Western culture, then compensation must be sought — the West must also accept elements of the Chinese world view. With her reformation, China would have a unique role to play upon the world stage; China could make what Li called its "second great contribution to the reconstruction of world civilization." This nationalist motif underlay the entire essay. Li, for example, could not resist the temptation to quote a now obscure American professor on the superior qualities of Chinese civilization and to present various historical and geographical reasons why China rather than India must bear the responsibility for reconciling East and West.[36]

This point of view bears upon the question of the relationship between nationalism and traditionalism in modern China. Chinese nationalism no doubt originated in alienation from the traditional culture, as Joseph Levenson has so brilliantly argued.[37] But if nationalism and traditionalism proved intellectually irreconcilable for the previous generation of intellectuals, they nevertheless were emotionally compatible for Li Ta-chao and many of his contemporaries and successors. In the historical environment of modern China — where the West played the role of both teacher and oppressor — the two have, in fact, tended to be mutually reinforcing. When the national tradition was challenged by the values of the hostile West, the nationalist, however much he himself might have been alienated from traditional values, often felt compelled to defend the tradition, or at least certain parts of it. In the history of the Chinese Communist movement the most nationalistic Communists, such as Li and Mao Tse-tung, were generally those who had, or sought to acquire, the deepest roots in Chinese culture.

More important for the present discussion are political implications of Li's views on the question of the differences between East and West. His solution — the synthesis of the two conflicting cultures — may have been both unoriginal and quixotic, but it freed him from a politically inhibiting obsession with China's cultural "inferiority." The conception of a synthesis did not in itself encourage political participation, but neither was it a psychological barrier to political activity. Moreover, Li's almost messianic belief that China had a vital role to play in reconciling East and West to create a new, universalistic culture could not but give rise to a sense of hopefulness that encouraged his already politically activistic tendencies. Thus, Li was later able to receive Marxism without first having to overcome the feeling that the plight of China could not be resolved until China had undergone a complete cultural and moral renovation.

Metaphysics

Following his withdrawal from politics in late 1916, Li once again found the leisure to return to the philosophic speculations that he had undertaken during his last months in Japan. The activist psychology that was implicit in his essay "Spring," [38] written two years before, received firmer philosophic grounding in the essay "Now," published in the April 1918 issue of Hsin ch'ing-nien.

Li's pre-Marxian philosophy was built around a belief in a "tide of great reality" that was "everlastingly flowing without beginning and without end." It was infinite in space and eternal in time. This "tide of great reality" was a universal spirit, representing not the ideas of God but the natural life-force that is present in all phenomena. It was the essence of motion and change in all things in the universe. Although the life of the individual human body was finite, the "tide of great reality" was eternal. It passed through the lives and "egos" of innumerable individuals and in the process was forever "broadening, continuing, progressing, and developing." [39] It was the "spirit that restores youth and life, the spirit that moves mountains." [40]

Li's "tide of great reality" bore strong affinities to the philosophy of Henri Bergson. Like Bergson, Li was concerned with movement and the mode of experiencing time, which Bergson called "duration." The values of Li's philosophy, like those of Bergson, were the values of motion and change rather than static and nontemporal values. Like Bergson, Li conceived of reality as an all-pervasive life force that flowed unceasingly through time and through the personalities of individual men. Although Li did not explicitly draw Bergson's conclusion that reality is apprehended through introspection and intuition, this conclusion seems implicit in Li's pre-Marxian world view. The conclusion that Li did draw from his philosophic system was a rationale for political activity. It is interesting that many young French intellectuals who advocated "direct-action politics" in the period shortly before the First World War interpreted Bergson in the same light — although, as H. Stuart Hughes has pointed out, the notion of "direct-action politics" was contrary to Bergson's own convictions. [41]

Li's "tide of reality" progressed in dialectical rather than unilinear fashion: "since there is progress there is also retrogression, and hence arise the myriad different phenomena." Thus, there were life and death, prosperity and decline, youth and old age. But each phenomenon produced its opposite: from death came life, from decline came prosperity, from old age came youth. This was simply the "progress of spring . . . since the universe is eternal, spring is also eternal and so are we ourselves." The self-renewing process of life, death, and rebirth was, in Li's view, the essential characteristic of the life of nations as well as the life of nature and man. [42]

From this dialectical view of the universe Li deduced two principles. One was the concept of duality, according to which all things must develop through opposition; nothing could exist alone, everything must inevitably have its opposite, and the struggle between them must, just as inevitably, produce a new unity. The other was the belief that nothing could be completely lost in history. If a synthesis represented a unity of two opposites (more correctly, an infinite series of opposites), then however unique any

49

particular historical synthesis might be, it must retain elements of both the opposing phenomena that produced it. The past, and every event therein, was always a part of the present. Thus Li argued, "historical phenomena are always revolving and always changing and at the same time they still forever remain indestructible phenomena in the universe." [43] This thesis served as a philosophic support for his belief that one could not escape from one's cultural heritage, that traditional Chinese culture could not simply be made to disappear and then replaced by a whole new set of cultural values and methods borrowed abroad, because what resulted from the clash between the two opposing forces (or two opposing cultures) must inevitably contain parts of both of them.

The concept that historical phenomena were indestructible also led Li to postulate a rather harsh ethic of individual social and historical responsibility: "If one makes an error [*i-shih-t'iao* — literally, loses one's footing] then it will necessarily persist to accumulate evil seeds among innumerable men of the future and innumerable 'egos' of the future. One will never be able to remove it and never be able to repent." [44]

The essay "Now" was not intended simply as an inquiry into metaphysical knowledge. As in "Spring," Li was primarily concerned with the problem of encouraging human activity — that is, political activity — in order to solve the immediate problems of China. To do so, he must relate intimately his conception of dialectic evolution with the actual life-process of the individual. It had to be shown that concrete individual activity was both necessary and meaningful in the vast dialectical movement of universal forces. Li approached one aspect of this problem when he argued that all historical phenomena were indestructible and that therefore each individual was responsible to history for his every action. In "Now" he dealt with another aspect of the problem — the psychological barriers to human activity.

Li's discussion of this question was based upon the dialectical principle that the present includes both the past and the future: "Unlimited 'pasts' all find their resting place in the 'present,' and unlimited 'futures' all originate in the 'present.'" He declared that the present or "now" was the "most precious thing in the world," and he quoted Emerson on why the present was to be loved. Moreover, because everything in the universe was constantly changing, the "now" was the thing most easily lost. "Is it not pitiful, there-fore, if we take 'now' and recklessly throw it away?"[45]

Li enumerated three general types of attitudes that prevented men from truly appreciating the present. There were those who hated the present and looked to the past; those who hated the present and looked to the future; and those who simply enjoyed the present. While the members of the first group dissipated their efforts in a vain attempt to restore antiquity, those of the second "float along as in a dream, throwing away a great many 'presents' where they might have exerted their efforts, and instead sink into the empti-ness of illusions. Neither of these two groups are able to contribute to progress; on the contrary, they obstruct progress." Finally, those who enjoyed "now" were people who were satisfied with the present and therefore saw no need for change. Since they could not appreci-ate the true significance of "now," they impeded the "tide of prog-ress" as much as those who hated "now": "Enjoying 'now' is a form of inertia; it is necessary to advance a step further to understand that the reason for loving 'now' is wholly dependent upon being able to strive to create the future; it definitely cannot be attained [in a state of] contented passivity."[46]

Thus, the whole of Li's philosophy can be seen as an expression of his own strongly activist impulses. Its purpose was to stimulate human activity — to encourage others to appreciate the opportuni-ties that lay in the present in order to "strive to create the future." This, he declared, was "the basic duty of human life." By activity in the present the individual could become identified with the great progressive "tide of reality" and reach a future where "the universe is the ego and the ego is the universe."[47]

But if the individual was to be active in the present, how was this activism to be expressed in the concrete historical conditions of twentieth century China? If the law of universal dialectical progress was constantly developing to higher and higher levels, toward what historical goals and purposes was it moving? Li was not yet able to answer these questions. Nationalism alone was clearly an inadequate goal for such universalistic forces. Not until the Bol-shevik Revolution presented Li with an all-embracing vision of the future, as well as with practical methods of individual activity for realizing that future, was he able to find answers to some of the issues posed by his pre-Marxian world view.

CHAPTER III THE RUSSIAN REVOLUTION AND THE INTRODUCTION OF MARXISM

THE FIRST passages from the writings of Karl Marx to be translated into the Chinese language were ironically the ten measures in the second section of the *Communist Manifesto* that Marx had proposed for "the most advanced countries" following the success of the proletarian revolution. The translator of this portion of the *Manifesto* was Chu Chih-hsin (1884–1920), a young Chinese student who was a member of Sun Yat-sen's revolutionary group in exile in Japan. Chu appended the proposals of Marx to the first of a series of two articles he wrote late in 1905 entitled "Short Biographies of German Social Revolutionaries." The first article — published in the January 1906 issue of *Min-pao* (People's paper) the organ of the T'ung-meng hui exiles in Japan — consisted of biographical sketches of Marx and Engels. The second dealt with one of Marx's most prominent socialist rivals, Ferdinand Lassalle.[1]

Even before the appearance of Chu Chih-hsin's article, some anti-Manchu Chinese reformers and revolutionaries had become acquainted with at least the name of Marx. Liang Ch'i-ch'ao was the first prominent Chinese intellectual to refer to Marx — although briefly and in highly critical tones — in an essay dealing with the English social philosopher Benjamin Kidd, written in 1902.[2] At about this time more radically inclined Chinese students and exiles in Japan began to read Japanese socialist writings. In 1903 two popular Japanese accounts of European socialist history and thought that were sympathetic to Marxism were translated and published in Chinese.³ Not until the Russian Revolution of 1905, however, did socialist influences in Chinese revolutionary circles become widespread. The exiled followers of Sun Yat-sen, stirred by the example of the Russian upheaval, began to feel a certain kinship with the Russian revolutionaries, which they were fond of expressing by drawing a parallel between the struggle against Czarist absolutism and their own struggle against the tyranny of the Manchus. It was under the stimulus of this general interest in socialist theory that Chu Chih-hsin wrote his article on Marx.

Among the many socialist doctrines considered by radical Chinese intellectuals in the period between 1905 and the Bolshevik Revolution of 1917, Marxism seemed to attract the least attention. There were strong anarchist influences in Chinese revolutionary circles during these years and a widespread if vague sympathy for socialism, but not a single figure emerged who could even be remotely identified as a Marxist. Chu Chih-hsin appears to have lost interest in Marxism soon after the appearance of his article. He later became identified with the left wing of the Kuomintang and did not again write on Marx or Marxism. Those among the small band of Chinese revolutionaries who continued to look to the Russian revolutionary movement for inspiration were largely attracted to the terrorist exploits of the Russian Socialist Revolutionary party rather than to the Russian Marxists. Preoccupied with the immediate need to overthrow the Manchu dynasty, the Chinese revolutionaries were interested in methods and ideologies that promised quicker solutions than those offered by Marxist doctrine.

However, along with the celebration of Russian terrorist activities appearing in the pages of Chinese radical journals during these years is evidence of at least a sporadic interest in the writings of Marx and Engels. In 1908 a Chinese translation of the first chapter of the *Communist Manifesto* and Engels' introduction to its English edition appeared in *T'ien-i-pao*, a magazine of anarchist inclinations published by Chinese students in Japan. That same year *T'ien-i-pao* carried a translation of the second chapter of Engels' *The Origin of the Family, Private Property, and the State*. In 1912 a translation of Engels' *Socialism: Utopian and Scientific* was published in the Shanghai periodical *Hsin shih-chieh* (New world).⁴ This was the extent of the works of Marx and Engels available in Chinese before

1919, although Chinese readers of Japanese and Western languages were of course able to gain access to a much wider range of Marxist writings if they chose.[5]

As in the case of Chu Chih-hsin, neither the Chinese translators of the writings of Marx and Engels nor their readers felt sufficiently moved by the doctrine to undertake actively its propagation; nor, it would appear, were they curious enough to study it seriously. This cannot be accounted for by any reluctance on the part of Chinese intellectuals to support radical ideas. During these years there was no lack of passionate declarations in favor of the most extreme forms of anarchism and nihilism, and there were some who did not hesitate to advocate, and occasionally even practice, political terrorism. The reason for the lack of interest in Marxism is not difficult to discern and has been frequently noted: in the period before the October Revolution Marxism, in its pre-Leninist form, presupposed the existence of capitalist economic relations and a well-developed urban proletariat. In the absence of these conditions Marxism could not yet serve as a guide to meaningful political action. To those members of the intelligentsia who were attracted to socialism, Marx appeared simply as one among many Western socialist thinkers — indeed, one who was held in considerably less esteem than Kropotkin and Bakunin or even Saint-Simon and Henry George. Thus, Marx was known to Chinese intellectuals in the early years of the century, but his theory clearly failed to strike a responsive chord.

After the Revolution of 1911 there seems to have been a general decline of interest in socialist theories. Many of the members of the T'ung-meng-hui who had earlier been influenced by anarchism, such as Wang Ching-wei (1883–1944), tended to abandon the anarchist faith as they became preoccupied with the practical political affairs of the Kuomintang. With the emergence of the new group of intellectuals associated with *Hsin ch'ing-nien* and the development of the New Culture movement after 1915, the question of socialism seemed even further removed from the relevant issues confronting the intelligentsia. Concerned with the problem of transforming traditional cultural values, the new intellectuals looked to the existing democratic institutions and scientific culture of the advanced countries of the West, not to the revolutionary political movements in the West that opposed the existing order.

This does not imply the existence of widespread antisocialist predispositions. On the contrary, the westernized intelligentsia's admiration for contemporary Western thought and political institutions rarely extended to an admiration for the underlying capitalist social and economic system. There was a general sympathy for socialism as an ultimate goal, even though it was rarely discussed. Ch'en Tu-hsiu's view of socialism in the years immediately preceding the Bolshevik Revolution was fairly typical. In 1915 Ch'en saw socialism as one of the three most advanced intellectual tendencies of modern Western civilization, along with the doctrine of human rights and the theory of evolution. Modern socialism, he wrote, had originated in France as a movement to achieve social and economic equality, had been developed in Germany by Marx and Lassalle (between whom he made no distinction), and was now, he hoped, serving to encourage the governments and wealthy classes of the European nations to carry out the social reforms necessary to harmonize capital and labor.[6] When in 1917 a reader of *Hsin ch'ing-nien* wrote that he believed socialism represented the most advanced form of modern thought and inquired as to why there was so little discussion of it by the contributors to the magazine, who usually promoted the most advanced theories, Ch'en briefly replied: "The ideals of socialism are very high and its schools of thought are very complex. I can only say that China, compared to Europe, is very retarded. Because [China's] industry is not yet flourishing, socialism cannot yet be put into effect."[7]

In the years preceding the October Revolution Li Ta-chao found socialist theories little more relevant to the needs of China than did Ch'en, although he expressed some passing interest in them. Shortly before he left for Japan in 1913, Li is said to have had some sympathy for Chiang K'ang-hu's (b. ca. 1883) mildly reformist "Socialist party,"[8] an inconsequential and short-lived group founded in late 1911. Li was also sympathetic to Sun Yat-sen's "Principle of Peoples Livelihood" (*min-sheng chu-i*). Regardless of whether this expression was originally intended by Sun as a synonym for socialism, it seems clear that Li used it to mean little more than a general concern for the welfare of the people and the promotion of the national economy — principles traditionally supported by Chinese political thinkers for over two thousand years. In Japan Li came into contact with more substantial socialist influences, such as the writings of Saint-Simon and especially the Japanese utopian "New Village" movement, which had a particularly strong following at Waseda University where Li studied.[9]

Li's first exposure to Marxist theory occurred during his student days in Japan, although the extent of his early acquaintance with it does not appear to have been significant. Kao I-han (1885 —), the well-known liberal political philosopher who was a frequent contributor to *Hsin ch'ing-nien*, has written that when he first met Li in Japan in early 1916 — when the latter came to enlist Kao's participation in the movement against Yüan Shih-k'ai — Li was engaged in the study of Marxian political economy. According to Kao's account, Li, "his hand not releasing the volume for whole days at a time," was ardently reading the works of Kawakami Hajime, the famous Japanese interpreter and translator of Marx.[10] Despite Kao's somewhat dramatic description of Li's first encounter with Marxist theory, it would seem that the impact of Marxism was something less than overwhelming. Although Li no doubt read Kawakami, probably in the course of his formal studies in political economy, no traces of Marxist influences can be found in his writings before the end of 1918, nor was Marx even mentioned until then. Li was apparently not sufficiently impressed with the doctrine to investigate it further until after the Bolshevik Revolution. During his last year in Japan, Li was concerned with the problem of finding a philosophic support for his desire for immediate political action, and it is hardly likely that he could have found anything in orthodox Marxist political economy to encourage him in this quest.

The absence of a Marxist Social-Democratic tradition in China, as well as the lack of any appreciable Marxian influence on the thought of intellectuals before 1918, had important implications for the way in which the Bolshevik Revolution and Marxist doctrine were received in China. Unlike European and Russian Marxists, who had usually immersed themselves in years of study of the fine points of Marxist theory before committing themselves to a course of political action, those who came into the Communist fold in China were committed to a "Marxist" revolution long before they had accepted even the basic assumptions of the Marxist world view. This meant that they responded to the message of the Bolshevik Revolution almost completely outside of the framework of Marxist categories of thought. Not being wedded to orthodox Marxist formulations, many found it comparatively easy to revise and transform those formulations to fit the needs of the Chinese situation.

Although it is generally true that the impulse to revolution preceded the commitment to Marxist ideology in China, this fact did not prevent the future members of the Chinese Communist intelligentsia from responding to the Bolshevik Revolution in very different ways. The differences reflected not only dissimilarities in pre-Marxian world views and in personalities but also divergent attitudes towards one of the more immediate issues confronting the intelligentsia — the First World War. Before a consideration of the impact of the October Revolution, therefore, it is necessary to turn to the intellectual scene in China during the last years of the war.

The First World War and the Russian February Revolution

In the months preceding the Russian October Revolution of 1917 Peking replaced Shanghai as the center of the new intellectual movement in China. In December 1916, Ts'ai Yüan-p'ei (1876–1940), a man of generally libertarian views, became chancellor of Peking University and proceeded to reorganize the university upon the principle of "freedom of thought" and "the policy of tolerating everything and including everything." Concerning the appointment of professors, Ts'ai declared, "their knowledge is the main thing . . . their words and actions outside the university are entirely their own affair. This university never makes inquiries nor takes responsibility for such words and actions." [11] In this liberal atmosphere Peking University became a haven for the radical intelligentsia. In early 1917 Ts'ai Yüan-p'ei appointed Ch'en Tu-hsiu as dean of the School of Letters. A year later, in February 1918, Li Ta-chao was appointed chief librarian of the university upon Ch'en's recommendation. [12] He concurrently became professor of economics and later professor of history. [13] Most of the other leading figures identified with *Hsin ch'ing-nien* also became associated with Peking University at this time.

As the radical intellectuals were gathering in Peking in 1917, the First World War was entering its fourth year. The results of the war drastically changed the perspectives and assumptions held by many leading members of the westernized intelligentsia. The war not only made possible Lenin's seizure of power in Russia, but it also led to the erosion of the Chinese intelligentsia's image of a rational, stable, and democratic West where a scientific culture served the social progress of mankind. It was not so much the carnage of the war itself as the war's aftermath that tarnished this image. When the Allied Powers cynically sanctioned Japanese ambitions in North China at the Versailles Peace Conference in 1919, the indignation of Chinese intellectuals and students made many receptive to the anticolonial and anticapitalist appeals of Marxism-Leninism.

Even before the betrayal of Chinese interests at Versailles had turned the attention of Chinese intellectuals to the dramatic developments in Russia, at least one member of the new intelligentsia was looking abroad for omens of revolution. When the democratic February Revolution of 1917 overthrew the monarchy in Russia, Li Ta-chao interpreted it as the harbinger of a similar revolution in China. "Today the blood of the Russian people," he stated in March 1917, "is washing away the dirt accumulated over the years in the Russian political world and indirectly providing the embryo for our own country's freedom; it will cause the old bureaucrats to recognize definitely that the dictatorship cannot be revived, that the sovereignty of the people cannot again be repressed, that the republic cannot once more be destroyed, and that the imperial government cannot be resurrected . . . objectively speaking, the success of this revolution in Russia cannot avoid influencing the next revolution in China." [14]

Li was not alone in his interest in the February Revolution. The other members of the Chinese democratic intelligentsia unanimously welcomed the downfall of the czarist system and the establishment of a democratic republic in Russia. But whereas Li hoped that the Russian Revolution would provide the stimulus for a political transformation in China, others were more concerned with its implications for the outcome of the European war.

The question of China's participation in the war had become a burning political issue and a hotly debated topic in Chinese intellectual circles during the early months of 1917. In February the Peking government broke off diplomatic relations with Germany in preparation for a formal declaration of war, which was made in August. Most intellectuals associated with *Hsin ch'ing-nien* approved the government's policy of bringing China into the war, for they interpreted the war as a struggle of the Anglo-French forces of progress and democracy against German militarism and monarchism. The victory of humanism over militarism and democracy over monarchism, they assumed, would have a salutary influence upon political conditions in China. As it turned out, this conviction that the Allied Powers were fighting for the cause of justice in the world only served to intensify their eventual disillusionment with the West.

But in 1917, to men like Ch'en Tu-hsiu who favored a Chinese declaration of war against Germany, a revolution in Russia was mainly significant insofar as it might affect the course of the war. Thus, Ch'en's article "The Russian Revolution and Our Nation's Awakening" had relatively little to say about either the February Revolution or the awakening of China. It was essentially concerned with arguing that China should join the Allied cause. It was every bit as necessary for China to fight against Germany in 1917, Ch'en declared, as it had been to oppose Yüan Shih-k'ai a year earlier. As for the February Revolution itself, Ch'en stated: "I praise its success. I believe that it [the Russian provisional government] will not need to enter into separate peace negotiations with Germany, which represents monarchism and militarism, that it will oppose the pro-German clique of the old government, and that it will fully favor the spirit of democracy and humanism. I believe that the democratic nations will come to its aid and that it will fight against Germany and all the immoral monarchist and militarist states." [15]

Unlike Ch'en's essay, Li's article on the February Revolution was unconcerned with the fate of the Allied cause. In fact, he suggested that an Allied victory would not be a victory for democracy but would only benefit "those who champion bureaucratic government." [16] Li's attitude toward the war was in large measure determined by the element in his "dialectical" philosophy that maintained that history was an unending cyclic process of the inevitable rise and decline of nations. This conception of history, inspired by a faith that the forces of rebirth within old China were preparing the way for the resurgence of a young China, convinced Li that the advanced nations of the West were in decline and that the future belonged to the newly emerging nations, which had not yet found their way to the center of the world historical stage. Thus a year earlier in 1916 Li had written: "Such prominent nations of Europe as Italy, France, Spain, Portugal, Holland, Belgium, Denmark,

Sweden, Norway and England have all had a long history, a long life. They had their vigorous youth when their distinctive genius was brought into full play; but now their day has gone, their fame and glory have declined into mere empty shells. Thus these nations are past travellers in the caravan of human civilization."[17]

With the notable exception of Russia, the list of "declining" nations included all the major powers on the Allied side in 1916. Germany and Austro-Hungary were pointedly excluded. In fact, Li predicted a German military victory, since Germany was a comparatively "newly emergent" nation on the world scene. Although whatever sympathy Li may have felt for Germany in 1916 was short-lived (at least pro-German sentiments did not appear again in his writings), it is evident that he did not share the sympathy of Ch'en Tu-hsiu and the other members of the *Hsin ch'ing-nien* group for the Allied cause.

The October Revolution

The different attitudes of Li and Ch'en on the war were reflected in their responses to both the February and October Revolutions in Russia. Believing that the Allied Powers were engaged in a just struggle for democracy and humanism, Ch'en could wholeheartedly welcome the February Revolution not only because it was a democratic revolution (which made more plausible his view of the nature of the war), but also because the Russian provisional government was determined to keep the Russian armies in the war against the Central Powers. But Ch'en could hardly have been enthusiastic when the Bolsheviks came to power in Russia determined to sign a separate peace with Germany — a development that seriously threatened the Allied position. Lenin's description of the war as a conflict among equally rapacious and aggressive imperialist states must have at first appeared to Ch'en as a repudiation of the democratic West in which he so fervently believed.

Because Li Ta-chao did not share Ch'en's faith in the West or his view of the war, he could be more receptive to the possible political implications for China of the two Russian revolutions of 1917. His response to the February Revolution foreshadowed his response to the October Revolution both in his inclination to look to Russia for signs of a forthcoming revolution in China and in the type of imagery he employed. He had already begun to use an historical image in which each century was carried along by a single, universal wave of revolution. Thus, in the February Revolution Li saw the first manifestation of a great antibureaucratic tide of the twentieth century that would inevitably spread to the far corners of the earth: "Just as the main aim of the revolution of the early part of the previous century was a revolt against monarchical and aristocratic government, so the main aim of the revolution of the early part of the present century is a revolt against bureaucratic government." [18] In his essay "Violence and Politics," which appeared on the eve of the Bolshevik Revolution and presented a rationale for revolution, Li again evoked the metaphor of universalistic waves. Democracy was a modern world tendency that "flows like a hundred rivers towards the East and nothing can stop it." [19] This historical image of century-long revolutionary waves was a prominent feature of his response to the Bolshevik Revolution and became deeply imprinted upon many of his student followers at Peking University.

Contrary to the impression left by recent Communist accounts of modern Chinese history, the Russian October Revolution did not strike the Chinese intellectual world with the force of a thunderbolt bringing sudden enlightenment. Except for Li Ta-chao, few Chinese found the revolutionary message of Bolshevism relevant to their own situation until after the events set in motion by the Versailles Peace Conference and the May Fourth Incident of 1919. Even Li, the first important Chinese intellectual to proclaim his allegiance to Bolshevism, did not publicly express his views on the significance of the October Revolution until the summer of 1918, seven months after Lenin had seized power.

This delay cannot be attributed to a lack of information about events in Russia. After the February Revolution both Li and Ch'en had published their interpretations of that event within a few weeks. Accounts of the October Revolution appeared in Chinese newspapers three days after the Bolshevik victory,[20] and events in Soviet Russia thereafter were fairly regularly reported in the Chinese press and were followed with close interest by Chinese intellectuals of diverse political inclinations.

The Russian Revolution seems at first to have aroused more interest in Kuomintang circles than among those intellectuals who eventually came into the Communist fold. On January 1, 1918, an

61

editorial expressing sympathy for the aims of the Bolsheviks appeared in the Shanghai Kuomintang organ *Kuo-min jih-pao* (Republic daily). Shortly afterwards, Sun Yat-sen sent a personal message of congratulations to Lenin.[21] Although the intellectuals associated with *Hsin ch'ing-nien* remained silent, one may well suspect that many members of the new intelligentsia were attracted to the example of the Bolshevik Revolution long before they were willing to comment upon it publicly. They could not fail to be impressed by the social and political similarities between Russia and China, by the Bolshevik promise rapidly to transform an economically backward land, and by the dazzling vision of a classless, nonbureaucratic society in which all men would enjoy equally the benefits of the most advanced levels of civilization. Opposing these attractions were several factors, such as their sympathy for the Allied cause in the First World War and their overriding concern with the need for implanting Western cultural values in China as a prerequisite to social reform and political action. As a result of these conflicting attitudes, views on the October Revolution remained ambiguous and unexpressed until the climactic events of 1919; the new intellectuals neither praised nor criticized Bolshevism. In the meantime, they held to their faith in democracy and science and waited to see what the end of the war would bring.

Although Li Ta-chao did not share his fellow intellectuals' hopeful view of the war or their preoccupation with the deficiencies of Chinese culture, he shared other less deep-seated concerns that contributed to his reluctance to rush immediately to the Bolshevik banner. There was, to begin with, considerable doubt that the Bolsheviks would be able to maintain their precarious hold on political power. Press reports filtering into China from Europe presented lurid and often highly exaggerated accounts of the political disorders and economic chaos that had followed in the wake of the revolution. If the Bolsheviks were not overthrown by the civil war that threatened them from within, it was widely assumed that the European powers would intervene to crush the revolution from without. Thus, even among those who were most attracted to the Bolshevik example, the fear that the revolution might prove abortive tended to inhibit commitments.

Responses to the Russian Revolution were further inhibited by the predisposition to look to the advanced countries of the West for political and intellectual guidance. Unlike the older nationalist intellectuals of the T'ung-meng hui era, who had found a certain spiritual identity with the Russian revolutionary movement, the new intellectuals had displayed relatively little interest in Russia (with the exception of Russian literature). To turn away from the political and social thinkers of France, England, and America, where democracy and science seemed triumphant, in order to accept ideological and political leadership from backward, peasant Russia, required a psychological reorientation that could not be accomplished at once. Even though Li was less enthusiastic about Western democracy and science than his colleagues, he too had drawn his main intellectual inspiration from the thinkers of the advanced Western nations. Except for Tolstoy, he had been little influenced by Russian thought.

Finally, the Marxist and Leninist terminology that emanated from Petrograd was largely unfamiliar to Chinese ears. How were the Chinese in 1917 to interpret such expressions as "the dictatorship of the proletariat" and "dialectical materialism"? China, after all, had no Marxian Social-Democratic tradition that might have provided some basis for interpreting and responding to the Leninist program. The very strangeness of both the pattern of events in Russia and the ideology that accompanied it at first provoked curiosity rather than passionate declarations of approval or denunciation.

It was perhaps because of these factors that not until the summer of 1918 was Li willing to express his views on the October Revolution. When he did so, however, in an article entitled "A Comparison of the French and Russian Revolutions," he left no doubt that he had formed a deep emotional commitment to the universalistic Bolshevik message. For Li the October Revolution represented no less than a "manifestation of the general psychological transformation of twentieth century humanity." [22] He drew a parallel between the French Revolution as heralding the historical tendencies of the nineteenth century and the Russian Revolution as performing a similar role for the twentieth century. This model of comparison was to be repeated again and again by the young intellectuals of the May Fourth period.

Although in Li's view the two revolutions were reflective of the historic tendencies of their respective centuries, the Russian Revolution represented an incomparably higher level of development. The

French Revolution had been basically a nationalistic revolution with "a social revolutionary flavor," but the Russian Revolution was fundamentally a socialist revolution with "a world revolutionary color." The revolution of 1789 had been motivated by "the spirit of French patriotism," but the revolution of 1917 was based upon "the Russian spirit of humanism": "the spirit of the French of that day was the spirit of loving their country; the spirit of the Russians today is the spirit of loving man. The former was based upon nationalism; the latter tends toward internationalism. The former has always been the source of war; the latter promotes the dawn of peace." [23] Whereas the influences of the "nationalistic" French Revolution had by-passed China, the internationalist character of the Russian Revolution was to be of universal significance. Under its influence China could enter the stage of world history and join the great tide of universal progress.

Li's emphasis upon the internationalism of the Russian Revolution may at first appear to be a disavowal of his strongly nationalistic and patriotic tendencies. Yet nationalism was very much involved in this interpretation. The October Revolution, he proclaimed, was the first great step in the "reconstruction of a third great civilization" — a reconstruction in which China and the Chinese cultural tradition had a special and essential role to play. For Li in 1918 the primary appeal of the October Revolution lay in the belief that the "spirit of Russia" was uniquely qualified to "harmonize Eastern and Western civilizations" because Russia bordered on both Europe and Asia and had therefore been influenced by both Eastern and Western civilizations. "The creation of a new civilization in the world that simultaneously retains the special features of Eastern and Western civilizations, and the talents of the European and Asian peoples, cannot be undertaken except by the Russians." [24] Thus, if Russia had a messianic mission in world history, it was a mission to which China was to make a distinctive contribution. Through the medium of Russia China could preserve her national identity and at the same time join the universal forces of progress. Through "internationalism" China could accept the advanced material civilization of the West without surrendering the essence of her own nationhood. With this assurance Li proclaimed, "we have only to raise our heads to welcome the dawn of the new civilization of the world, and turn our ears to welcome the new Russia that is founded upon freedom and humanism, and to adapt ourselves to the new tide of the world." [25]

One further aspect of Li's initial response to the October Revolution should be noted since it is important to an understanding of the appeal of the revolution in China and the later evolution of Chinese Marxist ideology. Li believed that backwardness was a positive advantage — that the very backwardness of nations like China and Russia held the seeds of youth and progress — whereas the material maturity of the West was a prelude to decline and decay. Li applied this conception to the history of Russia as follows:

From the point of view of the history of civilizations, any particular national civilization has its period of flourishing and its period of decline. The countries of Europe, like France and England, have reached a period of maturity in civilization. They no longer have the strength to advance any further. German civilization is today like the sun in the heavens controlling the forces of the world . . . [but] according to the history of the past, a period of flourishing is followed by a period of decline. Even though Russia geographically occupies a position on the European continent, in comparison with the other countries of Europe the rate of progress of Russian civilization has been slow for the past three centuries. History tells us that the Mongolian invasions stopped the growth of Russian civilization, caused it to return to barbarism and stagnate. Therefore the European Renaissance had no influence on Russia and Russia became completely isolated from European civilization. Because of this isolation, Russia's progress in civilization was comparatively slow with respect to the other nations of Europe, *and just because of its comparative slowness in the evolution of civilization there existed surplus energy for development* [My italics].[26]

Since Li believed the backwardness of Russia had resulted in the accumulation of "surplus energy," how much more "surplus energy" he must have felt was stored in China, where the rate of progress had been even slower! Thus, we are confronted with the paradox of China's pioneer Marxist treating as advantages the very characteristics of the Russian environment that created the most severe ideological and psychological dilemmas for the Russian Marxists; namely, the backwardness of Russian economic and social development and what Lenin and Trotsky frequently disparaged as the still "Oriental" characteristics of Russian thought and culture.

The promise of the Russian Revolution to transform a backward society soon began to appeal to a growing number of Chinese intellectuals. For Li Ta-chao this appeal was all the greater and more immediate because of his philosophy of dialectical evolution and rebirth. All the philosophic assumptions behind his conception of a resurgent young China suddenly and dramatically breaking out of its dead shell predisposed him to look favorably on the Russian Revolution. It confirmed his own pre-Marxian world view. The spectacle of the most backward country in Europe suddenly appearing as the advance guard of modern civilization in defiant challenge of the West was not only emotionally satisfying to Li as a nationalist but also intellectually satisfying to him as a dialectician, who saw all phenomena as producing their opposites. The rebirth of backward Russia was merely the prelude to an even more dramatic rebirth of China.

Li's argument that the backwardness of Russia (and China) foreshadowed an imminent leap into the forefront of civilization bears certain affinities to Trotsky's theory of permanent revolution. Trotsky maintained that in the era of international socialist revolutions the working classes of the backward countries were potentially more revolutionary than their counterparts in the mature societies of the West. Because of the weakness of the bourgeoisie in the economically underdeveloped areas, the proletariat, however small in numbers, might gain control of the "bourgeois democratic" revolution against the "feudal" state power and almost immediately transform the revolution into a socialist revolution that would result in the establishment of a proletarian dictatorship. This, in turn, would provide the stimulus for proletarian revolutions in the "advanced" countries. It was possible that "in a backward country with a lesser degree of capitalistic development," Trotsky declared in his classic inversion of Marx in 1906, "the proletariat should sooner reach political supremacy than in a highly developed capitalist state."[27]

Li and Trotsky began from very different premises. Trotsky developed the theory of permanent revolution within the framework of Marxist categories and sanctioned it by an analysis of the material conditions of life; Li still thought in terms of the movement of spiritual forces and the accumulation of "surplus energy." Trotsky insisted that the revolution would essentially be the work of the proletariat (however embryonic its stage of development); Li was not yet concerned with the role of social classes. And Trotsky, unlike Li, assumed that the survival of socialist revolutions in the economically backward areas would ultimately depend upon successful proletarian risings in the capitalist states of the West. Despite these differences, the two arrived at certain strikingly similar notions. Both found in backwardness the source of the most rapid political and social progress, and both assigned to the economically backward lands the really creative role in the great drama of global revolution. On a nondoctrinal level, at least, Li was something of a "Trotskyist" before he was a Marxist. At the same time he was also a precursor of "Maoism." In his belief that China's backwardness offered immense advantages for both the tempo and content of her future advance, and that all the evils of old China were on the verge of being "reborn" into their opposites, Li foreshadowed one of the major themes of contemporary Chinese Communist ideology.

"A Comparison of the French and Russian Revolutions" leaves no doubt that by mid-1918 Li was emotionally committed to the October Revolution, but it offers nothing to suggest that he had even begun to consider seriously Marxist theory. The forces of history and revolution, as he then perceived them, operated in the realm of spiritual changes and psychological transformations. For example, Li explained that there were differences between the French and Russian revolutions simply because "the spirit of the times are not the same." History, he flatly declared, "is a record of universal psychological expression." [28] Thus Li had not yet accepted even the fundamental materialist premise of Marxist doctrine. This in itself indicates the superficiality of his earlier contact with Marxist writings and suggests that the appeal of the October Revolution preceded the influence of Marxist theory. In the summer of 1918 Li hardly even seemed aware of the socialist goals of the October Revolution. Rather, he was attracted to Bolshevism because he saw in it the triumph of "freedom and humanism" and the beginnings of a great synthesis between Eastern and Western civilizations.

Shortly afterwards, however, Li came to the realization that his acceptance of the universal message of the October Revolution demanded the acceptance of the universal validity of Marxist theory as well. By the time he wrote his influential article "The Victory of Bolshevism" in November 1918, Li could announce — almost in tones of having made a discovery — that the Bolsheviks were followers of the doctrine of "the German socialist Marx." The great struggle in the world could no longer be looked upon as a clash between different "spirits of the time"; it had become "the class war . . .

between the world proletarian masses and the world capitalists." The aim of Bolshevism was no longer simply the reconciliation of Eastern and Western cultures; it had become "the destruction of the presently existing national boundaries which are barriers to socialism and the destruction of the capitalist monopoly-profit system of production." [29]

In "The Victory of Bolshevism" Li ridiculed China's participation in the World War — a war in which not a single Chinese soldier had fought and in which Chinese generals had commanded no troops. He scoffed at those Chinese who were then celebrating the Allied victory; only the foreigners living in China, he bitterly remarked, had cause to applaud the Allied success. Even their celebration was meaningless, for the Western powers were destined to follow German militarism to destruction. The real victory would be "the victory of humanism, pacifism, and reason; the victory of democracy, socialism, and Bolshevism; the victory of the red flag, the working class of the world, and the new tide of the twentieth century." [30]

Li's response to the October Revolution was imbued with a chiliastic feeling that the world stood on the brink of a gigantic transformation. Bolshevism was a great, irresistible wave about to sweep over the world: "Such mighty rolling tides are indeed beyond the power of the present capitalist governments to prevent or stop, for the mass movement of the twentieth century combines the whole of mankind into one great mass. The efforts of each individual within this great mass . . . will then be concentrated and become a great, irresistible social force . . . In the course of such a world mass movement, all those dregs of history that can impede the progress of the new movement — such as emperors, nobles, warlords, bureaucrats, militarists, and capitalists — will certainly be destroyed as though struck by a thunderbolt." In his fondness for drawing analogies from nature, Li maintained that the revolution in Russia signaled this oncoming destruction as certainly as the fall of the first leaf signals the coming of autumn. "From now on," he cried, "every place in the world will see the victorious flag of Bolshevism and hear the triumphal song of Bolshevism. The bell of humanitarianism is sounding. The dawn of freedom has arrived." [31]

Li's response to the Russian Revolution cannot be understood solely in terms of the influence of new ideas. He did not become such an ardent advocate of Bolshevism simply because of the impact of the doctrines of Marx, Lenin, and Trotsky. Rather, he was inspired by the very act of revolution, by his expectation that the millenium was being realized in the present. His articles of July and November 1918 were less concerned with what the millenium was to look like than with the fact that it was being created in the here and now. He conceived of the revolution not so much as a revolt against particular oppressors but as a great, universal, and elemental force that was transforming the entire world order. In "The Victory of Bolshevism" the presumably class character of the revolution as an uprising of workers against capitalists was mentioned almost incidentally. The main thrust of the article was the feeling that the "spirit" of Bolshevism "embodies what can be regarded as a common awakening in the heart of each individual of twentieth century mankind."[32] For Li in 1918 the revolution itself was the only real source of value and truly creative force.

Karl Mannheim has written, "the only true, perhaps the only direct, identifying characteristic of chiliastic experience is absolute presentness . . . for the real chiliast, the present becomes the break through which what was previously inward bursts out suddenly, takes hold of the outer world and transforms it."[33] There is no better way to characterize Li Ta-chao's response to Bolshevism. Chiliastic experiences are involved in all great revolutions and they were particularly characteristic of the Bolshevik Revolution, with its universalistic pretensions. There already existed precedents for such a response in Li's pre-Marxian world view. Both his faith that China was on the verge of a rebirth and his feeling of exaltation for the present moment, drawn from Emerson's concept of time, predisposed him to view the October Revolution in particularly ecstatic terms.

In view of his emotionally charged image of a single, global wave of revolution, it is not surprising that Li was at first attracted more by the writings of Trotsky than by those of Lenin. Trotsky was the great apostle of world revolution, and his melodramatic vision of the Russian Revolution as a spark that would ignite a world conflagration was very much in accord with Li's own feelings. In "The Victory of Bolshevism" Lenin was mentioned only once, but Trotsky's book, *The Bolsheviki and World Peace* (written in 1915) was discussed at length, and Li quoted a passage in which Trotsky declared that "ours will be the one and only creative force in the future."[34] Trotsky was singled out for special praise for his view that "the Russian Revolution is to serve as a fuse to world revolution" as well as for his "love for the world proletarian masses."[35]

Convinced that the "Russian form of revolution" was a drama destined to be played upon a global stage, Li was no less sanguine than the Bolshevik leaders in perceiving signs of imminent revolution in Europe. He saw evidence of forthcoming revolutions not only in Germany, Austria, and Hungary, but in Holland, Sweden, and Spain as well.[36] But what of China? Li could hardly fail to have been struck by the contrast between the mighty wave of revolution that he imagined to be sweeping the world and the situation that confronted him at home. The stranglehold of the warlords on Chinese politics seemed as tight as ever, and the political apathy of the Chinese masses, which had remained largely undisturbed since the Boxer uprising of two decades before, offered little promise for revolution from below. Even the most advanced, politically conscious intellectuals were applauding the military victory of the Western capitalist powers rather than the victory of the Bolsheviks.

In a speech delivered at a meeting celebrating the end of the war, Li indicated that he was indeed concerned with this dilemma. The world, he proclaimed, was on the verge of a gigantic historical transformation; it was about to become a workers' world in which only those who worked would have the right to eat. How, in such a world, he asked, "will an avaricious and lazy people such as we be able to find a place to stand?" Li's only answer to this question was the advice he offered to his listeners at the conclusion of the speech: "Gentlemen! Quickly go out and work!"[37]

CHAPTER IV   THE POPULIST STRAIN

In the last months of 1918, as Li Ta-chao hopefully waited for the revolutionary waves of Bolshevism to reach China's shores, a small but soon to be very influential group of Peking University students began to gather around him. By the end of the year Li's library office had become the central meeting place for the new radical student groups that were preparing the way for the May Fourth movement of 1919 and the establishment of the first Chinese Communist groups in 1920. In the autumn of 1918 Li had encouraged the formation of the Hsin ch'ao-she (New tide society) and turned over a room in the university library for its activities. One of Li's favorite students, Lo Chia-lun, an editor of the society's journal and later a high Kuomintang official, was then enthusiastically echoing Li's image of the Russian Revolution as the great tide that was about to sweep over all mankind.[1] Li also promoted the activities and publications of the Chiu-kuo-hui (Save the country society), which was organized late in 1918 by another of his student followers, the future Communist labor organizer Teng Chung-hsia.

About this time Li first began to study Marxism in earnest. The product of his labors was a long article entitled "My Marxist Views," which appeared on May 1, 1919, in *Hsin ch'ing-nien's* special issue on Marxism. Although Li looked at Marxist doctrine with considerably less enthusiasm than he had displayed in greeting the Bolshevik Revolution, he was convinced of the necessity of propagating what he called "the orthodox teaching . . . accompanying the great transformation of the world."[2] In order to encourage the young students around him to study this "orthodox teaching," Li organized the Marxist Research Society (Ma-k'e-shih chu-i yen-chiu-hui), the first group in China founded specifically for this purpose.[3] The date of the formation of the Marxist Research Society — which should be distinguished from the later Society for the Study of Marxist Theory (Ma-k'o-ssu hsüeh-shuo yen-chiu-hui) — has never been definitely established. There is no firm evidence to support the often repeated statement of Hatano Ken'ichi that the Marxist Research Society was organized as early as the spring of 1918.[4] In view of the fact that Li did not use Marxist phraseology or even mention Marx or Marxism in his first article on the October Revolution, which appeared on July 1, 1918, it is highly unlikely that he would have organized a Marxist group the previous spring. On the basis of his writings, it seems clear that Li did not become seriously interested in Marxism until some time between July and the appearance of "The Victory of Bolshevism" in November. The Marxist Research Society was in all probability not founded before the last months of 1918.

There is no doubt, however, that Li had begun to conduct informal discussions on Marxist theory with students of Peking University by the end of 1918. The discussions were held secretly in Li's office in the university library, usually in the evening. At the first of these meetings, according to one account, Li gave a report on Marx's *Capital*.[5] The biographer of Mao Tse-tung's early life has reported that during his first visit to Peking Mao participated in the discussions of a Marxist group that met in Li's office.[6]

Mao had come to Peking in September 1918 and had been introduced to Li Ta-chao by his former teacher at the Hunan Normal School and future father-in-law, Yang Ch'ang-chi, then a professor at Peking University. "Li Ta-chao," Mao reported in his autobiography, "gave me work as assistant librarian, for which I was paid the generous sum of $8 a month." Mao remained in Peking until early 1919. "Under Li Ta-chao, as assistant librarian at Peking National University," he later said, "I had rapidly developed towards Marxism."[7]

In addition to Mao, many young students at Peking University who later became leaders of the Chinese Communist party were introduced to Marxism through Li's discussion group in the months preceding the May Fourth Incident of 1919. Among them were

Ch'ü Ch'iu-pai, a student of Russian literature, Teng Chung-hsia, and Chang Kuo-t'ao. Teng and Chang, who were Li's students as well as his political disciples, later became prominent figures in the northern branch of the Communist party led by Li, and both, like Li, were destined to come to tragic ends.[8] These and other students came to Li's office to seek intellectual and political guidance and secretly borrow books from the collection of Marxist literature that he had begun to assemble. The office of the chief librarian of Peking University soon became known as the *hung-lou* or "Red Chamber."

In spite of the ferment at Peking University, Li was troubled by a growing sense of isolation and loneliness. In the early months of 1919 the messianic confidence with which he had greeted the Bolshevik Revolution gave way to darkly pessimistic moods. The great tide of revolution that had seemed about to sweep over the world the year before showed no signs of approaching China. He continued to believe that the Bolshevik Revolution represented the "dawn of a new era," but the dawn now appeared to be no more than "a tiny ray of light" in "this dark China and this dead and silent Peking of ours."[9] He began to brood upon an inertia that not only pervaded China but also seemed to be a universal human condition. In January 1919 the usually optimistic Li wrote: "The general unprogressive pattern of mankind is really due to the existence in society of a force that does mischievous things. This force is inertia. Its strength is really much greater than the force of progress."[10] Li remained convinced that the revolutionary tide would engulf the world, but it now seemed to be coming to China by a more circuitous route: "it can definitely be said that sooner or later [the tide of social revolution] will enter Western Europe and cross the Atlantic to take a look at America and then cross the Indian Ocean and the China Sea to visit Japan. Our China can expect to see its approach from the northwest land mass and the southeastern sea coast." The decline of Li's revolutionary expectations was in part the result of contemporary events in Europe. The revolution had failed to spread to Western Europe, and it seemed on the verge of extinction in Russia itself. By the end of 1918 the Bolshevik government was threatened from without by foreign intervention and from within by growing political and economic chaos. These developments, noted in Li's writings in early 1919, severely shook his confidence. He felt compelled to proclaim that the revolution, despite immediate appearances, could not possibly stop for long "in a corner of Europe," and he expressed grave concern over the rise of counter-revolutionary forces in Russia.[11]

Equally unpromising was the political situation in China. In early 1919 republican China seemed to be sinking deeper into political chaos, which was compounded by the economic dislocations that followed the end of the world war. The cynical struggle of the warlords and their parliamentary puppets for control of the shadowy remnants of the republican central government at Peking continued unabated. To Li, Chinese political life had become a "slaughterhouse form of politics in which our people are taken as pigs to be slaughtered and in which our blood, flesh, and bones are given to the civilian and military wolves to feast upon." [12] More ominous was the fact that there appeared nothing either to counter the tendencies toward internal political fragmentation and economic disintegration or to oppose effectively the growing menace of Japanese ambitions in Shantung. Threatened from without and disintegrating within, Chinese society seemed to Li to be paralyzed.

In all probability the intensive study of Marxist theory that he had embarked upon also contributed to his pessimistic outlook during these months. However he may have interpreted Marxism, he could hardly have failed to notice the contradiction between his revolutionary expectations for China and the objective laws of social and economic development that were set down by the doctrine to which he had committed himself. Although aspects of the Marxist world view later served to make Li confident that the laws of history were inexorably working to bring about a socialist future, it seems likely that the immediate impact of Marxist theory caused him to view the world revolutionary tide as receding even further from the shores of China.

As Li's doubts about the immediate prospects for revolution grew, he became increasingly concerned with the problem of the isolation and impotence of the intellectuals in Chinese society. The intellectual and political ferment that so totally occupied his time and energies, as well as those of his young student followers, hardly seemed to extend beyond the walls of Peking University. Compared to other countries, where the "new tide of thought is like a fire," China was a place where "both the old and the new are sunk in a deep atmosphere of death." The cause of this, Li lamented, was that China's "inert and slavish character is too deep, and we are unable to use our own powers of reason to maintain our own existence." [13]

With the ebbing of his chiliastic vision of world revolution Li began to search for concrete ways to activate the intellectuals and end their social isolation. Still largely unencumbered by the demands of Marxist theory, Li first turned to the peasantry. In a series of four articles published in February 1919 in the Peking *Ch'en-pao* under the title "Youth and the Villages," Li called upon the young intellectuals of China to leave the cities and "go to the villages" in order to liberate the great mass of Chinese peasants.[14] In retrospect, "Youth and the Villages" can be seen as one of the most important documents in the development of Communism in China. Since Li's proposals were explicitly advanced to encourage young Chinese intellectuals to follow the example of the Russian Populist "go to the people" movement, it seems appropriate before examining "Youth and the Villages" to consider briefly the nature of the Russian Populist movement that Li wished Chinese youth to emulate. Since Populist conceptions were to impinge deeply upon Li Ta-chao's interpretation of Marxism, it might also be relevant to point out some of the major differences between Populist and Marxist ideologies.

Populism and Marxism

Inspired largely by the writings of Alexander Herzen and Nikolai Chernyshevskii, Russian Populism emerged as a distinct ideology in the 1860's and rapidly became the dominant mode of thought of the revolutionary intelligentsia. In its pristine form, the *narodnik* movement reached its climax in the 1870's when groups of young, radical intellectuals, motivated by the perhaps conflicting desires to both enlighten and "fuse" with the peasantry, went to the villages of Russia to liberate what they assumed to be the revolutionary energies and innate socialist strivings of the rural masses. Met by the indifference and frequent hostility of the peasants, as well as by the harsh repression of the Czarist police, the movement soon foundered. By the close of the decade many of these radicals had abandoned direct work in the villages for terrorist tactics to overthrow the Russian autocracy, which, they argued, was the main obstacle to the cultivation of the socialist ideals of the peasants.

75

Others were coming under the influence of Marxism; the conversion of George Plekhanov from a Populist to a Marxist shortly after 1880 was a turning point in the history of the Russian socialist intelligentsia. Those who remained true to the Populist creed split into various political groups, some of which moved in reformist directions, while others turned to political terrorism.

After a decade of decline the Populist movement staged a revival at the end of the century, and in 1901 various *narodnik* groups combined to form the Socialist Revolutionary party, which had an important influence upon the revolutionary movement in China in the first decade of the century. Although the tactics of the Socialist Revolutionaries, who openly advocated and practiced terrorism, were far removed from the "go to the people" movement of the 1870's, they became the principal heirs of the Populist tradition.[15]

Despite the diffuse and heterogeneous nature of Populism, it is possible to identify several common beliefs and assumptions. One essential element of the Populist creed was an emotional attachment to the peasantry and a conviction that the peasants themselves embodied the vital forces and revolutionary energies of society. However vague the Populists may have been on the question of what the future socialist order was to look like, and however widely Populist groups differed in the tactics they employed, they were united in the faith that the peasantry was to be the main beneficiary of the revolution and the mass base for the construction of a socialist society.

Closely related to this peasant orientation was the Populist belief that European capitalism was an evil that Russia could and should avoid. Agrarian Russia would not be forced to go through all the phases of European social development but could circumvent capitalism and move directly to a socialist order by developing the collectivistic instincts of the peasantry that were embodied in the *mir*, the Russian village commune. Behind this conception lay the Populist assumption that Russia's economic backwardness was an advantage for the realization of socialism. Russia's relative insulation from capitalist economic forces and the absence of a strong Russian bourgeoisie had brought the Russians nearer to socialism than were the peoples of Western Europe.

The emphasis of the Russian *narodniks* on the role of the *mir* in the transition to socialism points to a third feature common to

Populist movements — the assumption of national uniqueness in historical development. In arguing that Russia was following a special historical path that would enable it to bypass the hated capitalism of the West, the revolutionary Populists adopted highly nationalistic assumptions of the distinctiveness of Russian civilization and psychology, which frequently were not far removed from the Slavophile idealization of the early forms of Russian national life.

The Populist movement was also characterized by a romantic voluntarism, which assumed that the active factor in history was the conscious and purposeful intellectual. In the *narodnik* view the course of social and political events could be determined by "critically thinking individuals" who would stimulate the innate socialist strivings and revolutionary energies of "the people." Whereas Populist groups differed widely on how the socialist revolution was actually to be carried out, all assumed that the intervention of the intelligentsia could decisively influence the course of history.

The Populist belief that the Russian peasantry was communist by instinct and tradition is very similar to the anarchist notion of a "general will." Indeed, the terrorist tactics of the later forms of Populism, particularly those of the Socialist Revolutionaries, had their ideological basis in the anarchist assumption that the innately communist "will" of the people was suppressed by the "unnatural" force of the state and the "alien" force of capitalism; once these exterior obstacles were removed by the action of the revolutionary intelligentsia, the socialist ideals of the people would be released and the socialist revolution would be consummated.

Most of the beliefs and assumptions that have been outlined here are of course not peculiar to Populist movements. Many were shared by anarchists, and others merged with Russian Marxism. Trotsky also found in Russia's economic backwardness a favorable condition for revolution — although only if the revolution there was followed by a general socialist uprising in the industrially advanced countries. Lenin was profoundly influenced by the writings of Chernyshevskii and drew much of his voluntaristic and elitist approach to revolution from Populist ideas.[16] The idea of bypassing the capitalist phase was certainly not foreign to Marxist thought even before Lenin. In 1881 Marx himself had toyed with the idea that Russia might be able to utilize communal village institutions to proceed directly to a socialist reorganization of society.[17] Yet Populism remains identifiable as a distinct ideological tendency by its fundamental peasant orientation — the view that the truly creative forces of society are embodied in the peasantry. Only in the context of this basic emotional tie to the peasantry and rural life can the various other beliefs and assumptions suggested here as characteristic of the Russian Populist movement be used to define the term "Populism" in a historically specific manner.

Despite the fact that Populists and Marxists professed to be working for the same socialist goal, and however much Lenin may have been influenced by aspects of the Populist creed, the Populist and Marxist world views remained profoundly different. These differences, which involved not only the question of the role of the peasantry in the revolution but also fundamentally different assumptions on the nature of history, revolution, and the state, were delineated at length in 1884 by Russia's pioneer Marxist, George Plekhanov in his famous work *Our Differences*. Plekhanov criticized the *narodnik* intellectuals for wishfully attributing to the people their own socialist ideals and basing their revolutionary hopes on an atavistic idealization of the "primitive" forms of Russian life. He accused the Populists of having implicitly adopted conspiratorial Blanquist notions and thereby attempting to substitute the will of the intelligentsia for the forces of history — "to replace the initiative of the *class* by that of a *committee*, and to change the business of the whole working population of the country into the business of a secret organization." [18] Plekhanov further argued, as Lenin later did at even greater length in his *Development of Capitalism in Russia*,[19] that the communal village institutions which were so central to the Populist faith were rapidly being undermined by the inexorable workings of modern economic forces. Through the development of commodity production, capitalism was not only destroying the remnants of the *mir* and inevitably giving rise to class conflict within the village, but it was also transferring the center of political struggle from the countryside to the cities. The growing forces of the Russian bourgeoisie, Plekhanov believed, would inevitably come into revolutionary conflict with the Czarist autocracy. At the same time the development of an urban proletariat was creating the necessary conditions for the true Russian road to socialism.

Because of the *narodniks'* idealization of the village commune, their faith in the "communist instincts" of the peasantry, and their special emphasis upon the revolutionary will of the intelligentsia in making history, Plekhanov maintained that the Populists ignored the class character of the revolutionary struggle in Russia. It should be noted that the Populists did not categorically deny the validity of the Marxist concept of class struggle; many were disposed to accept its applicability to Western Europe. Nor did the Populists deny the existence of class divisions in Russia. But they attributed these divisions to "unnatural" and "external" factors, particularly to the intervention of the state in Russian society. Here was one of the fundamental differences between the Marxist and Populist outlooks. The Populists believed that the state structure brought classes and their struggles into existence; the Marxists held that class struggles and the economic relations that produced them gave rise to the state.

This basic difference on the question of the relationship between political and economic forces underlay all the differences in the Populist and Marxist programs. The Populists believed that the village commune was disintegrating under the impact of external political forces and that this disintegration would end with the removal of the state; the Marxists viewed the disintegration of the commune as a natural process determined by the immutable laws of capitalist development. "No historical peculiarities of our country," Plekhanov declared, "will free it from the action of universal social laws." [20] For Plekhanov and his Marxist followers the forces of economic progress were preparing the necessary preconditions for a socialist revolution; for the Populists the Russian road to socialism lay in the preservation of the social conditions based upon Russia's economic backwardness. The Populists pinned their revolutionary hopes on the innate socialist traditions of the peasantry; the Marxists looked to the cities and the urban proletariat. The Populists trusted in the revolutionary will and consciousness of the intelligentsia; orthodox Marxists such as Plekhanov anchored their socialist faith in the forces of history. In Li Ta-chao's attempts to adapt Marxism to Chinese conditions there reappeared many of these ideological problems that were debated by the Populists and the Marxists in Russia.

"Youth and the Villages"

Unlike the Chinese revolutionaries of the T'ung-meng hui period, who had been influenced principally by the terrorist exploits of the Russian Socialist Revolutionary movement,[21] Li Ta-chao was drawn to the earlier "go to the people" movement of Russian Populism — to the messianic and self-sacrificing spirit of the young Russian intellectuals who had tried to "fuse" with the peasantry. Like the early Russian Populists, Li was motivated by an overriding concern with the problem of the isolation of the intelligentsia from the masses of society. Thus, "Youth and the Villages" began with the proposition that if "contemporary culture" was to be brought to Chinese society, it was imperative that the intelligentsia unite with the "laboring classes" (*lao-kung chieh-chi*). To achieve this unity, Li suggested that the "go to the people" movement of nineteenth century Russia be the model for the educated youth of twentieth century China. Noting that a revolution was not something that could be accomplished in one's leisure time but required long years of effort by totally dedicated men, Li argued that the success of the Bolshevik Revolution was based upon the earlier activities of the young Populists in the Russian villages. Russia, he wrote,

had a great many cultured and determined men who entirely gave up the happiness of living with their own families, and not fearing bitter hardships . . . went to the villages of the countryside to spread the principles of humanism and socialism. Sometimes they used their leisure periods to talk with the village people, and at other times they bled and sweat working together with them. Sometimes they gathered together the old and the young, the women and the children, and talked with them before candlelight, discussing their hardships and advancing their knowledge. When the police discovered them, they either fled or were imprisoned. But in the Russia of those dark days, where was the new heaven and earth where these young men were active? It was in the villages of Russia.[22]

Although Li acknowledged that conditions in China might be different from those in Russia of a half-century before, he proposed that "our youth ought to go to the villages, adopt the spirit of the Russian youth in the Russian village propaganda movement of those years, and without delay begin the work of developing the villages."

Anticipating Mao Tse-tung by almost a decade, Li also predicted that the Chinese revolution would be a peasant revolution: "Our

China is a rural nation and most of the laboring class is made up of peasants. If they are not liberated, then our whole nation will not be liberated; their sufferings are the sufferings of our whole nation; their ignorance is the ignorance of our whole nation; the advantages and defects of their lives are the advantages and defects of all of our politics. Go out and develop them and cause them to know [that they should] demand liberation, speak out about their sufferings, throw off their ignorance and be people who will themselves plan their own lives." Having identified the liberation of China with the liberation of the peasantry, Li did not claim that the peasants would rise spontaneously. The educated youth were to awaken them from their stupor and "cause them to demand liberation." "Except for our youth," Li wrote, "the whole nation is in darkness." The peasantry was to be the base for the regeneration of China, and the young intelligentsia was to provide the spark and set the direction. Li attributed the ignorance of the peasantry and its inability to resist the oppression of the gentry and the bureaucrats to the fact that the "youth of the intellectual classes have run to the cities." Instead of returning to the rural areas, the young intellectuals "only think of begging a livelihood among the bureaucrats . . . After a while these youths sink into the mire of the city and become treacherous men. In the villages no trace of the intellectual classes can be seen; the villages have become hells, and life in the bright, beautiful fields is buried in darkness . . . Who can be held responsible for this other than our lazy youth?"[23]

To encourage the young intellectuals to return to the villages, Li appealed not only to youth of socialist inclinations but also to those who believed that the plight of China could be resolved through the establishment of constitutional government. Under a democratic form of government, Li pointed out, the great majority of voters would be in the villages; only if the peasants understood and participated in the electoral system could democracy be made to work in China. The corruption of the electoral system under the republic, he argued, was owing to the fact that "in the villages there are no youths who are the true companions of the peasants and who can inform them of the purposes of elections and prepare them to run for office." Thus, those "elected" to parliament under the republic were "city vagrants and city robbers . . . [who] accumulate ill-gotten wealth and then come to cheat the elders of the villages."

The only hope for democracy in China was for the youth of the cities to recognize their responsibility to awaken the peasants:

Constitutional youth! If you want to establish constitutional government, there must first be a constitutional people. If you want to have a constitutional people, you must first change the dark villages into enlightened villages, change the despotically controlled villages into constitutional villages. If the modern youth are in the villages creating the line of advance of modern culture, then the peasants will not abdicate and misuse their right to vote and will not endure the oppression of the local gentry and city vagabonds . . . Then those who come to parliament to speak for the common people will themselves be common people . . . This kind of village will be fertile soil for the cultivation of democracy, and in this activity the youth will be the workers who plant the tree of democracy.[24]

By going to the villages the young intellectuals would not only fulfill their responsibilities to Chinese society but also remove themselves from the corrupting influences of the city. Li described the life of young people in the cities in particularly somber tones. They drifted about aimlessly, begging for the favors of influential people, and vainly prepared for careers as bureaucrats. Soon they could not "even get a bowl of rice to eat," their youthful spirits disintegrated, and they became "men who have lost their way." He wrote: "My young friends who are idle in the cities! You should know that while the cities have a great many evils, the villages have a great many happinesses. The dark aspects of life in the cities are many; the bright aspects of life in the villages are many. City life is virtually the life of the devil, whereas village life is a wholly human life. The air of the city is filthy, whereas the village air is clear."[25]

It is hardly necessary to emphasize the contrast between Li's sympathy for rural China and the contempt for the "idiocy of rural life" that runs through most European Marxist literature. Yet a belief in the essential purity of the countryside, coupled with a feeling of revulsion against the corruption of the city, remained a prominent theme in Li's writings after his conversion to Marxism. As late as 1922 — when Li's Marxist credentials were no longer in doubt — he was still presenting a rather idyllic picture of rural life in traditional China: "Previously the places of production were the villages, the mountains, the forests and the pastures. In these places of work the air was clear and fresh, the scenery was beautiful, time and nature were joined together, and thus worry and fatigue were reduced. Now the places of production are big factories located in big cities. The noise of the machinery is crushing and people are crowded together. Although machine power has replaced human power, spiritual fatigue and worry have increased." [26]

In "Youth and the Villages" Li wove together these antiurban sentiments with the moral injunction that the young intelligentsia was duty-bound to awaken the villages and merge with the peasantry:

How can you not hurry and pack your belongings, liquidate your debts, and return to your villages? Every day in the cities you seek a bit of compassion, and if you are lucky enough one day to obtain some, then is that really happiness? . . . If you return to the countryside soon, then no matter whether you engage in mental labor or physical labor, cultivate the land or become a teacher in a primary school, your own lives will become simpler. Each day you will be engaged for eight hours in work that will benefit the people and will benefit yourselves as well, and you can devote your leisure time to the development of the village and to the reform of the life of the peasants; thus, on the one hand, you will be engaged in labor, and, on the other hand, you will join with your fellow workers . . . to discuss the higher principles of human life. Only if the intellectuals enter the laborers' organizations will the laborers' organizations become enlightened; only if large numbers of youths return to the villages will there be any hope of reforming village life; and only if village life is effectively reformed will there be progress in social organization. Those robbers who plunder the rural workers and cheat the peasants will then disappear . . . Youth! Hurry to the villages! Each day go out and work in the fields and then return to rest, till the fields and eat, dig wells and drink . . . In these places you [should] settle yourselves and find your destiny. [27]

There is nothing in Li's early writings to suggest that he was ever directly influenced by Russian Populist theories. Before the Bolshevik Revolution it is unlikely that he was even aware of the existence of the *narodnik* movement in Russia. Rather, Li's knowledge of the Russian revolutionaries who "went to the people" was undoubtedly gained from secondary historical sources when, under the impact of the Bolshevik Revolution, he began to study the history of the Russian revolutionary movement. It was not Russian Populist theory but the romantic example of a past revolutionary heroism that captured Li's imagination and seemed relevant to the immediate situation in China. Yet there are certain remarkable intellectual and theoretical affinities between "Youth and the Villages" and early

Russian Populism. Like the Populists, Li assumed that China would not be forced to endure a capitalist phase of development before the achievement of socialism. In "Youth and the Villages" he stated that the purpose of the intellectuals in "going to the villages" was to "spread the principles of humanism and socialism." Later he explicitly argued that it was possible — indeed necessary — for China to bypass the capitalist stage and proceed directly to a socialist reorganization of society.

There were also certain nationalistic implications in the picture Li drew contrasting the vices of urban life with the purity of village life. Modern Chinese cities (and many of their evils) were to a large degree foreign creations and were widely regarded as such in Chinese intellectual circles. By equating the virtues and defects of the Chinese peasantry with those of the Chinese nation, and by contrasting city and rural life, Li emphasized the conflict between foreign imperialism and Chinese national traditions. Virtually all Chinese intellectuals opposed foreign imperialism and condemned the injustices of life in foreign-dominated cities, particularly Shanghai, but nothing could have been further from the world view of the urbanized, westernized Chinese intellectual than to find anything of positive value in Chinese rural life. It is true that certain more conservative intellectuals, such as Chang Shih-chao, and some Kuomintang intellectuals, such as Liao Chung-k'ai, did look to the countryside to find elements of the Chinese tradition that were relevant to modern conditions.[28] But among the radical intelligentsia Li's sympathetic view of village life and his picture of the cities as "the life of the devil" was unique. It recalls the Russian Populist view of urbanization as representing the intrusion of the alien forces of Western capitalism upon the national traditions of Russia.

Li's view of the role of the intelligentsia in the liberation of the peasantry also bore significant resemblances to the revolutionary voluntarism of the Russian Populists. Despite the deterministic injunctions of historical materialism, Li was not inclined to wait for economic forces to solve the problems of China. By "going to the villages," the young intellectual could satisfy his desire to take immediate action and play a crucial role in the liberation of society. As in early Russian Populist ideology, the frustrated intellectual of the city was to find salvation in the village. But Li did not consciously recognize the elitist implications of the role that he assigned to the intellectuals; he did not possess what Stuart Schram has so aptly referred to as Mao Tse-tung's "natural Leninism." [29]

Finally, like most of the Russian Populists, Li tended to see the peasantry as a single and united entity whose common interests overrode whatever class differences might exist within the villages. In the one passage in which he discussed class differentiation Li treated the village landlord as a part of "the common people" and suggested that discord within the village was a result of external political intervention:

The corrupt officials and bureaucrats and the evil gentry depend entirely upon the police and the local rascals and their hangers-on to feast upon the common people. These common people are all ignorant people and they do not know how to unite together and defend themselves. Among them are peasants who own just enough land to be self-sufficient; some are landlords who rent land to others; some are farmers who have small pieces of land of their own and also work as agricultural laborers for others; some are only hired [agricultural] laborers. Not only do they not know how to organize themselves to resist the bureaucrats and gentry and repel the police and the local rascals, but they cheat each other according to their status in order to gain the favor of these bureaucrats, the gentry, the local rascals, and police.[30]

In his later writings on the peasant question Li continued to pay relatively little attention to the question of rural class differentiation and emphasized the external enemies of the village.

Despite these important similarities, there were several significant differences between "Youth and the Villages" and early Russian Populist thought. The *narodniks* looked to the *mir*, the traditional village commune, as the distinctive Russian road to socialism, but in the relatively well-developed system of private property in agrarian China there was no institution that could be used as a symbol of the "innate socialist strivings" of the peasantry. Although Li later argued that people who worked with the soil were naturally predisposed towards "humanism," [31] he never claimed that the Chinese peasantry was socialist by instinct and tradition. And although he was most sympathetic to the virtues of rural life, he did not romanticize the traditions of the Chinese village. On the contrary, the villages of China had been subjected to centuries of oppression and ignorance, which it was the duty of young intellectuals to dissolve. The peasants, in Li's view, had to be educated toward socialist

85

ideals — there was no native collectivist social and economic base for a quick transition to socialism.

Furthermore, Li did not fully share the Populist aversion to Western-style industrialization. Although he looked fondly upon the rural, preindustrial life of traditional China, the attachment was more a romantic one than a fundamental political orientation. He was committed not to the Chinese past but to a socialist, industrialized future. He was not tied, as were many of the Russian Populists, to the ideal of small-scale village industry.

Finally, in raising the "go to the villages" slogan, Li did not anticipate the immediate revolutionary explosion that many of the more anarchistic and militant Russian Populists confidently predicted. It was, in fact, because his apocalyptic vision of imminent liberation had been tempered by international events and the grim realities of Chinese politics that Li urged young Chinese intellectuals to follow the example of the Russian Populists of the 1870's. By suggesting that the revolutionary movement in China was only in its Populist stage, Li implicitly recognized that the Chinese road to socialism might be longer and more difficult than he had at first anticipated.

Notwithstanding these differences, "Youth and the Villages" is probably the most faithful expression of the spirit of early Russian Populism to be found in modern Chinese intellectual history. The significance of this Populist strain in Li's thought was not confined to the question of whether young Chinese intellectuals should go to the villages or remain in the cities. Many of the theoretical assumptions identified with the Populist outlook and implicit in "Youth and the Villages" profoundly influenced Li's interpretation of Marxist doctrine and his view of how a socialist revolution in China was to be carried out. Li was not simply a Populist, but the Populist tendency that he introduced became a powerful current within the Chinese Marxist movement.

In the tactics of modern Chinese revolutionary politics, "Youth and the Villages" represents an innovation of considerable significance. Although Chinese revolutionaries had long talked about the liberation of the common people, their methods had been confined mostly to military conspiracies, assassinations, attempted coup d'etats and usually ill-fated alliances with warlords. In 1918, Ts'ai Yüan-p'ei, Ch'en Tu-hsiu, and Li Ta-chao had rejected these particular methods by raising the slogan of the "dignity of labor" and urging a program of mass education to bridge the gap between the intellectuals and the common people.[32] But Li was the first to present a specific proposal for action to achieve the "unity of the intellectuals with the laboring masses." In the early months of 1919 Li repeatedly turned to this theme. He urged the young intellectuals to "go out and put forth your efforts in human activity" and to recognize that "in labor there is unlimited happiness . . . [I] fear that the most suffering and most tragic people are the laboring people. Therefore we ought to adopt the spirit of seeking to go where we hear the sounds of suffering and tragedy. We ought to know who these suffering people are, what kind of thing their suffering is, and the causes of their suffering. We ought to think about what methods to use to eliminate their suffering. If we are unable to rescue them, then who would be able or willing to rescue them?"[33]

Li's Populist response to the problem of bridging the gap between the intelligentsia and the common people was not a passing fad. In September 1919 he elaborated upon the call to "go to the villages." Declaring that China required both spiritual and material reform, Li urged the intellectuals:

not to drift about in the cities and become cultured vagrants existing outside of working society. We ourselves ought to go to the villages . . . and take up hoes and plows and become companions of the toiling peasants. During periods of rest . . . we ought to take the opportunity to teach and comfort them. It should be known that the term "dignity of labor" is certainly not applicable to those people who talk but don't do a bit of physical work. Those intellectuals who eat but do not work ought to be eliminated together with the capitalists. The condition of China today is that the cities and the villages have been made into two opposite poles and have almost become two different worlds. The village people have not the slightest relation with the problems that develop in the cities and the spread of culture. Generally the city people are wholly unconcerned with life in the villages and are completely unaware of their conditions . . . In countries with a comparatively low level of culture [the spread of culture] depends entirely upon the propaganda activities of self-conscious youth who labor together with the peasants . . . The peasants, who are in close daily contact with the world of nature, come naturally to believe in humanism. By working together with them, not only can we informally influence them and spread culture, but also the cultural tools that are produced in the cities, such as publications, will necessarily follow in the footsteps of the youth and enter the countryside. In periods of agricultural slack we ought to come to the cities to study, and in times when the peasants are busy, we ought to work in the fields . . . then the atmosphere of culture will merge together with the shadows of the trees and smoke of the village chimneys, and those quiet, depressed old villages will become transformed into lively, active new villages. The great unity of the new villages will be our "Young China." [34]

The first to respond to Li's appeal for the intellectuals to "unite with the laboring classes" were several of his own students at Peking University. In March 1919 a group of students that included Teng Chung-hsia, Chang Kuo-t'ao, and Lo Chia-lun organized the Mass Education Speech Corps (P'ing-min chiao-yü chiang-yen t'uan). The purpose of the Corps, the students stated, was "to advance the knowledge of the common people and awaken the consciousness of the common people." The Corps at first established four lecture halls in the working-class sections of Peking, where popular literature was distributed and weekly lectures, generally on Sundays, were held on such topics as socialism, the theory of "mutual aid," the threat of Japanese aggression, the significance of reading, the need to eliminate superstitious beliefs, and the commemoration of Labor Day. In early 1920 the student lecturers extended their activities to the villages in the vicinity of Peking. [35]

After the May Fourth Incident of 1919 the example of the Mass Education Speech Corps in the Peking area was emulated in other parts of China. Various radical student groups, some with specifically rural orientations, were organized to promote the merger of the intelligentsia and the masses. One such group declared that the reformation of Chinese society was solely the responsibility of the peasants and workers themselves; thus, "all of the awakened members of the intelligentsia ought to destroy the very concept 'intelligentsia,' throw themselves into the world of labor and completely join together with the laborers." [36]

In the summer of 1920 young students in Shanghai gathered together with the aim of "going to the countryside to do agricultural work together with the peasants." [37] A year later the young Communist P'eng P'ai, who like Li had been influenced by the Japanese agrarian socialist tradition while a student at Waseda University, began the organizational work among the peasantry of Kwangtung province that culminated in China's first agrarian soviet. Beginning in Canton, in 1925, vacationing students of the Socialist Youth

Corps went to the villages in what was at first a spontaneous effort to establish peasant unions, which provided the organizational basis for the vast peasant movement of the next two years.[38]

Except for the Peking group, Li had no direct organizational connections with these movements. However, since he was the acknowledged leader of the pro-Bolshevik intelligentsia in 1919, it seems likely that his passionate appeal to young intellectuals to unite with the peasants and achieve the reformation of China had a powerful impact in the highly emotional atmosphere of the May Fourth era. In view of the direction that Chinese Communism took, "Youth and the Villages" can be seen as a pioneering effort in preparing the intellectual climate for very unorthodox Marxist approaches to the question of the role of the peasantry in the Chinese revolution. In 1926, seven years after he had written "Youth and the Villages," Li took a most important step in that unorthodox direction.

CHAPTER V   MARXISM AND THE MAY
FOURTH MOVEMENT

Hsin ch'ing-nien's "special issue" on Marxism, edited by Li Ta-chao, appeared on May 1, 1919, just three days before the May Fourth Incident. Yet far from foreshadowing the rapid spread of Marxist influence that was to follow in the wake of that event, the articles in the "special issue" reveal how limited was the appeal of Marxism at the time. Except for Li, none of those who were soon to be prominent in Chinese Marxist circles were among its contributors; nor did any, with the exception of Li, come forward as advocates of Marxism. The articles were generally rather uninspired, scholarly presentations of various aspects of Marxist theory. Several were distinctly critical of Marxism. One followed Eduard Bernstein's revisionist critique of Marx, and another repeated both Bernstein's and the anarchist Kropotkin's objections to Marxist doctrine.[1]

Li's lengthy article, "My Marxist Views," was largely a summary of some of the main concepts of orthodox Marxist theory, which he drew from Japanese translations of Marx's *The Poverty of Philosophy, Communist Manifesto*, the Preface to *The Critique of Political Economy*, and at least a part of *Capital*.[2] Before the appearance of the essays on the materialist conception of history by the Kuomintang leader Hu Han-min in the autumn of 1919,[3] Li's article was by far the most systematic and serious treatment of Marxism to be published in Chinese.

Li presented much of his summary of Marxist theory without comment. However, his discussion does serve to reveal his initial impressions of the doctrine to which he was now committed and also suggests which aspects of Marxism he found attractive and which he was reluctant to accept. Some of the specific theoretical problems that Li raised in this article will be treated more fully in Chapter 6.

"My Marxist Views" is a rather curious document in that it was something less than a wholehearted endorsement of Marxism. Li found Marxist theory to be "the motive force of world reform" and "the orthodox teaching . . . accompanying the great transformation of the world." [4] But in describing this "orthodox teaching," he proceeded to make several significant departures from orthodoxy.

In general Li was disposed to accept those elements of Marxism that emphasize the importance of political activity and the consciousness of men, that is, those elements that promise a relatively rapid revolutionary transformation. He was critical of the deterministic aspects of Marxist doctrine, which seemed to him to encourage passivity or imply the necessity for a long period of economic development as a prerequisite for revolutionary political change. Thus, Li was immediately receptive to the theory of class struggle, which, if separated from the economic preconditions underlying it, places heavy emphasis upon the role of conscious political activity in the making of history. Li viewed the phenomenon of class struggle in relatively simple terms; it was the eternal conflict between the propertied and the unpropertied, between the oppressors and the exploited. The theory of class struggle, moreover, was an inevitable manifestation of the universal drive toward progressive self-expansion in both biological and social phenomena. Li therefore implied that Marx's concept of class struggle was not really alien to the Chinese intellectual milieu since it was supported by evolutionary theory in general and by the writings of Spencer in particular — theories with which Chinese intellectuals had long been familiar. However, Li was aware of certain ambiguities in Marx's treatment of the class struggle. He noted that whereas Marx denied that class activity determines the movement of economic forces, Marx also declared that all history has been the history of class struggle and affirmed that the activities of social classes can influence the whole direction of the social process. Li was quite clearly drawn to the latter formulation; he preferred to believe that the class struggle itself was the truly creative force in historical development. The particular importance that Li attributed to the theory of class struggle is suggested by his frequent references to it as the "golden thread" tying together the various parts of Marxist doctrine.[5]

Li also looked with favor upon Marx's general description of the nature of capitalist exploitation and the tendencies of modern capitalist development. He was fully attuned to the "law" of the concentration of capital, which decrees that the productive forces of capitalist society must necessarily come into the hands of an ever smaller group of oligarchs, and that this must be accompanied by the progressive pauperization of the workers, leading inevitably to a dramatic, final struggle between the proletariat and the bourgeoisie. This belief that the "natural and unavoidable" tendency for capitalism is to sow the seeds of its own destruction was particularly appealing.[6]

Li was rather less well-disposed toward the materialist conception of history. He was willing to accept historical materialism as a general explanation of historical development, and he was attracted to the promise that history is inexorably moving toward a brilliant future, but he was concerned with the deterministic implications of the materialist conception of history, especially the Marxist injunction that all elements of the "superstructure" of society — politics, ideas, and spiritual phenomena — are no more than reflections of the economic "base" and its underlying motive force, the "mode of production." In dealing with this question, Li both supported and criticized Marx. He understood Marx in a particularly mechanistic and economically deterministic fashion, and thus at one point he inaccurately described the doctrine of historical materialism as decreeing that the elements of the superstructure can have absolutely no influence upon the economic base — a proposition that he clearly was unwilling to accept. On the other hand, he defended Marx from the oft-repeated criticism that because conscious class activity becomes meaningless in a scheme in which all of history is determined by the forces of production, there exists a fundamental contradiction between the materialist conception of history and the theory of class struggle. This apparent contradiction was self-explanatory, Li argued, because Marx maintained not only that "social relations change in accordance with changes in the productive forces [but also that] changes in social relations depend upon the activity of the class that is in an economically disadvantageous position. Thus it can be seen that Marx really put class activity within the framework of changes of the economic process itself." Li acknowledged that there were "several places where there are still forced arguments and contradictions," but he attributed them to the exaggerations that inevitably accompany the promotion of a new theory. "But these small defects," he remarked, "are unable to obscure his [Marx's] great achievement." [7]

As for his own views on the question of the relationship between base and superstructure, Li made it clear that he believed the two could influence each other. Drawing upon examples from European history, such as the influence of the Norman invasions upon the English landed property system, he took particular pains to argue that political forces and "self-conscious group activity . . . can change the tendency of economic phenomena." [8] Having not yet clearly distinguished Marxism from economic determinism, Li was uncertain whether his own views were in accord with those of Marx. Thus, at the same time that he quoted Marx to support a politically activistic position, he left the impression that he felt it was still necessary to revise the materialist conception of history. The problem that Li raised here — the whole question of the relationship between political and economic forces in history — is one of the most complex problems in Marxist ideology, and one that was to prove particularly vexing for its Chinese adaptors.

Although Li's treatment of the materialist conception of history was rather ambiguous, he left no doubt that he found wholly unpalatable the Marxist de-emphasis on the role of ethical and spiritual factors in history. He noted that the Marxian conception of socialism had deep ethical roots, but he was critical of Marx for relegating the role of ethics to the postrevolutionary future when a "truly human history" will have replaced the "prehistory" of class struggles. On the contrary, Li argued, "in this period of transition, ethical and humanist movements ought to redouble their efforts to eliminate the evils of the earlier periods of history . . . We cannot rely upon material change alone." On this point he bluntly stated that Marxist theory should be revised so that Marxists would recognize that the reformation of the human spirit must accompany the transformation of the economic organization. Apparently referring to the attempts of certain German and Austrian socialists to fuse Kantian ethics with Marxism in the pre-World War I era, Li hopefully professed to see the rise of a new emphasis upon ethical and humanistic factors as the latest tendency of European socialist thought.[9]

Li also expressed "great regret" that Marxism had been erected on so shaky a foundation as the labor theory of value.[10] Although this question was not to loom very large in the history of Marxist thought in China, it was indicative of the critical tone that marked Li's first response to Marxist doctrine. Finally, he saw Marxism, like all ideas and ideologies, as a product of a specific historical milieu — in this case, the milieu of the industrial revolution when economic influences had become dominant over political and religious influences: "These economic phenomena were reflected in the creation of Marx's theories and principles, and yet Marx himself forgot this point. To speak frankly, Marx's theory was really a product of a certain age; in Marx's time it truly was the greatest of discoveries. But today, of course, we cannot take the theory that was created in the environment of one period and use it to explain all of history, nor apply the whole of the theory to our existing society."[11]

It is noteworthy that the Marxism that Li discussed in "My Marxist Views" was orthodox pre-Leninist Marxism. Nowhere in either of the two parts of this lengthy article is there any discernible influence of specifically Leninist theories. Whereas the orthodox conceptions of original Marxism were also the formal orthodoxies of Leninism, there is nothing in this article to suggest that Li was aware of the distinctive ideological "contributions" of Lenin. Nowhere did Li deal with the Leninist theory of imperialism, the Leninist conception of a vanguard revolutionary elite, or the whole complex of ideological innovations that were intended to make "Marxism-Leninism" a revolutionary ideology relevant to the conditions of nations where capitalism had not yet fully matured. This does not mean that Li was not attracted to some of the distinctive ideas of Lenin; but the fact that Leninist influences were not apparent in an article in which Li purported to describe "the orthodox teaching . . . accompanying the great transformation of the world" does lend support to the view that Li became a partisan of Bolshevism and a supporter (albeit a lukewarm one) of Marxist theory not because of the impact of Marxist-Leninist ideas but rather because he was inspired by the very act of revolution in general, and by the universalistic message and revolutionary mystique of Bolshevism in particular.

In "My Marxist Views" Li clearly approached Marxist theory in a far different spirit from that which characterized his response to the October Revolution. Having ardently embraced the Bolshevik victory as the signal for the imminent liberation of humanity, he was reluctant to submit this vision to the test of the cold economic and historical laws of orthodox Marxist theory. While proclaiming himself a Marxist and committing himself to the propagation of Marxism in China, he reserved the right to decide which elements of the theory were to be accepted and which might have to be revised or discarded.

If Marxism is primarily interpreted as a method of social analysis rather than as revealed dogma, there is much in the writings of Marx that would lend support for changing and modifying the original theoretical formulations as they are applied to different and changing historical conditions. The Marxist conception of the relation between theory and practice does, in fact, presuppose that theory will be modified as it is tested in revolutionary practice. In this sense Li's criticisms of Marxist theory in 1919 cannot necessarily be taken as a rejection of Marxism. Many of the criticisms were soon to disappear from his writings or at least become less explicit. Yet "My Marxist Views" raised several key questions in the adaptation of Marxism to the Chinese environment and foreshadowed certain fundamental departures from Marxist and Leninist orthodoxy in not only Li's thought but also the whole Maoist evolution of Chinese Marxist ideology.

The May Fourth Incident

In the spring of 1919 Li Ta-chao stood virtually alone as an advocate of Bolshevism and a promoter of Marxism in China. Except for a few student followers, no figure prominent in Chinese intellectual circles had yet responded to Li's passionate vision of the October Revolution as heralding the imminent reconstruction of world civilization. As Li admitted in March 1919: "To be frank, at present even the most advanced discussions in our country are separated from Bolshevism by several thousand *li*." [12] Even Ch'en Tu-hsiu, who was to become the cofounder of the Chinese Communist party and its first secretary-general, had confined himself to a few brief and noncommittal comments on the Bolshevik Revolution and had yet to show any interest in Marxist theory.

This situation was dramatically transformed by the stormy train of events that began on May 4, 1919. On that fateful day more than five thousand university students in Peking, incensed by the cynical decision of the Allied Powers at the Versailles Peace Conference to turn over to Japan the former German concessions in Shantung province, staged a demonstration of protest that culminated in an attack upon the homes of several cabinet ministers of the Peking government who had become notorious for their collaboration with the Japanese. The violent clashes with the police and the arrests that followed led to massive student demonstrations, which rapidly spread to all the major cities in China. Although the movement began as a protest against Japanese aggression and suspected traitorous activities within the Chinese government, all China was soon engulfed in a violent wave of nationalism directed against imperialist encroachments in general. The students were soon joined by many of their professors as well as by industrial workers and merchant associations. The months of May and June saw an endless series of demonstrations, riots, strikes, economic boycotts, and mass arrests. Chinese society, which had for so long seemed dormant, was suddenly seething with political and intellectual ferment.[13]

The Versailles decision on Shantung was not merely a blatant violation of the much celebrated principle of national self-determination. It posed a particularly ominous threat to China in view of the much wider Japanese colonial ambitions that had been evidenced in the Twenty-One Demands of 1915 and in the continuing Japanese claims to a "special position" in China. The bitter resentments provoked by the peace treaty among the members of the hitherto pro-Western democratic intelligentsia soon drew many of them into the revolutionary political movements that emerged from the student demonstrations.

When the Allied decision on the Shantung question became known in China, Li Ta-chao professed the same feelings of surprise and disappointment as did most of his fellow intellectuals: "When the war ended we had dreams about the victory of humanism and peace; [we thought] that the world would not be a world of robbers or at least that there would be a little bit of humanity in the world. Who could have known that these terms were all only the false signboards of the robber governments? When we look at what has been decided at the Paris Conference, where is there the slightest shadow of humanity, justice, peace, or brightness? Where have the freedom and rights of the small and weak peoples not been sacrificed to a few big robber states?" [14]

This posture of shock and outrage was probably something less than truly reflective of Li's feelings. Li had never shared the new intelligentsia's faith in the West, and the betrayal of Chinese interests at Versailles must have come to him as less a disillusionment than a confirmation of the deep-seated suspicions and intense distrust with which he had long looked at the Western world. As early as 1914 he had come to the conclusion that all foreigners were "prejudiced and filled with hate" and that the problems of China "cannot be discussed with foreigners." [15] In the years that followed there is nothing to suggest that he had altered this view of the relationship between China and the West — a view that was expressed partly in his hostility to the Allied cause in the World War and partly in his receptiveness to the anti-imperialist appeals of Lenin and Trotsky.

In the months preceding the May Fourth Incident, moreover, Li's writings echoed the call of the Soviet leaders for the peoples of Asia to rise up against "the European imperialist robbers." [16] In January 1919, Li wrote that only "overthrowing the capitalist classes of the whole world" would do away with an international order that practiced such "demoniacal things" as "secret diplomacy" and "constant war preparations." In the meantime the imperialist powers, "always wearing a devilish mask, plot with mutual suspicion how to swallow up and cruelly oppress small peoples. They are always organizing such things as peace conferences and disarmament negotiations and what have you, but even here they still adhere to the old pattern of killing people and destroying nations." [17] A month later Li half anticipated the betrayal of Chinese interests at what he was to call "the European divisions-of-spoils conference" when he warned: "If the Europeans and Americans do not follow a reasonable course [but instead] think in terms of sacrificing the peoples of the East, then we will unite to resist them without delay. If they reject the problems of Asia and do not [agree to] a just solution and equal treatment, then that really would be the common problem of the peoples of Asia and we ought to unite the whole strength of the Asian peoples to solve it. A struggle for justice that leads to war is no misfortune." [18]

97

Thus, the outcome of the Versailles Conference must have been conclusive proof for Li that Chinese problems could be solved only by the Chinese. This was a theme that he had long been preaching, and he seized the opportunity to repeat it shortly after the May Fourth Incident:

In foreign affairs we have always believed in "using barbarians to control barbarians" and in internal matters [believed in] "relying upon extraspecial force." These were both fundamentally great mistakes. We have never realized how much shame, grief, defeat, and heartbreak has been buried in these two phrases. On the other hand, all the weakness, inertia, deceit, and vulgarity of our nation are revealed by these two phrases . . . [In dealing with the Shantung problem] we were weak and submissive, and today we hope that other people will come to lend us a helping hand; but it should be known that even in a period of justice, humanism, and brightness people without will and backbone who are unable to help themselves will not be helped by other people; and in a robber world they will suffer even greater misfortunes. Yet we still dream that someone else will come to help us. This shame of having lost our independent nature is a thousand times deeper than the shame of losing territory.[19]

The significance of the events that followed the May Fourth Incident lay precisely in China's recovery of the "independent nature" whose loss Li Ta-chao had lamented. The May Fourth movement of 1919–1921 marked the emergence of a new Chinese intelligentsia, who abandoned their emotional and intellectual dependence upon the West and rediscovered the ability of the Chinese to determine their own future. The movement marked not the height of the influence of Western liberal and democratic thought in China, as has often been supposed, but the beginning of what was to prove its rapid demise. It is true that the students of the new generation had been nurtured on the Western liberal and democratic ideas disseminated in *Hsin ch'ing-nien*; and as Chow Tse-tsung has pointed out, the May Fourth Incident was in many respects the practical expression of the efforts of the leaders of the westernizing New Culture movement of 1915–1919.[20] Yet the May Fourth movement was not simply the logical and inevitable result of earlier intellectual trends, for the new young intellectuals rejected many of the most fundamental and cherished beliefs of their teachers. Whereas the intellectuals of the *Hsin ch'ing-nien* group in the period 1915–1919 had professed to be liberal internationalists and were mostly unconcerned with the question of foreign imperialism, the students of the May Fourth era were, above all, revolutionary nationalists who saw themselves defending China from the imperialist menace. Whereas most of the members of the *Hsin ch'ing-nien* group had abjured political participation because of their preoccupation with the problem of the cultural and moral renovation of China, the new student generation lived in an environment permeated with the spirit of political activism; they demanded immediate action to solve China's most pressing problems and looked to total solutions for what was a total social crisis. Although the student activists were no less antitraditionalist than the older intellectuals who had instructed them, they were less willing to wait patiently during the long years that would be required to reeducate the Chinese people and to implant a whole new culture; they were particularly impatient when their immediate enemies — Chinese warlords and foreign imperialists — were both so threatening and (with the early successes of the movement) so seemingly vulnerable.

The members of the younger generation still passionately believed in democracy and science and still looked to the West for intellectual guidance, but they no longer saw the West in the same light nor were they attracted by the same Western ideas and ideologies. For many of the students and young intellectuals of the May Fourth era the image of a liberal and progressive West that would instruct China in the principles of democracy and science had been forever submerged under a wave of nationalism and anti-imperialism. Inflamed with the passion to "save the nation," most of them found it increasingly difficult to accept the West in its dual role of teacher and oppressor. Unlike the earlier generations of Western-educated intellectuals, they were no longer overwhelmed by the power, the wealth, and the culture of the West; they were now more impressed by the defects. Thus, the Western ideas and ideologies that became most prominent after the May Fourth Incident were ones critical of the existing order in the West.

The more conventional and less politically-oriented theories of Darwin, Mill, Huxley, and Spencer, which had exercised so pervasive an influence upon the thought of westernized Chinese intellectuals during the first two decades of the century, were increasingly overshadowed by a variety of socialist doctrines. The utopian

socialism of Saint-Simon, the Christian socialist and agrarian socialist doctrines inspired by Tolstoy, the anarchist theories of Kropotkin and Bakunin, the guild socialism of Bertrand Russell and
G. D. H. Cole, and the revolutionary socialism of Marx and Lenin
were the ideas and ideologies that the new student generation responded to with the most enthusiasm. Although these new theories
differed profoundly from each other, both in their assumptions
and in the methods by which they proposed to reach their presumably common goal of socialism, their popularity reflected one of the
important changes that had taken place in the Chinese intellectual
world in the period after the May Fourth Incident — the anticapitalist predispositions that had been implicit in the thought of the
earlier generation were now explicit and formalized in the adoption
of socialist ideologies. As Bertrand Russell observed in the course
of his lecture tour of China in the autumn of 1920: "There is,
among the young, a passionate desire to acquire Western knowledge,
together with a vivid realization of Western vices. They wish to be
scientific but not mechanical, industrial but not capitalistic. To a
man they are socialists, as are most of the best among their Chinese
teachers." [21]

The appeals of socialism were not purely intellectual; more often
than not they reflected profound nationalistic resentments against
the capitalist West. For most, socialism was the highest, still unreal-
ized form of Western democracy, but a form that rejected the existing social and political order of the West and the existing relationship between China and the Western powers. Socialist beliefs thus
affirmed the westernizing intellectual inheritance of the new generation and yet were in harmony with the powerful undercurrents
of nationalism and anti-imperialism that molded the intellectual
and political temper of the times. In socialism the young intellectuals
found a means to reject both the traditions of the Chinese past and
the Western domination of the present.

From the new intellectual atmosphere of the May Fourth movement — an atmosphere dominated by the formidable combination
of nationalism, socialism, and the impulse for political action —
there emerged the two major political forces of modern Chinese
history: the revitalized Kuomintang and the Chinese Communist
party. Although the differences between them eventually led to a

long and bloody civil war, in 1919 the future leaders of both parties met on the common ground of nationalism and anti-imperialism.

Among the intellectuals prominent in the period prior to the May Fourth Incident, no one had done more than Li Ta-chao to foreshadow and inspire the later intellectual and political tendencies. The nationalistic and bitterly anti-imperialist passions that permeated his writings and the politically activistic implications of his world view had sharply distinguished him from the other members of the *Hsin ch'ing-nien* group. And with his conversion to Bolshevism and Marxism in 1918, Li became the pioneer of the revolutionary ideology that proved the most important of the newly popular socialist doctrines.

The need for young Chinese intellectuals to be both anti-imperialist and politically active was the main theme in Li's writings in the months prior to the May Fourth Incident. He continued to promote the activities of the politically oriented discussion groups that he had first encouraged his students to organize in 1918, besides passionately urging the youth to "go to the villages" to liberate the Chinese peasantry. Typical of Li's efforts to activate the students and to instill among them a feeling of social responsibility was his article "The Direction of the Activities of the Present Generation of Youth," which appeared in the Peking *Ch'en-pao* in mid-March 1919. In highly emotional tones Li called upon the youth "to go where you hear the cries of grief and suffering . . . The dawn of the new era has appeared . . . our zealous youth, quickly rise up! Go forth and devote your efforts to human activity . . . Shine your brightness upon the vast areas of darkness; even if you are surrounded by evil conditions and are forced to make sacrifices, good results will necessarily be achieved. I only wish that your brightness shall never be destroyed and that the darkness of the world shall one day be destroyed completely. Put forth your efforts! Advance! My dear youth!" [22]

On almost the eve of the May Fourth Incident Li wrote an article entitled "Thoughts on May Day," which he called a day of dedication for "direct action" (*chih-chieh hsing-tung*). Although Li admitted that few Chinese were yet moved by the spirit of "direct action," he predicted that "in the years to come it may be different, perhaps greatly different." [23]

Since Li had done everything within his power to encourage the students to become politically active, it is hardly surprising that many of them looked to him for leadership after the Fourth of May. On the evening of the first demonstration the student leaders went to Li's library office, which was already known as the "Red Chamber," to report to him on the events of the day. During the next two months the Red Chamber became one of the meeting places where the students made plans for their activities. At the same time Li asked members of the Marxist Research Society to go to other cities to spread the movement. Among those who responded to this request was Teng Chung-hsia, Li's student and a future Communist luminary, who departed for Shanghai and participated in the working-class strikes that took place in that city early in June.[24]

The emergence of a politically conscious Chinese urban proletariat was one of the developments of the May Fourth period that greatly facilitated the spread of Marxist influences. Although there were still relatively few urban workers in 1919 — certainly no more than two million — their numbers had increased dramatically during the World War when the interruption of foreign imports had stimulated Chinese industrialization. The intelligentsia was not completely unaware of the new proletariat even before May Fourth. Tsai Yüan-p'ei, as well as Li Ta-chao, Ch'en Tu-hsiu, and others, had begun to promote the slogan "the dignity of labor" in 1918.[25] In February 1919, Li wrote two articles on the "labor education question" in the Peking *Ch'en-pao* in which he argued that the capitalist usurpation of the workers' leisure time necessary for "social and spiritual cultivation" was even more shameful than the economic exploitation of labor.[26] In March 1919 he reported on the coal miners in Hopei province. The living conditions of the miners, he concluded, were inferior to those of the mules and horses used in the mining operations.[27] In this same month Li encouraged a group of his students to organize the Mass Education Speech Corps, which engaged in educational and propaganda activities in the working-class districts of Peking. However, not until June, when workers in Shanghai went out on strike in support of the student movement, did the radical intellectuals begin to grow dimly aware of the political potentialities of the urban proletariat. As this awareness gradually developed during the May Fourth period, it lent plausibility to the idea of a proletarian revolution in China and thus to the relevance of Marxist doctrine.

When he later assessed the significance of the movement, Li Ta-chao called May Fourth the "May Day" of the Chinese student world. It was the day when "Chinese students employed direct action to resist tyranny," [28] and the day that marked "the students' reconstruction of the political atmosphere." [29] This new atmosphere was filled with hope, the spirit of self-sacrifice, and a strong sense of mission. It made it possible to see China as being reborn and participating fully in the transformation of the modern world — a prospect that was quite in accord with Li's vision of a universal tide of revolution in which China, like Russia, would play a distinctive and essential role. Since events of mid-1919 demonstrated the ability of organized students and workers to influence the course of events, they promoted a spirit of political activism and made increasing numbers of Chinese intellectuals responsive to the Marxist-Leninist message.

As a direct result of this politically charged, anti-imperialist atmosphere, Ch'en Tu-hsiu and many others who were to become prominent in the Chinese Communist movement were drawn into the Marxist-Leninist fold. Ch'en Tu-hsiu had, in fact, begun to abandon his posture of political noninvolvement in December 1918 when he joined Li Ta-chao as co-editor of *Mei-chou p'ing-lun* (Weekly critic).[30] *Mei-chou p'ing-lun* provided a forum for Ch'en and Li to comment on current political events unencumbered by the restrictions imposed by the *Hsin ch'ing-nien* editorial board. Ch'en's writings took on an increasingly radical tone in the early months of 1919, but not until the student demonstrations of May Fourth was he willing to participate personally in politics. He became so deeply involved in student political activities after the May Fourth Incident that he was arrested on June 11, 1919, while distributing leaflets in the streets of Peking. Accused of having published Bolshevik materials, Ch'en was imprisoned for eighty-three days. Li Ta-chao felt personally responsible for the imprisonment because Ch'en, as chief editor of *Hsin ch'ing-nien*, had approved the publication of Li's "Victory of Bolshevism." Replying to Hu Shih in *Mei-chou p'ing-lun*, Li wrote: "Perhaps my article caused trouble for my colleagues on *Hsin ch'ing-nien*. It is really my fault that Ch'en Tu-hsiu is still in prison and that you [i.e., Hu Shih] have been falsely accused of being a Bolshevik."[31] When Ch'en was released in September, Li welcomed his return with a poem:

> We rejoice
> That you are now out of prison
> Their brute force and intimidation
> Never will be victorious over truth
> Neither prison nor death
> Can conquer you.
> Because you have upheld truth
> There have been a great many fine youths
> Who have put in practice your words:
> "Out of the research institute to enter prison,
> Out of prison to enter the research institute."
> If they all enter prison
> Then the prisons will become research institutes;
> Even if one is in prison forever
> Then one need not grieve in solitude without companions.[32]

Upon his release from prison Ch'en, fearing rearrest, resigned his professorship [33] and left Peking for Shanghai, where less than a year later he announced his conversion to Marxism. With the departure of Ch'en, Li became the acknowledged leader of the radical intelligentsia in Peking.

Unlike Ch'en, Li had proclaimed his support for Bolshevism and Marxism before rather than after the May Fourth Incident. Although the May Fourth movement was not therefore responsible for his conversion, it did confirm for him the relevance of his new creed. Under the impact of the exhilarating events of mid-1919, Li overcame the concern with the inertia of Chinese society that had so deeply troubled him in the early months of the year, and he acquired a renewed feeling of hopefulness for the future. At the same time many of his reservations about Marxism that had appeared in the article "My Marxist Views" were submerged beneath the new waves of political activism.

As the May Fourth movement assumed increasingly radical overtones, the unity of the *Hsin ch'ing-nien* group began to break down. The split between the liberals and the Marxists was heralded by the "Problems and Isms" controversy, which was initiated by Hu Shih in the summer of 1919. During the course of this debate Li Ta-chao, Hu Shih's main antagonist in the controversy, fully committed himself to a revolutionary Marxist program of political action.

Problems and Isms

Professor John Dewey happened to be lecturing in China in the summer of 1919 when his most notable Chinese disciple, Hu Shih, raised the slogan "More Study of Problems, Less Talk of Isms." Clearly disturbed by the growing popularity of socialist doctrines, Hu argued that the energies of intellectuals should be devoted to the difficult task of studying individual, practical social problems rather than to the easy repetition of "fanciful, good-sounding isms." All doctrines, he contended in the July 20 issue of *Mei-chou p'ing-lun*, were the product of the specific social needs of their time and were not necessarily applicable to the conditions of other times — a principle neglected by those who imported foreign theories without understanding the background in which those theories had originated. Isms were especially dangerous because they could be easily utilized by unprincipled politicians to promote their selfish ends. Particularly ominous was the use of such abstract terms as socialism and anarchism, which were subject to widely differing interpretations. Although Hu maintained that he did not wish to discourage the study of theories and isms, the major thrust of his argument was that doctrines advocating all-embracing and fundamental solutions not only were irrelevant but actually hindered finding the real solution of social problems.[34]

Li Ta-chao quite correctly interpreted Hu's article as an attack upon his own Bolshevik and Marxist beliefs. In a long letter to Hu, written from Chang-li-wu-feng (a remote mountain area near Li's native village in Hopei where he frequently retreated during periods of political repression in Peking), Li replied that problems could not be separated from isms because "the solution of social problems necessarily depends upon the common movement of the majority of the people." How were the people to solve social problems? It was first necessary, Li argued, to instill a sense of consciousness among them so that they would relate their own individual problems to the problems of society as a whole. It was here that isms had an indispensable role to play, for they provided the people with "an idealism" and a "common direction" through which social problems could be understood and solved. Therefore Hu Shih, the pragmatist, was the really impractical one: "Your exhaustive study of your social problems has no relation with the majority of people in society.

Therefore, there can never be any hope of solving these social problems, and thus your study of social problems can have no practical influence." [35]

On one point — the futility of purely theoretical discussion — Li agreed with Hu. Yet from an apparent area of agreement the two drew wholly opposite conclusions. Hu's argument strongly implied that the intellectual should remove himself from the political arena so that he could dispassionately study "practical problems," but Li's position was permeated with the desire for political action: "I recognize that my recent discussions have mostly been empty talk [existing only] on paper with little involvement in practical problems. From now on I vow to go out and work in the practical movement."

To leave no doubt that his commitment to the "practical movement" meant participation in socialist politics, Li went on to advocate that socialist theory should be used in China "as a tool to eliminate the nonlaboring bureaucratic robbers." He gave further evidence that he approached Marxist theory with the assumption the theory would be changed in the process of its adaptation to the Chinese environment: "A socialist, in order for his ism to influence the world, must study how he can apply his ideals to the real conditions surrounding him. Therefore in contemporary socialism there are a great many attempts to take its spirit and change it into practical forms to meet the needs of the present. This proves that within the basic nature of an ism there exists the possibility of adapting it to practice . . . Thus the danger of isms that you [Hu Shih] have spoken about is not something that is inherent in the isms themselves, but rather lies with the people who engage in empty talk about them." [36]

The real point at issue between Li and Hu Shih was not the philosophic problem of the relation between theory and practice nor the question of the value of commitments to isms; Hu was himself fairly committed to a number of isms, including liberalism, pragmatism, and experimentalism. The heart of the debate was the more practical and immediate question of whether China's problems should be solved by political revolution or by slow, evolutionary, and essentially nonpolitical social reform. In "More Study of Problems, Less Talk of Isms," Hu was particularly vehement in his objection to any doctrine that advocated "fundamental solutions."

Such doctrines, he declared, were "the dreams of self-deceived and deceptive persons, ironclad proof of the bankruptcy of Chinese thought, and the death-knell of Chinese social reform!" [37] In another article Hu elaborated upon this theme: "Civilization was not created *in toto*, but by inches and drops. Evolution was not accomplished overnight but in inches and drops. People nowadays indulge in talk about liberation and reform, but they should know that there is no liberation *in toto*, or reform *in toto*. Liberation means the liberation of this or that system, of this or that idea, or this or that individual; it is reform by inches and drops. The first step in the recreation of civilization is the study of this or that problem. Progress in the recreation of civilization lies in the solution of this or that problem." [38]

Li, on the other hand, reaffirmed his belief that a basic political transformation was a prerequisite to the solution of specific social problems: "it is first necessary to have a fundamental solution, and then there will be hope of solving concrete problems one by one. Take Russia as an example. If the Romanoffs had not been overthrown and the economic organization not reformed, no problems could have been solved. Now they are all being solved." [39]

Neither Hu Shih's concern with the solution of individual concrete problems nor Li Ta-chao's advocacy of "fundamental solutions" can be considered apart from the particular Chinese situation to which these opposing methods were to be applied. Hu Shih had formulated his ideas in terms of the American philosophical and sociological tradition. That tradition had grown out of the experiences of a stable and progressive society that could realistically view its problems (in the words of Karl Mannheim) as "discrete technical problems of social readjustment." [40] The philosophy and sociology of John Dewey did not need to be concerned with the structure of society as a whole because in the American social context it could be optimistically assumed that the whole would take care of itself. Dewey's program was essentially conservative, assuming that reform would take place within the framework of existing institutions; but it was the product of a society that could afford conservatism, a society that could solve particular social problems because there already existed a viable social structure and a general consensus on the direction of social progress.

As applied to China, Dewey's program was neither conservative nor radical but largely irrelevant. After the Revolution of 1911 China was confronted with a crisis of social, cultural, and political disintegration of massive proportions. The extreme poverty and widespread illiteracy of the masses of the Chinese people and the lack of even the rudiments of responsible political authority negated the possibility of the general social consensus that Dewey's program presupposed. Because of the overwhelming social crisis within and the threat of foreign aggression from without, the very existence of the Chinese nation was in doubt at the time Hu Shih and Li Ta-chao debated the matter of "problems and isms." To advocate the study of particular problems and to call for social reform by "inches and drops" was to assume that there existed or would soon arise a viable social and political structure within which problems could be studied and reforms implemented. This assumption was unwarranted either by the existing situation or by any realistic hopes for the immediate future. In view of the total crisis of Chinese society, Dewey's program was doomed to failure.

This failure was made even more certain as the echoes of the "problems and isms" controversy were still reverberating in Chinese intellectual circles. Although Hu Shih had proposed Dewey's philosophy as a method to solve Chinese social problems, he and his fellow liberals turned in the 1920's not to social problems but rather to more esoteric matters, such as archeological investigations, the study of ancient Chinese philosophy and history, and the textual criticism of traditional literature. It is ironical, as Chow Tse-tsung has so perceptively pointed out, that "in 1920, just after their suggestion of 'more study of problems,' very few liberals joined the social survey or labor movements, whereas many of the socialists and their associates began to go among the workers and peasants to study their living conditions." [41]

To say that their program was doomed to failure is not to question the sincerity and good intentions of Hu Shih and his fellow liberals. Although Hu was by temperament and philosophic training opposed to revolutionary ideologies and revolutionary politics, he was also deeply concerned with the grave social and economic problems of his country. That he failed to make any substantial contribution to the solution of these problems suggests only that Hu had fallen victim to the same error that he had perceived in his more radical colleagues, the error of importing foreign theories without paying sufficient attention to the social environment in which these theories had been created.

In rejecting political participation and emphasizing the study of concrete problems, Hu Shih remained very much in accord with the intellectual tendencies dominant in the earlier New Culture era. He also continued those tendencies by his distrust of nationalism and his refusal to regard imperialism as a serious menace to China, by his preoccupation with the transformation of traditional cultural values, and by his preference for evolutionary rather than revolutionary approaches to social reform. As the May Fourth movement gathered momentum — as nationalism, political activism, and the impatient search for immediate solutions to the plight of China became the dominant themes of the intellectual climate — Hu Shih increasingly seemed like the voice of an intellectual era that had passed.

Lurking in the background of the "problems and isms" debate was the problem of choosing between two irreconcilably opposed maxims of conduct that have been defined by Max Weber as the "ethic of ultimate ends" and the "ethic of responsibility." The believer in the "ethic of ultimate ends" is committed to abstract standards of personal morality. His is the ethics of conscience in which the individual reserves his personal freedom to interpret social reality and acts to change that reality only in ways that are consistent with the preservation of his own moral standards. Thus, he does not consider that his primary responsibility is the practical social consequences of his actions (or his inaction) but feels that his primary responsibility is the preservation of the purity of his own intentions. Followed to its logical conclusion in a world in which most issues are at best morally ambiguous, this is the ethic of the Sermon on the Mount, the ethic of the saint who has withdrawn from the sordid affairs of the world. The political activist who is a man of conscience must, on the other hand, follow the "ethic of responsibility." He is responsible not only to the demands of his conscience but also to society, and he must accept responsibility for the immoral means and sometimes the evil results that are often involved in attempting to attain "good ends." He must recognize that "he is responsible for what may become of himself under the impact of these paradoxes." [42]

The problem of choosing between the "ethic of ultimate ends" and the "ethic of responsibility" is in part the problem of choosing between the life of a scholar and the life of a politician. It is a dilemma of particular relevance for understanding the psychological background of the appeals and conflicts involved in the Chinese intelligentsia's response to the Marxist-Leninist program of political action. There are strong echoes of this dilemma in the Chinese tradition. It appeared in the Confucian literatus' ideal of state service, which required the scholar's participation as a functionary in a political organization based upon the use of violence, although the moral precepts of his Confucian faith taught that government should be based upon the example of moral virtue and good conduct in the ruler. It appeared even more sharply in the contrast between the scholar-official, dedicated to participation in public affairs, and the Taoist recluse, dedicated to the cultivation of his own inner life and the goal of knowledge. Even within the Confucian tradition itself, as Benjamin Schwartz has pointed out, there existed a tradition of protest and withdrawal from public life.[43]

The influence of the Confucian spirit of public service on Li Ta-chao's early intellectual life, and the emphasis that he placed upon the need for immediate political participation in his debate with Ch'en Tu-hsiu on the problem of "consciousness" in 1915, have already been noted. In the "problems and isms" controversy, Li made a final commitment to the "ethic of responsibility." In choosing to pursue the political life, he was now prepared to sacrifice many of his own beliefs and principles to attain the "good end" of Bolshevism, with which he identified the forces of universal regeneration. In doing so, he was deeply conscious of his own personal responsibility to Chinese society and to Chinese history.

Hu Shih would have liked to follow the "ethic of ultimate ends." He would have liked to remain a pure scholar engaged in the study of "concrete problems" with which he would be involved only as a scientific observer and nonpartisan guide. He did not wish to soil his hands in the dirty and irrelevant business of politics. As it turned out, however, Hu Shih and other liberals were unable to maintain either of these two ethics. The pressures for political commitment in the revolutionary turbulence of modern China proved too strong to permit a life of pure scholarship. Hu Shih eventually came to an accommodation with the Kuomintang, and many other liberals eventually turned to (or, more precisely, were driven into the arms of) the Communists. In modern Chinese politics the liberals were more often used by the contending parties than they were able to influence them. They were thus denied both the possibility of maintaining the personal standards of integrity dictated by the "ethic of ultimate ends" and the possibility of assuming responsibility for the political roles that they reluctantly undertook.

Shortly after the publication of Li's article "Again on Problems and Isms" in *Mei-chou p'ing-lun* on August 17, the periodical was suppressed by the warlord-controlled Peking government. The debate was carried on by Hu Shih in the Shanghai monthly *T'ai-p'ing yang* (The Pacific Ocean). The Chinputang (many of whose supporters were then advocates of guild socialism) was represented in the controversy by the journalist Lan Kung-wu, who was critical of Hu Shih, maintaining that the study and encouragement of all isms was the first step in the solution of problems.[44] The controversy continued until the end of the year.[45] By the time of its conclusion, Li Ta-chao was no longer concerned with, or had at least concealed, the objections he had raised to Marxist doctrine in "My Marxist Views." He was firmly committed to the Marxist-Leninist program of political action.

This change was already evident in his first reply to Hu Shih on the question of "problems and isms" in August 1919. Challenged in his Marxist beliefs by Hu and deeply stirred by the magnetic atmosphere of the May Fourth movement and the activistic impulses that it had liberated, Li was no longer disposed to quibble over his philosophic reservations with respect to Marxism. In his reply to Hu Shih's objection to "fundamental solutions," Li's treatment of the materialist conception of history showed no trace of the belief — which he had insisted upon two months before — that material reform must be accompanied by spiritual reform: "According to the historical materialist point of view of Marx, all the spiritual constructions of society such as laws, politics, ethics, etc., are part of the superstructure. Beneath lies the economic structure, which is the whole basis upon which they rest. If there is a change in the economic structure, then all [the elements of the superstructure] will follow it in changing. In other words, *the solution of the economic problem is the fundamental solution.* As soon as the economic problem is solved, then all political and legal problems and the problems of the family system, women's liberation, and the workers' liberation can be solved."[46]

Li, to be sure, was prompt to emphasize that the economic revolution could not be achieved unless there was a conscious movement of the masses expressed in the form of class struggle. But this was simply good Marxism. In the following months Li was drawn even closer to the Marxist world view. His article "Material Change and Ethical Change," published in December 1919,[47] contended that all ethical systems were no more than reflections of the material conditions of life. In another article he dismissed Confucianism as the tool of the traditional ruling classes and attempted to explain all intellectual changes in modern China as the inevitable result of changes in the Chinese economy. The new ideas, he asserted, "arise from the new demands of society which must meet the new conditions of the economy."[48] By the end of 1920 he had refined this ultradeterministic approach by clearly distinguishing between historical materialism and economic determinism. In an essay entitled "The Value of the Materialist Conception of History in Modern Historical Study,"[49] Li attempted through the agency of the theory of class struggle to find a place for his belief in the power of human activity and consciousness within the Marxian scheme of the workings of the material forces of production. It was here that Li achieved some measure of intellectual harmony with Marx.

Ch'en Tu-hsiu's conversion to the Marxist-Leninist program came later and more abruptly, but it was no less total than Li Ta-chao's. Throughout the year 1919 Ch'en remained virtually silent on the subject of the Bolshevik Revolution. Indeed, during the "problems and isms" controversy Li criticized Ch'en as well as Hu Shih for their reluctance even to discuss the October Revolution.[50] Li's criticism was not wholly justified, for Ch'en did occasionally comment on the Russian Revolution, although very briefly and without making commitments, in the "Random Thoughts" columns of *Mei-chou p'ing-lun* and *Hsin ch'ing-nien*. On one occasion, in April 1919, Ch'en wrote: "The political revolution of eighteenth century France and the social revolution of twentieth century Russia were both subject to the extreme abuse of the men of those times; but later historians regarded them as great turning points in the change and evolution of human society."[51] In December 1919, Ch'en was content to define briefly the origin of the term "Bolshevism" and to defend the Bolsheviks from the charge that they threatened world peace.[52] Yet at this very same time Ch'en wrote an essay supporting

John Dewey's gradualist program for building political and social democracy upon the foundations of small self-governing groups. He still hopefully believed at the end of 1919 that China could use England and America as her model.[53]

Within a few months, however, Ch'en's perspectives shifted away completely from Dewey's proposals for gradual reform and settled firmly on the "labor question."[54] The image of the West he presented was no longer one of progressive, democratic nations but one of imperialist states in which capitalists mercilessly exploited workers. "The number one task of contemporary society," he declared, "is the establishment of a working-class state."[55] Dewey's program, as Benjamin Schwartz has pointed out, would have required "years of prosaic and undramatic work" and the willingness of the intelligentsia "to play a modest role in the background with no hope of immediate spectacular results."[56] The highly emotional and activistic atmosphere of the May Fourth era did not encourage Ch'en to resign himself to such prospects. Moreover, his faith in Western democracy had never really recovered from the shock of Versailles. Thus, by the middle of 1920 Ch'en was firmly in the Marxist-Leninist camp. In replying to an anarchist critic on the question of "State, Politics, and Law" in November 1920, Ch'en left no doubt of his commitment to the Communist program of political action and to the goal of establishing a proletarian dictatorship. Democracy, which hitherto had occupied so central a place in his thought, was dismissed as no more than a "tool that the bourgeoisie formerly used to overthrow the feudal system and which they presently use as a device to swindle mankind in order to maintain political power."[57]

Ch'en's conversion to Bolshevism, which came almost two years after Li's, was not accompanied by the same passionate and chiliastic enthusiasm for the October Revolution that had marked the response of his younger colleague. Nor did Ch'en's treatment of Marxist theory display any of the doubts and unorthodoxies that appeared in Li's writings. Ch'en accepted Marxism *in toto,* in much the same spirit that he had earlier accepted democracy and science. For him Marxism had replaced democracy as the most advanced expression of contemporary Western thought.

But Marxism demanded political as well as intellectual commitments. "The philosophers," Marx declared, "have only interpreted the world . . . The point, however, is to change it."[58] In its Leninist metamorphosis, this activistic injunction had come to the very forefront of the doctrine. In his reaction against the West during the May Fourth period Ch'en gradually overcame his inhibitions on the question of political participation. By mid-1920 he was no less eager than Li Ta-chao to assume the role of political organizer and revolutionary leader.[59]

Early Communist Organization

In 1920 the organizational as well as ideological foundations for the Chinese Communist party were laid. The early period of the organization of Communist activities in China is tangled in a web of obscurity that Chinese Communist historians have done little to unravel. Since in the Communist pantheon Mao Tse-tung is both the Lenin and Stalin of China, relatively little attention has been paid to those aspects of party history in which Mao was not directly involved. Yet before his attendance at the meeting that formally established the party in July 1921, Mao played only a minor role in Chinese Communist affairs.

The inception of Communist organizational activities in China is generally attributed to the intervention in Chinese affairs of the Comintern, whose agent, Gregori Voitinsky, arrived in Peking early in 1920. Before the appearance of Voitinsky, however, the stage had been set. After the May Fourth Incident radical intellectual and political activities multiplied and left-wing student organizations proliferated. Many of the future leaders of the Chinese Communist party were active in 1919 in such politically oriented organizations as the Social Welfare Society, the New People's Study Society, and the Awakening Society, as well as various "work and study" groups. Some of the student groups, such as the Mass Education Speech Corps, had as their aim "the awakening of the consciousness of the common people." In late 1919 student groups in the Shanghai area were organized for the purpose of achieving the unity of the intelligentsia and the laboring classes.[60]

The origin of the Communist labor movement in North China can be traced to the spring of 1919, when several of Li Ta-chao's students (led by Teng Chung-hsia and Chang Kuo-t'ao) began agitational and educational activities in the working-class districts of Peking. They established a lecture hall in the town of Chang-hsin-tien, a railroad center on the outskirts of Peking, which became the center for the organization of the Peking-Hankow Railroad Workers' Union. In 1919 Li and his student followers also began to organize dock workers in Tientsin. According to Russian sources, two young Russian Communists, who found themselves in North China rather accidentally as a consequence of the civil war in Siberia, assisted Li in these efforts in the year preceding the Voitinsky mission. One of them, A. A. Muller, has written of these activities by himself and N. Bortman, a fellow member of the Russian Communist party, in Peking and Tientsin in 1919–1920:

Bortman, even before my arrival, had fairly wide ties with progressive Chinese students from the higher educational institutions and colleges in Tientsin and Peking, and personally with Professor Li Ta-chao, whom Bortman spoke of as an excellent Marxist . . . When I met Bortman in September 1919, the ties with the students were maintained as before, and one group after another visited our apartment nearly every evening.

We acquainted the Chinese students with Lenin's work *Imperialism, the Highest Stage of Capitalism,* often touching on problems relating to China, analyzed the works of Sun Yat-sen, and told them about the leading role of the working class in the October Socialist Revolution in Russia.

It was not difficult for us to prove to the students that they must establish close ties with the textile and dock workers of Tientsin and engage in the organization of trade unions, which at that time did not as yet exist. This question was a subject of Bortman's discussions with Li Ta-chao.

At the beginning of January 1920, before our departure from China, a group of four students had already established ties with dock workers and had begun the practical formation of a trade union.[61]

The dissemination of Marxist theory also increased rapidly in the wake of the May Fourth Incident. In February 1919 Li Ta-chao was appointed editor of the Peking *Ch'en-pao's* weekly supplement *Ch'en-pao fu-k'an,* which he shortly turned into an instrument for the popularization of Marxism. In addition to Li's writings, between May 9 and June 1, 1919, *Ch'en-pao fu-k'an* printed Marx's "Wage Labor and Capital," the first Chinese translation of Marx to appear since 1912.[62] Also in 1919 Yün Tai-ying (later a leader of the Communist Youth Corps) translated and published Kautsky's *Class Stuggle,* and in April 1920 the first complete Chinese version of the *Communist Manifesto* (translated by Ch'en Wang-tao) was published in Shanghai.[63] The first of the writings of Lenin to appear in Chinese was translated late in 1919.[64]

The Marxist Research Society that had been established by Li Ta-chao in late 1918 was superseded in December 1919 by the more broadly based Society for the Study of Socialism (She-hui-chu-i yen-chiu-hui). The latter, which claimed 110 members, mostly students of various colleges in Peking, also held its meetings under Li's auspices in the Peking University Library. The Society for the Study of Socialism, which included anarchists, syndicalists, and guild socialists as well as Marxists, shortly broke up into its component parts. The Marxists regrouped under Li in March 1920 in a new organization known as the Peking Society for the Study of Marxist Theory (Ma-k'o-ssu hsüeh-shuo yen-chiu hui). According to Chu Wu-shan, a Peking University student who was a member of the group, Li's role was rather that of a faculty adviser for a student debating society. At its meetings Li usually sat in a corner, limiting his participation to answering the questions that students directed to him. Although many of the future leaders of the Chinese Communist party were members, its membership was not confined to Marxist activists; at one of its sessions a heated debate ensued over the question of whether China was really ready for socialism.[65]

Although Li and his student followers had not yet come to appreciate the virtues of a Leninist-type party organization, they had already initiated the activities that a Communist party in China would be expected to undertake, that is, the propagation of Marxism and the attempt to organize the working class. Thus, when Voitinsky arrived in Peking with his Chinese interpreter Yang Ming-chai, a native of Shantung who had migrated to Siberia before the October Revolution and there joined the Russian Communist party, he set foot upon already fertile soil.[66]

Through a Russian professor teaching at Peking University, Voitinsky was introduced to Li Ta-chao.[67] The exact date of Voitinsky's arrival has never been verified, but according to a recent Chinese Communist account, in March 1920 — the month that Li organized the Society for the Study of Marxist Theory — Li and Voitinsky discussed the formation of a Chinese Communist party in Li's library office.[68] Li was apparently receptive to the purposes of the

Comintern mission but suggested that Voitinsky first contact Ch'en Tu-hsiu. Voitinsky thereupon proceeded to Shanghai where he won the support of Ch'en, who organized a Communist group consisting of seven members in May 1920.[69] Then Ch'en invited Li and other Marxist intellectuals to Shanghai to lay plans for the organization of a national party. At this meeting it was agreed that Ch'en would assume primary responsibility for the organization of the party in the southern provinces, while Li would undertake the task in the North. The slogan "Nan-Ch'en, Pei-Li" (Ch'en in the South and Li in the North) became generally accepted within party ranks. During the summer and early autumn of 1920 small Communist groups using a variety of names were established in Peking, Wuhan, Changsha, Chinan, and Hangchow.[70] At the end of the year a Communist group was organized in Canton by Ch'en Tu-hsiu after he had accepted the invitation of Ch'en Ch'iung-ming, the new warlord of Kwangtung, to become chairman of that province's education commission.[71]

These early Communist groups were something less than models of the proper Leninist distillation of dedicated and disciplined revolutionaries. Among their early members were a good number of anarchists and such ultranationalist "Marxist-Leninists" as Tai Chi-t'ao, who later became a leader of the Kuomintang right wing and Chiang Kai-shek's chief ideologist. Li Ta-chao's group in Peking originally consisted of eight members, of whom six were said to be anarchists.[72]

Within a few months, however, the anarchists (and Tai) left the party and were replaced by the more dedicated student followers of Li and Ch'en. During its early years the Chinese Communist party was principally a student party. Except for Ch'en, who was forty-one years of age when the party was organized, and Li, who was thirty-two, the party members were mostly university students in their early twenties. At Peking Li recruited a number of his favorite students, including such future Communist notables as Teng Chung-hsia, Chang Kuo-t'ao, Lo Chang-lung, Ho Meng-hsiung, and Liu Jen-ch'ing (later leader of the Chinese Trotskyists). According to Chinese Communist accounts, Mao Tse-tung was in close contact with Li while engaged in Communist organizational activities in Hunan in 1920, following his second visit to Peking in February of that year.[73] Chou En-lai was also in contact with Li while active in the Awakening Society in Tientsin and in the

Society for the Study of Socialism in early 1920, shortly before Chou left to study in France, where he joined the Communist group organized among Chinese students in Paris by Ts'ai Ho-shen.[74]

Li Ta-chao's recruitment of many of the leading Chinese Communists was greatly facilitated by the very close personal relationships that he had developed with the student activists shortly before and after the May Fourth Incident. To his students Li was not only a teacher, an intellectual guide, and a political oracle but also a fatherly adviser on personal matters and financial problems. Something of the nature of this latter relationship as well as Li's own personality is suggested by an incident related by the liberal political philosopher Kao I-han, a professor at Peking University. In 1918 Li had taken the initiative in organizing a society to aid financially distressed students, and he frequently lent or gave his own money to needy students. Li's generosity evidently occasioned some domestic discord. At one point the situation became so serious that Li's wife went directly to the university chancellor, Ts'ai Yüan-pei, to complain that there were not sufficient funds for the most elementary household necessities. Thereafter Ts'ai gave Li only a part of his salary, insisting upon turning over the greater portion of it directly to Mrs. Li.[75]

Thus, the Communist movement in China grew in part out of the close student-professor relationships that had developed during the May Fourth period. The movement was led by two professors who recruited the core of their followers from among their own students. The new Communist groups, however, undertook immediate efforts to remedy their rather unproletarian origins. In Shanghai, Ch'en Tu-hsiu began to promote the organization of trade unions among the dock workers and in August 1920 began to publish a workers' magazine, *Lao-tung chieh* (The World of Labor). In Peking Li Ta-chao founded a similar publication, *Lao-tung yin* (The Sound of Labor), and met with considerable success in organizing railroad workers around the laborer's school that had been established in Chang-hsin-tien. On May 1, 1920, Li led the workers of Chang-hsin-tien in a May Day demonstration and shortly thereafter assisted in the organization of a union, first known simply as the Workers' Association (Kung-jen chü-le-pu).[76]

The early Chinese Communist groups engaged in other activities that the Comintern expected of a member party. A Communist youth organization, the Socialist Youth Corps, was established in Shanghai in August 1920 and in Peking in September. Publishing facilities for the printing of Marxist-Leninist literature were established. *Hsin ch'ing-nien* became a party publication with the July 1920 issue, and in November an official party organ, *Kung-ch'an-tang* (The Communist), was established in Shanghai.

Neither Li nor Ch'en attended the meeting held in Shanghai in July 1921 that has come to be celebrated as the Party's official birthday. Ch'en was still in Canton, and the Shanghai Communist group was represented by Chou Fu-hai (later a follower of Wang Ching-wei and a member of the latter's puppet government during the war). Li sent Chang Kuo-t'ao to represent the Peking group. In all, twelve delegates, representing a total of fifty-seven members, formally launched the Chinese Communist party at a secret "Congress" that opened in a girls' boarding school in the French Concession of Shanghai and closed on a houseboat on a lake in Chekiang province. The Congress approved the standard Leninist methods of party organization and discipline, established a central committee, and elected Ch'en to the position of secretary-general.[77] Despite this Leninist facade, the party during its early years was neither ideologically nor organizationally a united entity. The northern branch, under Li's leadership, remained largely independent of, although not in direct opposition to, the Central Committee at Shanghai. The slogan "Nan-Ch'en, Pei-Li" was tacitly accepted within the party until 1927.

Although the Chinese Communist party was to grow dramatically after the spring of 1925, the relatively small number of people actually engaged in its early activities[78] reflected one factor in the Chinese environment that was of immense significance in conditioning the development of Marxism in China. Unlike the Communist parties formed in Western European countries after the Bolshevik Revolution — parties organized on the basis of the left wing of older Marxian Social Democratic parties — China totally lacked a Social Democratic tradition. Except for individual intellectuals and students who were attracted to the Marxist-Leninist message, there was little basis for the recruitment of Communist cadres. To the early Chinese Marxists and their Russian advisers this appeared to be a great handicap since it not only hampered recruitment but was also responsible, the Russians complained, for the "immaturity" of the Chinese Communists in the understanding of Marxist theory. In current Chinese Communist writings the absence of a Marxist Social Democratic party is treated as an important advantage since it protected China from the baneful influences of the revisionist Second International.

Although the advantages or disadvantages of the absence of a Social Democratic tradition are a matter of dispute, there can be no question that the Communist movement in China benefited from the traditional Chinese hostility to commercial pursuits and an almost innate anticapitalist predisposition. Most Chinese intellectuals would have heartily endorsed Benjamin Franklin's dictum (which Marx was so fond of quoting) that "war is robbery and commerce cheating in general." The Western-educated Chinese intelligentsia's admiration for Western political systems and democratic ideas did not extend to the capitalist economic system upon which democracy rested. Nor did there exist in China, as there did in Czarist Russia after 1900, a liberal political movement advocating democracy within a capitalist economic framework that could compete with Marxism for the loyalties of the intellectuals. These factors in the Chinese environment made the passage from Western democratic beliefs to Marxism-Leninism much less difficult than it might otherwise have been.

The formal conversion of Li and Ch'en to the Marxist-Leninist program posed the question of whether Marxist theory was really relevant to the Chinese situation. Both Li and Ch'en had already expressed serious reservations on this point in their different ways and at different times. In the spring of 1919, after he had already declared his support for the Bolshevik Revolution, Li had objected to the deterministic features of Marxist doctrine that conflicted with his fundamentally activistic predispositions. Before 1920 Ch'en had looked upon socialism as perhaps a worthy goal but one that was appropriate only to an advanced industrial nation. The impulse to political action generated by the May Fourth movement had temporarily submerged these doubts, but with the beginning of Communist political activities the problem reappeared. Now it was necessary to test Marxist theory in the Chinese environment. It was necessary to apply the new doctrine to the practical task of organizing a revolutionary political movement.

It might have been argued that the question of the relevance of Marxism would be settled by the success or failure of the political movement that was guided by it. But to intellectuals who undertook the practical work of creating the movement, the problem did not appear in so simple a form. Before they could wholeheartedly propagate Marxist theory and effectively employ it in politics, the theory had not only to provide a plausible explanation of the situation in which they found themselves but also to sanction meaningful forms of practical activity. This problem of achieving some correspondence between theory and practice was demanded by the very premises upon which Marxist doctrine rested as well as by the intellectual and emotional needs of the individuals who were involved in Marxist-Leninist politics. The manner in which Marxism was interpreted to meet these needs had very much to do with the way in which the practical movement developed and with its successes and failures.

PART TWO

THE REINTERPRETATION OF MARXISM

CHAPTER VI DETERMINISM AND ACTIVISM

EVEN BEFORE he was won over to the brilliant vision of a world-wide revolutionary transformation that the Bolshevik victory seemed to promise, Li Ta-chao had come to believe profoundly in the ability of the human spirit and human activity to change the circumstances under which men live. His whole pre-Marxian world view was built upon the faith that conscious Chinese youth, as carriers of the seed of national rebirth, were "capable of everything." "When the young have seen the light," he declared in 1916, "they should break the meshes of past history, destroy the prison of old ideas, and suffer no corpses to restrict their activity."[1] He pleaded for immediate action in the present, unencumbered by traditionalist sentiments for the past or by hopelessly utopian dreams about the future.

Upon the basis of this activistic world view Li had received the universalistic and messianic message of the October Revolution. The success of the Russian Revolution was to be but the first wave of a revolution that would wash away the dead shell of old China and release the pent-up energies of young China. The Russian upheaval, he believed, foreshadowed an imminent upheaval in China itself.

When Li had first seriously considered Marxist theory in the early months of 1919, he was willing to abandon his belief in the spiritual and psychological basis of historical change and to accept, at least in form, the general principles of Marx's materialist explanation of history. He refused, however, to renounce his faith in the ability of conscious, active men to remake society in accordance with their wills. Nor could he wholeheartedly accept what he perceived to be the Marxist belief in the inexorable workings of the economic laws of history.[2] To do so would have been to condemn China to a long and dreary period of capitalist development, and also to resign himself to the role of a passive observer of this painful process.

Both Li Ta-chao and Ch'en Tu-hsiu had adopted the new Marxist creed with the expectation that the revolutionary movement they proposed to create would lead to a more or less rapid transition to a socialist society. Li and Ch'en (and many other Chinese intellectuals) were brought into the Communist fold not only by the nationalistic appeals of Lenin's theory of imperialism but also by the assumptions best formulated in Trotsky's theory of permanent revolution. This theory, which Lenin had implicitly adopted in 1917, held out the hope that an economically backward country could be rapidly transformed and, by virtue of its very backwardness, advance to the forefront of world civilization. Yet the contradictions that existed between the desire for immediate revolutionary action to rescue China and the demands of certain fundamental principles of Marxist theory could not be ignored, for the materialist conception of history brought to the new Chinese converts to Bolshevism the very disheartening message that Chinese society lacked almost totally the material conditions for the realization of the Marxist socialist program.

For no one was this message more disheartening than for Li Ta-chao. All the activistic implications of his pre-Marxist world view and the chiliastic spirit with which he had greeted the Bolshevik Revolution rebelled against any doctrine that seemed to limit the role of human consciousness and activity or seemed to suggest that the millennium might be far off. Thus, in his essay "My Marxist Views" Li quite candidly raised the problem of the conflict between the economically deterministic assumptions of Marxist theory and the Marxist emphasis on the importance of political consciousness: "We are unable to consider correct historical materialists who say that economic phenomena have an unshakeable and unbending nature and that the ideas and activities of groups must entirely submit to them." He insisted that political forces could change the direction of economic developments and argued that socialism must be based upon ethical principles and aim to achieve a spiritual as well as a material reformation. Above all, Li was concerned with the fatalistic conclusions that might be drawn from the Marxist view of history: "Some people say that historical materialists regard the movement of the economic process as inevitable, and this can not but give [their theories] a kind of fatalistic color . . . the [European] Marxist socialist parties, because of their belief in a fatalistic theory, proposed nothing, undertook no activities, and only waited for the natural maturation of the productive forces, until today the socialist parties of the various [European] countries have entered a period of great crisis. This can be said to be a defect left by Marx's materialist conception of history." [3]

Li had embarked upon the propagation of Bolshevism and Marxism as a matter of individual responsibility and, at first, had felt relatively free to amend or even reject those aspects of Marxist doctrine that seemed to conflict with his hopes for revolution. But after the "problems and isms" controversy, when he began to form firmer political commitments, and especially after the organization of the first Chinese Communist groups in 1920, it was no longer possible simply to disregard those deterministic Marxist dicta that were opposed to his own activistic impulses. If Marxism was to serve as a guide to political action, it had to form a reasonably coherent body of doctrine whose fundamental precepts were accepted, or at least rationalized. It was therefore necessary to reconcile Marxian determinism with the desire for immediate revolutionary action, and this reconciliation had to take place within the framework of Marxist categories of thought.

The problem of the conflict between determinism and activism raised by Li Ta-chao in 1919 is one of the most complex and fundamental problems of Marxist theory. It is a problem that involves such vital issues as the Marxist view of the role of human consciousness and human activity in history, the nature of the theory of class struggle, and the question of the relationship between political and economic forces. On all of these questions Li Ta-chao made radical departures from the European and Russian Marxist traditions. The significance of his departures cannot be fully appreciated without some understanding of the nature of the theory with which he was concerned. Thus, before an examination of Li's interpretations, it is necessary to consider the origins — in the thought of Karl Marx and his successors — of some of the theoretical problems that Li encountered as he attempted to fashion Marxist doctrine to the cause of revolution in China.

Determinism and Activism in Marxist Theory

Marxism is a peculiar amalgam of deterministic and activistic elements, for it is both a theory of the general laws of socio-historical development and a philosophy of revolutionary practice. In the Marxist world view, man is both the object and the subject of history; he is the product of his past, but he is also the producer of his future.

Although Karl Marx presented his theory as a universalistic science of the impersonal and objective forces determining the activities and ideas of men, his doctrine begins with, and is permeated by, philosophic premises that are concerned primarily not with impersonal forces but with the state of man. It is a philosophy concerned with man's loss of his human identity, his regaining of his human essence, and his active role in shaping social reality. These deterministic and activistic elements converge upon the socialist goal to which Marxist theory is tied. Marx looked to the objective forces of history to explain that socialism was desirable, necessary, and inevitable, but he also emphasized the subjective factors of human "self-consciousness" and human "self-activity" as essential to the achievement of socialism.

Formal Marxist theory is dominated by the deterministic "laws" of history set forth by Marx — "laws" that were made more deterministic by his immediate successors. Yet the activistic elements of original Marxism have important implications for the interpretation of the theory as a whole and they have served to inspire and justify the attempts of later Marxists to adapt the theory to new and changing historical circumstances. These activistic elements are particularly relevant to the vital question of how and under what preconditions the socialist utopia of the future is to be realized. The purpose of this discussion will be to identify some of the contradictory deterministic and activistic strands in Marxism.

The starting point from which Marx began his critique of society and his analysis of history was the concept of alienation. The term "alienation" was used by Marx to describe a condition in which the powers and products of men come to confront their producers as alien and independent entities. History, for Marx, was the process not only of man's self-creation but also of his ever-growing self-alienation. Man, according to Marx, becomes increasingly estranged from himself and from other men and more and more enslaved to the products, the ideas and the institutions that he himself has produced as the result of the growing complexity of the social division of labor. Religion, the family, private property, and the state are all forms of human self-alienation; they are institutions originally created by man that have come to rule over him and prevent him from achieving a truly human life. The capitalist mode of production is but the most recent and most severe form of human self-alienation, for under capitalism labor has become fully alienated. The worker has become an appendage of the machine, and the very product of his labor, in the abstract form of capital, oppresses and exploits him. "The more the worker expends himself in work," Marx wrote, "the more powerful becomes the world of objects which he creates in face of himself, the poorer he becomes in his inner life, and the less he belongs to himself." [4]

Although capitalism is the most severe form of human self-alienation, it is also the final one — for capitalism has given rise to the modern industrial proletariat, a class so totally alienated and dehumanized that it is forced to recognize the conditions of its existence and strive to overcome them. In doing so, the proletariat must play a universalistic role for it cannot liberate itself without liberating the whole of society; indeed, it must liberate the whole world.[5] Upon the basis of these premises several of the most important Marxist beliefs rest: a faith in the proletariat as the agent of historical redemption, a conviction that capitalism inevitably produces its own "gravediggers," and the internationalism that was so vital a part of the original Marxist vision.

The concept of alienation, which underlies all the major doctrines of Marx, suggests a world view that emphasizes the importance of consciousness and the active role of man in making the future. If man is alienated from himself, from other men, and from the world he has created, then the overcoming of that alienation (that is, man's understanding of the situation in which he finds himself and his recognition that the powers he has attributed to outside forces are in reality his own) must be taken as a prerequisite for the revolutionary activity necessary to change his situation.

It is important here to distinguish, as Marx did, between the terms "consciousness" and "self-consciousness." Consciousness is an attribute of all men at all times and in all places. Whether it be the direct expression of social class interests or merely the religious phantoms that haunt men's minds, consciousness is no more than a reflection of the alienated conditions of human existence. It is, in effect, "false consciousness" — false because it fails to recognize and realize man's human potentialities. "Self-consciousness," on the other hand, is man's conquest of his alienation and the regaining of his human essence. It is not merely the product of the socialist utopia of the future but also a transformation that is essential to the process of attaining that utopia. Just as man's "consciousness" is transformed into "self-consciousness" in this process, man's "activity" is transformed into "self-activity." Thus, in his "Theses on Feuerbach" Marx stated, "the coincidence of the changing of circumstances and of human activity or self-changing can only be comprehended and rationally understood as revolutionary practice." It is through the very act of revolution against the existing alien world, through the coincidence of "change of self" and "change of circumstances," and through the unity of theory and practice that man overcomes his alienated condition and is able to realize his truly human potentialities. Marx then concluded his 'Theses" with the activistic injunction: "The philosophers have only interpreted the world differently, the point is, to change it." [6] To be sure, Marx believed that man's self-alienation is rooted in the material conditions of his life and the division of labor in society; but the conditions of man's material life have been created by man himself and can only be changed through human action. The "change of self," that is, the acquisition of "true consciousness," is an essential element in the Marxist conception of the revolutionary process leading to the future communist utopia.

If human alienation is to be overcome and freedom is to be achieved by the conscious and purposeful revolutionary action of men, how does consciousness arise? How does man achieve the "self-consciousness" necessary for meaningful "revolutionary practice?" Marx answered this question by attributing to the proletariat the ability to transform itself into its opposite. Marx argued, in effect, that it is precisely because the worker is so completely dehumanized that he is bound to become fully human. He is destined to achieve the "self-consciousness" necessary to lead mankind from the realm of "prehistory" to the realm of a "truly human history." However, the proletariat has not arrived upon the historical scene as *deus ex machina.* He is the product of a specific form of economic organization, namely, the capitalist mode of production, which is itself the result of many centuries of historical development. To explain the origins of capitalism and the appearance of the modern proletariat, Marx set forth an interpretation of history that was later and somewhat inaccurately called the "materialist conception of history." This theory propounds a number of "laws" that universally govern the development of society and the activities of men. It also provides an answer to the question of what forces determine man's consciousness; its answer presumably applies to the exercise of proletarian consciousness as well as to earlier forms of consciousness. In this view of history the tension between the conflicting deterministic and activistic strands inherent in the Marxist system of thought is most sharply revealed.

The materialist conception of history attempts to establish a relationship between man's consciousness and the material processes of production. Its basic assumption is the proposition that "being determines consciousness." "Being," for Marx, is essentially economic being, that is, the stage of the development of the productive forces of society and the way in which these forces are organized. The "forces of production" constitute the economic "base" upon which is erected the legal, political, and ideological "superstructure." "Consciousness," which is part of the superstructure, includes not only the general ideas and ideologies that correspond to the base and the other elements of the superstructure, but also class consciousness, which is the prerequisite for political activity. Thus, in what Marxists still regard as a classic statement of the theory, Marx described the process of historical change in the following manner:

At a certain stage of their development, the material productive forces of society come in conflict with the existing relations of production, or what is but a legal expression for the same thing — with the property relations within which they have been at work hitherto. From forms of development of the productive forces these relations turn into their fetters. Then begins an epoch of social revolution. With the change of the economic foundation the entire immense superstructure is more or less rapidly transformed. In considering such transformations a distinction should always be made between the material transformation of the economic conditions of production, which can be determined with the precision of natural science, and the legal, political, religious, aesthetic or philosophic — in short, ideological forms in which men become conscious of this conflict and fight it out. Just as our opinion of an individual is not based upon what he thinks of himself, so can we not judge such a period of transformation by its own consciousness; on the contrary, the consciousness must be explained rather from the contradictions of material life, from the existing conflict between the social productive forces and the relations of production . . . mankind always sets itself only such tasks as it can solve . . . it will always be found that the task itself arises only when the material conditions for its solution already exist or are at least in the process of formation.[7]

This fundamental statement of the materialist conception of history would seem to dictate that all forms of consciousness and conscious political activity are wholly determined by the economic structure of society and its changes. Yet these deterministic implications undergo considerable modification when viewed in the light of the philosophic premises of the early thought of Marx, which emphasize "self-consciousness" and human activity as the truly creative forces in the contemporary historic process. Although these activistic premises tend to become subject to an increasing number of economic determinants in the writings of the "mature" Marx, they never really disappear. Even his most deterministic writings are set within the framework of a radical critique of existing social reality and the explicit assumption that society will be transformed not through the preordained workings of an abstract process of "history" but through the revolutionary action of men. It is men, Marx repeatedly emphasized, who make history.[8] Although Marx turned to the objective material world to solve the problem of human self-alienation, he always recognized that this world had been created by men and could only be changed through the self-conscious activity of men.

The recognition that it is "people and their consciousness" who are "the effective bearers of historic development" is of vital importance for interpreting the principle that "being determines consciousness." As one of the most eminent of contemporary Marxist theoreticians, George Lukacs, has written, the question of the relationship between being and consciousness must "pass beyond the purely theoretical and pose the problem of 'praxis.' For it is only when the core of being is revealed as social process that being appears as the product, in the past unconscious, of human activity, and this activity is seen as the decisive element in the transformation of being."[9]

From this dialectical point of view the rise of man from the realm of "necessity" (where man is dominated by the alien world he has created) to the realm of "freedom" (where rational man becomes the master of his own externalized nature) is a process that cannot be separated from man's attainment of "true consciousness." Marx believed that the socialist revolution would be dependent upon the development of a high level of material civilization, but he also believed, as Herbert Marcuse has so perceptively pointed out, that these objective conditions "become revolutionary conditions . . . only if seized upon and directed by a conscious activity that has in mind the socialist goal. Not the slightest natural necessity or automatic activity inevitably guarantees the transition from capitalism to socialism . . . The realization of freedom and reason requires the free rationality of those who achieve it." [10]

On this problem of Marx's view of the relationship between the material conditions of life and conscious human activity, Karl Lowith has written: "It is true that man's self-alienation is conditioned by the type and degree of the development of the material conditions of production, by the division of labor and by the sum of the concrete conditions of his life. But these conditions are structurally united in the social nature of man, who is his own world and whose self-consciousness is a world consciousness. The sum of conditions cannot be derived from abstract economic factors; the latter must be integrated into the concrete of historic human conditions . . . In his true reality man is an essence which has to be brought into existence through action." [11]

It lies beyond the scope of this study to enter into the complicated and rather scholastic question of whether Marx should be properly divided into an activistic and humanistic "young Marx" and a more deterministic "mature Marx." [12] However, it is highly relevant to the problems involved in the adaptation of Marxism in China to recognize that many of the most fundamental and widely read works of Marx either are explicitly based upon his early philosophic conceptions or can be interpreted to support a revolutionary, non-deterministic world view emphasizing the role of consciousness and human activity rather than simply the workings of impersonal economic forces. This activistic strain is particularly evident in the *Communist Manifesto*, with its essentially chiliastic call to revolution, and in the frankly utopian spirit of *The Civil War in France*, a commentary on the Paris Commune of 1871. In early Chinese

Marxist circles these were among the most influential of Marx's writings.[13] Even as seemingly a deterministic work as *Capital* is explicitly based upon the concept of alienated labor.[14] In China, *Capital* was read not so much as a scientific exposition of the laws of capitalist production as a moral indictment of the injustices and dehumanizing influences of capitalist industrialization.

The deterministic implications of the injunction that "being determines consciousness" are subject to further modification in considering the problem of the relationship between political and economic forces. In formal Marxist theory this relationship is cast in formulations as deterministic as those between "being" and "consciousness." Marx and Engels, of course, always held that economic phenomena were part of the social "base," the motivating force in historic development, whereas political forces were part of the "superstructure." Although after Marx's death Engels conceded that they had at times laid undue emphasis upon the economic factor in history (because, Engels claimed, their adversaries had completely ignored economics), he reaffirmed, as every Marxist still must do, that in the final analysis economic forces are decisive. In describing the relationship between economics and politics in Marxist theory, Engels wrote in 1890:

The economic situation is the basis, but the various elements of the superstructure — political forms of the class struggle and its results, to wit: constitutions established by the victorious class after a successful battle, juridical forms, and even the reflexes of all of these actual struggles in the brains of the participants, political, juristic, philosophical theories, religious views and their further development into systems of dogma — also exercise their influence upon the course of the historical struggles and in many cases preponderate in determining their form. There is an interaction of all these elements in which, amid all the endless hosts of accidents . . . the economic movement finally asserts itself as necessary.[15]

The relations between economic and political forces in Marxist theory were summed up more succinctly by Plekhanov: "Indisputably, political relations influence economic development; but it is no less indisputable that before influencing this movement, they are created thereby."[16] Although this proposition appears prominently in the writings of Marx and his successors, an examination of Marx's treatment of specific historical topics and his responses to contemporary political events suggests that he held a considerably more flexible view of the relationship between political and economic forces. That Marx believed political power plays a largely independent role in history under certain conditions is evident in his treatment of the absolutist states that emerged during the transition from feudalism to capitalism in Europe,[17] in his interpretation of the French Revolution of 1848 and the dictatorship of Napoleon III,[18] and in his application of the concept of "Oriental despotism" to traditional Indian history.[19] On a number of other topics, such as the history of European overseas expansion, Marx went to considerable effort to demonstrate the economic effects of the employment of political force.[20]

Of more significance is the fact that the nondeterministic strain in Marx's thought was reflected in his willingness to entertain hopes for revolution wherever the existing political situation seemed promising, even if the objective economic prerequisites were lacking. This tendency appeared in Marx's early belief that Germany, then one of the most economically backward of the Western European countries, was closer to a proletarian socialist revolution than were the more economically advanced countries of France and England.[21] The lack of any complete correspondence between economic and political forces was also evident in Marx's long-standing view of England as the model of economic development and France as the classic country of political revolution. The impatient revolutionary activism of Marx was even more dramatically revealed in his flirtation in the 1870's with the notion that a revolution in Russia might bypass the capitalist phase of development and proceed directly to a socialist reorganization of society,[22] and even in his little-known article of 1853, "Revolution in China and Europe," where he suggested that the T'ai-p'ing Rebellion might serve as a stimulus to a socialist revolution in the West.[23] Whereas taken as a whole, the writings of Marx do suggest a correlation between a given level of economic maturity and political ripeness for revolution, numerous statements and formulations lend support to more voluntaristic approaches.

The point to be emphasized is that the original doctrine of Marx does not have the iron-like consistency often attributed to it. The deterministic injunctions on the relationships between "being" and "consciousness" and between economic and political forces are challenged by the philosophic humanism of the early writings of Marx as well as by the revolutionary activism that remains a prominent feature of many of his later writings. Even the idea that the proletariat is the agent of human liberation — a conception that is at the very core of the Marxist world view — contains within itself these contradictory deterministic and activistic streams. The subjective elements of "self-consciousness" and "self-activity" are central to the Marxist notion of the proletariat and the process of proletarian revolution, even though the emergence of the proletariat and the preconditions for its revolution are seen as the result of the workings of objective economic forces that develop as a matter of historic necessity. In the final analysis the doctrine of Marx cannot free itself from the paradox that man, the maker of history, is also the object through which the objective laws of history express themselves. The problem of reconciling the consciousness and practical political activities of man with a theory of historical inevitability was a dilemma Marx faced throughout his intellectual life, and the dilemma was left basically unresolved for his successors.

The fact that Marx did not fully reconcile the conflicting deterministic and activistic elements of his thought is a matter of less importance here than recognizing that these contradictory elements existed and could be drawn upon for different purposes by later Marxists of differing intellectual predispositions, living in dissimilar historical circumstances. All Marxists have upheld, at least in form, the deterministic formulas of Marx; but the manner in which they have perceived this determinism has not always been the same, and their views of the relationship between "being" and "consciousness" have differed profoundly. All Marxists have recognized that the attainment of a socialist or "true" consciousness is a necessary element for the achievement of socialism; but they have interpreted differently the origins and preconditions for the development of such a consciousness. The proletariat has always been involved, but it has been involved in very different ways. These differences have influenced profoundly the manner in which other aspects of Marxist doctrine have been interpreted and the way in which Marxism has been applied to political practice.

As long as Marxism was confined to the industrialized nations of the West, the rise (or anticipated rise) of socialist consciousness and revolutionary activity could be assumed to be the inevitable result of the maturation of capitalist economic forces. Thus, the

Marxian Social Democratic movements of Western Europe were, for the most part, content to adhere to the deterministic heritage of Marx. Although Marxism was not originally a doctrine of materialist determinism, it became primarily that in its orthodox European metamorphosis in the late nineteenth and early twentieth centuries.[24] This deterministic orientation was already apparent in the later writings of Engels, which tended to shift the emphasis of the Marxist system from history (where conscious man is the actor) to the world of nature (ruled by scientifically determinable laws of evolution). The development of the concept of "dialectical materialism" by Engels in such works as *Anti-Duhring* and *Dialectics of Nature*, and his tendency to equate the laws of history with those of nature, made the achievement of socialism seem not so much the work of man as the inevitable result of an abstract process of natural evolution. This tendency for Marxism to become a doctrine of universal, scientific laws was carried further in the writings of Karl Kautsky and George Plekhanov, the two leading Marxist theoreticians after Engels. As a result, orthodox Marxism blunted the utopian character of Marx's thought and became less a philosophy of revolutionary action than an ideological system based upon faith in necessary and natural laws of historical evolution.

As Marxist influences moved eastward into Russia, where the material preconditions for the realization of socialism were largely absent, the "scientific" determinism of the orthodox theory became increasingly untenable. To maintain the orthodox Marxist perspective in the economically and socially backward Russian environment required a faith in the forces of history that only the most patient of revolutionaries could bear. Lenin was anything but a patient man. Neither by temperament nor intellectual predisposition was he capable of acquiring the confidence in the reasonableness of the determining forces of history that marked the thought of his Marxist teacher and later political rival, Plekhanov.[25]

In response to peculiarly Russian conditions and influences Lenin, at an early point in his intellectual development, arrived at the notion that "socialist consciousness" was not primarily an attribute of the proletariat itself (as in Marx), nor a product of "history" (as in orthodox Marxism), but an attribute of an elite of revolutionary intellectuals whose historic duty was to inject this "consciousness" into the "spontaneous" movement of the proletarian masses.[26] The revolutionary strategy that Lenin derived from this notion marked a major break in the Marxist tradition, and the revolution he led formed the bridge for the passage of Marxism from Europe to Asia.

It has been frequently observed that Marxism came to China in its Leninist form. Yet this observation is not without its ambiguities. It is one thing to assert that the impact of the Leninist revolution in Russia turned Chinese intellectuals to the study and propagation of Marxist doctrine, as has been demonstrated in the case of Li Ta-chao. It is quite another to assume that the writings of Lenin were what made Marxism seem relevant to Chinese intellectuals. This proposition has yet to be proved and is subject to doubt on a number of counts.

There is, first, the matter of the very nature of Leninism. Lenin's main "contributions" to the Marxist tradition lay not in the realm of theory but in the realm of political strategy. The methods of political organization and the revolutionary strategy and tactics evolved by him have been the subject of many studies and need not be repeated here. What these studies often fail to point out, however, is that Lenin did not revise the doctrines of Marx to correspond to his innovations in Marxist political practice. Certainly one of the most striking features of Leninism is that Lenin failed to draw the theoretical conclusions from the new strategy he advocated.[27]

Lenin did, of course, employ a variety of theoretical rationalizations to justify his revolutionary strategy. In part, he did so by turning to the activistic and utopian elements of the Marxist tradition that had been neglected in orthodox Marxist theory. He drew upon the Hegelian origins of Marxism to reinforce his own faith in the powers of the human will and the conscious and purposeful activities of men.[28] He emphasized the revolutionary utopianism of Marx, most notably in *State and Revolution,* a work modeled principally on the *Communist Manifesto* and *The Civil War in France.* Although these efforts were departures from the orthodox Marxism of Kautsky and Plekhanov, in no sense were they revisions of Marx.

At the same time Lenin reaffirmed the deterministic doctrines of Marx, often in the most rigid fashion. Much of the "theory" of Leninism is, in fact, an attempt — partly deliberate, partly perhaps unconscious — to conceal and obscure the theoretical implications of Leninist strategy behind a deterministic Marxist facade and so to condemn all conflicting strategies as distortions of Marx. Leninism thus broke down the deterministic strictures of Marxism more in practice than in theory. Although Leninist practice had vital implications for Marxist theory, these implications were not explicit and could hardly be recognized by the new Chinese converts to Bolshevism, unfamiliar as they were with the Marxist tradition.

The point to be emphasized is that the "Marxist-Leninist" doctrine inherited by the Chinese Communists upheld all the fundamental theoretical formulations of Marx. With the messianic message of the October Revolution there came to China the Marxist theory of class struggle, including the principle that the socialist revolution was to be the work of the urban proletariat. The Chinese Marxists also inherited the materialist conception of history with all its deterministic injunctions on the relationships between "being" and "consciousness" and between economic and political forces, as well as the entire scheme of the historically necessary stages of social development.

These theories, which were the common bequest of both Marx and Lenin, concerned Li Ta-chao and his Communist colleagues most in the early years of the adaptation of Marxist theory to the Chinese environment. In fact, in the period in which Li Ta-chao resolved to his own satisfaction the problems involved in adapting Marxian determinism to the Chinese situation, he read fairly widely in the works of Marx and Engels but had only the most cursory acquaintance with the writings of Lenin. In the years 1919–1921 Li arrived at certain basic views on a number of key questions of Marxist doctrine. By the end of 1921 he had interpreted (or more precisely, reinterpreted) the nature of the theory of class struggle, the question of the role of man's ideas and consciousness in history, and the problem of the economic prerequisites for the realization of socialism in China. These interpretations characterized his treatment of Marxist theory and were reflected in his political activities during the remaining years of his life. Yet in an article written in the summer of 1921 Li quite frankly admitted that of the writings of Lenin he had read only a short collection of recent speeches of Lenin and Trotsky published under the title *The Revolution of the Proletariat*, Lenin's *Outline of the Soviet Government,* and his *State and Revolution*.[29] Of these books (all of which Li read in English translation), only *State and Revolution*, Lenin's highly utopian vision of the future stateless workers' commune, is of any theoretical significance; and even its significance does not lie in any departure from the Marxist tradition.

It is hardly surprising, therefore, that Li neither quoted from Lenin nor made use of specifically Leninist formulations in his writings during these crucial early years. Far more important than the influence of Lenin in Li's interpretation of Marxist doctrine were the assumptions of his pre-Marxian world view and his concern with the immediate needs of China.

The Theory of Class Struggle

When Li Ta-chao first attempted to reconcile the deterministic tenets of Marxism with his ardent faith in the ability of conscious, active men to shape social reality, he was immediately drawn to the theory of class struggle. Although he had been quite candid in his criticisms of the deterministic and fatalistic implications of the materialist conception of history when he wrote "My Marxist Views" early in 1919, Li had no reservations about the doctrine of class struggle. That doctrine, he declared, was "a great achievement of Marxism" because it proved that the realization of socialism is impossible "if it is separated from the people themselves." [30] By supporting the principle of class struggle, Li believed that he could satisfy the formal commitment to Marxist theory demanded by his acceptance of the Bolshevik Revolution without being forced to abandon his own activistic predispositions.

The activistic role that Li attributed to the doctrine of class struggle was underscored by him during the debate with Hu Shih on the question of "problems and isms": "if one only took the first part of the materialist conception of history, and only believed that economic changes are necessary and inevitable, and paid no attention to the second part — the theory of class struggle — then there would not be the slightest possibility of using this doctrine as a tool in the actual movement for working-class unity, and I fear that the economic revolution would never be realized; and even if its realization were possible, I don't know how long it would be delayed. A great many Marxists and socialists have been deceived by this concept." [31] Li seized upon the theory of class struggle since it explicitly recognized that men consciously participate in the making of history. In Marxism it is the link between the basic economic laws of history and the practical political activities of men.

Yet in Marxist theory the elements of consciousness and political activism that Li perceived in the concept of class struggle are strictly limited by objective circumstances. The formation and development of social classes is only a function of the development of the material forces of production, and the political consciousness and activities of these classes must correspond to their actual economic and social positions. "The existence of revolutionary ideas in a particular period," Marx decreed, "presupposes the existence of a revolutionary class." [32]

It is true that in Leninist ideology the relation between social groups and the productive forces tends to become less strict, and more weight is given to moral, psychological, and pragmatic criteria in describing the social nature and assessing the political role of classes. But here again the changes are not made explicit in theory. Leninist theory strictly upheld Marxist economic preconditions for the formation of classes and the existence of class consciousness. Lenin never abandoned the original Marxist belief that in the final analysis the proletarian revolution would be the work of the proletariat itself, even if a true socialist consciousness had to be brought to the proletariat "from without." It should again be emphasized that although Chinese Marxists may have been attracted by Leninist practice, it was Marxist theory that they were called upon to adapt to their own situation.

In Li Ta-chao's hands the theory of class struggle tended to break away almost completely from its socio-economic moorings and to become almost wholly centered upon the element of consciousness. At the same time the theory took on highly nationalistic overtones. To understand Li's treatment of the theory of class struggle, it is necessary to return to a subject thus far only briefly touched upon — Li's attitude toward Social Darwinism and the influence of Kropotkin's theory of "mutual aid."

Even before his conversion to Marxism Li Ta-chao had not shared the new intelligentsia's affinity for Social Darwinism.[33] The terminology of Social Darwinism had become widespread in the rhetoric of the Chinese intellectual world, and this terminology did on occasion appear in his writings, but the concepts of Social Darwinism had no significant influence on the development of his thought. Li's optimistic faith in the ability of man to master his environment and in the power of the human conscience to mold social reality was too deeply rooted for him to accept an outlook that appeared to be both deterministic and pessimistic.

In Kropotkin's theory of "mutual aid" Li found an instrument to counter the influence of Social Darwinism: "All of the preceding discussions about natural evolution centered about [the problem of] the survival of the fittest and [advocated that] the weak are the prey of the strong and that one ought to sacrifice the weak for one's own existence and happiness . . . Now we know that these discussions were greatly mistaken [because] biological progress does not arise from struggle but from mutual aid. If humanity wishes to strive to exist and if it wishes happiness and prosperity, then it must have mutual friendship and ought not to rely upon force for mutual extermination." [34] The idealistic assumptions of Kropotkin's theory were in sharp contrast to Social Darwinism. Instead of coming through struggle, progress was achieved through the spirit of co-operation; and man, instead of being controlled by the harsh, unalterable laws of nature, could be the master of his own fate. Despite all the evil influences of history, man's spirit of "mutual aid" persisted as a reflection of his inalienable conscience and pointed the way to his true liberation.

Li had referred to the idea of "mutual aid" during his student days in Japan, but it was not, paradoxically, until after he had announced his conversion to Bolshevism that it became a prominent theme in his writings. This may be attributed in part to the generally eclectic character of the reception of Western ideas in China. It is also apparent that Li found in Kropotkin's theory not only a weapon against Social Darwinism but also a weapon to blunt the deterministic implications of Marxism by recasting the theory of class struggle so that it would conform to his own views on the efficacy of conscious human activity. Thus, in an article entitled "Class Struggle and Mutual Aid," written in the summer of 1919, Li undertook to reconcile Marx and Kropotkin: "The roots of all forms of socialism are purely ethical. Cooperation and friendship are the general principles of the social life of man . . . We ought to recognize that human social life will always be controlled by these general principles, and it can be discovered that they are always hidden in the premises commonly and generally recognized by socialists at any time and in any place. Not only utopian but also scientific [socialism] . . . establish their concepts upon these premises." [35]

Although Li observed that the theory of class struggle might seem to be opposed to the theory of mutual aid, he contended that in reality they were complementary. Marx did indeed say that all history had been the history of class struggle, but Li noted that he excluded both ancient communal society and postcapitalist society from its application. The doctrine of class struggle, Li stated, pertained only to the "prehistory phase of human history [i.e., the presocialist phase] and was not applied to the whole of human history . . . [Marx] believed that the first page of the true history of man would begin with the [establishment] of the economic organization of mutual aid." [36]

In this period of "prehistory," when man was alienated from himself and when society was divided by the struggle between social classes, Li wrote, the idea of "mutual aid" had nevertheless remained alive in man's spirit. Now that the world was on the brink of the final class struggle, which would forever destroy the class nature of society and usher in a truly human history, the "spirit of mutual aid" had an indispensable role to play: "In this prehistory period of human history, the spirit of mutual aid has definitely not been destroyed even though it has been maligned throughout the world because of the [nature of] social organization . . . After the true history of humanity has begun, these evil sprouts of selfishness and private profit . . . will be burned away by the spirit of mutual aid . . . The final class struggle is the means to reconstruct the social organization. The principle of mutual aid is the creed that will reconstruct the human spirit. We advocate the reconstruction of both matter and mind, the reconstruction of spirit and flesh together." [37]

Li thus reconciled, to his own satisfaction, the doctrines of class struggle and "mutual aid." He firmly believed that class conflict was both necessary and desirable in the present, but he conceived of this struggle as being dependent as much upon the forces of the human spirit as upon the forces of the productive system. He categorically stated, in fact, that "the power of human conscience is completely spontaneous." [38] The rise of revolutionary socialist consciousness, therefore, need not be wholly dependent upon any pre-determined level of economic and social development. In the Chinese situation this implied that one might look for signs of proletarian consciousness even if the existence of the Chinese proletariat was in doubt.

Li's search for revolutionary consciousness was facilitated by his tendency to see the class struggle not as a process taking place within individual countries, where social classes must be defined upon the basis of specific national economic and historical conditions, but as a single, climactic, and final world struggle. This struggle was between the forces of darkness, represented by international capitalism, and the forces of regeneration, expressed in the universal tide of Bolshevism. Li's seemingly internationalist position had, however, a profoundly nationalistic content, which became evident in his idea that China was a "proletarian nation."

Li first put forward the "proletarian nation" theory in an essay that appeared in January 1920 under the imposing title "An Economic Explanation of the Causes of the Changes in Modern Chinese Thought." Much of the essay was cast in formulations as deterministic as its title suggests. Yet Li presented one argument that changed the whole import of his seemingly economic interpretation of Chinese history. The crucial factor in modern Chinese history, he contended, was that economic changes in China resulted from the intrusion of outside forces, in contrast to the Western countries where economic changes arose from internal developments. Thus, the suffering of the Chinese people under the pressure of world capitalism was far more severe than that of the proletarian classes of the various Western nations, who were oppressed only by their own national capitalist classes. So great, in fact, was the impact of imperialism upon the Chinese economy, and so severe the oppression of the Chinese people, that "the whole country has gradually been transformed into part of the world proletariat." [39]

The implications of this argument were quite clear: if China was a proletarian nation, China was entitled to a proletarian world view. In summarizing the main points of his article, Li stated, "in the world economy of today China really stands in the position of the world proletariat," and then he reaffirmed that the "new ideas" that were becoming prevalent in China "arise from the new demands of society to meet the new conditions of the economy." [40] These "new ideas" were obviously the revolutionary socialist ideas that Li himself was propagating — the ideas that corresponded to China's status as a proletarian nation. In Li's view, then, China was both economically and ideologically qualified to participate fully in the world proletarian revolution, its economic backwardness and agrarian social structure notwithstanding. China as a nation had been transformed into the revolutionary class that in Marxist theory was the prerequisite for the existence of revolutionary ideas. Thus, an economically deterministic dictum had been employed to justify a position that was, in the Chinese context, at once voluntaristic and nationalistic.

Whereas Marx had looked to the proletariat itself for the emergence of socialist class consciousness, and whereas Lenin had found that the bearers of this consciousness were revolutionary intellectuals who would impose it upon the proletarian movement, Li Ta-chao searched for wider and deeper sources. Li saw socialist consciousness both as an attribute of the Chinese nation as a whole (by virtue of China's proletarian status in the world economy) and as an almost innate characteristic of the human spirit.

Li's transfer of the class struggle from a class to a national basis, and his view that this struggle would be played out in the international rather than the national arena, had far different political implications from those of a somewhat similar conception later developed by the right-wing Kuomintang ideologist Tai Chi-t'ao. Tai transformed the theory of class struggle into a war between nations, and he used this nationalist version of the theory to deny that there could be class conflict within China.[41] Li, on the other hand, called for the intensification of the internal class struggle, never its cessation. Even in its most nationalistic form, Li's concept of China as a proletarian nation excluded bureaucrats, "evil gentry," and Chinese compradores representing foreign imperialism from membership in the nation. As in later Maoist ideology, in Li's approach to the class struggle both nationalism and revolutionary voluntarism were reflected. His expansion of the role and sources of consciousness served the purpose of releasing the theory of class struggle from its deterministic Marxist bonds and allowed it to be applied to the Chinese scene with maximal flexibility. Thus, when the political situation seemed appropriate, the theory could be reconciled with the promotion of internal class harmony for nationalist ends (which often coincided with Communist ends as well), but it could also be utilized to foster internal revolutionary class conflict in ways and in situations that orthodox Marxist-Leninist theory had not foreseen.

The Role of Consciousness in History

After he had debated the question of "problems and isms" with Hu Shih in the summer of 1919, Li Ta-chao announced his unconditional conversion to the materialist conception of history and the Marxist world view. He wrote lengthy essays whose ostensible purpose was to prove that all the elements of man's consciousness were no more than reflections of material reality. "Matter is always changing," he declared, "and the spiritual structure follows it in changing. Therefore, thought, ideology, philosophy, religion, ethics, and law are unable to limit economic and material transformations; rather material and economic [phenomena] determine thought, ideology, philosophy, religion, ethics, and law." [42] In another article he contended that all the new intellectual movements in China resulted from the transformation of the Chinese economy under the impact of Western imperialism. [43]

Having thus formally made his peace with Marxian orthodoxy, Li was nevertheless not content to leave the future of China in the uncertain and impersonal hands of the economic laws of history, nor was he prepared to abandon his faith in the abilities of self-conscious men to change objective reality. After his acceptance of the Marxist world view there appeared throughout his writings an unresolved tension between his pre-Marxist faith in the human conscience and the materialist demands of Marxist philosophy. In the very essay which purported to demonstrate that ethics was merely a function of changing material reality, Li also suggested that ethics was both an innate human characteristic and an independent social force. "The natural sciences, law, politics, religion, and philosophy," Li wrote, "are all things one knows after studying them; they definitely do not possess any natural authority. Only ethics is the kind of thing that has natural authority." This "natural authority" was not God-given; it was "the voice in man's heart" and the spirit of self-sacrifice. Although ethical principles had originated in man's struggle with nature, once having come into being, they had become a fixed "social ability" that provided men with a spirit of "self-sacrifice" and the "willingness of the individual to contribute to the good of the social whole." Without this spirit the existence of human society was inconceivable.[44]

Not only were ethical principles necessary to maintain the fabric of society, but they were also a source of social development: "This spirit of mutual aid, this ethic, this social ability, is able to cause human progress. Moreover, with human progress the content [of this spirit] develops greatly . . . Because the ethics of men has been a powerful social ability since the most ancient period of human life, there has developed in the human heart a voice of authority that down to the present day still echoes in our own hearts. It has a mysterious quality that is not due to the stimulus of the outside world, nor is it a matter of advantage or disadvantage; [rather] it is a naturally produced authority. Its mysterious nature is similar to the mystery of sex, the mystery of mother love, and the mystery of sacrifice." [45]

Yet nowhere did Li attempt to reconcile the contradiction between the independent and creative role that he attributed to the powers of the human conscience and the major thesis of his essay, which was that the ideas and ethical principles of men were merely reflections of their material existence. Li's refusal fully to identify man's consciousness with the conditions of his material life reflects one of the basic tendencies of his pre-Marxian world view, but it also indicates his continuing concern with the political implications of such an identification for the immediate situation in China. The materialist demands of Marxism would have denied the possibility of the development of socialist consciousness and socialist ethics in the materially backward environment of China.

Li's attempt to uphold the deterministic formulas of Marx and at the same time maintain a belief in the creative historical role of conscious human activity was particularly evident in his essay "The Value of the Materialist Conception of History in Contemporary Historical Study," published in *Hsin ch'ing-nien* in December 1920. In this essay Li undertook to reconcile the conflicting deterministic and activistic elements of his thought by emphasizing the role of the Marxist view of history as a spur to revolutionary action rather than as a preordained scheme of historical development. He contended that all idealist, pre-Marxist interpretations of history were either superficial narrations of historical facts or theological interpretations, which paralyzed "the moral powers of the individual" by attributing historical events to forces beyond the sphere of human control. All such interpretations of history served the interests of the ruling classes by teaching the common people that their plight was predetermined and by counseling them to bow to established authority.[46]

The materialist conception of history, however, had a "completely different effect on the human spirit" because it searched for the motive force of history in the actual material life of society; it looked to "the nature of the people themselves and certainly not to any outside force." Since the Marxist view of history interpreted social change as the result of man's own efforts, Li argued, it gave man "great hope and courage." Man was able to see that "all progress is able to come only from the unity of progressive people . . . from the self-consciousness of his own power, his own position in society, and from his acquisition of new attitudes." In all other theories of history man was "only a passive and negative animal," but according to the materialist view of history he was "an active and positive element," who recognized his own creative potentialities and was ready to "put his shoulder to the wheel of life and push directly forward . . . This concept can make a man a person who belongs to himself and a person who can rise up to obtain satisfaction in life and be useful in society."[47] The appeal of the Marxist notion of man overcoming his alienation through the achievement of "self-consciousness" was quite evident in this discussion of the influences of Marxist historical theory.

Having interpreted the materialist conception of history to the satisfaction of his own activistic needs, Li was not disposed to bother with the troublesome question of the economic preconditions for the exercise of man's self-consciousness. He dismissed in advance any possible criticism of the apparent contradiction between his acceptance of the Marxist view that the motivating forces in social and intellectual development were basically economic and his emphasis on the independent role of conscious human activity by implying that such objections would merely reflect a misunderstanding of Marxism: "There are some people who misinterpret the materialist view of history by saying that social progress depends only on natural material changes. [They therefore] disregard human activity and sit around to wait for the arrival of the new situation. Moreover, there are other people who are generally critical of the materialist conception of history who also use this as an excuse to talk [and take no action], and then they say that fatalistic views of human life result from the evil influences of the materialist conception of history. This is an especially great error because the influence of the materialist conception of history on human life is precisely the opposite." [48]

Thus the dominant activistic impulses of Li Ta-chao's pre-Marxist world view — which resulted in his explicit rejection of certain deterministic features of Marxism in his first encounter with the theory — were not submerged by his formal conversion to the materialist view of history. On the contrary, he merely reinterpreted Marxism to suit his own conception of the role of consciousness and human activity in history. Even the deterministic aspects of Marxism were harnessed to the cause of promoting immediate revolutionary action in China.

The dominance of the factor of consciousness in Li's world view colored his entire conception of the nature of the socialist movement. For Li, socialism was not something to be defined primarily in economic terms but was rather a phenomenon that arose out of the knowledge, the emotions, and the wills of men. In 1922, for example, Li explained the origins of socialism in the following manner:

Socialism and communism are still in their period of pregnancy, and therefore we are still unable to know what kind of system will finally emerge. But we can search for the roots [of socialism] in three aspects of our psychology. In the aspect of knowledge, socialism is a critique of the presently existing order. In the aspect of feeling, socialism is an emotion that makes us capable of replacing the present order with a comparatively good new order; this new order is the result of our intellectual critique of the capitalist system . . . In the aspect of will, socialism causes us to exert our efforts in the objective world [upon the basis] of things that are already known to us in our intellectual and emotional images, that is, to exert our efforts to replace the capitalist order, which is the final form [of government] possessing the characteristics of ruling and authority, with a workers' administration. [49]

The Debate on Industrialization and Socialism

In the history of the Russian revolutionary movement the question of the economic prerequisites for the realization of socialism was raised first by Plekhanov and later by Lenin in their polemical struggles against the Populists. The growth of capitalism, both Plekhanov and Lenin argued, was an inevitable and progressive phase of historical development, which was creating the necessary preconditions for socialism. Later, standing on the firm ground of Marxist orthodoxy, Plekhanov and the Mensheviks repeated many of Lenin's own arguments to oppose the Bolshevik program for revolution.

In China, which lacked a Marxist Social-Democratic tradition, the problem of the economic preconditions for socialism was brought up for public debate by non-Marxian socialists and even nonsocialists. The Chinese opponents of Marxism paradoxically employed arguments similar to those that had been used by orthodox Marxist theorists in the Russian debate.

In December 1920 the journalist and philosopher Chang Tung-sun, one of a number of guild socialists associated with the Chin-putang, opened a heated debate on whether it was necessary for China to undergo a capitalist phase of development. Chang argued that China's poverty could be overcome only through industrialization, with which his Marxist opponents were the first to agree. But Chang's principal thesis was that the development of a native Chinese capitalism was the most efficient road to industrialization. Only after a lengthy period of economic development and the formation of a strong industrial working-class, he contended, would socialism be suitable for China.[50]

Chang Tung-sun's arguments were principally inspired by the views of John Dewey and Bertrand Russell. While lecturing in China in 1919–1920, Dewey had not only questioned the relevance of isms in general but had stated that Marxism and socialism in particular could have no roots in China because of the low level of industrial development.[51] Russell, who had been invited to lecture in China by Liang Ch'i-ch'ao and other members of the Chinputang, arrived in October 1920 for nearly a year's stay. His critical comments on the Soviet economic system (and his opinion that Russia would soon revert to capitalism), as well as his argument that under Chinese conditions industrialization could best be accomplished through a partly nationalized capitalist system, served to intensify doubts about the relevancy of Marxism.[52] The fact that Russell himself was known to be a socialist undoubtedly gave added weight to his views among many young Chinese intellectuals who were sympathetic to socialism. Chang Tung-sun's articles specifically referred to Russell's writings and lectures in many places.

Although the arguments of the Chinese critics of Marxism were quite in accord with the demands of orthodox Marxist theory on the question of the relationship between economic and political forces, the Chinese Marxists had not adopted their new revolutionary faith only to promote the development of Chinese capitalism. Chang Tung-sun's perspective of a capitalist path to industrialization immediately drew the fire of Ch'en Tu-hsiu and a number of younger Marxists in Shanghai. Ch'en maintained that as a result of the Russian October Revolution, China was in the fortunate position of being able to choose between the new socialist methods of industrialization and the old, exploitative capitalist methods. It was highly questionable that the latter method offered any real alternative since Chinese capitalists were only the agents of foreign capital, and foreign capitalism was a principal cause of China's poverty. Therefore, Ch'en argued, only an independent working-class government could promote industrial development in China. He declared that the experience of Soviet Russia proved that it was possible to achieve a rapid transition from feudalism to socialism.[53]

Li Ta-chao did not participate directly in the debate on the economic prerequisites for socialism (which took place in Shanghai), but he did address himself to the issues involved early in 1921 in a letter to Fei Chüeh-t'ien, a member of the Society for the Study of Socialism. The letter was later published under the title "Chinese Socialism and World Capitalism." Since it set forth some of the principal ways in which the problem of the relevance of socialism was later to be rationalized by many Chinese Marxists, Li's letter is here translated in full:

Whether or not China is able to put socialism into effect at the present time, that is, whether or not the economic conditions of today's China are prepared for the realization of socialism, is a very important question that we ought to study seriously. My views on this can be briefly stated as follows: If one asks whether or not the economic conditions of present-day China are prepared for the realization of socialism, it is first necessary to ask whether or not present-day world economic conditions are tending toward the realization of socialism, because the Chinese economic situation really cannot be considered apart from the international economy. The contemporary world economy is already moving from capitalism to socialism, and although China itself has not yet undergone a process of capitalist economic development such as occurred in Europe, America, and Japan, the common people [of China] still indirectly suffer from capitalist economic oppression in a way that is even more bitter than the direct capitalist oppression suffered by the working classes of the various [capitalist] nations. Although within China the relations between capital and labor still have not developed into a very great problem, the position of the Chinese people in the world economy and in the ever-growing storm of the labor movement has already been established, and it is really impossible to think of preserving the capitalist system either in theory or practice. If we again look at the international position of China today, [we see] that others have already passed from free competition to the necessary socialist-cooperative position, while we today are just at the point that the others have started from and are following in their footsteps. Others have reached maturity, while we are still juveniles; others have walked a thousand *li*, while we are still taking the first step. Under these kinds of conditions, if we want to continue to exist and adapt ourselves to the common life [of the world], I fear that we will be unable to succeed unless we take double steps and unite into a socially cooperative organization. Therefore, if we want to develop industry in China, we must organize a government made up purely of producers in order to eliminate the exploiting classes within the country, to resist world capitalism, and to follow [the path of] industrialization organized upon a socialist basis.[54]

The argument that Li presented here was based on the same assumption that he had used for his theory that China was a "proletarian nation." Though lacking the industrial preconditions for socialism, China was ready for a Marxist socialist movement and could join with the forces of the world proletarian revolution because the Chinese people as a whole suffered under the yoke of international capitalism.

In arguing that a socialist revolution was relevant to the Chinese situation, Li did not employ the pretense — which Trotsky was later to use — that social relations in China were already predominantly capitalist in nature. He acknowledged, in fact, that "within China the relations between capital and labor still have not developed into a very great problem." But he did anticipate Trotsky's application of the "law of uneven development." Writing in 1927, Trotsky rejected the argument that China did not yet have the economic prerequisites for a socialist revolution. The establishment of the dictatorship of the proletariat, Trotsky contended, was determined not by the internal economic conditions of a single country but rather by "the trend of world development." The political situation would in the final analysis prevail over the economic: "The concrete historical, political and actual question is reducible not to whether China has economically matured for 'its own' socialism, but whether China has ripened politically for the proletarian dictatorship. These two questions are not at all identical. They might be regarded as identical were it not for the law of uneven development. This is where this law is in place and fully applies to the interrelationship between economics and politics." [55]

Li Ta-chao's efforts to resolve the dilemma that Marxian determinism posed for the Chinese Communist movement shared significant affinities with the views that Trotsky later set forth on the nature of the Chinese revolution. Like Trotsky, Li contended that it was not only the internal Chinese situation but international political tendencies that made possible a socialist revolution in China. Moreover, his reinterpretation of the theory of class struggle and his emphasis on the activistic influences of the materialist conception of history clearly implied that it was not China's economic maturity but the Chinese political situation — the political consciousness of the Chinese people and the practical activities of men — that would in the final analysis determine whether the Marxist program would be realized in China.

More important than these affinities, perhaps, were the differences between Li and Trotsky. Although Trotsky's search for political radicalism in situations produced by economic backwardness was a fundamental departure from orthodox Marxism, he still believed that in the end the decisive factor in world revolution would be the long-anticipated proletarian risings in the industrialized states of Western Europe. Li, however, largely ignored this link with the orthodox Marxist tradition. Furthermore, whereas Trotsky's conception of a socialist revolution in China, as in Russia, presupposed the action of an actual proletariat, however tiny, Li's notion that China was a "proletarian nation" dispensed with the necessity for a real proletariat. Indeed, the very idea of a "proletarian nation" would have been anathema to Trotsky, since he was committed to the genuinely internationalist traditions of Marxism.

The impulse to identify the Chinese nation with the international proletarian movement, which so decisively influenced Li Ta-chao's interpretation of Marxist theory, was implicit in his original response to the Bolshevik Revolution. From perceiving Bolshevism as a portent of the long-awaited rebirth of the Chinese nation it was but a short step to perceiving this national rebirth as an integral part of the universal forces of regeneration, represented by the world proletarian movement. Although certain aspects of Marxian historical determinism had appeals of their own, Marxist theoretical considerations were not to be allowed to stand in the way of China's alliance with the new forces of historical reformation. In Li Ta-chao's optimistic and dialectical world view, disadvantages were converted into advantages to consummate this alliance with history. If China lacked a developed urban proletariat to carry on the class struggle, then the whole nation must be looked upon as part of the world-wide forces of proletarian revolution. If the economic preconditions for the realization of socialism were absent in China, then the socialist reorganization of Chinese society was all the more necessary to achieve these very preconditions.

CHAPTER VII   PHILOSOPHY OF HISTORY

"IF ONE wishes to obtain a true view of human life," Li Ta-chao wrote in 1920, "it is first necessary to obtain a true interpretation of history."[1] It is not surprising that Li attached importance to the study of history, for the will to shape history inevitably gives rise to the desire to understand it. Indeed, in the very article in which he first announced his support for the principles of the Bolshevik Revolution, he remarked, "if one can write the history of billions of people, then one can have the authority to move the minds of billions of people."[2] That the study of history should serve political ends was a conviction that the first Marxist historian of modern China shared with his Confucian predecessors.

Even before his conversion to Marxism Li's desire to promote action in the present had been accompanied by a need to understand the forces that had molded the past. After he had argued against Ch'en Tu-hsiu in 1915 that it was necessary for "self-conscious" Chinese intellectuals to participate in politics to achieve their ends,[3] Li had turned to the development of a transcendental philosophy purporting to identify the motivating forces of history. The historical world view that emerged from his philosophic speculations was used to support his demand for political participation.

As a Marxist, Li became even more committed to an understanding of history. Marxism rests on the proposition that an understanding of the general laws of historical development provides the insights into contemporary historical reality that are necessary to guide the activities of men in the present and to enable them to create the socialist utopia of the future. Li accepted this commitment with enthusiasm. From 1920 until his death seven years later his main intellectual interest in Marxism revolved about the study of the materialist conception of history. A major portion of his writings during these years was devoted to problems of historical interpretation, including his only book-length manuscript, *The Essentials of Historical Study*, published in 1924.[4] At Peking University he lectured on the Marxist view of history and its application to the Chinese past, and he accumulated a considerable personal library of Western-language works on historical theory.

Li's efforts to promote and popularize the materialist conception of history were perhaps surprising since he had so bluntly criticized the determinism of this view of history in "My Marxist Views" early in 1919. Although his objections to the materialist conception had no longer been so explicit in the period after the May Fourth Incident when he became more firmly committed to the Communist program, his emphasis on the factors of consciousness and human activity in his treatment of Marxist theory indicated that his earlier reservations about Marxist determinism were not fully overcome and that the activistic impulses of his pre-Marxian world view remained very much a part of his Marxist mentality. Yet in his writings on history in 1920 and after Li upheld all the deterministic formulas he implicitly rejected in many of his other writings. Time and again in a variety of ways he repeated the view that "changes in the social superstructure completely follow the changes in the economic base, and therefore it is impossible to explain history except from economic relations."[5] Since Li's purpose in promoting the materialist conception was not to recite these well-known formulas, it is unnecessary to deal here with his efforts to popularize the historical doctrines of Marx. His aim, rather, was to find support for his own politically activistic needs and his voluntaristic interpretation of Marxist theory.

The historical theory of Marx was able, in part, to serve his purposes because it is not just a scheme of periodization and a collection of "laws" purporting to prove that all history is determined by the inexorable movement of the forces of production. It is also a philosophy of history, which begins with the assumption that "man makes history" and ends with the vision of a future socialist utopia in which man for the first time fully realizes his truly human potentialities. It is a philosophy that views history as the process of man's self-creation in his struggle to master nature, his self-alienation growing out of that struggle, and finally his attainment of the true self-consciousness that is to make possible the passage of mankind from the "realm of necessity" to the "realm of freedom."

Like Hegel, Marx found an inner logic and an objective meaning in history. History was seen as progress through necessary and ever higher stages of development leading to the inevitable triumph of reason. The content of Marxist historical philosophy is, of course, profoundly different from the Hegelian philosophy of history. For Hegel the true subject of history was the *Weltgeist*, a power that moved through the actions of men; for Marx it was men themselves, and the productive forces they had created. Yet for both Marx and Hegel history was logically moving toward a final utopian goal, however much they differed on the definition of that goal.

It would be impossible to explain the appeal of the materialist conception of history, or the role that it has played in Chinese Communist ideology, if it were seen as no more than a method of analyzing historical reality upon the basis of objective economic criteria without reference to its utopian goals. As Croce has pointed out, if historical materialism were deprived of the elements of finality and inevitability, it could not provide support for socialism or any other form of society. It would remain silent, as Robert Michel has written, on the "outcome of the struggle it has traced through history."[6] It is precisely the utopian vision of the future, sanctioned by an analysis of history, that gives the materialist conception its dynamic appeal. By this means the Marxist view of history has inspired men to transform the existing historical situation.

The terms "materialism" and "determinism" as applied to the Marxist conception of history are often quite misleading. Marx's "historical materialism" is a unique variety of materialism, for it is based on the premise that all material forces and objects are merely the expressions, or materializations, of human activity. Marxism is deterministic to the extent that socialism is considered historically inevitable, but it demands the participation and activity of men to realize the "inevitable." "History does nothing," Marx declared, ". . . it is not 'history' which uses men as a means of achieving . . . *its* own ends. History is nothing but the activity of men in pursuit of their ends."[7] The notion that "man makes history" lies at the very core of the Marxist world view.

It should also be pointed out that the Marxist emphasis on change in history (that which is historical in the Marxist sense is defined as that which is constantly changing and in the process of becoming) does not refer simply to a variety of evolutionary change. The notion of quantitative to qualitative change that Marx derived from Hegel manifested itself in the belief that at certain stages in its development human society undergoes quick and sudden transformations. The Marxist concept of revolution is not simply a matter of the slow maturation of economic and social forces; it is conceived as a radical break with the past. The socialist revolution is to be a "leap" from man's "prehistory" to his "truly human history."

These were the strains in the materialist conception of history — the belief that man is the producer as much as the product of history, the utopian goals towards which the historic process is inevitably moving, and the promise of radical, revolutionary breaks with the past — that Li Ta-chao could and did draw upon to support his voluntaristic predispositions. In his writings on the Marxist view of history he was hardly ever concerned with the question of historical periodization, and he was content to repeat in a purely formal way the "objective laws" of historical development set down by Marx. For Li the Marxist view of history was above all a conception for encouraging the activities of men and inspiring them to create the future.

This approach was already present in Li's first writings on Marxism in early 1919. In the essay "My Marxist Views," which was sharply critical of many of the deterministic formulations of the materialist conception of history, Li had nevertheless found that the great contribution of the Marxist view of history was that it recognized that "the realization of socialism is completely impossible if it is separated from the people themselves."[8] The notion that men make their own history was of the greatest appeal to Li from the very beginning of his Marxist intellectual life.

One striking feature of Li's historical writings was that he was less concerned with what happened in the past than with the views men hold of the past and how these views might influence their activities in the present. In the essay "The Interpretation of History," written in 1920, Li developed this theme by emphasizing the importance of a "true view" of the past for the life orientation of the individual. The essay began with echoes of the cosmic tones of "Spring," written four years earlier: "It is not known how the history of humanity began, and it is not known when it will end. In this long tide of history [which is] without beginning and without end, there is still myself and my own life. The future and the past are limitless, and thus if I do not clearly examine the nature of history in order to understand its tendencies, then my life will be without a shred of significance . . . I will be like a solitary boat being thrown about in a wild and limitless ocean, having lost its way. An interpretation of history, therefore, is really the standard to measure human life."[9]

Li traced the beginnings of "the true interpretation of history" to the European scientific revolution. The ideas of Kepler and Newton, he wrote, gave birth to a new historiography, which was developed by Condorcet, Saint-Simon, and Comte and which culminated in the materialist conception of Marx. The purpose of the new historiography was "to pluck out from men's minds" the traditional theological interpretations that attributed historical events to forces beyond the sphere of human activity and human control. This was a particularly important task in China, Li argued, because Confucian historiography had instilled in the minds of the Chinese a "retrogressive view of history," which looked back to a golden age in antiquity and emphasized the power of the gods and the role of great men.[10] These baneful Confucian influences still lived in the Chinese present, for Li found evidence of the traditional "retrogressive view of history" in the thought of such eminent contemporary intellectuals as Liang Ch'i-ch'ao and Chang Shih-chao.[11]

The activistic role that Li assigned to historical theory was reflected in the definition of the nature of history that appeared at the beginning of *The Essentials of Historical Study*. History, Li declared, "is the process of human life, the succession of human life, the changes in human life, and the evolution of human life. It is a thing of life, activity, progress, and development . . . it is not old volumes of books, old pieces of paper, dead rocks and dried bones . . . What we study should be living history, not dead history. Living history can only be obtained from human life and cannot be sought in old pieces of paper."[12]

Partly because of this preoccupation with the psychological implications of historical world views, Li sometimes adopted a highly relativistic position in dealing with the question of what constitutes historical truth. In the same essay in which he claimed that "Marx discovered the true meaning of history," he also wrote: "In rewriting and revising history, do we dare determine what is unchanging truth? History has a life which dead and old records are unable to express . . . [The expression] of this life is completely dependent on the new historical conceptions of later men . . . But although later men arrive at new understandings and make new discoveries, we still cannot know whether that which we now recognize as true will not later be regarded as mistaken. The facts that we recognize as true and our view of truth are certainly not fixed but rather are relative." [13]

Li did not deny that there was an objective historical process apart from man's perception of it, although certain statements seem to lend themselves to such an interpretation. In *The Essentials of Historical Study*, for example, he wrote that an historical fact is "past and cannot be revived. But our understanding of that fact is always in the process of movement and can change at any time. The so-called historical fact is thus the fact that is perceived. Perception is active and has a progressive nature. Even if one had a complete record of the past, it could not be considered historical truth. In order to have historical truth, it is necessary to have complete perception." Moreover, he added, "historical truth is only temporary." Further in the same passage Li acknowledged that there was indeed a "real past," but he argued, "the real past is dead and gone, the affairs of the past have been made and completed, and the men of the past are dead and can never be revived; a change in these is forever impossible. What can be expanded and broadened is not the past itself but our knowledge of the past." [14] In an earlier essay Li had put the matter more succinctly: "Facts are dead and unchanging but explanations are alive and always changing." [15]

Li was not seriously concerned with the metaphysical problem of whether historical reality exists independent of man's cognition of it. He did, in fact, believe that there was an objective historical reality, and he tried to believe that there were scientifically discoverable laws according to which the historic process proceeded. But the actual history of the past always remained a matter of far less concern to him than how men of the present interpreted the past. His preoccupation was with the need to create an intellectual and psychological atmosphere that would encourage political action in the here and now, and it was this need that his writings on historical theory were intended to serve. It was also this need that lay behind the great appeal of Marx's notion that history is made by men and not determined by "outside forces."

The Problem of Inevitability

Both before and after his conversion to Marxism, Li Ta-chao's faith in the ability of men to shape historical reality was coupled with a seemingly contradictory belief in the existence of impersonal and immutable forces that determined the course of historical development. In his pre-Marxian phase Li saw the determining principles of history as essentially spiritual forces, which moved on cosmic levels and manifested themselves both in the "egos" of individuals and in the cyclic process of the inevitable rise and decline of nations. The cyclic theory of history had supported his pre-Marxian faith in the inevitable rebirth of China and in the equally inevitable decline of the materially powerful nations of the West.

With his conversion to Marxism his idealist assumptions as to the causal factors in history were replaced by materialist assumptions. His earlier view of history as a cyclic process gave way to the view that history moved in a progressive fashion. Correspondingly, his faith in the inevitability of the rebirth of China was replaced by a newly found faith in the inevitability of world socialism, a process with which Li now identified the rebirth of China.

The influence of Marxism also led Li to proclaim that there were laws of history that could be scientifically determined. "There is no difference," he wrote in 1920, "between the study of history and the natural sciences . . . With Marx's materialist conception of history, the study of history has been raised to the same position as that of the natural sciences. This accomplishment really opens a new era in the world of historical studies." [16] In arriving at the conviction that there were scientifically verifiable laws governing objective reality, Li drew not only upon Marx but also upon the whole line of universalistic historians who began with Turgot and Condorcet and continued with Saint-Simon and Comte. Li had read Saint-Simon during the years he studied in Japan, and possibly Condorcet and Comte as well, and his interest in Marxist historical theory encouraged him to return to the works of these and other

European historical theorists. In 1923 he published two essays on Condorcet and Saint-Simon, both of whom he regarded as important precursors of the Marxist conception of history. The essays are of interest because they suggest the reasons for the appeal of the more deterministic elements of Marxist historical theory.

Among the virtues of Condorcet enumerated by Li were "his natural optimism" and his belief that the process of "enlightenment and social progress is unlimited" and that its direction can be predicted. "In Condorcet's eyes," Li observed, "the study of the history of civilization has two uses. One is to enable us to construct the factual record of progress, and the other is to enable us to determine its future direction and from this to increase the velocity of progress." Condorcet believed, Li stated, that "if the universal laws of social phenomena were known to men, it would be possible to predict changes. These laws can be sought in the history of the past." [17]

However, Condorcet's search for universal laws of historic development was unsuccessful, not because such laws did not exist but because his methodology and assumptions were unscientific. He saw social progress as the result of intellectual progress; thus, his efforts to predict the future remained in the realm of philosophic speculations. Instead, Li suggested, it was necessary to look to "the masses of humanity" for the sources of historical progress.[18] "The human race is wholly dependent upon the results of its own work, which is the accomplishment of the masses of the people. The true subjects of history are these masses." Li found this Marxist notion in embryo in Saint-Simon, particularly in Saint-Simon's later historical writings, which emphasized economic factors. Saint-Simon, Li declared, "recognized that the productive classes were the basic classes of society and the motivating force of history." Furthermore, Saint-Simon elevated Condorcet's belief in the existence of universal laws of historical development and the inevitability of social progress to a more scientific plane when he became convinced that "the laws of history and the historical process could only be explained by changes in the organization of property and that the society of the future could be foreseen only by [studying] the tendencies in the development of property . . . Later Marx inherited these clues and built the theory of the materialist conception of history." [19]

Li did not write a separate essay on Comte, but he frequently referred to Comte as the successor of Saint-Simon and one of the direct predecessors of Marx. Whereas Li praised Comte's search for "definite laws of history,"[20] he was by no means drawn to the mechanistic materialism of the Positivist outlook, nor did he write anything to suggest that he was aware of the elitist role of the "enlightened educator," which is implicit in the writings of both Saint-Simon and Comte. Like Marx, Li saw history as the product of human activity; unlike Saint-Simon and Comte, he found "the masses" to be "the true subject of history."[21] Taken as a whole, Li's historical writings affirmed the view that history is a process of the interaction of man and his material environment — a view that Marx expressed so well in his critique of mechanical materialism in his "Theses on Feuerbach": "The materialist doctrine concerning the change of circumstances and education forgets that circumstances are changed by men and that the educator himself must be educated."[22]

Li drew from the writings of Condorcet, Saint-Simon, and Comte the same beliefs that Marx shared with these historical theorists — an optimistic faith in the intrinsic rationality of man and history, a conviction that historical development was essentially progressive in nature, and an assurance that the triumph of reason, equality, and freedom was inevitable. Above all, Li drew from them the confidence that the future could be foretold, and this confidence served to reinforce his belief in the inevitability of socialism: "Scientific socialism has taken as its basis the materialist conception of history, and by investigating the process of human historical development, it has discovered the necessary laws of history. On the basis of these laws it has advocated the social necessity of socialism. From this it can be said that a socialist society, no matter whether men want it or not . . . is a command of history."[23]

Li's assertion that there were "necessary laws of history" inevitably moving toward the realization of socialism was not necessarily incompatible with his faith that conscious human action could shape historical reality. The combination of a doctrine of inevitability and an emphasis upon human activity is hardly a unique phenomenon in the history of human thought. The Calvinist doctrine of predestination, for example, taught that salvation was predetermined, that even before the creation of the world God had chosen the elect and condemned the damned. But in Calvinism, as Max Weber has written, "it is held to be an absolute duty to consider oneself chosen

. . . since lack of self-confidence is the result of insufficient faith . . . The exhortation of the apostle to make fast one's own call is here interpreted as a duty to attain certainty of one's own election and justification in the daily struggle of life . . . In order to attain that self-confidence, intense worldly activity is recommended as the most suitable means." [24] Thus although salvation was predetermined, the evidence for salvation was to be sought in the activities of men on earth.

This combination of a doctrine of inevitability with an exhortation to activity also appeared in different forms in many secular philosophies. The Russian "Realists" of the 1860's, for example — men such as Chernyshevskii, Dobrolyubov, and Pisarev — firmly believed that society proceeded towards a rational end in accordance with the logical laws and scientific principles of objective reality. Yet their "realistic" faith in objectivity was combined with a demand that a few men of will and perception transform the world in the image of their consciousness.[25] Marxism itself combined a faith in socialism as the inevitable result of processes immanent in history with a call to revolutionary action. In Leninism these two elements coexisted in exaggerated form, for Lenin's emphasis upon subjective factors — the consciousness and will of the revolutionary intellectual in particular — was coupled not only with the generally deterministic formulations of the materialist conception of history but also with his own particularly strong appeal to a concrete and objective reality. If a belief in a doctrine of inevitability is logically inconsistent with a world view that emphasizes the importance of the active participation of men in making history, the inconsistency has nevertheless proved psychologically compatible in a variety of very different intellectual systems and historical situations. It was an inconsistency that Li Ta-chao shared with many of his Marxist predecessors.

Nevertheless, Li was not unaware of the problems posed by the doctrine of the inevitability of socialism. He was ever fearful that other men might draw from the materialist conception of history the fatalistic conclusion that the future was assured regardless of their own activities. Thus, he was continually preoccupied with the question of the psychological impact of the Marxist view of history. Time and again he felt compelled to repeat that it would encourage "self-consciousness" and human activity and not lead to quietism.

Li never acknowledged that there existed any contradiction between his belief in the historic inevitability of socialism and his demand for political action. Just as in his pre-Marxian world view his faith in the inevitable rebirth of China was combined with a demand for individual political participation, he now saw no conflict between the historical necessity of socialism and the need for human activity to achieve it. In 1919 he had drawn a parallel between the efforts necessary to achieve socialism and the spread of Christianity. Since the Christian's faith in the coming of the millenium did not hinder his efforts to propagate the gospel, there was no reason why the socialist's belief in the inevitability of socialism should impede his efforts to achieve socialism.[26] On a later occasion Li declared, "the Marxist economic interpretation of history is especially valuable in that it is able to provide people with a belief in the necessity of the realization of socialism."[27] For Li, as for Marx and Lenin, the recognition of "necessity" was merely the first step in a program for action.

That a Marxist believes there are determining forces in history which must inevitably produce socialism is of less importance in describing his thought than the manner in which he perceives this determinism. Although Marx no doubt arrived at the desirability of socialism before he proclaimed its inevitability, his economic and historical studies gave him the fullest confidence that socialism would be the necessary result of the contradictions of capitalist society in general, and the arrival of the proletariat upon the historical scene in particular. For Marx, the social and economic structure was an absolute reality which determined the direction of the historical process — a direction inexorably moving toward the realization of socialism.

Li Ta-chao never succeeded in acquiring this Marxist confidence in the determining forces of history. One need not doubt the sincerity of Li's declarations that socialism would be the inevitable result of the laws of history, for he was certain from the beginning that the millenium was approaching; but his faith in the forces of history was never firm enough to allow him to test that faith by applying Marxist criteria to a serious examination of Chinese historical realities. His historical studies were always directed to promoting what he regarded as a true historical world view rather than to understanding concrete historical processes. Moreover, his emphasis on the consciousness and practical activities of men (and his concomitant de-emphasis on material preconditions), as well as his continued insistence that spiritual change was no less important than material change, suggest that his confidence in the workings of the laws of history was something less than absolute. There were laws of history, but these laws were not objective forces to which the activities of men had to conform; they were merely expressions of conscious human activity, and the evidence for their existence was to be sought, in the final analysis, in the consciousness and the actions of men.

The Concept of Time

An element of particular significance in Li Ta-chao's historical world view was his concept of time, for in this area he made a most important departure from the Marxist outlook. As noted before, his earlier concept of time had been derived from Emerson. Li drew from Emerson the feeling that the present moment is "the most precious thing in the world" and that any given "present" offers unlimited opportunities for human creative activity. The purpose of Li's pre-Marxian philosophy, like his later interpretations of Marxism, was to encourage the activity of men in the here and now, to inspire men to take full advantage of the potentialities existing in the present in order to create the future. He was harshly critical of all mentalities that failed to appreciate the vital forces latent in "now."

Li's concept of time was originally set within the framework of a transcendental philosophy based upon a belief in an unceasing "tide of great reality," a universal spirit of youth that flowed through limitless time and space and through the "egos" of innumerable individuals. This tide moved in a dialectic fashion, manifesting itself in higher and higher levels of "rebirth," which were always expressed in an infinite series of "nows." After his conversion to Marxism strong echoes of this transcendental philosophy appeared in Li's writings. Moreover, his feeling of exaltation for the present moment survived the influence of Marxism virtually intact.

Early in 1923 Li wrote an essay entitled "'Now' and 'Antiquity,'" which began with a restatement of certain themes of his pre-Marxian philosophy: "Both the destiny of the universe and the history of man can be seen as the torrential flow of a great reality (*ta shih-*

tsai), which has no beginning and no end and which is in continuous motion and circulation. The past is gone and can never return, and the changes of the future will never end. Time has a present and a past, man has a present and a past . . . attitudes toward the present and the past differ, and the debate between the present and the past continues." This "debate between the present and past" was the concern of the essay. Li's aim was to combat the influences of what he termed the "recalling-the-past school" of historiography, for which purpose he turned to an examination of the writings of a number of seventeenth and eighteenth century European philosophers — such diverse figures as Jean Bodin, Francis Bacon, Descartes, and the English theologian George Hakewill — who were lumped together as the "venerating-the-present school." From Bodin Li drew support for his opposition to "the theory of a golden age" existing in the past, and in Bacon he found confirmation that "the cyclic theory [of history] is the greatest obstacle to the development of knowledge, for it causes men to lose their faith and hope." Descartes was praised for his critical attitude toward the authorities of the past, and Hakewill was commended for recognizing that "the theory of [historical] regression can numb the vitality of man . . . drown man's hopes and dull his efforts." [28]

The reasons that these and other philosophers of the Enlightenment had "an optimistic and activistic view of history and human life," Li suggested, was that they shared a common conception of time, that is, they "venerated the present." Their views appeared to Li to be very much in accord with Emerson's concept of time — the concept that "yesterday is beyond recall and tomorrow is uncertain; the sole thing within our grasp is today." This view of time, Li concluded, could stimulate "the efforts of the men of the present to become the vanguard of the future." [29]

In an essay entitled "Time," written late in 1923, Li attempted more explicitly to relate the manner in which time is perceived to the way in which history is understood. Here again the reappearance of his pre-Marxian world view was quite striking: "The best part of life is youth, and the best part of morning is the dawn . . . heaven and human life everywhere move unceasingly, waxing and waning, in a contradictory and a complementary fashion. The dead and the living all enter into the present, the fulfilled and the unfulfilled are just beginning to develop into the future. Time is the vastness of nature without beginning and without end. Time is a boundless great reality . . . Time is the great creator and also the great destroyer. The stage of history is its creative work-place, and the ruins of history are the remnants of its destruction. Life and death, success and failure, and flourishing and decline among men are all but the metamorphosis of time." [30]

The concept of time had an almost mystical significance for Li. Taoist and Western philosophers, psychologists, mathematicians, and physicists had all grappled with the problem of explaining time but had provided only partial answers. This was because "the problem of time cannot be studied and, moreover, it is unnecessary to study it. When all is said and done, the problem of time is really beyond conception." If "time" was so elusive and transitory a phenomenon that it could not really be apprehended, then one must grasp what he could of it — the present moment. Thus, the past and the future, Li wrote, existed only in the present. Only the present or "now" (*chin*) was "alive." "Now is powerful, active and creative. If in any given instant there is no activity and no movement, then this instant of the present becomes nothing, and the life of this instant is equivalent to death." [31]

This feeling that all moments were unique led Li to the view that men were presented with an infinite series of unique opportunities and that in order for such opportunities not to be wasted they must be taken advantage of at the very moments they occurred. The ability to appreciate the creative opportunities in the present had very much to do with how history was interpreted, Li believed, for a mistaken view of time inevitably gave rise to a mistaken view of history. The failure to appreciate the present resulted in a view of history that was "retrogressive and motionless, [one] which disavows the developing aspects of nature and reality and which looks back to the past and loses the future." But "if you want to know the essence of time, then you must look not to antiquity but rather to the present, and not flee towards the vast and limitless past but rather towards the vast and limitless future." One who was able to understand the present as the "essence of time" was thereby capable of achieving "an energetic and exciting view of history and an optimistic and striving view of human life." [32]

There was much in Li's concept of time that could be reconciled with the Marxist outlook. The notion that the past lived in the present and that the future was being prepared in the present, as well as the need to look to a utopia located in the future, were very much in accord with the Marxist world view. In Marxism, however, the process leading to the future socialist utopia is disciplined by a relatively strict sense of historical time. The past is highly differentiated in time according to specific and necessary stages of historical development, stages that are the result of the movement of concrete economic and social forces. Not only the past but also the future is differentiated, for the arrival of socialism is placed at a specific point in time — the period of the collapse of the capitalist system.

In Marxism, moreover, the determining objective forces of history apply not only to the past and the future but also to the present. Man makes history, Marx believed, but only under pre-existing conditions: "men are not free to choose their productive forces — which are the basis of all their history — for every productive force is an acquired force, the product of former activity. The productive forces are therefore the result of practical human energy; but this energy is itself conditioned by the circumstances in which men find themselves, by the productive forces already acquired, by the social form which exists before they do, which they do not create, and which is the product of the preceding generation." [33]

For the Marxist, therefore, not all moments are favorable for revolution; indeed, favorable moments are relatively rare, determined as they are by the movement of the forces of production. It is only at certain crucial times· that these forces give rise to the social and political conditions that make revolution possible. Thus, in the Marxist world view, as Karl Mannheim has pointed out, time is experienced as "a series of strategic points" [34] and not, in the manner that Li Ta-chao experienced it, as a series of equally significant "nows." The activity of the Marxist revolutionary is not to be undertaken on impulse but rather is to be based upon, and restrained by, the recognition of the determining, objective forces of history and the concrete analysis of such forces at any given time. Marxists, of course, have differed profoundly in the prescriptions for political action that they have presumably drawn from their analyses of these determining forces of history. However, to a greater or lesser degree, the need to act in conformity with objective historical forces, and the discipline and restraint that such a need imposes upon the revolutionary impulse, has been a characteristic feature of the Marxist mentality.

The almost total absence of such a sense of discipline characterized Li Ta-chao's historical world view. His concept of time mostly precluded the differentiation of time on the basis of the development of objective historical forces, because the present alone was vital and creative. In envisioning the process of the realization of socialism, Li did not look to the objective forces of history but rather to the revolutionary will and consciousness of men. One of the most important elements in acquiring this will and consciousness, he believed, was a proper concept of time, that is, the ability to appreciate the potentialities inherent in the present moment. For Li the "now" was pregnant with meaning, and men needed only to grasp that meaning to realize through action its unlimited latent opportunities. Since there was an infinite series of "nows," Li's concept of time was a philosophy of permanent activity.

Li's view of history was also a philosophy of activity. History was to be studied not primarily to discover the tendencies of objective forces as the basis for political action but rather to create the proper psychological atmosphere for political action. The role of historical theory was not so much to gain scientific insights into history as to provide men with the spiritual energy to create the future. For Li Ta-chao, men, inspired by a "true" historical world view (and a true concept of time), were to shape history; they were not to be bound by history.

Chinese History

Although Li Ta-chao often called on historians to study the Chinese past from the point of view of the materialist conception of history, he himself found few opportunities to undertake such efforts. Although he lectured on traditional Chinese history at Peking University, where he retained his professorship in the history department until the political repressions of March 1926, the published notes based on those lectures offer little to suggest that specifically Marxist assumptions were fruitfully employed. The major product of his own research on Chinese history — an attempt to analyze very ancient Chinese society on the basis of passages in the Chinese classics — might just as well have been written without any knowledge of Marxism.[35] As the leading figure in the Communist party in North China, Li had little leisure for serious historical research; and his death in 1927 at the age of thirty-eight canceled whatever opportunities the future might have held. Yet one suspects that because of his complete preoccupation with the need for a proper historical world view rather than with the historic process itself, the application of the materialist conception to Chinese history would in any case have remained a matter of secondary concern.

Although Li lacked the opportunity, and perhaps the inclination, to engage in serious historical research, he was not reluctant to express his views on Chinese history in his political writings or his writings on historical theory. Two themes emerged from these writings which bear upon the questions posed by the Marxist historical outlook, and which are also relevant to the problems encountered by later Chinese Communist historians; first, his rejection of a universalistic pattern of historical development, and second, his highly nationalistic interpretation of modern Chinese history.

The notion that the history of all mankind has proceeded according to the pattern of evolution Marx outlined for Western European history — i.e., the passage from primitive communism to slavery, feudalism, capitalism, and finally socialism — is a dogma to be found in the writings of neither Marx nor Lenin. Marx, of course, quite explicitly denied that his scheme of historical periodization had universalistic applications. It was, he argued, only an "historical sketch of the genesis of capitalism in Western Europe" and not "an historico-philosophic theory of the *marche generale* imposed by fate upon every people, whatever the historic circumstances in which it finds itself."[36] Although Lenin had been disposed to magnify the degree of capitalist economic development in Russia, he never argued that Marx's scheme of periodization was fully applicable to Russian history, much less to the histories of Asian lands. The theory of a unilinear pattern of historical development is, in fact, a distinctive product of Stalinist ideology. By the time the Chinese Marxist Kuo Mo-jo wrote his *Study of Ancient Chinese Society* in 1929,[37] Stalin's control of the international Communist movement had hardened and the unilinear scheme was generally, although still by no means universally, accepted in world Communist circles.[38]

In the early 1920's, however, in its pre-Stalinist phase "Marxist-Leninist" doctrine did not demand universalistic assumptions as far as the past was concerned, and Li Ta-chao felt no compulsion to make such assumptions. Nowhere does one find Li searching for evidence of a slave society in ancient China; nowhere did he categorize the traditional Chinese socio-economic structure as feudal; nowhere did he feel the need to look for signs of incipient capitalism in prenineteenth century China. He was content to describe traditional Chinese society only in the most general terms — as an "agrarian economic organization" that had remained "unchanging" for two thousand years.[39] As late as 1926 Li pointed out that private property in land (a form of property relationship wholly incompatible with the Marxist definition of feudalism) had been the predominant type of landownership in China since the late Chou era.[40] Whereas Chinese Marxists have since devised various schemes to encompass the traditional Chinese system of private landownership within the scope of "feudalism," Li himself constructed no such rationalizations.

Far from attempting to fit Chinese history within the Marxist scheme of periodization, Li always stressed the divergencies in historical development. After his conversion to Marxism, Li saw no need to revise his earlier views on the sharp differences between Eastern and Western civilizations, even though the matter was no longer of great concern to him. He assumed that Marxist historical theory would be interpreted in a fashion sufficiently broad to take into account the divergent historical patterns of East and West. Moreover, he called upon Marxist historians to construct a new, general "theory of national experience" that would include within its scope all national peculiarities in historic evolution.[41]

Li attributed differences in historical development to essentially geographic factors. He argued that the generally favorable natural environment of China produced a relatively stable and static agrarian system, which served as the base for traditional China's distinctive social, political, and ideological "superstructure." Conversely, "deficiencies in nature" stimulated the commercial and industrial activities in the West.[42]

Li did not derive these views from Marxism, but he could have found considerable support in Marxist historical writings for an emphasis upon geographical and climatic factors in history. Marxists have been quick to deny that geography, which is unchanging, can account for historical change, but the geographical environment is in fact the starting point of the Marxist analysis of history. Marx himself attached considerable importance to "the natural conditions in which man finds himself — geological, orohydrographical, climatic and so on." "All historiography," he wrote, "must begin from these natural bases and their modification in the course of history by men's activities."[43] It is well known, moreover, that Marx believed that capitalism could only have developed in the temperate zone.[44] The importance of geographic factors has been emphasized by many of the successors of Marx. Plekhanov, for example, wrote, "The peculiarities of the geographical environment determine the evolution of the forces of production, and this, in its turn, determines the development of economic forces, and therefore the development of all the other social relations."[45]

The influence of the geographic environment was also the basis of Marx's theory of the "Asiatic mode of production." This theory purported to explain the peculiarities in historical development of at least a part of the non-Western world on the basis of the economic need for large-scale irrigation works managed by the state. The theory appeared in various writings of Marx, including *Capital*, as a general sociohistorical concept, which Marx employed to describe traditional Indian and other societies[46] but which he did not apply to China and Japan.[47] However, in one case — the well-known Preface to *The Critique of Political Economy* — Marx mentioned the "Asiatic mode of production" as one stage (the one preceding slavery) in his general scheme for the periodization of Western history.[48]

Despite his rejection of a unilinear scheme of historical development, and despite his emphasis on geography as the main factor determining the differences between East and West, Li Ta-chao did not employ the concept of the "Asiatic mode of production" to explain these differences. Although he had read *Capital*, Li chose to treat the "Asiatic mode," as Marx had in the Preface, simply as an ancient antecedent of modern Europe.[49] It played no part in his view of traditional China.

Whereas Li rejected the notion that mankind had developed in the past according to a single, unilinear scheme, he was insistent that the revolutionary future of all mankind would be the same. He had the fullest confidence that the road to socialism would lead to world unity, which would forever destroy the national and racial distinctions that had developed in the course of historic evolution. However, since the Chinese past had been different from that of the Western countries, and since Chinese society had been "unchanging" for more than two thousand years, what assurance was there that the Chinese future would now converge with the future of Europe and the rest of the world? Li's pre-Marxian belief that future world unity would rest upon the synthesis of Western and Eastern (i.e., Chinese) cultures would clearly no longer suffice after he became a Marxist. If China had become part of the mainstream of world history, as he now believed, it had to be explained upon the basis of economic not cultural factors. It was here that the agency of foreign imperialism was invoked. The pressure of foreign economic power, Li argued, had transformed China's "unchanging agricultural economic organization" and its entire social, political, and cultural "superstructure," which thereby thrust China onto the stage of modern world history.[50] More than once he pointed out that the forcible entry of Western guns, technology, and ideas had awakened China (and all of Asia) from its millennial slumber.[51]

The admission that foreign imperialism had played an objectively "progressive" role in Chinese history was an uncomfortable notion for a Chinese nationalist to hold. This admission, however, did not prevent Li from treating modern Chinese history — as Chinese Communist historians do today — as essentially the history of Chinese national resistance to imperialist aggression. Like his Marxist successors, Li paid particular attention to the T'ai-p'ing Rebellion, which he interpreted not primarily as an anti-Manchu dynastic movement but rather as the opening chapter of the popular struggle against Western imperialism. Virtually every important event in China since the time of the T'ai-p'ings was viewed by Li through the same anti-imperialist prism. Even the more traditionalist movements, such as the activities of the Triads and other secret societies in the post T'ai-p'ing era and the Boxer Rebellion, were seen as part of "the Chinese peoples' national revolutionary history of resistance to imperialism."[52]

The details of Li's interpretation of modern Chinese history need no discussion here since his views were quite similar to more recent Chinese Communist interpretations. It should be pointed out, however, that Li's purpose was not simply the glorification of Chinese nationalism. "From the beginning," he argued, "the Chinese national revolutionary movement was a part of the world revolution. The success of the Chinese revolution will have the greatest influence upon Europe and the whole world." [53] Li was inclined to place "the beginning" of Chinese participation in the international revolution at a very early period in modern Chinese history. He sought, and claimed to have found, concrete links between certain secret societies connected with the T'ai-p'ings and Marx's First International. [54] Moreover, he drew upon the authority of Marx's own writings on China to support his nationalistic interpretation of the T'ai-p'ing Rebellion. [55] The identification of Chinese nationalism with world socialism was the essential message that Li's comments on modern Chinese history were intended to convey.

CHAPTER VIII NATIONALISM AND INTERNATIONALISM

KARL MARX believed that nationalism was a temporary and unnatural phenomenon that was one of the manifestations of human self-alienation. The division of men into antagonistic nation-states not only separated them from each other through artificial national boundaries but also alienated man from his own human nature, since in the formation of national loyalties man had attributed his own powers to an entity (the nation) which he no longer recognized as his own creation. In short, Marx regarded patriotism and nationalism as forms of idolatry, that is, man's worship of and submission to a creature of his own making.[1]

Although Marx made various concessions, in both theory and revolutionary strategy, to the actual existence of the nation-state system and nationalist feelings,[2] he remained convinced that the foundations of nationalism, and indeed the nation-state itself, were rapidly being undermined by the "cosmopolitan" forces of modern capitalism and industrialism.[3] As he optimistically wrote in the *Manifesto*: "National differences and antagonisms between peoples are already tending to disappear more and more, owing to the development of the bourgeoisie, the growth of free trade and a world market, and the increasing uniformity of industrial processes and of corresponding conditions of life."[4]

Not only were the forces of modern capitalism exerting unifying influences and creating a "world after its own image," but more important, industrialization had produced the modern proletariat,

176

the class destined to overcome all forms of alienation (including nationalism) and regain its "human essence." Marx's famous dictum that "the workers have no country" was meant not to deny that workers might have nationalistic and patriotic feelings but rather to affirm the principle that the historical role of the proletariat was to be universalistic. Its task was not simply the liberation of one class or one nation but the liberation of all humanity. The proletarian socialist revolution was to be internationalistic in aspiration and content as well as world-wide in scope.

It is characteristic of the paradoxes that have attended the modern fate of the doctrine of Karl Marx that the first Chinese supporter of this profoundly internationalistic creed was a young intellectual who, even within a highly nationalistic milieu, was noted for his frankly nationalistic and even chauvinistic inclinations. Indeed, the present alliance between Marxism and Chinese nationalism began to be forged from the very time that Li Ta-chao proclaimed himself a Bolshevik and undertook to organize a Marxist study group at Peking University.

It would be absurd to argue that nationalism was the sole factor responsible for Li Ta-chao's conversion to Communism, for while most Chinese intellectuals were nationalists at the time of the May Fourth movement, few then became Communists. Yet nationalism was centrally involved in Li's response to the Bolshevik Revolution and his interpretation of Marxism, and although his response was not typical of all the early Chinese Communists, it is clear that nationalistic impulses were also very much present in the motivations of the other founders of the Communist movement in China. Even Ch'en Tu-hsiu, who was perhaps closer to the genuine internationalist traditions of Marxism than any other leading Chinese Communist, at first responded to the Marxist-Leninist message for essentially nationalistic reasons. During the New Culture era Ch'en Tu-hsiu had proclaimed himself a "cosmopolitan," but he had not then expressed any interest in the cosmopolitan doctrines of Karl Marx. Not until after he had been caught up in the nationalistic passions generated by the Shantung question and the May Fourth movement did he find Marxism relevant to the Chinese situation.

The paradox of Chinese intellectuals adopting an internationalistic ideology for nationalist reasons and using it for nationalistic ends is only one aspect of the relationship between Marxism and nationalism in the Chinese environment. If one compares the views of the cofounders of the Chinese Communist party — Li Ta-chao and Ch'en Tu-hsiu — on the subject of Chinese patriotism and nationalism in the years 1919–1920, a further paradox emerges. During those years Li Ta-chao, hitherto an ardent nationalist, rejected patriotic loyalties and proclaimed himself a devoted Marxian internationalist. During the same period, Ch'en Tu-hsiu, who had been in the forefront of internationalist tendencies among the intellectuals associated with the periodical *Hsin ch'ing-nien*, for the first time openly expressed his previously latent nationalistic impulses. Although before long Li again proved himself a more fervent nationalist than Ch'en, and Ch'en's interpretation of Marxism became more compatible with the traditions of Marxian internationalism than was Li's, their attitudes in 1919–1920 suggest that just as the nationalistic impulse was not wholly absent in Ch'en's pre-1919 world view, so the strongly nationalist component in Li's thought was not an immutable entity that could never be modified by new experiences and ideas. When Li's virulent nationalism later re-emerged, it did so in combination with his new commitments to socialism and world revolution; and those commitments profoundly influenced both the form and content of his nationalistic predispositions and the ends to which they were put. The combination of Marxism and nationalism is perhaps an unholy alliance, but it has nevertheless proved to be a highly potent political formula.

The Internationalist Phase

When Li Ta-chao in 1918 declared his support for the October Revolution, he was immediately confronted with the task of reconciling the nationalistic impulses that had originally driven him to becoming a Bolshevik with the principle of "proletarian internationalism," for the latter was then a central element in Bolshevik ideology. In the years immediately following Lenin's seizure of power, before the notion of "socialism in one country" had emerged, a spirit of genuine internationalism and an expectation that world revolution was imminent were very real elements in the mentalities of the Bolshevik leaders and their supporters. World revolution was, after all, not only a cornerstone of Marxist theory but also a practical necessity for the success of the revolution in Russia, as Lenin

himself insisted. It was when this spirit of "proletarian internationalism" and the hopes for world revolution were at their height
that Li Ta-chao announced his conversion to Bolshevism and his
acceptance of Marxism.

It is hardly necessary to emphasize the incompatibility between
the internationalist principles of Li's newly adopted Marxist creed
and the nationalistic and antiforeign strains that were so deeply
imbedded in his thought. A faith in the inevitable rebirth of a
"young China" had been the emotional core of his pre-Marxian
world view. Except for his interest in particular Western thinkers,
his concern with the world outside of China had been largely confined to attributing China's predicament to the intrusion of "evil
foreigners" and to comforting himself with the notion that the
rebirth of China would be accompanied by the decline of the
materially powerful but overly mature nations of the West.

Not until 1918, when he set forth his views on "The Basic Differences between Eastern and Western Civilizations," did Li's perspectives move beyond this exclusive concern with the present condition and the future glory of the Chinese nation. He then had called
for the creation of a new, unified world civilization based on the
synthesis of Eastern and Western cultures. Quite possibly Li's essay
was influenced by the two Russian revolutions of 1917, for he
mentioned in passing that Russia was uniquely situated to mediate
between East and West,[5] but the essay was essentially inspired by
the same nationalistic motives that had earlier made Li pose
as a reluctant defender of the Chinese tradition against the advocates of all-out westernization. In calling for a synthesis of East
and West, Li was replying to Ch'en Tu-hsiu and other members
of the new intelligentsia who insisted that there was little or nothing
of value in the traditional culture. Li argued in effect that not only
were there worthwhile elements in the Chinese tradition but these
elements had unique and essential contributions to make to world
civilization.

However desirable Li may have thought the goal of world harmony
to be, the conception did not impinge deeply on his immediate
concern with the plight of China. Nor did it influence his views on
how that plight might be resolved. Indeed, he admitted that the
achievement of world unity would be a difficult and lengthy process
at best.[6] Not even the most general program for action could be

drawn from a vague notion of the desirability of an ultimate harmonization of Eastern and Western civilizations.

Although the idea of a future synthesis of East and West did not make a significant impact on Li Ta-chao's intensely nationalistic concern with the Chinese present, his response to the internationalist appeals of the October Revolution immediately transformed his view of the nature of the problems China faced. The Bolshevik-Marxist message provided a new explanation of both the external threat to China and her internal crisis, as well as a comprehensive program for political action from which a variety of proposals for immediate, practical activity could be derived. It also provided the goal of world socialism towards which such activity was to be directed, as well as the faith that this goal was guaranteed by history and that its realization was near at hand.

Li had earlier attributed China's misfortunes to the "guns of the Europeans," but he now identified the more impersonal force of international capitalism as the major culprit. Before he had been exclusively concerned with the fate of China; now he linked the Chinese future with the future of the world socialist movement. His earlier goal of world unity based on the synthesis of Eastern and Western cultures had been placed at some remote time in the future; now he envisioned the Bolshevik Revolution as a great elemental tide sweeping over the world immediately. For Li in 1918 the international socialist revolution had become an imminent reality, which conditioned all his ideas and attitudes.

Among the Chinese intellectuals drawn to the Bolshevik program, no one was more sanguine than Li about the prospects for world revolution. Even as the first flush of revolutionary enthusiasm began to subside, he remained confident that, despite external appearances, the millenium was fast approaching. "The militarism and capitalism of the world," he wrote in December 1919, "is built like the T'ang-shan coal mine. Its outer form is imposing but its foundations have been dug away by the workers and it may suddenly collapse." [7]

Li's nationalistic proclivities were at once submerged under this wave of faith in the imminence of world revolution. In his very first comments on the significance of the October Revolution, Li attached particular importance to the internationalist goals of Bolshevism. He argued in July 1918 that the Russian Revolution was a much higher order of revolution than the French Revolution of 1789 had been precisely because the Russian upheaval was internationalistic in content, whereas the French had been only nationalistic. The French revolutionaries, he wrote, had been motivated only by "patriotism," but the Russians were inspired by "humanism." [8] There was, nonetheless, a strong nationalist motivation in this apparent internationalist position, for Li had first interpreted the October Revolution as the beginning of a great reconciliation between Eastern and Western civilizations, in which he believed China had a very special role to play. However, this notion of the reconciliation of conflicting civilizations was soon abandoned. When Li wrote "The Victory of Bolshevism" in November 1918, the Russian Revolution no longer appeared to be the first step in the harmonization of East and West but was rather the harbinger of "the destruction of the presently existing national boundaries which are obstacles to socialism." [9]

By this time Li had become very much concerned with the incompatibility between the antiforeign and nationalistic passions that had marked his earlier writings and the Marxist doctrines he now embraced. In the years 1919–1920, the period of the inception of Communist organizational activities in China, Li was intent upon identifying himself as a "proletarian internationalist." He no longer spoke about the rebirth of China but rather about "the whole history of humanity" and the "great mission of mankind." His goal was no longer simply the reformation of China but the realization of world socialism. Typical of his new perspective was the view he offered in January 1919 of the essence of contemporary world politics: "The working classes are uniting with their compatriots of the whole world to create a single rational association of producers in order to destroy national boundaries and overthrow the capitalist classes of the world." [10]

Most striking was the transformation of Li's attitude on the question of patriotism. In his brief polemic with Ch'en Tu-hsiu in 1915 Li had argued that patriotic feelings were not a barrier to the intellectual's achievement of "self-consciousness" but the necessary precondition for it. His writings in the years that followed were entirely consistent with this point of view. Yet in the months after the betrayal of Chinese interests at the Versailles peace conference, at the very time when China was engulfed in a wave of nationalistic resentments and patriotic zeal, Li made special efforts to counsel Chinese intellectuals to eschew patriotic passions. Opposition to the Versailles decision, he wrote a few weeks after the May Fourth Incident, should be based "not on narrow and selfish patriotism but rather upon resistance to aggression and to the robberlike behavior of the robber world." [11] In November 1919 Li declared that it was erroneous to interpret the May Fourth movement as "simply a patriotic movement" for "it is really a part of the movement for the liberation of all humanity." [12]

He later elaborated on this view of the May Fourth movement: "We are unable to recognize the Chinese student movement as a patriotic movement. We love the Japanese working class, common people, and youth just as we love the working class, common people, and youth of our own and other countries . . . the state is not based on the principle of love. A patriotism that kills people and steals their lands is a betrayal of humanism and opposed to reason. We recognize the Chinese student movement only as a movement to resist the [imperialist] powers." When the new Soviet leaders renounced the privileges obtained in China by the czarist government, Li argued that it should not become an occasion for patriotic celebration: "It is not because we have recovered a bit of material power that we are grateful to them [the Russians]; rather it is because in this world of powerful states they were able to express their humanist and internationalist spirit." [13]

Li's study of the history of the international socialist movement — a subject on which he frequently wrote in the early 1920's — seemed to reinforce his growing disenchantment with the value of patriotism. In *Hsin ch'ing-nien's* special issue on labor, published in May 1920, he noted: "With the outbreak of the Great War in 1914 the faith in working-class liberation was at once trampled underfoot by patriotism. Many of the European socialist parties, in a fierce tide of patriotism, loyally capitulated before the capitalist governments." [14]

Li propagated his new internationalist faith among the members of the Young China Society (Shao-nien Chung-kuo hsüeh-hui), a stronghold of nationalist sentiment in the ranks of the Chinese intelligentsia. Li had been one of the principal founders of this influential organization of returned students in the spring of 1918 and had fully shared its highly nationalistic proclivities. [15] Indeed, through the great popularity of his essay "Spring" he had become personally identified with the notion of a "young China." Yet in September 1919 in the pages of the Young China Society's journal, Li urged his fellow members to eliminate the narrowly nationalistic content of the concept of a "young China" and to look beyond to the greater goal of international brotherhood:

[Just as we] do not want to be bound by the corrupt family system [so we] should not be shackled by a narrow patriotism. Our new life should be one that will fulfill our own individual [potentialities] and, on a larger scale, one that plans for the happiness of the world. The sphere of our family has already expanded to include the world . . . [thus] we ought to make the life of the world the life of one family. We ought to know that the movement of man is more important than the movement of patriotism. Our concept of "young China" should not be to make China a stage for our youth to struggle for dominance with other countries. Rather it is to integrate the territory of China with the world so that we will be able to shoulder our responsibility in the reformation of the world. The scope of our "young China" should definitely not be limited to China. We should join hands with the youth of the rest of Asia for a common movement of Asian youth and at the same time join hands with the youth of the whole world to create a common movement of world youth. This is all part of the task of our "principle of young China"! [16]

As Li was about to embark upon the organization of the first Chinese Communist groups in 1920, patriotism apparently no longer seemed to him to be the essential attribute of the "self-conscious" intellectual that it had in his debate with Ch'en Tu-hsiu five years earlier.

It is significant that Li Ta-chao's new internationalist faith was accompanied by a harshly critical re-evaluation of the Chinese tradition. Although Li had earlier assailed the Confucian tradition as authoritarian and unsuited to modern conditions of life,[17] he had been inclined to salvage as much of the past as possible. In such essays as "The New and the Old" and "The Differences between Eastern and Western Civilizations," both of which were written on the eve of his conversion to Marxism, he had attempted as best he could to reconcile traditional Chinese values with modern economic forces and Western ideas. But through the new prism of world revolution and the cosmopolitan values of Marxism he now saw a different picture of traditional China. By the beginning of 1919 Li had come to the conclusion that "for thousands of years"

Chinese life had been "without a bit of significance, without a bit of interest, and without a bit of value." "The new era has arrived," he proclaimed, and the old life was to be completely swept away.[18]

Typical of Li's new view of the Chinese past was his description of the traditional Chinese foreign policy of "using barbarians to fight barbarians" as expressing not only "the weakness and inertia" but also "the deceitfulness and vulgarity" of old China.[19] He dismissed all of Chinese history as "the record of the union of hypocrites [hsiang-yüan] * and big robbers." "If the big robbers [ta-tao] had not united with the hypocrites, they could not have established an emperor. If the hypocrites had not united with the big robbers they could not have become sages."[20]

There are many other such sarcastic comments on traditional China in Li's writings of 1919–1920. Significantly, many of these attacks were launched not from a strictly nationalist standpoint but rather from the standpoint of Li's Marxist principles. He did not argue that old values and customs had to be destroyed merely because they had become fetters on the progress of the nation and could not serve the cause of China's survival in the modern world. Rather, he emphasized the Marxist view that all presocialist ethics reflect the alienation of man from his true self. He attacked Confucian philosophy, for example, because instead of promoting "man's realization of his individuality, [it exists] for the purpose of man's sacrifice of his individuality."[21] In a similar vein he condemned the traditional civil service examination system because it "trampled down the human personality."[22] Having derived from Marx the view that under capitalism the relations between men become "almost wholly a relation between commodities" and that therefore "men regard each other as abstract things," Li proceeded to lump together traditional Chinese values and Western bourgeois values and call for a new system of universalistic ethical standards. Neither the ethics of the Chinese family system nor the ethics associated with Western-style nationalism, he declared, could possibly exist "in the age of a world economy."[23] This demand for the complete elimination of traditional Chinese values — a demand so opposed to the whole tenor of Li Ta-chao's pre-Marxian thought — was quite consistent with the posture of "proletarian internationalism" he had

---

* The term hsiang-yüan, literally "rural honesty," is a derisive reference to the landed scholar-gentry class.

assumed and the arrival of the world socialist order he confidently anticipated.

New Asianism

Much of the internationalism that was so prominent in Li Ta-chao's writings in 1919–1920 was the product of his essentially chiliastic view that the Bolshevik Revolution heralded the approach of a world-wide revolutionary transformation. When the prospects for world revolution grew dimmer after 1920, the internationalist themes in his writings began to recede, but in the early phase of his Marxist career, Li's desire for international solidarity and unity was no less genuine than his hopes for world revolution.

Just as Li's original view of the October Revolution had been drawn more from the bold visions of Trotsky than from Lenin, so his internationalism and the specific proposals that he advanced to achieve a world socialist order bore the imprint of Trotsky's conceptions. The views that Li presented in late 1918 in his essay "The Victory of Bolshevism" were, as previously noted, inspired in large measure by Trotsky's book of 1915 *The War and the International*, which Li read in English translation under the title *The Bolsheviki and World Peace*. From this book Li had drawn the conclusion, "it is clear that Trotsky holds that the Russian revolution is to serve as a fuse to world revolution. The Russian revolution is but one [revolution in the process of] world revolution; numerous revolutions of other peoples will successively arise." [24]

In the same book Trotsky argued that the outbreak of the world war signaled the downfall of the nation-state, that the proletariat no longer had any interest in defending an antiquated national fatherland, and that the task of the proletariat was therefore to create a "republican United States of Europe, as the foundation of the United States of the World." [25] The proposal for a "United States of Europe," Isaac Deutscher has pointed out, "came to be regarded as a hallmark of Trotskyism," reflecting Trotsky's unshakeable faith in the international character of the coming revolution. The proposal had in fact given rise to a controversy in Russian Marxist circles in the prerevolutionary period. In 1915 Lenin criticized Trotsky's use of the phrase "United States of Europe" on the grounds that it seemed to imply that a revolution in Russia could only occur as part of a simultaneous rising in Western Europe. It was probable, Lenin argued, that the revolution might first succeed in a single country.[26]

The differences between Lenin and Trotsky on this point reflected differences in temperament and emphasis rather than any important disagreements over Marxist theory or revolutionary strategy. Both agreed that the revolution would be victorious first in Russia and that the success of the Russian revolution would stimulate revolutions elsewhere in Europe. The major difference was that Trotsky, who was always more sanguine about the prospects for world revolution, assumed that the Western response to the Russian spark would be much more immediate than Lenin thought likely.

Li Ta-chao was in all probability wholly unaware of these differences when in 1918 he came across the notion of a "United States of Europe." He immediately seized upon Trotsky's controversial proposal, which he undoubtedly assumed to be an accepted principle of Bolshevik doctrine, and expanded it into a universal scheme of socialist reorganization. If there was to be a socialist "United States of Europe," then why not a similar socialist federation for the nations of Asia? The very idea of federalism became appealing once it seemed to be sanctioned by Bolshevik theory. In an article that appeared in the periodical *Hsin-ch'ao* in February 1919, entitled "Federalism and World Unity," Li presented various theoretical and historical arguments in favor of federalist-type organizational structures in general. On the basis of these arguments he advocated the establishment of three separate continental federations: one for Europe, another for Asia, and a third for the Americas. These three federations would then serve as the foundation upon which "mankind will organize a single federation that will completely destroy all boundaries between countries. This is our fervent prayer for world harmony."[27] Li acknowledged that the self-determination of individual nations might be a necessary first step for the oppressed lands of Asia, but he emphasized that it should be only a first step. National self-determination was not an end in itself but only the prelude to the formation of extranational organizations and eventual world unity.

Li adopted the expression "New Asianism" (*hsin Ya-hsi-ya chu-i*) to describe his proposal for an Asian federation in order to distinguish it from Japanese-sponsored movements for "Pan-Asianism" or "Greater Asianism" (*ta Ya-hsi-ya chu-i*). The purposes and methods of the two, he declared, were absolutely opposed. Pan-Asianism was no more than a Japanese attempt to dominate Asia by invoking an Asian version of the Monroe doctrine. It was "not a principle of peace but a principle of aggression; it is not national self-determination but an imperialism that swallows up weak and small peoples; it is not an organization suitable to world organization but rather a seed that will destroy world organization." New Asianism, on the other hand, was to be a free union of the peoples of Asia and a pillar for the construction of "a world federation to promote the happiness of all mankind." [28]

Li emphatically denied that the concept of New Asianism had any racial overtones. It was to be based on strictly geographical rather than racial criteria. "When we define the boundaries of Asia," he wrote, "we do not want to draw a boundary between the yellow and white races. We only want to identify the area where we live and where it is our responsibility to carry out the work of reconstruction." [29] Europeans and Americans living in Asia, Li took pains to point out, would be included in the future Asian federation, as would Russians living in the Soviet Far East. [30]

Asian unity was particularly necessary, Li argued, because the most immediate threat to the freedom of the peoples of Asia came not from Westerners but from other Asians: "I advocate New Asianism in order to oppose Japanese Greater Asianism . . . if within Asia the tyranny of Asians against Asians is not removed, there is no hope of ending the tyranny of those from other continents . . . we only hope that all Asians will together rise up to destroy Greater Asianism. This is a responsibility that falls not only to Chinese and Koreans but one that is to be shared by all Asians, even enlightened Japanese." [31]

Li was quick to reject the criticism that New Asianism would separate the Asian from the non-Asian socialist movements. "New Asianism," he argued, was only a means to "destroy racial and state boundaries and cast away all the jealousies and alienations that have been imposed upon us by the ruling classes." [32] Far from separating Asia from the rest of the world, the movement for Asian unity would be "part and parcel of [the movement to create] world unity and a world organization. It does not turn its back on internationalism but harmonizes with internationalism. We vigorously oppose

Asians who oppress other Asians and Asians who oppress Africans. Tyranny is our enemy, justice is our friend . . . All men are our compatriots, none are our enemies." [33]

Nationalistic motivations were undoubtedly involved in the concept of New Asianism for Li assigned to Asia a role equal to that of the industrially advanced West in the realization of world socialism. This position, of course, could hardly have been justified in terms of orthodox Marxist criteria or, for that matter, even by any strict application of Marxist-Leninist theory. Yet Li's call for a federation of Asian socialist states seemed to him no bolder a proposal than Trotsky's call for a socialist "United States of Europe." Li was asking for no more than equality for Asia in the world revolution. Within the context of the imminent world-wide revolutionary transformation he confidently expected, the notion of New Asianism seemed fully in accord with the Marxist internationalist principles he then embraced.

Class, Nation, and Race

At the time that the internationalist themes in Li Ta-chao's writings were still very prominent, he began to develop the theory that China was a "proletarian nation." As previously noted, he first put forward the idea in January 1920. Because of the oppression of international capitalism, he argued, the entire Chinese nation had been transformed into part of the world proletariat and China was thereby qualified to fully participate in the international proletarian revolution.

The highly nationalistic overtones of this theory are quite obvious. Implicit was the assumption that class differences within China had dissolved in the face of China's external enemies. If the entire Chinese nation was "proletarian," then national struggle and class struggle were synonymous, and nationalistic interests and motivations were sanctioned as legitimate forms of China's contribution to the world revolution. Furthermore, the theory implied that China had a special role to play in the international proletarian struggle. If the whole Chinese nation had been proletarianized, then China was presumably more revolutionary than the capitalist nations of the West. The latter might have large proletarian classes, but they nevertheless appeared on the world scene as imperialist aggressor states. Thus, the position of equality that Li had provided for China in the world socialist revolution through the concept of New Asianism was elevated into a position of superiority vis-à-vis the Western nations by virtue of the "proletarian nation" theory, for the revolutionary struggle was no longer between oppressor and oppressed classes but between oppressor and oppressed nations. Among the latter, "proletarian" China stood in the vanguard.

At first these nationalistic implications were muted. As long as Li still held to the hope that a world-wide socialist upheaval was imminent, China's special "proletarian" position was only temporary, for it could be assumed that all national differences would soon dissolve in a great global tide of revolution. Not until this chiliastic vision of world revolution was smashed by the hard realities of European and Chinese politics was the essentially chauvinistic content of the "proletarian nation" theory revealed. The Comintern-sponsored alliance between the Chinese Communists and the Kuomintang set the stage for this disclosure.

In January 1924 Li Ta-chao was elected to the Central Executive Committee of the reorganized Kuomintang, which formally consummated the united front between the two parties that had been in the making since the summer of 1922. The alliance had grown out of the new Comintern strategy of promoting nationalist movements and national "bourgeois-democratic" revolutions in Asia and the Middle East — a strategy that had resulted directly from the failure of the revolution in Central and Western Europe. Li Ta-chao's role in this alliance and his interpretation of it are subjects for later discussion. Here it need only be noted that within the political framework of this alliance with the Kuomintang the internationalism that Li had embraced when he first accepted Marxism distintegrated and gave way to a new and virulent nationalism.

Since the policy of collaboration with the Kuomintang emphasized the common interests of all "democratic" Chinese in opposing foreign imperialism, it seemed to many Chinese Communists fully to justify the expression of their own nationalistic resentments and, in some cases, their chauvinistic inclinations. Li Ta-chao took the lead in promoting these tendencies in Chinese Communist ranks, but he was by no means alone. As Stuart Schram has pointed out, Mao Tse-tung also appears to have gone through an ultranationalistic phase at this time.[34]

The resurgence of nationalism was at first reflected in the disappearance from Li's writings after 1922 of his earlier view that Chinese patriotism was incompatible with the principles and purposes of the Chinese revolution. No longer did he voice suspicions about the value of patriotic feelings, nor did he continue the attacks on the Chinese tradition that had accompanied his internationalist phase of 1919–1921. He began to express a renewed nationalistic appreciation for the traditions of the Chinese past. In *The Essentials of Historical Study*, written in 1924, Li called upon Chinese historians to develop a "theory of national experience" and to engage in "the study of national psychology." "I think," he wrote, "that the particular characteristics of a nation can determine the particular history of that nation. National characteristics constitute a most powerful motivating force in the special experience of each nation."[35]

These re-emerging nationalistic tendencies culminated in a lecture on "The Race Question" that Li delivered before a meeting of the Peking University Political Study Society (Pei-ta cheng-chih hsüeh-hui) in May 1924.[36] This lecture attempted to provide a quasi-Marxist justification for a virulent Chinese nationalism and even marked the reappearance of strains of Li's pre-Marxian antiforeignism. Li began the lecture in moderate tones, discussing in a rather academic manner the problems involved in defining the terms *kuo-min* (people), *min-tsu* (nation), and *jen-chung* (race). The scholarly manner, however, soon gave way to a violently anti-Western tirade. National antagonisms were everywhere increasing, Li cried, and behind these antagonisms there lay profound racial differences and racial prejudices. Who was responsible for injecting the racial issue into world politics? The blame rested entirely with "the world view of the Europeans." For the Europeans "there is nothing else to speak of except Christianity, and as far as their world view is concerned, they think that there is only the white man's world." According to the "European world view," all nonwhite peoples were destined to occupy a position of permanent inferiority.[37]

Needless to say, Li was not at a loss to find evidence in support of these charges. There was, of course, the ever-present example of foreign domination in the treaty ports and the humiliations that the Chinese were forced to endure in their own cities at the hands of privileged and often arrogant foreigners. Moreover, there was no lack of European racist literature. In his lecture Li referred, among others, to Gobineau's infamous *Essay on Racial Inequality* and Putnam Weale's *The Contest of Colours*. The latter, he noted, predicted the inevitability of a war of extermination between the white and nonwhite races.[38] From this "world view of the Europeans" only one conclusion was to be drawn — the Marxist class struggle had been transformed not only into a struggle between nations but also a struggle between races:

The white peoples [see themselves] as the pioneers of culture in the world; they place themselves in a superior position and look down on other races as inferior. Because of this the race question has become a class question and the races, on a world scale, have come to confront each other as classes . . . the struggle between the white and colored races will occur simultaneously with the class struggle. The Russian Revolution is evidence of this. Although [members of] the white race participated in the Russian Revolution, the oppressed-class colored races also took part, and the object [of the revolution] was to resist the oppressor-class white race. Thus, it can be seen that the "class struggle" between the lower-class colored races and the upper-class white race is already in embryonic form, and its forward movement has not yet stopped.[39]

Near the end of his lecture Li took a somewhat more restrained view of the nature of the "class struggle." He called upon the Chinese to work together with "the peoples of the world" and join the world-wide socialist struggle. But even this plea for Chinese participation in the "international" revolution was filled with watchwords of modern Chinese chauvinism. China was to take part in the world revolution in a spirit of "national resurrection" and with "new culture and new blood pouring into our nation." In joining the tide of "world history," moreover, the Chinese were fully to display their "national characteristics" and "national spirit."[40]

On the question of how seriously Li took the theory that the class struggle had become a war between the "white" and "nonwhite" races, it should be noted that the lecture of May 1924 was the only time when he publicly and explicitly discussed the class struggle as a conflict between races. On that occasion, moreover, he was addressing a non-Communist group of nationalistically-inclined students at a time when the prospects for the Kuomintang-Communist united front seemed at their brightest. The racial appeal was no doubt a potent weapon in inspiring enthusiasm for the anti-imperialist crusade among young Chinese who had already become painfully aware of the racist attitudes that were so widely-held in the West. Nevertheless, although Li was undoubtedly attempting to manipulate racial resentments for immediate political ends, it seems inconceivable that he could have spoken in such extreme and bitter terms if he did not himself harbor similar resentments. Moreover, the conclusions that Li arrived at in his lecture "The Race Question" seem but a logical extension of his theory that China was a "proletarian nation." If the class struggle could be interpreted as a confrontation between nations, then it could also be interpreted as a confrontation between races. It was, after all, only too apparent to non-Western nationalists of every variety that whereas most of the capitalist and imperialist nations were "white," their victims, as Li Ta-chao noted, were members of the "yellow and dark races." [41] The notion of proletarian races was implicit in the theory of proletarian nations.

For Li Ta-chao the triumph of Chinese nationalism over Marxist internationalism was complete by mid-1924. Yet as profoundly incompatible as were his ultranationalistic views with the original Marxist world view, Li had not become simply a nationalist in Marxist guise. He retained vital elements of the Marxist revolutionary outlook, which determined the ends towards which his nationalistic impulses were directed and the way those impulses were involved in practical political activities. The antiforeignism and Chinese chauvinism that had marked Li's pre-Marxian thought were resurrected in 1924, but not in pristine form. They were combined with elements of Marxist ideology and political strategy and blended into a highly explosive revolutionary mixture.

Li remained as firmly committed as before to the goal of socialism. As much as he bent Marxist theory to accommodate his nationalistic predispositions, he manipulated nationalist sentiments to serve Communist purposes. If his earlier support for the principle of "proletarian internationalism" could hardly have survived the onslaught of his lecture on "The Race Question," his commitment to world revolution could survive; although now Li made it quite clear that it was to be the "nonwhite" peoples, and especially the Chinese, who were to march in the vanguard of the world proletarian movement. Much of Li Ta-chao's original enthusiasm for the Bolshevik Revolution had been derived from Trotsky, but Li was an early Chinese exponent of the very tendency that Trotsky had long before warned Marxists against, the tendency Trotsky called "that national revolutionary messianic mood which prompts one to see one's own nation-state as destined to lead mankind to socialism." [42] This tendency has more recently received fuller expression in the hands of Mao Tse-tung who, like Li, is also committed to both Chinese nationalism and world revolution and has also identified class struggle with national and racial conflict. [43]

What is of considerably more importance insofar as Li's Marxist credentials are concerned is that he did not abandon completely the concept of class struggle. The logical political conclusion to have been drawn from attributing proletarian class status to the "yellow and dark" races in general and the Chinese nation in particular would have been to deny the existence of class conflict within China. Yet Li always drew back from taking this fateful step, which perhaps more than anything else distinguishes the pure nationalist from the Marxist who is also a nationalist. Early in 1920 when he was first putting forward the theory that China was a "proletarian nation," Li had begun to organize the few genuinely proletarian elements to be found in North China. Until the bloody suppression of the Peking-Hankow railroad workers' strike in 1923, his main energies were devoted to the promotion of the proletarian class struggle. Even after 1923 he continued to condemn Chinese capitalists no less vigorously than he did foreign capitalists, and the attacks he levied against such members of the presumably "proletarian" Chinese nation as militarists, bureaucrats, and landlords were no less bitter than was his opposition to foreign imperialism. In 1926, he emerged as an ardent advocate of a revolution of peasants against their Chinese class oppressors. If Li actually believed that China had become a "proletarian nation," this did not prevent him from promoting class struggle within the nation in every way that he could. If he really thought that the class struggle was proceeding along racial lines, this did not seem to him inconsistent with finding Japanese imperialism an even greater evil than the imperialism of the "white oppressor classes." Between Li's theories on the nature of the class struggle and his political practice there lay a huge abyss.

In the European Marxist movement nationalism has generally been associated with conservative and revisionist Marxist tendencies. Most revolutionary Marxists took it for granted that nationalism was inevitably bound up with conservatism. Trotsky, for example, frequently employed this proposition in his critiques of Stalinist policies. The theory of "socialism in one country," Trotsky declared, "would serve to justify, to motivate, and to sanctify all the tendencies directed towards restricting the revolutionary objectives, towards quenching the ardor of the struggle, toward a national and conservative narrowness." [44]

As valid as this association between nationalism and conservatism may have been in the European Marxist context — in fact, the histories of both the Second International and the Soviet state offer much evidence to support this view — it has nevertheless not been borne out by the Chinese experience. In the Chinese Marxist milieu nationalism has been identified not with the more moderate and conservative political tendencies but with the most radical and voluntaristic tendencies. Li Ta-chao's nationalistic impulses, and Mao Tse-tung's as well, did not lead to any "quenching of the ardor of the struggle" but rather to the intensification of revolutionary struggle. Nationalism has not only widened the popular appeal of Communism in China but it has provided the Communist movement with a vitality, and its leaders with a heightened sense of mission, that they could not have otherwise possessed. More important, nationalistic predispositions enabled Li, and those who followed his lead, to appreciate more quickly and fully where the real opportunities for revolutionary success in China lay. Nationalism provided the opening to the mass movement through the "united front" strategy and was intimately involved with the factors that eventually impelled the Chinese Communists to look to the countryside and the forces of peasant revolt.

PART THREE

POLITICS

CHAPTER IX   LENINISM AND POPULISM

"THE RESOLUTION of theoretical contradictions is possible only through practical means, only through the practical energy of man. Their resolution is not by any means, therefore, only a problem of knowledge, but is a real problem of life." [1] In these lines the youthful Karl Marx put forward a fundamental concept of the Marxist world view — the concept of the unity of theory and practice — which has survived the many strange transformations his theory has since undergone.

For Marx, knowledge and action were intimately related and mutually dependent. True knowledge of the world was impossible except through revolutionary practice that aimed to change the world. Theory was valid only insofar as it could guide men in practical life, that is, promote the revolutionary action that was necessary to transform historical reality in line with its potentialities. Theory, Marx believed, was to be tested by men acting in the real historical situation and revised in the light of that situation and its changes. The new and presumably higher level of theory that emerged was then to be employed in guiding men to higher and more meaningful levels of revolutionary practice. [2]

The notion of the unity of theory and practice has played a dual role in the history of Marxist thought. On the one hand, it has demanded of Marxists political as well as ideological commitment; it has stimulated revolutionary activism and held special attraction for those with politically activistic predispositions. On the other hand, it has served as a built-in justification for those who have undertaken to revise Marxist theory to meet what they perceived to be new and changing historical circumstances. The revisionism of Lenin and of Eduard Bernstein have been equally well served by the demand that Marxist theory must be kept in accord with practical realities.[3] Since Li Ta-chao had come to Marxism with strong politically activistic impulses, and since he had accepted Marxism on the assumption that the theory would be revised to fit the realities of Chinese society, it is hardly surprising that even in the very early stages of his assimilation of Marxist doctrine he was attracted to the idea of the unity of theory and practice.

Li made much of this aspect of Marxism in his debate with Hu Shih on the question of "problems and isms" in the summer of 1919. He argued that it was insufficient "for people only to talk about isms, for no matter how lofty are their words, they must also search for a practical experiment." Regardless of what ism one might follow, "only if you are willing to devote your efforts in a practical movement can it be correct and have an effective result." Li assumed that the theory would be revised in the process of being employed for practical ends. Noting that "an ism has the two aspects of theory and practice," he argued that when a theory "is adapted to practical politics, there arise differences due to time, place, and the nature of conditions . . . If we take this or that ism and use it as a tool in the practical movement . . . it will change and adapt itself to its environment."[4]

In the months and years after the "problems and isms" debate Li himself contributed much to the changes in Marxist theory that he had implied were necessary and inevitable in its adaptation to the Chinese environment. Yet as much as his reinterpretation of Marxism was influenced by his pre-Marxian intellectual proclivities, it was not undertaken to satisfy purely intellectual needs. He was above all motivated by the desire to mold Marxism into a body of ideas that could be fruitfully applied to the practical tasks of promoting a socialist revolution in China, for Li fully shared Marx's eagerness to transform philosophy into a practical movement to change the world.

To understand the revolutionary strategy that Li Ta-chao came to advocate in the 1920's, it is first necessary to deal with the question of whether he proceeded from specifically Leninist assumptions and upon the basis of the revolutionary strategy prepared by Lenin, for Lenin has frequently been credited by both his disciples and his critics with fashioning Marxism into a theory of revolution relevant to the conditions of China and other areas of the "non-Western" world. As a revision of Marxist theory and strategy, Leninism contained two elements that were particularly relevant to the Chinese situation. The first was the attempt to draw within the strategic framework of the world revolution the anticolonial nationalist movements of the "backward lands." This aspect of Lenin's revolutionary strategy was given a general theoretical sanction by his theory of imperialism. The second element was Lenin's attempt to include the peasantry within the scope of the revolutionary process through the formula of the "democratic revolution."

However, more general and basic to Leninism were the theoretical assumptions underlying his concept of party organization. Simply as a method of political organization designed to facilitate the seizure of power by a revolutionary elite, Lenin's concept of party organization and the principle of "democratic centralism" had no organic relationship to the Marxist tradition and could exist quite independently of Marxist premises. It is well known that Leninist methods of organization have appealed to, and been effectively utilized by, political movements far removed from Communist or Marxist orientations. Yet to treat Leninism as no more than an efficient organizational means for attaining power without reference to the Marxist tradition would be to convert a diverse assortment of power-seekers into "Leninists." As a specifically Marxist method of political organization, however, the Leninist concept of the party rested upon a theoretical framework that had the most vital implications for Marxist doctrine. Although Lenin never fully and explicitly stated these implications, he quite candidly outlined his theoretical assumptions in his treatise of 1902, *What Is to Be Done?* Only in this work did Lenin state the central ideas upon which his concept of the party and his later departures in the realm of revolutionary strategy rested.

What Is to Be Done? dealt directly with the problem of how there came into being the consciousness that Marx regarded as necessary for the realization of socialism. Lenin attempted to resolve the problem by identifying the two categories of "spontaneity" and "consciousness" with the two social groups with which he was mainly concerned, the urban proletariat and the Marxist-oriented intelligentsia. The workers, Lenin argued, were capable only of "spontaneous" strivings. At best the "spontaneous" evolution of the proletariat was "consciousness in embryonic form." Left to itself, the workers' movement could only develop "mere trade union consciousness," which eventually led to "its becoming subordinated to bourgeois ideology."[5] Whereas the "spontaneous" movement of the workers (which followed inevitably from objective material factors) was an essential prerequisite for socialist revolutionary activity, true socialist consciousness could only be brought to the proletariat from the outside. A segment of the bourgeois intelligentsia was the carrier of the socialist world view and imposed "consciousness" upon the amorphous movement of the masses. This process, in Lenin's view, was essentially one of the evolution of ideas:

We have said that there could not yet be Social-Democratic consciousness among the workers. It could only be brought to them from without. The history of all countries shows that the working class, exclusively by its own effort, is able to develop only trade union consciousness, i.e., the conviction that it is necessary to combine in unions, fight the employers and strive to compel the government to pass necessary labor legislation, etc. The theory of socialism, however, grew out of the philosophical, historical and economic theories that were elaborated by the educated representatives of the propertied classes, the intellectuals. According to their social status, the founders of modern scientific socialism, Marx and Engels, themselves belonged to the bourgeois intelligentsia. In the very same way, in Russia, the theoretical doctrine of Social-Democracy arose quite independently of the spontaneous growth of the working-class movement, it arose as a natural and inevitable outcome of the development of ideas among the revolutionary socialist intelligentsia.[6]

This emphasis on the revolutionary role of ideas and the consciousness of the intelligentsia is the most striking feature of Leninism. Like the young Marx, Lenin derived his stress on the importance of consciousness from Hegelian philosophy. As Leopold Haimson has pointed out, voluntarists such as Lenin drew from Hegel the belief that consciousness was not merely a reflection of nature but a phenomenon external to it.[7] But whereas Marx tended to attribute consciousness to the proletariat itself, and many later Marxists simply looked to the more or less automatic workings of "history," Lenin unhesitatingly identified the rise of consciousness with the emergence of an elite of revolutionary intellectuals whose historic role was to inject it into the spontaneous proletarian movement.

From this view of the relationship between the "consciousness" of the intelligentsia and the "spontaneity" of the masses Lenin derived his concept of party organization. Because he feared that the "consciousness" of the socialist intelligentsia was in constant danger of being overwhelmed by the "spontaneity" of the working-class movement, and that therefore the workers and the intellectuals were both imperiled by the temptation to follow nonrevolutionary paths, Lenin called for an organization of "professional revolutionaries" to impose its socialist goals and world view on the mass movement and assume the leadership of that movement. "The spontaneous struggle of the proletariat," he declared, "will not become its genuine 'class struggle' until this struggle is led by a strong organization of revolutionaries."[8]

Only a centralized organization of professional revolutionaries operating under military-like discipline could guarantee the growth of consciousness among the workers and ensure that their "spontaneous strivings" would develop into meaningful political action. "An attack," Lenin wrote, "means an assault by regular troops and not a spontaneous outburst of the crowd."[9] "The crowd," which here means the proletariat, was still an essential element in Lenin's program for revolution, but it was no longer the dynamic element. The real motivating force had become an elite of revolutionary intellectuals, who by virtue of their "consciousness" transformed "the crowd," or a portion of it, into "regular troops" led and disciplined by themselves. The essential feature of Marxism in its Leninist form was that the proletariat was converted from the subject to the object of the revolutionary movement.

To what extent were these elements of Leninism present in Li Ta-chao's view of the revolutionary process in China? It should be pointed out that Li began from very different perspectives than those of Lenin, for he never placed any great faith in the proletariat as either the subject or the main object of the Chinese revolution. For Li, the raw material of the revolution first included virtually the whole Chinese nation, and then the peasantry, which constituted the overwhelming majority of the nation. These are subjects to which the following two chapters are devoted. My immediate concern is the question of how Li thought this raw material of the revolution was to be organized, for here he revealed his attitudes toward Lenin's characteristic emphasis on the role of consciousness, the elitism inherent in the Leninist view of the role of the intellectual, Lenin's sense of discipline, and his special concern with matters of organization.

There is little doubt that Li attached the greatest significance to the element of consciousness in the revolutionary process. In stressing the importance of subjective factors, Li went well beyond Lenin's departure from the orthodox Marxist outlook and was even less concerned than was Lenin in finding objective correlatives for his faith in the conscious actions of men. His emphasis on consciousness quite clearly implied that it was the intelligentsia who would mold history and become the driving force in the revolutionary movement, for consciousness was the attribute of the "enlightened" intellectual, as Li had made quite clear long before his conversion to Marxism. Nor was Li reluctant to express this view after he had declared his support for the Bolshevik cause. When in 1919 he called for the liberation of the peasantry, he addressed himself not to the peasants but to the young intellectuals of the cities. The intellectuals were to go to the villages and awaken and educate the peasants.[10] Li assumed that "the suffering and tragic people" could not be expected to liberate themselves solely by their own efforts. In urging his students to go among the masses, Li asked: "If we are unable to rescue them from their suffering, then who would be able or willing to rescue them?"[11]

These views were ready-made for the adoption of Leninist phraseology. As early as January 1920 Li used the notion of a revolutionary "vanguard." As a result of the May Fourth movement Li wrote, "the victory of the intelligentsia has been confirmed. We very much hope that the intelligentsia will become the vanguard of the masses and that the masses will become the rear shield of the intelligentsia. The significance of the intelligentsia is that a part of it becomes loyal to the masses and becomes the vanguard of the mass movement."[12]

Although the use of the word "vanguard" clearly reflected the influence of current Bolshevik doctrines, there is little reason to believe that Li's general emphasis on the role of consciousness and the importance of the intelligentsia was derived from Lenin. A faith in the ability of "self-conscious" intellectuals to fashion reality in accordance with their ideas and wills was an integral part of Li's pre-Marxian world view, and this faith was reflected in the voluntaristic interpretation of Marxism he had arrived at mostly without reference to the writings or formulations of Lenin. Therefore, though Li's assumptions concerning consciousness and the intellectual showed strong affinities with the Leninist conception, they were essentially the product of the peculiarities of his own intellectual development and the needs of the Chinese situation as he perceived it. This point is important because it bears upon certain vital differences between Li's view and the Leninist view of the nature of revolutionary process.

Some of these differences were suggested in an article Li wrote in 1921 on the history of the Russian revolutionary movement, in which he discussed the life and contributions of Lenin at some length. The most striking feature of the seven-page section on Lenin was that it dealt less with Lenin then with his martyred elder brother Alexander. Alexander had been a member of the revolutionary Populist group Narodnaya Volya (Peoples will) and was executed in 1887 after he was implicated in a plot to assassinate the czar. Li described Alexander in particularly heroic terms. Alexander was his model of the self-sacrificing revolutionary who was willing to give up the comforts of a middle-class home and the prospects of a brilliant career to devote his life to the cause of the people. Li noted that Lenin had rejected terrorist methods, but on the whole the picture of Lenin was similar to the one he had drawn of Alexander. He devoted considerable attention to Lenin's youth and home environment, which he characterized as being marked by close and affectionate family ties. Li emphasized the influence of Alexander and the impact of his death in determining the revolutionary course of the younger Lenin. Drawing a further parallel between the two brothers, Li praised Lenin's profound cultural and intellectual interests, the nobility of his personality, and his willingness to sacrifice all in order to liberate the oppressed masses.[13] In short, what emerged from this picture was a heroic and self-sacrificing revolutionary, not a hard-boiled revolutionary organizer.

Li was not wholly unaware of Lenin's special interest in the problem of party organization. In tracing the high points of Lenin's revolutionary career, he observed that in 1903 Lenin had advocated a centralized party structure. But this fact was mentioned almost in passing, and Li attached no special significance to it. He also listed the titles of nineteen of the most important works of Lenin, but

admitted that he had read only one of them, *State and Revolution*.[14]
Nowhere in this essay was there anything to suggest that Li suspected that Lenin's writings had made special contributions to or
changes in Marxist theory.

Li's view of Lenin as more a revolutionary hero than an organizer
and theoretician did not change in later years. In contrast to Marx,
whose theories and writings were constantly invoked, the name of
Lenin appeared only infrequently in Li's writings. When Li did
refer to Lenin, he added to the earlier picture only one new theme:
Lenin's sympathy for Asian nationalism. On learning of Lenin's
death in 1924, for example, Li wrote: "Lenin was the liberator of
the oppressed peoples of the world, and his death is the greatest loss
for the oppressed classes and peoples of the world, especially for
the oppressed nations of the East, like China."[15] On another occasion he stated, "Lenin was the good friend of the weak and
small peoples, the loyal servant of the oppressed, a benevolent and
brave fighter who devoted himself to the world revolution."[16] In
Li's eyes the significance of Lenin lay in his revolutionary heroism
and his presumed friendship for Chinese national aspirations rather
than in his innovations in the realm of Marxist theory and revolutionary organization.

Li's failure to appreciate Lenin as an innovating Marxist theoretician was in part the result of his very limited acquaintance with
the writings of Lenin. Moreover, the one work with which Li was
most familiar and which did influence his thought, *State and Revolution*, was distinguished by its reaffirmation of the original Marxist
viewpoint rather than by any departures from the Marxist tradition.
Even if Li had been more fully acquainted with the writings of
Lenin, it is unlikely that he would have readily perceived their
unorthodoxies, for the revolutionary voluntarism that distinguished
Leninism was usually only implicit in Lenin's writings and often
deliberately obscured by orthodox Marxist formulations. Even one
who was much more fully immersed than Li in the Marxist tradition
would have found it most difficult to recognize the essential unorthodoxies of Lenin simply by reading his works, unless he had
read *What Is to Be Done?* (which Li had not).

If it is not difficult to understand why Li failed to perceive Lenin's
theoretical innovations, it is astonishing to find that he had little
appreciation of Lenin's emphasis on the need for organization and

the role of the party. This is all the more surprising in view of the strong affinities between the two men on the question of consciousness and the role of the intellectual, the very elements on which the Leninist concept of the party rested. Yet one characteristic of Li's writings, in striking contrast to those of his disciple Mao Tse-tung, was his almost complete unconcern with matters of organization. Instead, he was drawn primarily to the spontaneous forces of revolution within Chinese society and had very little to say about the role of the party in the revolutionary process.

This deficiency in Li's Leninist credentials cannot be explained on the grounds of either Lenin's ambiguity or Li's unfamiliarity with Leninist doctrine. If there was one area in which Lenin made himself unmistakably clear, it was the area of party organization; and Li was aware of his views on this subject. In fact, Li himself was a principal founder and leader of a party organized on Leninist principles. Instead, the differences between Li and Lenin on this question may be traced to the different conclusions the two drew from the common Populist core of their initial assumptions, or more precisely, Li's failure to draw all the logical conclusions from these assumptions.

It has often been pointed out that Lenin's voluntarism derived from Russian Populist sources, most particularly from Chernyshevskii, the spiritual and ideological godfather of the Russian Populist movement. From the works of Chernyshevskii Lenin arrived at the conviction that men of firm will and the proper consciousness could mold historical reality in accordance with their ideals. The impatient revolutionary activism reflected in this belief, and its implied emphasis on subjective factors, were blended with the more deterministic formulas of Marx to become a characteristic feature of the Marxist-Leninist world view.[17]

Up to this point Li was in accord with what Lenin had derived from Populism. He shared with Lenin the Populist belief that the intellectuals and their powers of consciousness were to play a decisive role in the revolution. But from this general Populist assumption Lenin had drawn a radically new conclusion. He had posited the "consciousness" of the intellectuals and the "spontaneity" of the masses as opposing and, in part, conflicting forces. Lenin's conception of spontaneity not only reflected a lack of faith in the revolutionary capacities of the proletariat but also implied, as Leopold

Haimson has pointed out, "a basic distrust in the ability of any man to outgrow his 'spontaneous' elemental impulses, and to act in accord with the dictates of his 'consciousness' without the guidance, and the restraint, of the party and its organizations." [18] The imposition of the consciousness of the intellectuals upon reality could not be guaranteed unless their consciousness was organized into a centralized party structure that would discipline the spontaneity of the masses, and even discipline the ever-present impulse toward deviation within the ranks of the revolutionary intelligentsia itself.

It was this conclusion that Li Ta-chao never fully accepted, for Li's emphasis on the role of the self-conscious intellectual was combined with an element of the original Populist faith to which Lenin was never drawn — the feeling that the people themselves possessed a latent "consciousness" that could and must be liberated from its artificial restraints. This aspect of the Populist creed appeared in Li's early writings in the form of his belief that there was a "common will of the people" that had been suppressed by the unnatural forces of history,[19] and in his advocacy of the notion of "only-peopleism" (wei-min chu-i).

After his conversion to Marxism Li did not abandon his predisposition to treat the people as an entity possessing a "common will." It survived and was reinforced by his adoption of Kropotkin's theory of "mutual aid," which presupposed the existence of a "common will" in the form of man's inherent and inalienable spirit of cooperation. Li employed the "mutual aid" theory when reinterpreting Marxism in order to loosen the theory of class struggle from its concrete socio-economic foundations and thereby extend the sphere of potential "proletarian" qualities to virtually the whole Chinese people.

If the people as a whole were seen as possessing a "common will" and a latent "consciousness," it implied that the role of the intelligentsia in the revolutionary process, however essential, was still limited. Its function might be little more than that of a catalytic agent to release the spontaneous feelings of the masses. Thus, when Li called upon young Chinese intellectuals to "go to the villages" in February 1919, he said nothing about the need for any form of organizational apparatus to achieve the liberation of the peasantry. Rather, he assumed that once the "darkness" of the villages had been dissolved by the "enlightenment" brought by the intellectuals, the peasants would become "people who will themselves plan their own lives." [20] A month later, when he urged his student followers to go among "the suffering and tragic people," he assured them that despite "the evils and poisons" of society all men possessed "an indestructible human nature." The young intellectuals needed only to "go forth with pure, clear, and bright hearts and do [their] utmost to shine [their] brightness upon the vast areas of darkness . . . then the darkness of the world will one day be completely destroyed." [21] Rather than one of imposing organizational restraints upon the "spontaneity" of the masses, Li saw the role of the intellectuals as one of releasing the spontaneous forces of regeneration that were presumably latent in man's "indestructible human nature." With these essentially Populist notions Li began his Marxist career, and they remained basic to his view of the revolutionary process.

They were reinforced by a radical democratic strain that also endured as a prominent theme in Li's thought long after his conversion to Marxism. His works abounded in such romantic descriptions of democracy as the following, written in 1922: "Democracy is a kind of temperament, a kind of spirit, and a kind of general view of life. It is not only a political system but is actually an abstract philosophy of human life. It is not purely a product of the faculty of reason but is really imbued with the brightness of the deepest human emotions. . . . Democracy expresses a kind of poetic flavor that is forever striving . . . to grasp arms with Shelley and Whitman and soar to the heavens." [22]

The statement that democracy was "not only a political system" reflected Li's general antipathy to organizational restraints of any sort. It also reflected his Populist conception of democracy as essentially the uninhibited expression of the spirit and will of "the people" rather than simply a formal political structure. He argued in 1923 that true democracy was not a system by which the majority imposed its will over the minority but rather a means by which society arrived at a naturally produced "general consensus." He therefore insisted that democracy be translated as *p'ing-min chu-i*, which literally means "common peopleism," rather than as *min-chih chu-i*, the expression then generally used in China. *Min-chih chu-i*, Li acknowledged, was quite in accord with the Greek origins of the word *democracy*, for it incorporated the words *demos* (*jen-min* or "people") and *kratia* (*t'ung-chih* or "rule"). But the concept of democracy, he asserted, had evolved and changed since ancient times when it "included the idea of a compulsory system that suppressed unwilling peoples." Although the aspect of "rule" or *t'ung-chih* was still present in the existing capitalist versions of democracy, true contemporary democracy eliminated any sense of ruling and precluded any distinction between the governing and the governed.[23]

Li regarded "democracy" (in its modern form of *p'ing-min chu-i*) and socialism as converging waves in the same universal tide of revolution. Both, he asserted, had the same spiritual sources, and both aimed "to eliminate all relations of ruling and subordination and to destroy systems in which men are used as implements."[24] In constructing this vision of the future socialist democracy, he borrowed heavily from the utopian concepts of Lenin's *State and Revolution*. Li defined "true democracy" as "only the administration and management of things."[25] "Both officials and citizens," he wrote, "will be responsible for the management of the state. Everyone will be rulers, no one will be subordinates . . . those who are called rulers will be those who are responsible for managing affairs; it will not include the idea of ruling people."[26]

That Li derived from Lenin little more than the utopian notions put forward in *State and Revolution* is itself indicative of the essentially non-Leninist character of his political world view, for the utopianism of *State and Revolution*, although very much in accord with the original Marxist vision, was highly inconsistent with the assumptions and implications of the Leninist scheme of party organization. Whereas for Lenin the radical-democratic Marxism of *State and Revolution* was a temporary digression from the revolutionary road he had mapped, for Li those utopian notions were matters of faith at the very core of his revolutionary world view.

There were, to be sure, many important affinities between Li Ta-chao's conception of the revolutionary process and the Leninist outlook, even though Li had not derived the common elements from Lenin. Like Lenin, he placed great emphasis on the role of ideas and human, subjective factors in social and political change. Both men were voluntarists who took the Marxist injunction to "change the world" as a license to bend theory to serve immediate practical political needs. Both attributed to the intellectuals and their "consciousness" a "vanguard" role in the revolutionary process. Yet from this common emphasis on the role of "consciousness" vital differences emerged. Lenin resolved the conflicting elitist and democratic strains of the Populist tradition by opting in favor of the consciousness of the revolutionary intelligentsia, as organized in a centralized party, which would impose its world view on the masses and control and manipulate their activities. Li Ta-chao never succeeded in resolving these conflicting strains. The elitist role of the "vanguard" intelligentsia was tempered by his continuing faith that among the people there existed a latent "common will." This faith implied that consciousness was an inherent attribute of all people and not of intellectuals alone, and that the intervention of the intelligentsia was needed only to release this universal consciousness in order to bring forth spontaneous popular energies for revolution and reconstruction. The question of how much organizational control from above was to be involved in this process was one to which Li never really addressed himself. The Leninist injunction that the party must play the central role was ignored or at best left ambiguous.

Specifically Leninist elements intruded on Li Ta-chao's essentially Populist view of the revolutionary process, but he always remained reluctant to accept that stress on discipline and organizational restraint that was the essence of Leninism. On the whole, Li held more to the original Populist conception in which the relationship between the "consciousness" of the intelligentsia and the "spontaneous" energies and ideas of "the people" remained undefined. From these general intellectual differences with Lenin, differences in the interpretation of specific elements of Leninist revolutionary strategy were to grow.

CHAPTER X   NATIONAL REVOLUTION

IN MARCH 1921, four months before the founding congress of the Chinese Communist party, Li Ta-chao noted that China had "not yet experienced a capitalist industrial development like that of Europe, America, and Japan" and that "within China the relations between labor and capital have still not developed into a very great problem."[1] He thus acknowledged that the prospects for proletarian revolution in China were something less than promising. Yet it was precisely this "not very great problem" with which Li was preoccupied during the early years of the Chinese Communist movement. From late 1919 until early 1923 the greater part of his political energy was devoted to the task of organizing the Chinese urban working class. This activity was governed not by his own assessment of Chinese realities but by the demands of Marxist theory as well as by the "advice" that the Comintern first offered its fledgling Chinese party. This advice was officially adopted at the party's first congress. The sixty or seventy young intellectuals represented at that meeting were supposed to march at the head of "the revolutionary army of the proletariat." "To form industrial unions," it was determined, "is the chief aim of our party."[2]

As the leader of the northern branch of the party, Li's efforts to carry out this latter injunction were severely circumscribed by the fact that North China was the least industrialized part of a sparsely industrialized country. Yet his efforts were not entirely unrewarded. Building upon the foundations laid by his student followers — those who, inspired by his plea to "go among the suffering people," had organized the Mass Education Speech Corps in 1919 — Li, together with Teng Chung-hsia and Chang Kuo-t'ao, operated a Communist school at the town of Chang-hsin-tien for the workers of the Peking-Hankow railroad and published a workers' magazine entitled *Lao-tung yin* (The sound of labor). The railroad workers were soon organized in a union and formed the main proletarian base for the early Communist movement in North China. The activities of this union, as well as of several smaller workers' organizations established in Peking and Tientsin, were generally directed by Li in his capacity as head of the northern branch of the China Labor Union Secretariat, an organization set up after the first party congress for the specific purpose of uniting the small and scattered Chinese trade unions under Communist leadership.[3]

Even in this early period, however, Li Ta-chao's political activities were not confined to strictly proletarian endeavors. The Third International had also become interested in alliances with "bourgeois nationalist" forces in China; and a "bourgeois nationalist," according to the flexible Comintern definition, was virtually anyone who would agree to cooperate with the Communists. In 1921 the Comintern agent Maring (H. Sneevliet), while stopping in Peking to confer with Li en route to the first congress of the Chinese Communist party in Shanghai, found one such "class ally." He turned out to be the warlord Wu P'ei-fu, who dominated much of North China, and often the Peking government as well, in the almost continuous warfare between rival militarists that ravaged China after 1920. In return for Russian support against opposing warlord armies, Wu agreed to permit Communist organizational activities in the areas he controlled. Li Ta-chao played a central role in negotiating this loose accord and assumed the primary responsibility for maintaining it because of his close personal friendship with Pai Chien-wu, a former classmate at the Peiyang College of Law and Political Science who was then a political adviser to the northern warlord.[4] Although Li never revealed his own views about the wisdom of this particular piece of Comintern strategy, it may be assumed that he thought it expedient at the time for it greatly facilitated the organizational work in which he was then engaged. The successful establishment of the Peking-Hankow Railroad Workers Union was in large measure made possible by the agreement arrived at with Wu P'ei-fu.[5]

Its success was short-lived. On February 4, 1923, the Peking-

Hankow railroad workers went out on strike. Three days later the troops of Wu P'ei-fu intervened, brutally suppressing the strike in what has come to be known as the infamous "February Seventh" incident. Forty-four workers were said to have been killed and hundreds wounded; others were arrested or forced to flee from areas controlled by Wu's troops. In the general police repression that followed in the Peking area, numerous Communists were arrested and some executed.[6] For all practical purposes the proletarian base of the Communist party in the north had been abruptly and, as it proved, irreparably destroyed. This was the first of several bitter lessons that the Chinese Communists were to learn about the perils of Comintern-sponsored alliances with "bourgeois nationalists," especially when the latter possessed guns and the Communists did not.

For Li the "February Seventh" massacre was a particularly bitter experience. Not only had he known personally many of the men who were killed, but he felt that he himself bore part of the guilt for their deaths because of the leading position he had occupied in the ill-fated accord with Wu P'ei-fu. He interpreted Pai Chien-wu's role in the suppression of the strike as the betrayal of a sacred personal friendship and, in an angry letter to Pai, terminated all relations with him.[7]

For many months the tragedy continued to weigh upon Li's conscience for he felt that he had allowed the ties of friendship to blur his vision of political realities. In a speech in Canton in 1924 commemorating the first anniversary of the "February Seventh" incident, Li passionately revealed his own feelings of responsibility for it. He also compared the significance of the sacrifice of the dead workers to that of the seventy-two martyrs executed by the Manchu government on the eve of the Revolution of 1911. The blood shed by both groups, he cried, "has planted the seeds for a second revolution that will soon burst forth." [8]

The destruction of the Peking-Hankow Railroad Workers Union not only physically destroyed the proletarian movement in the north but also destroyed what faint hopes Li may have cultivated that the Chinese revolution would be a revolution of the urban working class. Yet even before the "February Seventh" incident events were unfolding in Europe and Moscow that would have drawn Li's attention away from the work of organizing the Chinese proletariat and have fastened it upon a very different kind of revolutionary strategy. As a result of the decline of Lenin's hopes for revolution in Europe, especially after the failure of the Communist bid for power in Germany in March 1921, Asia loomed increasingly large in Soviet strategic calculations. New and more concrete policies for Asian Communist parties were formulated as part of the general attempt by the Soviet regime to stabilize its international position and normalize diplomatic relations with the West. Diplomacy rather than world revolution became the order of the day in Moscow. Thus, it was quite logical to look to the already existing anti-imperialist forces in Asia — the forces of "bourgeois nationalism" — which might be expected to offer more immediate success for Soviet diplomacy than the still embryonic Asian Communist parties and the tiny proletarian movements they were attempting to organize. Accordingly, at the First Congress of the Toilers of the Far East, held in Moscow in January 1922, the representatives of the Chinese Communist party, among whom was Ch'ü Ch'iu-pai, were told that the Chinese revolution was still in its bourgeois-democratic phase.[9] Soon after, it was further determined in Moscow that the main vehicle of the bourgeois-democratic revolution in China was the Kuomintang, with whom the Chinese Communists were to cooperate in a common front against imperialism.

Although Lenin's personal role in formulating the Comintern's particular policies for China was perhaps limited because of his failing health and declining influence in Soviet affairs of state, those policies flowed directly from specifically Leninist elements of revolutionary strategy. Among European Marxists, Lenin had proved uniquely prepared to appreciate the revolutionary potentialities of Asian nationalism, but his interest in Asia was not based upon any particular sympathy for its nationalist aspirations. Actual and potential Asian nationalist movements were always viewed through the perspective of their possible influence on the revolutionary situation in Europe, particularly Western Europe, for it was there, Lenin remained convinced, that the decisive battles of the world revolution eventually would be fought. The very problem that impelled Lenin to turn his attention to the role of the "backward lands" in the world revolution revealed his basic preoccupation with the role of the advanced capitalist states. In looking to Asia, he was immediately concerned less with liberating the colonial peoples of the

East than with explaining the apparent viability of capitalism in the West. Lenin's theory of imperialism may have provided a rationale for Asia to play more than a passive role in the world revolution, but the questions to which this theory was addressed were questions that European Marxists had already wrestled with for several decades. Why had not the contradictions of capitalism torn the system asunder in the advanced industrialized states, as Marx had predicted? Why was not the Western proletariat responding to capitalist exploitation in the manner Marx had anticipated? These questions had been asked before by Eduard Bernstein. They were posed again by Lenin, who arrived at a very different set of answers.

The explanation that Lenin provided was, in brief, that the inherent contradictions of capitalism had been temporarily mitigated by overseas imperialist expansion. Through the exploitation of cheap labor and the acquisition of raw materials in the colonies, through the monopoly of markets that absorbed surplus production and surplus capital in areas under their political control or influence, the Western capitalist states had in effect constructed safety valves against internal explosions. Some fruits of colonial exploitation, moreover, had filtered down to the working classes of the metropolitan countries, which created an "aristocracy of labor" that sapped the revolutionary vitality of a portion of the proletariat and thus postponed the collapse of capitalism.[10]

From this explanation of the survival of capitalism in the age of imperialism, one general element of world revolutionary strategy was clearly suggested. The world-wide capitalist chain might be broken at its weakest links, that is, in the backward colonial and semicolonial lands. Movements of national liberation in the colonies would cut off the economic lifeblood of the capitalist-imperialist system and thereby stimulate proletarian revolutions in the advanced, industrialized states.[11]

If anti-imperialist revolutions were to have an important and perhaps indispensable role in the world revolution (even if not a decisive one), the question arose as to what kind of revolutions they were to be. What classes and what parties were to lead them? In the years before the Bolshevik Revolution Lenin's answer to this question was reasonably consistent. He assumed that the revolutions in the backward nations of Asia (in contrast to the revolution he envisioned in backward Russia) would be bourgeois-democratic revolutions led by the native bourgeois classes, who would attempt to unite other classes behind them under the common banner of nationalism.[12] After 1917, however, the question of the nature of potential revolutionary movements in Asia became much more complicated, for then the problem turned on the question of whether the model of the Russian Revolution of 1917 might not also be applicable to Asian nations, and if so, under what domestic and international conditions? Matters were further complicated by the attempt to apply to Asia theoretical formulas that Lenin had developed in the course of the Russian revolutionary experience — particularly his curious notion of a "democratic dictatorship of the proletariat and peasantry."

The theory of a "democratic dictatorship" grew out of Lenin's awareness that the Russian bourgeoisie was incapable of carrying out its historically appointed "bourgeois-democratic" tasks, that is, the overthrow of czarism and the elimination of feudal economic and social relationships. According to Lenin's formula, the peasantry was to assume the historical role of the bourgeoisie and, in alliance with the proletariat, realize the "democratic revolution." [13] Whereas this seemed like an ingenious way to speed up the course of history, the formula was ambiguous when it came to the essential questions of who was to hold political power under the "democratic dictatorship" and what its social aims were to be. Was it to be an alliance between the political representatives of the two social classes, who were to cooperate in a "democratic" manner? Or was the whole process to be guided and presided over by the superior "consciousness" of the party of the proletariat? Was the purpose of the "democratic dictatorship" simply to prepare the way for the development of bourgeois social and political relationships, or was it to transcend those limits and pass over to proletarian socialist aims?

All ambiguities were, of course, resolved in 1917, at least in practice, when political power was in fact seized and held solely by the proletariat, or more precisely by the party that proclaimed itself to be the incarnation of the proletariat's consciousness. The "democratic" phase quickly "grew over" into the socialist phase and all differences except terminological ones between Lenin's concept of the "democratic dictatorship" and Trotsky's theory of permanent revolution dissolved. But although the ambiguities were resolved in practice, they remained in Lenin's theoretical formulas; and both

Lenin's formulas and the model of the Russian Revolution were to be invoked by Communist revolutionary strategists in Asia.

Whereas Lenin had been quite clear in the period before the Russian Revolution in stating that national liberation movements in Asia would be "bourgeois democratic" in character and would mainly come under the leadership of the national bourgeoisie itself, he was not so straightforward when he returned to this question in 1920. At the Second Comintern Congress he put forward his views on the "national and colonial question," which became the official theoretical basis for later Communist strategy in China. These formulas were distinguished by the ease with which they could be interpreted differently for different purposes. On one occasion Lenin declared that in the backward countries "all Communist parties must assist the bourgeois-democratic liberation movement"; [14] and on another he held out the hope that soviets might be established immediately. He rejected the inevitability of a capitalist phase of development in countries "under the domination of pre-capitalist relationships" and at the same time denied the possibility of the rise of "a purely proletarian movement." Typical of the ambiguity that characterized his formulations was this statement: "There need not be the slightest doubt that every national movement can only be a bourgeois-democratic movement, for the overwhelming mass of the population in backward countries consists of peasants who represent bourgeois-capitalist relationships. It would be utopian to believe that proletarian parties, if indeed they can arise in these backward countries, could pursue Communist tactics and a Communist policy without establishing definite relations with the peasant movement and without giving it effective support." [15]

Thus, Lenin denied that Asian revolutions could be anything more than bourgeois-democratic in nature and yet still managed to offer the hope of carrying out a "Communist policy." If these revolutions were to be bourgeois-democratic, who was to lead them? Must they inevitably be confined to bourgeois-democratic limits because of the predominance of peasant economies, or could they soon be transformed into socialist revolutions? Were proletarian parties, "if indeed they can arise," to lead and organize peasants in a "Communist policy," or were they only to give "effective support" to an independent peasant movement led by presumably non-Communist forces? These are the key questions that Lenin's formulas left unanswered.

However one may wish to interpret these perhaps purposely contradictory statements, which were intended in part as concessions to satisfy the revolutionary expectations of the Asian Communists, one governing consideration was quite clearly evident. In 1920 Lenin's eyes were still firmly fixed on the anticipated proletarian revolution in Western Europe; thus, all the hints and half-suggestions of the possibility of a relatively rapid transition to socialism in Asian lands assumed the realization of socialism in at least some of the advanced industrialized nations. It should be remembered that Lenin still believed that even the Soviet state probably could not long maintain itself if the Western proletariat did not respond to the revolutionary spark that had been ignited in Russia.

In the light of this consideration, the united front strategy formulated for China in 1922 was not as radical a reversal of Lenin's 1920 views on Asia as it then appeared to many Asian Communists. Having predicated the possibility of a socialist revolution in Asia upon the likelihood of a revolutionary advance in the West, he was not inconsistent to deny that possibility when the events of 1921 demanded a less hopeful assessment of the political situation in Europe. Revolutionary theory as well as the immediate interests of the Soviet state made it quite logical to fall back on the bourgeois-democratic formula.

However much this formula satisfied Soviet needs, the notion of a bourgeois-democratic phase was alien to the revolutionary perspectives then held by the leaders of the Chinese Communist party. Among those leaders important differences on the question of the nature of the Chinese revolution had already begun to emerge, even though they were still obscured by vague theoretical formulations and had yet to manifest themselves in specific policy conflicts. Whereas Ch'en Tu-hsiu tended to visualize a struggle between Chinese workers and Chinese capitalists in classical Marxist terms, Li Ta-chao was predisposed to look to the revolutionary forces of the whole nation, which by virtue of China's "proletarian" status in the world economy would harmoniously unite with the forces of world revolution. But on one point both Li and Ch'en, and virtually all their followers, were agreed — China would follow a noncapitalist path to socialism. In 1921 in discussing the question of how China was to be industrialized, the two founding fathers of the Communist movement in China had both explicitly denied the necessity of a capitalist phase of development. Neither spoke of even the possibility of an intervening bourgeois-democratic revolution, for both in their different ways anticipated a direct and rapid transition to socialism. It was this hope that was rudely shattered by the Comintern in 1922.

In August of that year the new Soviet evaluation of the nature of revolutionary movements in Asia was transmitted directly to the leaders of the Chinese Communist party. Meeting in a special plenary session at Hangchow, the members of the party's central committee were told by the Comintern representative Maring that China was only entering the stage of a bourgeois-democratic revolution and that the Kuomintang was to be the nucleus of this revolution. Not only was the Communist party to cooperate with the forces of Sun Yat-sen in united actions, but individual Communists were actually to join the Kuomintang to carry out the "national revolution" and destroy the influence of feudalism, militarism, and foreign imperialism. For the purposes of the alliance the Kuomintang was looked upon, in a most un-Marxian fashion, not as the political representative of a single social class but as a multiclass grouping. These policies and formulas were officially adopted at the third congress of the Chinese Communist party in June 1923.[16]

The founders of the Communist movement in China, inspired by the chiliastic appeals of the October Revolution, had undertaken their political activities with the expectation that a socialist revolution was imminent. For two years they had believed their main task to be the organization of the Chinese proletariat in order to prepare for this transformation. It is thus hardly surprising that for most Communists it was with the deepest disappointment that they now heard that the revolution was really to be only a bourgeois-democratic revolution and that, moreover, even this was to be led not by themselves but by another party, which they were to join only as individual members. According to Ch'en Tu-hsiu's account written in 1929, all the Chinese participants in the plenary session of August 1922, including Li Ta-chao, opposed the new Comintern policies. Not until Maring had made it a matter of international discipline, Ch'en claimed, did the Chinese Communists agree to amalgamate forces with the Kuomintang.[17] An officially-inspired party history written in 1926 put it somewhat more cryptically: "The resolution was adopted unanimously, although some individual comrades were opposed to it." [18]

There is no doubt that Ch'en had the greatest misgivings over the united front policy from the first, although as party leader he felt duty-bound faithfully to carry out Comintern directives. His misgivings were probably shared by most leading Communists. Yet except for Ch'en's account of 1929, there is no evidence that Li Ta-chao was among those who objected to the new strategy. As an ardent nationalist who had already identified the whole Chinese nation with the world proletariat, he was in fact predisposed to seeking the unity of all Chinese. Early in the autumn of 1922 Li became the first Communist to join the Kuomintang, thereby setting a precedent for the form that this most unusual type of united front was to take more than a year before it was formally established.[19] In subsequent years he earned a well-deserved reputation as the principal Chinese Communist advocate of the alliance.

According to a standard early account, the Peking Communist group, led by Li, split into "radical" and "gradualist" factions in late 1922. The radicals originally included Chang Kuo-t'ao, Ho Meng-hsiung, Lo Chang-lung, and Chu Wu-shan, all of whom had been brought into the Communist fold by Li while students at Peking University. They argued that the main efforts of the party should continue to be devoted to the organization of the urban working class, that the democratic and national movements should come under the direct leadership of the party, and that it was therefore unnecessary for Communists to join the Kuomintang. The "gradualists," led by Teng Chung-hsia, contended that conditions within China were unsuitable for a proletarian class struggle, that it was first necessary to carry out a "national revolution," and that this could best be accomplished if Communists worked within the Kuomintang. The "gradualist" faction, it is said, was generally supported by Li as well as encouraged by the Comintern.[20] However, Chu Wu-shan, who was a member of the "radical" faction, has presented a somewhat different picture of Li's role. According to Chu, Li did not support one faction against the other but was a conciliator between them.[21]

However conciliatory Li's relations with his colleagues may have been (and they no doubt were, for that was characteristic of both his personality and his politics), it is nevertheless clear that he took an early and firm stand in favor of the Comintern proposal for an alliance with the Kuomintang, that he played a principal role in effecting the alliance, and that he eventually succeeded in winning over most of the Peking Communists to his position.[22] It was Li who dispatched Teng Chung-hsia to Shanghai early in 1923 to discuss with Sun Yat-sen the reorganization of the Kuomintang and formally to request the admission of the Communists.[23] When the delegates of the Kuomintang's First National Congress assembled in Canton in January 1924 to ratify the reorganization of the party and the alliance with the Communists, it was Li who reassured them that the Chinese Communists would not form a party within a party and would adhere to the principles of the Kuomintang.[24] At this congress Li was selected by Sun Yat-sen as the only Communist member of the five-man presidium and was one of three Communists elected to the twenty-four-member Kuomintang central executive committee.[25]

The role of chief spokesman for the Communist party in the Kuomintang was one for which Li was well suited by virtue of both ideology and personality. He was regarded with good reason by non-Communist intellectuals as a staunch nationalist despite his Marxist commitments. This reputation was enhanced by a widespread, if probably ill-founded, belief that Li had been a member of the T'ung-meng hui at the time of the 1911 Revolution. If Li had not actually joined the T'ung-menghui, he nevertheless had always cultivated close ties with the non-Communist nationalist intelligentsia. Long after his conversion to Bolshevism, he maintained these ties through his activities in the Young China Society. It was, in fact, a fellow member of that group, Chang Chi, who originally invited Li to join the Kuomintang in 1922.[26]

Equally important in Li's role in the alliance was the quality of amiability that marked his personal relationships and the feeling that he was "the friend of everyone." [27] Unlike his colleague Ch'en Tu-hsiu, who is frequently described as having been brusque and "fierce" in manner,[28] Li took particular pains to prevent political differences from degenerating into personal quarrels. For example, Li maintained cordial personal relations with Hu Shih despite their sharp exchange on the question of "problems and isms" in 1919 and the divergent political paths they subsequently followed. In 1921, when Hu Shih attempted to move the editorial offices of *Hsin ch'ing-nien* back to Peking from Shanghai, where Ch'en Tu-hsiu had converted it into a Communist organ, Li supported Hu's move in a vain attempt to prevent a final split among the original members of the *Hsin ch'ing-nien* group.[29] This almost innate propensity for "united front" type activities was expressed in 1920 and again in 1922 when Li joined with Hu Shih and other liberals in issuing manifestoes calling for political freedom and democratic government.[30] Despite the fundamental political differences that separated them, Hu Shih dedicated a volume of his collected works to Li's memory in 1930 in recognition of their unbroken ties of personal friendship.[31]

Because of these personal and political qualities, and especially because of the leading role he assumed in the alliance with the Kuomintang, Li has often been pictured as a moderate and gradualist in the ranks of the Chinese Communist party. Yet it is highly misleading to think of the Chinese Communists of this period as either "gradualists" or "radicals" on the basis of whether they tended to favor or oppose collaboration with the Kuomintang, for some of the most ardent supporters of collaboration — such as Li and Mao Tse-tung — proved to be the most radical Communists. All Chinese Communists eventually accepted the alliance with the Kuomintang because of Comintern demands, but the crucial question was not how wholeheartedly one supported the alliance, but how one interpreted its nature and purposes.

The reasons for Li Ta-chao's support of the alliance had less to do with his desire to maintain international Communist discipline than with his own particular ideological tendencies. Paradoxically, the very ideological tendencies that made Li find so appealing the notion of a national revolution and the policy of collaboration were eventually to express themselves in fundamental departures from the premises upon which those elements of Comintern strategy rested. How, then, did Li view the purposes of the alliance and the nature of the national revolution he so fervently promoted?

A clue to the answer is to be found in Li's evaluation of the revolutionary capacities of the Chinese urban proletariat. Although until February 1923 his main political energies were directed to the task of organizing the urban working class of North China, there is little to suggest that he even then shared Ch'en Tu-hsiu's early faith in the possibility of a strictly proletarian revolution in China. In his writings on the "labor question" there were moving expressions of sympathy for the conditions under which Chinese workers were forced to live and anger against their exploiters, but nothing to indicate that he interpreted these conditions to mean that China was ripe for a successful urban proletarian uprising. One revealing aspect of these writings was their strongly antiurban bias — a theme that had been evidenced earlier in his "Populist" writings of 1919. Here the theme reappeared in a different context. Rather than explicitly identifying the socialist cause with the proletariat, Li was content to contrast the wholesome life of the peasantry with the evils of urban industrial life. In 1919 while discussing the problem of raising the educational level of the working class, he had observed that the traditional village ideal of combining "tilling and studying" offered a Chinese precedent for the realization of the Marxist ideal of a "truly human life." [32] In 1922 he contrasted the evils of urban industrial life with the virtues of rural life where "time and nature were joined together." A year later he noted that whereas factory workers rarely lived to the age of forty or fifty, "white-haired old farmers always can be seen in every village." [33] When Li Ta-chao looked at the embryonic Chinese proletariat, he saw the evils of capitalist industrialization but not the agent of historical redemption.

That Li placed no great faith in the likelihood of a proletarian revolution in China was quite clearly indicated by a rather curious argument that appeared in an essay on Marxist economic theory written in February 1922, a year before the "February Seventh" incident. Explaining that it was in the nature of capitalist development for the proletariat to become concentrated and to "seek out the capitalists and struggle against them," Li observed, "the conditions of the workers of China are not the same [as in Europe] since there are no places where they are concentrated and they are unable to find capitalists to struggle against!" If the Chinese workers were "unable to find" their capitalist exploiters, how was one to explain their exploitation? Li did not directly raise this question but he provided an answer: the oppression of foreign imperialism was responsible for the misery of the Chinese workers. Returning to an earlier theme, Li argued that the intrusion of foreign capitalism had ruined native Chinese industrial enterprises and placed the Chinese working class under a form of "indirect" international capitalist oppression that was more cruel than the direct oppression from which the proletariat of the Western capitalist nations suffered. The same forces of foreign imperialism also had driven millions of

Chinese from their homeland to seek work overseas, where they again fell under the tyranny of foreign capitalists. For these reasons, Li contended, Chinese workers, despite the lack of native capitalist exploiters, had common aims and indestructible bonds of unity with the international working-class movement.[34]

Although Li ostensibly was concerned with the Chinese urban working class, his argument implied that he was looking to far wider sources of revolution. If international capitalism rather than Chinese capitalism was the main enemy, the revolutionary struggle was not confined to the Chinese proletariat but included virtually all social classes, since except for compradores and warlords all Chinese suffered under the yoke of imperialism. The implications of Li's argument (which appeared well before the Comintern proposal for a united front strategy was first raised at the second congress of the Chinese Communist party in June 1922) were similar to the implications of his theory that China was a "proletarian nation." Li no doubt attached considerable importance to the organization of the actual proletariat, but he was predisposed from the beginning to look to the potential revolutionary forces of the whole "proletarian" nation rather than of a single social class forming only a tiny portion of the nation. The idea of a revolutionary united front against foreign imperialism was, in fact, implicit in Li's conception of China's place in the world economy and the relationship between the Chinese nation and the world revolution.

If these ideological proclivities made the Comintern proposal seem particularly attractive to Li, this does not mean that he interpreted the nature and purposes of the national revolutionary alliance with the Kuomintang in the same way that it was interpreted in Moscow. To the Kremlin the policy of a Chinese Communist alliance with the Kuomintang was a tactic motivated primarily by its newly pessimistic evaluation of the prospects for world revolution and by the immediate interests of the Soviet state in the light of that evaluation. The policy received its theoretical justification from the formula that the Chinese revolution was in its bourgeois-democratic phase of development. When the revolution moved to a higher stage, it was assumed that the Communists would break the alliance and lead history on its inevitable ascent. As Stalin later rather crudely put the matter, the Kuomintang was to be "utilized to the end, squeezed out like a lemon, and then flung away." [35]

For Li the national revolution was not simply a discrete stage in the process of social and political evolution, nor was the alliance with the Kuomintang no more than a tactical maneuver. Rather, he thought of both as logical expressions of the particular nature of the Chinese revolution, which he perceived as fundamentally a mass uprising of the entire Chinese nation against the forces of world imperialism. It was a continuous revolutionary process, which had begun in the mid-nineteenth century with the T'ai-p'ing Rebellion and would inevitably and increasingly merge with the world proletarian revolution. As he wrote in November 1922:

Among the classes it is the proletariat who suffers from the oppression of world capitalism, and on the international level it is the weak and small peoples. In the past one hundred years the Chinese people have been trampled under the iron hoofs of the armed, aggressive imperialism of the developed capitalist states of Europe and America and [as a result] have been reduced to a weak and defeated position. We laboring, impoverished people were suffering under two types of oppression when suddenly the October Revolution called for the "overthrow of world capitalism" and the "overthrow of world imperialism"! . . . The October Revolution has the very greatest historical significance and should be commemorated not only by the laboring and impoverished masses but by all the people of oppressed countries like China, who ought to become aware of their responsibilities, resolutely hasten to achieve the alliance of a "democratic united front," establish a peoples government, and resist international capitalism. This is an integral part of the world revolution.[36]

In attempting to identify the Chinese revolutionary tradition with the world socialist revolution, Li went so far as to make the dubious claim that a traditional secret society, the T'ien-ti hui (Heaven and earth society), which had absorbed many of the defeated T'ai-p'ing rebels after 1865, actually became a Chinese branch of Marx's First International. "The fact that the T'ien-ti hui developed relations with the First International," he asserted, "proves that the T'ai-p'ing Revolution was a national revolution that had a class nature and also proves that from the beginning the Chinese revolution has had the tendency to join arms with the world proletariat." [37] This tendency received fuller expression in the movement led by Sun Yat-sen who, Li argued, inherited the revolutionary tradition of the T'ai-p'ings and purged T'ai-p'ing ideology of its superstitious elements,[38] which set the stage for the consummation of the merger between Chinese nationalism and the world revolution:

The success of the October Revolution caused Sun Yat-sen to become increasingly firm in his belief that the Chinese national revolution is part of the world revolution, and he increasingly exerted his efforts to unite the Chinese national revolutionary movement with the world proletarian revolutionary movement. In other words, the revolutionary tide of the Chinese people during Sun Yat-sen's later struggles definitely tended to draw near to the world revolutionary tide and completely merge with it; and under the leadership of Sun Yat-sen it entered onto the correct track of world revolution in order to carry out a gigantic reconstruction of human history.[39]

These attempts to identify the Chinese national revolution with the world socialist revolution might be dismissed as propaganda efforts motivated by the immediate political consideration of maintaining the alliance with the Kuomintang were it not for the fact that the identification flowed so logically from certain basic elements in Li Ta-chao's ideological world view before 1922. His nationalist-Populist predisposition to treat the people as a single entity with basically common interests and his description of China as a "proletarian nation" combined to make the identification seem only natural. His interpretation of the national revolution had the great virtue of satisfying both his nationalistic and his revolutionary impulses.

Li was not content simply to interpret the national revolution as a part of the world revolution; he was intent upon showing that the anti-imperialist movement in China might be a decisive force in determining the outcome of the entire world revolutionary struggle. To support this notion Li turned to what seems a most unlikely source — the writings of Karl Marx. In the articles on China that Marx wrote for the *New York Tribune* in the 1850's Li found what appeared to him to be confirmation of his own view of the special nature and world-wide role of the Chinese revolution.

Marx's articles on China presented a strikingly different picture of the role of Western imperialism in Asia than did his better-known writings on India. In the latter writings Marx described traditional India as a stagnant, semibarbaric society that revolved about unchanging, isolated, and economically self-sufficient village communes. This social structure served as the foundation for a parasitic "Orientally despotic" state that ruled over society and reflected as well as perpetuated its "semicivilized" conditions. Upon this situation the British intruded, and Marx's major point was that British imperialism, however mercenary its motives, was playing an historically progressive role by dissolving the traditional social and political order and bringing about a genuine social revolution.[40]

Marx also believed that imperialism was undermining the foundations of traditional Chinese society and creating there a world after its own bourgeois image, but the main concern of his articles on China was neither the historical role of Western imperialism nor the nature of traditional Chinese society. They revealed a very different strand of thought. The article "Revolution in China and Europe" considered the possible effects of the T'ai-p'ing Rebellion on the political situation in Europe. Referring to Hegel's "law of the contact of extremes," Marx began with a rather startling proposition:

Whether the "contact of extremes" be such a universal principle or not, a striking illustration of it may be seen in the effect the Chinese revolution seems likely to exercise upon the civilized world. It may seem a strange, and a very paradoxical assertion that the next uprising of the people of Europe, and their next movement for republican freedom and economy of government, may depend more on what is now passing in the Celestial Empire — the very opposite of Europe — than on any other political cause that now exists . . . Now, England having brought about the revolution in China, the question is how that revolution will in time react on England, and through England on Europe.[41]

The source of Marx's hope that events in China would influence the political situation in Europe was his expectation that the T'ai-p'ing Rebellion would diminish the China trade and thus intensify what he thought was the beginning of a general European economic crisis. "It may safely be augured," he wrote, "that the Chinese revolution will throw the spark into the overloaded mine of the present industrial system and cause the explosion of the long-prepared general crisis, which, spreading abroad, will be closely followed by political revolutions on the continent." Marx went on to muse over the possibility of the "curious spectacle" of "China sending disorder into the Western world while the Western Powers, by English, French, and American war steamers, are conveying 'order' to Shanghai, Nanking, and the mouths of the Great Canal." [42]

Besides suggesting the notion that a "spark" from the East might ignite a revolutionary conflagration in the West, Marx's articles on China were noteworthy for their strongly anti-imperialist tone. He viewed the relations between China and the Western powers from a highly legalistic and moralistic standpoint rather than in terms of the objectively "progressive" role of imperialism that had characterized his writings on India. He accused the British of "piratical hostilities" and of waging an "unrighteous war" (the Second Anglo-Chinese War) in which "the unoffending citizens and peaceful tradesmen of Canton have been slaughtered, their habitations battered to the ground and the claims of humanity violated." [43] Moreover, in an article actually written by Engels but approved by Marx and published under his name, the possibility was suggested that the Chinese might wage a "national war" against the English invaders, and the T'ai-p'ing Rebellion was described as "a popular war for the maintenance of Chinese nationality." [44]

The articles on China were in part the product of particular circumstances, especially Marx's bitter hostility to the foreign policy of Palmerston, which he thought was playing into the hands of czarist expansionism. But they also marked the beginning of a tendency to look beyond Western Europe for revolutionary stimuli — a tendency that reappeared in the 1870's in Marx's interest in the possibility of a revolution in Russia. They also foreshadowed important changes in his views on the entire question of colonialism and imperialism, which were formalized in a radical revision of his position on the "Irish question" in 1869: "For a long time I believed that it would be possible to overthrow the Irish regime by English working class ascendancy. I always expressed this view in the *New York Tribune*. Deep study has now convinced me of the opposite. The English working class will never accomplish anything before it has got rid of Ireland. The lever must be applied in Ireland. That is why the Irish question is so important for the social movement in general." [45] Marx also had second thoughts about the progressive role of the British colonization of India. In 1881 he wrote: "As concerns East India, for example, everyone . . . knows only too well that there the suppression of the communal ownership of land was only an act of English vandalism, which has brought not an advance, but a setback to the native peoples." [46]

Li Ta-chao was the first Chinese to recognize and to utilize this anti-imperialist strain in Marx. He had originally come across Marx's article "Revolution in China and Europe" as a reprint in an American socialist periodical. He immediately set about to translate it into Chinese and eventually published it, early in 1926, in the Peking Communist magazine *Cheng-chih sheng-huo* (Political life). Although Marx's views on China were fragmentary and his articles on China were of limited theoretical significance, they seemed to Li to offer authoritative support for his own interpretation of the role of China in the world revolution. "If we want a clear Marxist analysis of China's present national revolutionary movement," Li wrote in the introduction to his translation, "the best thing that we can do is to read Marx's articles concerning the Chinese revolution of his time." [47] Conveniently ignoring the fact that the "Chinese revolution" Marx wrote of was bourgeois rather than socialist, Li was particularly drawn to Marx's suggestion that China might provide the stimulus for revolution in Europe. This point was repeatedly emphasized in his concluding comments to the translation:

After reading this article by Marx we ought very clearly to recognize that in both theory and fact the Chinese revolution is part of the world revolution . . . The pressure of English imperialism on China has created the Chinese revolution, and the Chinese revolution has in turn influenced England and, through England, Europe, and thus has a role in the world revolution. The T'ai-p'ing Revolution, which occurred during Marx's lifetime, was like this, and today the explosion of the whole Chinese nation in the era of the anti-imperialist movement is also like this, and it will be like this until the world revolution is completed. The manifestation of [China's] role is daily becoming more obvious, and the tendency for the Chinese revolution to urge on the world revolution is increasing day by day. Since the revolution of the T'ai-p'ings the main tide of the Chinese national revolutionary movement has generally been pushing forward unceasingly. The imperialist oppression of the Chinese nation has intensified day by day, and therefore the Chinese national revolutionary movement has day by day become stronger . . . because the only reply to oppression is resistance, and the only response to the "order" with which they repress us is for us to resist their violence, and this means revolution. According to the courtesy of "gifts ought to be exchanged," disorder should be transported [from China] to Europe and all the imperialist states. If the imperialists intervene in the movement of the Chinese masses, then, as Marx so well put it, this will only cause the Chinese revolutionary movement to become increasingly militant and hasten to end the commercial enterprises of the powers in China. It has been seventy-three years since Marx wrote this article. Since then the Chinese revolutionary movement has day by day grown broader and the crisis of Europe has grown ever more severe. In the last two years the development of the proletarian political parties of China and England has had the character of "traveling 1000 *li* in one day," and in the competition of all the national proletarian movements of the world they have progressed the most. Now at the same time that the Chinese national revolutionary movement has spread throughout the whole country, the English workers have called an unprecedented strike of a million men . . . is this not the phenomenon of China returning [to the West] the violence that has been brought to us by the "order" imposed by the armies and warships of the English bourgeoisie? Is not the Chinese revolution the spark that will set off the land mine already planted in the overproduction of the European economic system? Is this not about to produce a gigantic explosion? In the revolution that is imminent, this historic fact will be proved.[48]

This vision, which attributed future revolutionary events in Europe to a revolutionary stimulus emanating from China, revealed how little Li's basic revolutionary perspectives had changed since the day he originally proclaimed his adherence to the Bolshevik cause. In 1918 he had indicated that China had a distinctive and essential contribution to make to the world-wide revolutionary tide that he believed was sweeping the world. Now he interpreted the role of the Chinese national revolution in the same fashion. In promoting the notion of national revolution and in supporting the united front with the Kuomintang, Li still considered the world revolution to be imminent and maintained the belief that China had a very special and creative role to play in this process of universal transformation.

It is significant that in referring to the Chinese revolution, Li used only the expression "national revolution," not "bourgeois-democratic revolution," both of which appeared interchangeably in the writings of other Chinese Communists during this period. From a strictly Marxist standpoint, a national revolution could not be anything but bourgeois-democratic in nature. Lenin had as much as admitted that the expression "national revolution" had been invented as a synonym for the bourgeois-democratic phase in order to satisfy the nationalist impulses of potential Asian allies. "There need not be the slightest doubt," Lenin wrote in 1920, "that every national movement can only be a bourgeois-democratic movement, for the overwhelming mass of the population in backward countries consists of peasants who represent bourgeois-capitalist relationships."[49]

Li was reluctant to designate the Chinese revolutionary movement as "bourgeois-democratic" because he never really accepted the possibility of a bourgeois-democratic phase for either the economic or political evolution of China. If the national revolution was not bourgeois-democratic, what in fact was its class character? On one occasion at least, in 1924, Li asserted that "only the proletariat is the vanguard of the national revolution." [50] Yet the meaning of this statement is nebulous in view of his assumption that China was a "proletarian nation." Li believed that the national revolution was proletarian in character and socialist in aspirations not because of the role of the actual proletariat or even because of the role of the Communist party as the incarnation of proletarian consciousness. Indeed, Li had attributed a proletarian "class nature" to the T'ai-p'ing Rebellion [51] although he knew very well that it had been a movement of peasants more than half a century before the birth of the Chinese Communist party. In describing the revolutionary process in China, Li was less interested in the actual class composition of the movement than in its inherent tendencies and subjective aims. The "national revolution" was "proletarian" in nature because he was convinced that its aims and tendencies reflected the elemental forces of the Chinese nation in revolt against the capitalist-imperialist world order.

The views on the subject of national revolution held by Ch'en Tu-hsiu, who was the leader of the party, reflected a very different ideological orientation in the early Chinese Communist movement. Although Ch'en was at first bitterly opposed to the Comintern proposal for a united front with the Kuomintang, he reconciled himself to it partly in deference to the demands of the Comintern and partly because the prospects for a strong proletarian movement seemed so dim after the "February Seventh" incident of 1923. Faced with external Comintern pressures and an internal situation that severely restricted the scope of Communist activities, Ch'en accepted the united front policy as the only practical alternative. [52]

But in justifying this policy, Ch'en adopted an essentially deterministic view of the Chinese revolutionary process and fell back upon orthodox Marxist formulas. There were, Ch'en declared, only two contemporary types of revolution — the bourgeois-democratic and the proletarian socialist. Although the former took a special national form in colonial and semicolonial countries, it was nevertheless a discrete political phase based upon objective economic developments and identified with the specific social class interests of the native bourgeoisie. Thus, the development of industry would impel the Chinese bourgeoisie to carry out the democratic revolution. Revolution, he emphasized, was produced not by subjective desires but by objective economic and social conditions.[53]

As for the proletarian revolution, it was a separate and, for China, a still distant stage of political development that would result from the further evolution of the same forces that were preparing the bourgeois-democratic revolution: "The objective strength of the proletariat expands with the expansion of the bourgeoisie [and thus] if the bourgeoisie of the colonial and semicolonial areas are unable to form a successful revolutionary force, there is no point in talking about the proletariat." From this new point of view Ch'en no longer saw the growth of capitalism in China as undesirable. "The economically and culturally backward countries," he asserted, "are not injured by the development of capitalism but rather by the lack of capitalist development."[54]

All this of course was good orthodox Marxism, and on the basis of these orthodox formulations Ch'en finally accepted the program of a national revolution to be carried out in alliance with the Kuomintang. But his acceptance was conditioned by his insistence that Communist collaboration with the Kuomintang should take the form of an alliance between two separate political parties representing the differing interests of two distinct social classes. He never fully reconciled himself to the notion that the Kuomintang was a supra-class political entity in which Communists were to participate as individual members. The proletariat, he believed, could and should cooperate with the bourgeoisie in carrying out the national revolution because the Chinese proletariat was still too small and immature to constitute an independent revolutionary force and because it was in the interests of both classes to oppose foreign imperialism. But the Communist party should maintain its class identity as the party of the proletariat until the day that the proletariat became sufficiently strong to carry out its own revolution. In 1923 that day still appeared to Ch'en to be far off: "The class consciousness of the working class rises with the development and differentiation of production. It cannot be produced by the human will." In the meantime there were to be no illusions about the real character of the national revolutionary movement. "The victory of the national revolution," Ch'en declared, "is naturally the victory of the bourgeoisie."[55]

The profoundly different interpretations of the concept of national revolution put forward by Ch'en Tu-hsiu and Li Ta-chao reflected the two opposing poles around which the early Chinese Communist movement tended to gravitate. Whereas Ch'en's qualified acceptance of the alliance with the Kuomintang grew out of his pessimistic evaluation of the prospects for a socialist revolution in China, Li's acceptance derived from his chiliastic faith in an imminent, universal, socialist transformation in which China was to be centrally involved. In accepting the policy of a national revolution, Ch'en also accepted the likelihood of a perhaps prolonged phase of capitalist development, but Li assumed that the forces of revolution within Chinese society, no matter what the actual social class composition of the revolutionary movement, inherently tended to be socialist in nature. Ch'en's loss of confidence in the immediate revolutionary capacities of the tiny Chinese proletariat was replaced by a newly-found Marxist confidence in the determining forces of history; Li continued to place his faith in the revolutionary will of men rather than in the workings of objective social forces. Ch'en was inclined to employ the orthodox formulas of the Marxist canon to defend his new, more patient view of the Chinese revolutionary process; Li drew upon the nondeterministic strains in Marx to support the radical characteristics he attributed to the Chinese national revolution. For Li, the Chinese revolution possessed what might properly be called a "permanent" character; it was a continuous revolutionary process proceeding inevitably in a straight line towards socialism, and he was convinced that it was intimately related to — even essential to — the world revolution. In this interpretation of the alliance with the Kuomintang, revolutionary voluntarism and Chinese nationalism met on common grounds.

If Ch'en Tu-hsiu's view of the Chinese revolutionary process tended to stray from Lenin's concepts in a Menshevik direction, Li Ta-chao strayed even further in the opposite direction. Although Leninist theory allowed for the possibility of a bourgeois-democratic revolution "growing over" to the socialist phase under certain conditions, it could hardly sanction a concept of revolution in which the stages of social and political development were totally blurred and the actual class composition of the revolutionary movement virtually ignored. More important, the Leninist concept of the transition from the bourgeois-democratic to the socialist phase of revolution assumed that as the revolution grew more radical, its social base would narrow and the direction of the revolutionary process would come increasingly into the hands of the proletariat or its political representatives. But as Li Ta-chao perceived it, the Chinese national revolution was proceeding in precisely the opposite fashion. It was the actual broadening of the national revolutionary movement and the growing participation of wider elements of Chinese society in the anti-imperialist struggle that would bring the movement closer to socialism and to unification with the forces of international revolution. The heart of their difference was that whereas Lenin looked to the organized proletarian consciousness of the Communist party to lead and discipline this phase of the revolutionary process, Li looked more to the inherent proletarian consciousness of the Chinese nation.

In Li's conception of the Chinese national revolution the Communist alliance with the Kuomintang was a logical but not an essential tactical element. Clearly, there was an urgent need for an organization capable of bringing together the elemental forces of the Chinese nation that were to rise up and destroy foreign imperialism and its Chinese warlord hirelings, but Li had no fixed ideas about what form the organizational framework should take. He genuinely admired Sun Yat-sen, but he was by no means uncritical of the Kuomintang. In 1923 he complained that the Kuomintang had not yet acquired the character of a national party for it still reflected too greatly its overseas Chinese origins and its original Cantonese composition; moreover, it failed to appreciate the true significance of the mass movement. Yet despite these defects, the Kuomintang seemed to offer the most promising organizational means to carry out the national revolution. The still tiny Communist party was itself clearly incapable of performing so gigantic a task, and there were no other actual or potential anti-imperialist political organizations of any consequence. Thus, Li called for transforming the Kuomintang into a "universal national" (*p'u-pien ch'üan-kuo*) organization truly capable of becoming the agency of the national revolutionary movement.[56] As long as he held to the hope that the Kuomintang might indeed become such an organization, he remained an ardent supporter of the policy of collaboration.

CHAPTER XI   PEASANT REVOLUTION

ALTHOUGH Li Ta-chao was perhaps the foremost Chinese Communist advocate of the alliance with the Kuomintang, he was also, ironically, one of the first to abandon it. His disenchantment with the policy of collaboration was in part the product of his own political miscalculations, for he had attributed to the national revolution aims more radical than it proved able to bear. But the immediate cause of Li's abandonment of collaboration grew out of the peculiarities of the political situation in North China.

The repressive control over much of North China and the Peking area exercised by the reactionary Peiyang warlord clique in the 1920's not only hindered the activities of the Communist party but also inhibited the growth of the Kuomintang in the northern areas, particularly those elements of the Kuomintang that were most disposed to cooperate with the Communists. The Kuomintang-Communist alliance had hardly been formally ratified when a right-wing faction unalterably opposed to collaboration with the Communists moved to gain ascendancy in the Peking Kuomintang organization. The Communists in North China were able to implement the alliance only with a minority left-wing Kuomintang faction which, unlike the Kuomintang in the South, could claim neither mass support nor military power.

The weakness of the Peking Communist organization itself undoubtedly contributed to the failure of the alliance. The suppression of the Peking-Hankow railroad workers' strike in February 1923 had thrown the affairs of the northern branch of the party into considerable disarray, from which it never fully recovered. Not only had it lost its main proletarian base, but the party organization was subject to severe, even though sporadic, police suppression. Li Ta-chao himself spent much of the final four years of his life in flight or hiding from the warlord-controlled Peking authorities. For example, when Li returned to Peking from Canton after attending the first National Congress of the Kuomintang in January 1924, the government issued a formal order for his arrest. He was forced to flee to Chang-li-wu-feng, a mountain retreat in the northeast corner of Hopei about 150 miles from Peking, where he hid in a Buddhist temple for three weeks. Accompanied by his eldest daughter, Hsing-hua, Li is said to have spent a part of this time writing poetry in the fashion of a traditional Confucian scholar in retreat.[1] When he returned to the capital, his position was still highly precarious. In June he secretly left for Moscow as leader of the Chinese delegation to the Fifth Comintern Congress. Posing as a merchant, he traveled across Manchuria to the Soviet border by train and horsecart.[2] Li remained in Russia for almost six months, during which time he wrote a highly laudatory account of Soviet life, which was published in the Shanghai newspaper *Kuo-min jih-pao*.[3]

When Li Ta-chao once again returned to Peking in December 1924, the political climate had improved considerably. In October, Feng Yü-hsiang, a warlord who was soon to prove receptive to Soviet offers of military aid, had occupied Peking, deposed Ts'ao K'un, the president of the republic, and installed a more moderate government under Tuan Ch'i-jui.[4] Primarily because of the presence of Feng Yü-hsiang's "National Army," the Communist movement in Peking experienced a brief revival in 1925. But even though repressive police measures against the Communists had ceased for the time being, the scope of party activities was severely restricted by other circumstances. In contrast to South and Central China, where a militant urban working-class movement assumed considerable proportions following the killing of twelve student demonstrators by British-led police in Shanghai in the "May Thirtieth" incident of 1925, in the North there were few signs of proletarian political activity. Moreover, in late 1925 and early 1926, at the very time the Kuomintang-Communist alliance in the South was reaching the peak of its power and tending in more radical directions, the effectiveness of the alliance in the North was being seriously vitiated by the increasing control of the conservative and strongly anti-Communist "Western Hills" faction over the Peking Kuomintang organization.

Li Ta-chao's activities in 1925 reflected these weaknesses of the Communist movement in the North. Although his writings attributed ever more radical aims to the national revolution, and he continued to cultivate the party's tiny proletarian following in Peking and to send party members to work in the peasant movement, he was for the most part occupied with less revolutionary matters. As a member of the central executive committee of the Kuomintang, he was concerned with national Kuomintang affairs and with Sun Yat-sen's efforts to reunify China through the convocation of a national assembly.[5] He further attempted to maintain a working relationship between the Communists and whatever left-wing Kuomintang elements were to be found in Peking. He also served as a principal intermediary between Feng Yü-hsiang and Leo Karakhan, the Soviet envoy to the Peking government.[6]

The contrast between Li's radical theory and his rather benign practice did not last for long. With the failure of Sun's mission to Peking in January 1925, the subsequent death of Sun in March, and the erosion of Feng Yü-hsiang's power in the latter part of the year, the Communist position in Peking once again became highly precarious. With the implicit support of Feng's National Army, the Tuan Ch'i-jui government moved in an anti-Kuomintang and anti-Communist direction, and Communist activities were again subject to government repression.[7] Moreover, the death of Sun had been the signal for right-wing elements fully to assert their dominance over the Peking Kuomintang organization. By late 1925 the right wing was openly demanding the termination of the united front with the Communists. According to Kuomintang accounts, Li Ta-chao was actually "expelled" from the central executive committee of the Kuomintang at a meeting organized by the right-wing faction in Peking in late 1925.[8] It was thus with good reason that the Peking Communist organization in November 1925 reported to party headquarters in Shanghai (from which vantage point the alliance then appeared to be moving from one success to another) that "a very thick reactionary atmosphere has prevailed in the Kuomintang in the North in the last few months."[9]

Confronted with the virtual collapse of the alliance with the Kuomintang, the lack of any substantial proletarian following, and a hostile warlord-controlled government, the Communist movement in the North by the end of 1925 was tending to return to the point of its origin — it was becoming more and more confined to the students and ex-students of Peking University. What Li Ta-chao had so greatly feared in the early months of 1919 — the isolation of the radical intelligentsia from Chinese society — again loomed as a major danger. And as in 1919, his response to this danger was to look to the countryside and the forces of peasant revolt to bridge the gap between the intellectuals and the people.

"Land and the Peasants"

Li Ta-chao's first attempt to find in the forces of agrarian revolution a new mass base of support for the Communist movement appeared in an article entitled "Land and the Peasants," which was published in the Peking Communist periodical *Cheng-chih sheng-huo* (Political life) in six parts between December 30, 1925, and February 3, 1926.[10] Almost seven years had passed since the early phase of Li's Marxist career when he had identified the liberation of China with the liberation of the Chinese peasantry and had urged young Chinese intellectuals to "go to the villages." During those seven years Li had commented little about the role of the peasantry in the revolution. It may be argued that a peasant orientation was implicit in the ideological framework from which he viewed the Chinese revolutionary process. In light of the fact that China was an overwhelmingly peasant nation, Li's nationalist-Populist concept of the Chinese nation as a fundamentally united "proletarian" entity in revolt against world capitalism may indeed have implied that the peasantry was to play a greater role in the national revolution than Marxist-Leninist orthodoxy could have allowed. Moreover, the persistently strong antiurban bias that appeared even in references to the Chinese proletariat was no doubt indicative of Li's personal sympathy for rural life and the aspirations of the Chinese peasantry.

Yet the few explicit comments he made on the peasant question between 1920 and 1925 did not depart from the orthodox Communist viewpoint. In tracing the history of the Russian Revolution, Li noted in 1921 that "practically none of the peasants participated in the revolutionary movement. The peasants actually formed a majority of the country's population and certainly were not satisfied with their position, [but] their one hope was to protect their rights of landownership, and they did not look to political reform. They hated the landlords and the officials but they did not hate the emperor. Therefore, the responsibility for the revolution . . . fell upon the shoulders of a minority of people." [11] In January 1923 he again suggested that peasants were of dubious value to the revolutionary cause because "they are unwilling to sacrifice the wealth they may have obtained." [12]

It is impossible to know whether these transitory remarks were truly reflective of the attitudes Li then held or whether he was simply repeating the customary Marxist doubts about the revolutionary capacities of the peasantry. It is interesting that on neither of these two occasions did Li refer specifically to Chinese peasants. On the first occasion he referred to the role of the peasantry in the Russian Revolution, and on the second he spoke of peasants in general in the course of an exposition óf Marxist economic theory. In any event, whatever doubts Li may have had about the potentialities of peasant revolution in China were completely laid aside by the end of 1925. In "Land and the Peasants" he returned to and elaborated his Populist-inspired views of 1919.

In comparison with the more radical call for agrarian revolution that Li was to make later in 1926, "Land and the Peasants" was written in a relatively moderate spirit. Much of it was devoted to an historical survey of the movement for the "equalization of land ownership" since the late Chou era and to a statistical analysis of contemporary conditions of land tenure and peasant livelihood. As in many of his other writings of this period, Li attached particular significance to the T'ai-p'ing Rebellion, which, he emphasized, was the opening of the era of the modern peasant revolutionary movement. He attributed the intensity of the modern agrarian crisis not only to imperialism and militarism but also to the defeat of the T'ai-p'ings and the failure of the regimes under the republic to implement Sun Yat-sen's program for the "equalization of land ownership and the control of capital." Thus, the solution of the agrarian crisis was dependent on "the forces of the contemporary Chinese workers' and peasants' revolution" and should be carried out under the slogan of "land to the peasants who till it." [13]

When he wrote "Land and the Peasants," Li was still thinking primarily in terms of the role of agrarian revolution in strengthening the national government at Canton and completing the national revolution. "If the great peasant masses of China are able to organize together and participate in the national revolution," he predicted, "the success of the Chinese national revolution is not far off." However, there were several indications that he was already beginning to depart both from the limitations imposed by the alliance with the Kuomintang and from the orthodox Communist evaluation of the revolutionary capacities of the peasantry. As Mao Tse-tung was to do more than a year later in February 1927 in his celebrated "Report of an Investigation into the Peasant Movement in Hunan," Li did not hesitate to assign to the peasantry the major role in the Chinese revolutionary process: "In economically backward and semicolonial China, the peasantry constitutes more than seventy per cent of the population; among the whole population they occupy the principal position, and agriculture is still the basis of the national economy. Therefore, when we estimate the forces of the revolution, we must emphasize that the peasantry is the important part." [14]

If the participation of the peasantry was thus vital to the success of the revolution, how were the peasants to be organized, and how was the agrarian revolution to proceed? First, Li suggested that a class struggle within the village was necessary: "For a long time there have been peasant groups within the villages [but] most of these groups [consist of] the propertied village aristocracy; all [such groups] are managed by the village gentry and simply serve to protect the class interests of the propertied classes of the village. Not only do [they] have no concern for the poor peasants, but they are really used to exploit the poor peasants." An agrarian revolution was impossible without "peasant associations that are organized by the poor peasants, tenants, and agricultural wage laborers themselves [for] only the peasant associations organized by the peasants themselves are able to protect their class interests." [15]

Although Communists were to work in the peasant movement and assist in organizing such associations, Li's eyes were mainly focused on the organizations that the peasants had created spontaneously without outside assistance. He noted that in the northern provinces the peasants instinctively felt that "it was necessary to organize a peasants' self-protection army" in order to resist the "disorders of warlordism and banditry created by the imperialists." The peasants of the provinces of Hopei, Jehol, Shantung, and Honan

239

had created a "citizens' militia movement" to oppose the rule of the Feng-t'ien warlords; and after the collapse of the Feng clique "the citizens' militia movement has at once flourished everywhere." In addition to these new organizations, Li approvingly noted, there had been a revival of armed activity among such traditional peasant groups as the Ko-lao-hui (Society of elder brothers) and the Hung-chiang-hui (Red spear society).[16]

Since the peasants thus appeared to be rising spontaneously and creating their own organizations, what was the role of the Communists in the agrarian revolution? Li answered in the following manner:

The young revolutionary comrades ought to bring [the armed peasant groups] together by going to the villages to help the peasants to improve their organizations and to resist the oppression from which they suffer. Following rural organizational work they ought to direct their attention to the problem of raising the cultural [level] of the countryside. The comrades who go to the villages ought to know how to utilize the period of agricultural slack, especially the month of the New Year according to the old calendar, to spread all kinds of general knowledge and revolutionary education. For this work to produce the most effective results, it is necessary to prepare pictures, simple songs, and magazines. It is also necessary to organize the village schools and open supplementary classes for the peasants.[17]

Li Ta-chao was not the only Chinese Communist who had become interested in the revolutionary potentialities of the peasantry by 1925. Early in that year Mao Tse-tung, his former assistant at the Peking University Library, spent several months organizing peasant associations in his native province of Hunan. And long before Mao's first venture into the countryside another young Communist, P'eng P'ai, had begun organizational efforts among the peasantry of Kwangtung province. By the time Li wrote "Land and the Peasants," the Kwangtung movement could already claim tangible successes.[18]

Nor were other leading Communists unconcerned with the peasant question. After 1922 the new Comintern evaluation of the Chinese revolution as "bourgeois-democratic" required that at least theoretical consideration be given to the role of the peasantry in the revolution. By 1926 the matter was no longer merely theoretical. As a result of the largely spontaneous revolutionary upsurge in the countryside throughout much of China, the peasant question suddenly intruded upon Communist strategic calculations and became centrally involved in the factional disputes developing in the party. Although all Chinese Communists were agreed that the peasants had some role to play in the Chinese revolutionary process, they differed profoundly on what that role was to be.

Ch'en Tu-hsiu and Ch'ü Ch'iu-pai on the Peasantry

The major internal struggle to emerge openly within the Chinese Communist party before the debacle of April 1927 concerned the opposition of Ch'ü Ch'iu-pai to the Ch'en Tu-hsiu leadership.[19] One ideological question involved in this factional dispute was the role of the peasantry in the Chinese revolution. The views of Ch'en and Ch'ü on the peasant question remained dominant (although by no means universal) in Chinese Communist ranks during Li Ta-chao's lifetime and were reflected in the party's official policies.

As already noted, Ch'en Tu-hsiu's conversion to Marxism was based on an explicit and complete rejection of Chinese traditions, in striking contrast to Li Ta-chao's conversion. The ignorance and backwardness of traditional China that Ch'en so deplored were nowhere more apparent than among the tradition-bound peasantry. However much he may have sympathized with the lot of the peasant masses, he could not conceive that the most backward element of society could play a significant role in the modernization of China. In 1919 nothing could have seemed to him less relevant to China's needs than Li Ta-chao's proposal for the intellectuals to "go to the villages." When in 1920 Ch'en embraced Marxism, he accepted it as the most advanced product of modern Western civilization; like most European Marxists, he assumed that the backward countryside would follow the political lead of the progressive cities. The urban proletariat and the urban bourgeoisie were to be the main antagonists in the struggle that would determine China's future.

In July 1923, when the newly imposed Comintern strategy demanded that a place be provided for the peasantry in the bourgeois-democratic revolution, Ch'en was forced to acknowldege half-heartedly that revolutionaries in the economically backward countries "cannot disregard the strength of the peasantry." But he warned that in a country like China, where the majority of peasants owned their own land, it would not be easy to initiate a revolutionary movement in the countryside.[20] In the months that followed, Ch'en's doubts about the revolutionary potentialities of the peasantry increased. In assessing the role of class forces in national revolutions in colonial and semicolonial lands, he noted, "the strength of the bourgeoisie is concentrated compared to that of the peasantry." He acknowledged that such revolutions must obtain peasant support to become mass movements, but he was less than sanguine about that possibility: "The peasants are scattered and their forces are not easy to concentrate, their culture is low, their desires in life are simple, and they easily tend toward conservatism . . . These environmental factors make it difficult for the peasants to participate in the revolutionary movement." He noted that "among the peasants the concept of private possession is extremely strong" and therefore it was useless to think of winning their support for a socialist revolution since it "fundamentally clashes with their interests." Even the landless tenants "are only semi-proletarians; they oppose the landlords but they are unable to go beyond replacing the property rights of the landlords with the psychology of their own rights of property ownership. The hired agricultural laborers do belong to the proletariat, but they are few in number and not concentrated." [21]

This pessimistic assessment of the possible contributions of the peasantry to the revolution followed quite logically from Ch'en's interpretation of the nature of the Chinese revolutionary process in general. When Ch'en accepted the policy of collaboration with the Kuomintang in 1923, he also accepted the inevitability of a bourgeois-democratic revolution in which the likely victors would be the national bourgeoisie. The peasantry could participate in this phase of the revolution only as an element subordinate to political forces in the cities, and only to the extent that the demands of the agrarian movement remained confined to improvements in the immediate economic conditions of the peasants. After the success of the bourgeois-democratic revolution Ch'en anticipated a period of capitalist development of undetermined length. [22] This period would see the development of capitalist relations in the countryside and the creation of an agricultural proletariat, as well as the development of industry in the cities. Thus, the conditions for a "social revolution within the villages" would be created at the same time that the stage was being set for the urban proletarian revolution. In this final phase of the revolutionary process the agrarian revolution would once again be subordinate to political developments in the cities, for although "a Communist social revolution will, of course, want to obtain the sympathy and assistance of the peasants," it would be essential "to have a strong proletariat as the main force in order to carry out this kind of revolutionary struggle."[23] Ch'en judged the Chinese political scene by these rather orthodox Marxist standards until the disastrous year of 1927. Neither in the bourgeois-democratic phase, nor in the socialist phase, did the role of the peasantry loom large in his conception of the Chinese revolutionary process.

In view of the violence of Ch'ü Ch'iu-pai's accusations in 1927 that Ch'en Tu-hsiu had ignored the revolutionary potentialities of the peasantry, it is surprising to find that Ch'ü viewed the Chinese revolution fundamentally from the same theoretical framework as did Ch'en. In a polemic attacking the agrarian orientations of the constitutionalist Chang Shih-chao, written in 1923, Ch'ü argued that Chinese economic relations were already capitalistic in nature and that China was rapidly being transformed into "a commercial bourgeois country." "According to the logic of history," Ch'ü confidently proclaimed, China was "passing from a clan-type agrarian nation to a commercial and industrial nation." In this process the peasants could be little more than passive objects in the hands of the immutable economic laws of history. China, he predicted, "will soon not only be a nonagrarian nation [but] its political movement will be one in which bourgeois democracy and proletarian socialism advance together." He declared that it was nonsense to believe that the reformation of Chinese society could start in the agrarian sector.[24] For both Ch'en Tu-hsiu and Ch'ü Ch'iu-pai, the urban bourgeoisie and the urban proletariat were the only two social forces to be seriously taken into account.

After the remarkable and entirely unexpected growth of the peasant movement in 1925–1926, official Comintern and therefore official Chinese Communist pronouncements on the peasant question employed increasingly radical terminology. However, as Benjamin Schwartz has demonstrated, Communist policy on the peasant question was consistently subordinated to Stalin's overriding concern with preserving the alliance with the Kuomintang.[25] All seemingly radical policies were qualified by the stipulation that they be carried out under the authority of the Kuomintang, which Stalin had decreed to be the party of Chinese bourgeois-democracy and therefore the party that would have at least nominal predominance in the peasant movement.[26] This meant that the Comintern representatives and the Chinese Communist party central committee in Shanghai were as much concerned with preventing the peasant movement from taking too radical a turn and perhaps thereby undermining the united front as they were with promoting agrarian revolution.

The party central committee at its second enlarged plenum, held in Shanghai in July 1926, responded to the rising tide of peasant revolt by complaining, "the peasant movement has developed the disease of left-deviation everywhere. Either the slogans are extreme or action is excessively left-inclined."[27] In accordance with this assessment, the plenum set about to check the revolutionary and independent character of the peasant movement. Using the pretext that "our policy is not to let the peasantry become isolated," the central committee called for a united front of self-cultivating peasants, hired farmers, laborers, tenant farmers, and middle and small landlords against the "reactionary big landlords," and it called merely for the neutralization of "those big landlords who do not actively engage in oppressive activities." Pursuing this nonrevolutionary, united front policy, it declared that "it is not permissible to establish organizations of a permanent nature because it would inevitably give rise to conflict with other groups (such as landlords, *min-t'uan* [militia] and military garrisons)." The military training of peasants was to be discouraged because it was feared that "the totally disorganized and untrained peasants, once in possession of arms, could easily exceed the objective limits of action."[28]

The activities of traditional, quasi-military peasant secret societies, such as the Red Spear Societies, were looked upon with particular distrust. "In view of [the Red Spear movement's] loose organization and addiction to superstition, it cannot stand the test of battle. Furthermore it is full of destructive tendencies and lacks constructive tendencies." It was argued that "the directing power of the Red Spears Association falls easily into the hands of the local bullies, the Red Spears becoming their tools. Furthermore, since they have the strongest force, the Red Spears Associations with bandit characteristics frequently become the basic mass fighting force of the local bullies." Although the central committee grudgingly conceded that the Red Spear movement in North China was "an important anti-militarist force in the National Revolution," the resolution was distinctly calculated to leave the impression that the Red Spears were more a danger than an asset to the peasant movement. The Red Spear groups might temporarily be utilized for limited purposes, but Communists working in the peasant movement were urged secretly to gain control of the organization in order to suppress it as an independent force. Party members were warned of the basically "reactionary character" of the Red Spears and counseled that "the seizure of local political power by force is absolutely not allowed." [29]

It is, of course, always embarrassing for a Marxist-Leninist party to appear less radical than the actual mass movement, but despite the radical terminology with which the resolutions on the peasant question were embellished, it was clearly the intent of the July plenum to restrain and restrict the spontaneous forces of peasant revolution. The difficulties that this created for Communists who were actually working in the peasant movement were hinted at in the following passage of the resolutions: "We should find means to know and bring up the demands of the peasantry. When the objective situation does not allow the raising of such demands, a full explanation (to the peasants) is necessary. We should inspire them so that they will not be disheartened. We must absolutely avoid resorting to outright suppression of their demands." [30] As late as March 1927 several Comintern representatives at Shanghai quite candidly revealed the substance of the official Communist peasant policy when they reported, "the old policy of curbing the struggle in the village and applying the brakes to the peasants' movement as a whole still prevails . . . the fear of the peasants' movement has existed and still remains in the party." [31]

There is no evidence that either Ch'en Tu-hsiu or Ch'ü Ch'iu-pai raised any real objections in 1926 and the early months of 1927 to the official policy of restraining the revolutionary tendencies of the peasantry. Ch'en, it is true, had never completely reconciled himself to the united front with the Kuomintang, so that he perhaps did not share the Comintern's fear that a radical agrarian movement would undermine the policy of collaboration. Rather, Ch'en's deemphasis on the revolutionary role of the peasantry was the product of his orthodox Marxist perspectives and his desire to preserve the urban proletarian class identity of the Communist party. Nonetheless, Ch'en was fully in accord with the Comintern policy of restraining the peasant revolutionary movement, even though for a different reason.

The differences that developed between Ch'en Tu-hsiu and Ch'ü Ch'iu-pai on the peasant question may be traced to the fact that in 1927 Ch'ü sensed the possibilities of using the peasant issue to attack the leadership of Ch'en. If Ch'ü thus proved his adroitness as a student of the Comintern line, he did not prove that his conception of the nature of the Chinese revolution and his attitudes toward the peasantry were much different from those of Ch'en. Even in his attack on Ch'en in 1927 all his seemingly radical agrarian proposals were made on the assumption that they would be carried out under the direction of the "National Government" at Wuhan [32] — a limitation that vitiated whatever radicalism they contained. Ch'ü's basic opposition to a radical peasant policy persisted even when the case for such a policy had become more compelling. In 1929, when the urban working-class movement had virtually ceased to exist, Ch'ü wrote a lengthy treatise on the peasant question in which he insisted that the agrarian revolution must be led by the urban proletariat. In order to ensure that the peasant movement would come under the proper leadership, he suggested that urban workers' groups form relationships with peasant groups such as those that exist between "an elder brother and a younger brother." Furthermore, in a thinly veiled attack on Mao Tse-tung he castigated the "petty bourgeois populists within the party" who had abandoned the proletariat.[33]

In short, Ch'ü Ch'iu-pai was little more disposed than was Ch'en Tu-hsiu to allow the peasantry more than a subordinate place in the revolutionary process. Both looked to the cities to supply the real impetus and leadership for the Chinese revolution. In this respect they both reflected and molded the attitudes of the early Chinese converts to Marxism, as well as the official policies of the Chinese Communist party in the period before the ascendancy of Mao Tse-tung.

"The Red Spear Societies of Shantung, Honan, and Shensi"

Although a member of the central committee, Li Ta-chao was not present when the second enlarged plenum met in July 1926 and issued the party's official pronouncements on the peasant movement.

He was then confined to the Soviet embassy compound in Peking, where he had taken refuge four months before to avoid arrest. Li's flight to the Soviet embassy came as the culmination of the deteriorating political situation in Peking. The growing tension between the Communists and the Tuan Ch'i-jui government in the latter months of 1925, Feng Yü-hsiang's retirement from Peking in January 1926, and the implicit support that Feng's army, the first Kuominchün, offered to the increasingly reactionary policies pursued by Tuan, led eventually to an open clash between the Communists and the Peking regime.[34] On March 17, 1926, representatives of various Communist and left-wing Kuomintang organizations petitioned the government to reject an ultimatum that had been presented by the Boxer Protocol powers for the removal of Kuominchün artillery at a harbor near Tientsin.[35] The Tuan government, which was moving to accept the ultimatum, dispatched troops to disperse the petitioners, several of whom were wounded in the encounter. On the next day Communist and left-wing Kuomintang leaders organized a mass demonstration at the T'ien-an men (Gate of Heavenly Peace) to protest the government's action. When the demonstrators (most of whom were students) marched on government offices, they were brutally attacked by troops and more than forty were killed. Li Ta-chao, who personally took part in the demonstration, suffered minor head wounds and barely managed to elude the grasp of pursuing soldiers.[36]

As part of the general political repression that followed what came to be known as the "March Eighteenth Massacre," the Tuan government ordered the arrest of the leaders of the demonstration, including Li Ta-chao. Many leading Peking Communists as well as some left-wing Kuomintang leaders fled to the south. Li, however, elected to remain in Peking[37] and found sanctuary in the Soviet embassy. Within the embassy compound he was provided a small house, where he lived with his wife and children for most of the final year of his life. From there, it is said, he continued as best he could to direct the now completely clandestine activities of the remnants of the Peking Communist organization.[38]

The demonstration of March 18, 1926, was the last significant effort of the Kuomintang-Communist united front in North China. The left wing of the Kuomintang in the North virtually ceased to exist after the March Eighteenth Massacre, and the Communist organization was in shambles. Amid these disasters there appeared only one hopeful sign — the growing militancy of the agrarian revolution. Although the more highly organized peasant movement in South and Central China is better known, equally vigorous forces of peasant revolt had burst forth in the northern provinces in 1925. In the South the forces of peasant revolution were harnessed to the peasants' associations, which originally had been organized by members of the Communist Youth Corps as early as 1922 and which remained mostly under Communist influence. Communists also participated in the peasant movement in the northern provinces — in fact, Li Ta-chao had sent Communist cadres to the countryside in 1925 [39] — but the northern movement took on a more spontaneous character because the main organizational forms were provided by the traditional peasant secret societies rather than by the Communist-led peasant associations.

Li Ta-chao had already turned his attention to this emerging peasant movement by the end of 1925, and after the disaster of March 1926 his revolutionary hopes rested entirely upon the forces of peasant revolt. Sometime in the summer of 1926 Li expressed these hopes in the last of his published political writings, an article entitled "The Red Spear Societies of Shantung, Honan, and Shensi." [40] In it he set forth his views on the course he believed the Chinese revolution should follow. It was written in a much more radical spirit than was his essay "Land and the Peasants," which had appeared about six months earlier. In the earlier article he had been concerned with the role of the peasant movement in strengthening the national government at Canton; in this he was drawn wholly to the spontaneous forces of peasant revolution. He had earlier called for the establishment of peasants' associations such as those that had been organized in the southern and central provinces; now his eyes were completely focused upon the possibility of an elemental mass uprising of the peasantry through the medium of the most militant of the existing peasant groups in the northern provinces — the armed peasant secret societies. [41]

Li's article of 1926 was permeated by the feeling that the peasantry itself was capable of carrying out the objectives of the revolution. The revolutionary ferment in the countryside, Li declared, "proves that the Chinese peasants have already become awakened and know that they can rely only upon their own combined strength to liberate themselves from the disorders . . . that have been created by imperialism and militarism . . . In this kind of peasant movement there is formed a gigantic force." Li's enthusiasm was quite candidly based upon the use of military power. "The fact that the Red Spear Societies are adopting new and modern forms of weapons," he predicted, "will open a new era in the history of the armed self-defence movement of the Chinese peasantry and can be regarded as a great advance in the Chinese peasant movement." He was confident that the armed peasant societies alone could rid China not only of the curse of warlordism but of imperialism as well, since the latter thrived on the political disunity of China. "The Honan Red Spear Society can destroy the warlord forces of the Second National Army, and the Shensi Red Spear Society can destroy the warlord forces of Liu Chen-hua." [42] The major obstacle to the military victory of the peasant revolutionaries was the disunity of the peasantry and the utilization of certain of the armed peasant groups by warlords; but "a united peasantry, if it protects its class interests, can defeat all the warlords." [43]

To achieve a united peasantry, Li argued, it was necessary to appeal to the class loyalties of those peasants who were serving in warlord armies. Such an appeal would not fall on deaf ears for "the localistic concepts of the peasants contain elements of class consciousness, and if the peasants have not forgotten their localities, they will not forget their class; even the peasants who are in the armies still have not completely broken off relations with their class." Thus, the peasant movement "not only can engage in class struggle to defeat the troops of the warlords, but can also employ its class strength to summon the peasants who are still in the warlord camp to return to their native places and protect their communities. Not only will this increase [the number of] able-bodied men in the villages; it will also destroy the power of the warlords." [44]

Nor were the potentialities of the peasant movement confined to a military victory over warlordism for the peasants themselves were capable of taking charge of administrative and social functions. In a brief but intriguing passage that suggested the possibility that the armed peasant societies might form the nuclei of new organs of political power, Li noted:

The townships of Wen Shang and Ning Yang in Shantung province were occupied by the Red Spear Societies for seven months, and in these places they controlled all of the temples, schools, and public organs. All of the food they ate they had brought themselves, and they did not cause the slightest bit of trouble for the people. The Red Spear Society of Loyang, at the time that Feng Yü-tung was garrison commander, assumed the responsibility for keeping order in the streets, suppressing bandits, and protecting travelers outside of the city walls. The places occupied by the Red Spear Societies, moreover, were especially peaceful.[45]

If the peasants were thus spontaneously capable of such substantial revolutionary initiative, what was the role of the Communist party in the peasant movement and what was the relationship between the agrarian revolution and political developments in the cities? It should again be noted that throughout this essay Li repeatedly insisted that the peasant revolution was a movement of the peasants themselves. The Chinese peasants, he asserted, could not look for "saviors" from the outside; they must understand that "they can save themselves only if they themselves rise up in revolution." At one point Li suggested the following battle cry to guide the revolutionary activities of the peasants:

> There has never been a savior.
> Neither the gods nor the emperors.
> Who can liberate us if not ourselves?
> We can only depend upon ourselves to save ourselves.[46]

But if the peasants had the capacity to liberate themselves, the Communists were the ones to make them fully conscious of this fact. The Communists were to counteract the passivity resulting from the peasants' traditional faith in the arrival of a "true ruler" (*chen chu*) by making the peasants aware that they possessed overwhelming power when they organized in mass political action.

There were other traditional "defects" in the peasant movement that the Communists were to correct. One was rural antiforeignism, which was to be transformed into revolutionary nationalism. Antiforeign sentiments, Li noted, were particularly strong in the Red Spear Societies and were basically "an expression of the opposition of the peasants to imperialism because they feel that since the foreigners came to China, China has suffered insecurity and disorder, which has brought difficulties and hardships to the peasants. They think [these hardships are due to] the foreigners rather than to imperialism . . . we ought to provide them with a correct understanding so that they will know the nature of imperialism and transfer their hatred to imperialism, which is oppressing and exploiting the Chinese peasantry." Such an understanding would eliminate the "narrow racial views" of the peasants and broaden their perspectives so that they would know that "the revolutionary peasant masses of the whole world are their friends." [47]

The superstitions of the countryside inhibiting the adoption of modern weapons was another defect the Communists were to combat. However, this problem the peasants were in large measure solving themselves since they had already learned through bitter experience that bamboo poles, swords, Confucian signboards, and images of gods were no match for guns. Moreover, Li observed that peasants who had learned to use modern weapons while serving in warlord armies were returning to their homes and introducing these new weapons among the villagers.

The major obstacle to the advance of the peasant revolution was the existence of village, local, and provincial loyalties, Li warned, for they could be "easily used by warlords and gentry to cause the peasant movement to destroy itself." Thus, the most important task of the Communists was to inoculate the peasants with a full consciousness of their common class interests: "We ought to make all the peasants understand their class position and have their localistic concepts gradually transformed into class consciousness [so that] they will know that the peasant organizations ought to be broad and not narrow, that they ought to be united rather than separated on the basis of village or district . . . In order to avoid clashes among [the peasants] themselves, we ought to cause them to have a centralized organization." [48]

In Li Ta-chao's conception of the peasant revolution there was that characteristically Populist contradiction between a passionate faith in the spontaneous energies of the people and a conviction that the revolutionary intellectual must bring enlightenment and leadership to the mass movement. Li asserted that the peasants must liberate themselves by their own efforts, but he also believed that Communists must perform the vital function of directing and guiding their energies into the proper channels. He viewed the local loyalties of the peasants as an embryonic form of class consciousness, but the intervention of the Communist intellectual was to overcome local loyalties and convert them into true class consciousness. On the one hand, Li was clearly drawn to the spontaneous forces of peasant revolt and the existing traditional forms of peasant organization; on the other hand, he called for the creation of a new "centralized organization" to ensure the success of the movement. However much Li desired the revolutionary intelligentsia to merge with the peasant masses, however much he stressed that the intellectuals should take up rural occupations and merely "assist" the peasants to improve the organizations they already had and the activities they had already begun on their own, he nevertheless implied that the intellectuals — by virtue of their superior organizing abilities and their superior understanding of the course of social and political development — would in fact become the leaders of the agrarian revolution and determine its direction.

The vital role that the Communist-oriented intellectuals were to play in the peasant revolution was reflected in the final paragraph of the article on the Red Spears — one of the last passages Li wrote:

Enlightened youth of the villages, elementary school teachers of the villages, intellectuals, and all who have gone to the countryside to participate in the peasant movement! You should hurry to join the masses in the Red Spear Societies, develop and assist them, and explain to them the reasons for the present poverty of the Chinese peasantry and the need to create Red Spear Societies. Allow them to understand clearly the position and responsibilities of the peasant class in the national revolutionary movement, to recognize who are their enemies and who are their friends, and to understand the nature of the Red Spear Societies and the road they ought to follow. [If these things are done] then this great movement of peasants that roars like the expanse of the ocean will not follow a mistaken road, its earlier defeats will not be repeated, and it will not be destroyed because peasants are misled into leaving their own camp and [allowing themselves] to be utilized by warlords and gentry. The peasants will then be able to break the bonds of backwardness, superstition, and obscurantism, and transform the old form of the Red Spear Societies into the dignified and correct representatives of the armed peasants' self-defense groups . . . Comrades, several hundred million peasants are waiting to be released from the deep waters of the sea and the hot fires of hell . . . They longingly wait for you to lead them out of this vile pit onto the road of brightness.[49]

Although the spontaneous peasant movement "roars like the expanse of the ocean," the peasants were to be led from "the hot fires of hell" by Communist intellectuals. But if the Communists were to lead the peasant movement, they were to do so in the villages, not from the cities. The revolutionary intellectuals were to go to the countryside, take up rural occupations, join the existing peasant organizations, and fashion them into instruments of revolution. Certainly one of the most remarkable features of Li's article on the Red Spears, as well as his article "Land and the Peasants," was the complete absence of any suggestion that the agrarian revolution was an appendage of, or even closely related to, political developments in the cities. Not even formal homage was paid to the current Comintern doctrine that the agrarian revolution was merely a part of the bourgeois-democratic revolution taking place in the cities (and that, therefore, the peasant movement should come under the leadership of the Kuomintang, or at least conform to the aims of the Kuomintang). Nor did Li once mention the role of the urban proletariat in the revolutionary process; he failed to pay even lip service to the notion that the Communists who were to go to the villages were really the representatives of the actual proletariat.

Li's lack of concern with the urban revolution was further reflected in his refusal to apply urban class designations to the different social strata within the village, as did almost all Comintern and Chinese Communist publications of this period. He divided the peasantry only into the categories of rich peasants, middle peasants, small owner-cultivators, tenants, and agricultural wage laborers.[50] Even Mao Tse-tung differentiated the peasantry on the basis of urban social class criteria in his "Analysis of the Classes in Chinese Society," written in March, 1926. According to Mao's classification, the owner-cultivators belonged to the petty bourgeoisie, while the semiowner cultivators, the tenants, and the poor peasants were described as semiproletarian.[51] By ignoring this type of classification, Li completely rejected the implication that the peasants were mere adjuncts of their urban counterparts.

On this key question of the relationship between the urban and rural revolutions, Li made a fundamental departure from Lenin's views on the revolutionary role of the peasantry. The place of the peasantry in Leninist revolutionary strategy has been the subject of heated controversy (precisely because his views on the question varied so greatly from time to time that they could be used to support conflicting interpretations), but he consistently maintained two conditions for the participation of the peasantry in the revolutionary process. First, no matter whether the revolution was defined as a purely bourgeois-democratic revolution or as a more radical transformation in which the bourgeois-democratic phase would rapidly "pass over" into the socialist phase, it was assumed that the peasants would be subordinate allies of the urban social classes, either the bourgeoisie or the proletariat. Second, especially when the conditions were ripe for the more rapid and radical revolutionary transformation, it was essential that the agrarian revolution and the revolutionary process in general be presided over by the "socialist consciousness" of the Communist party, which was to have its main social base in the actual proletariat.

Neither of these conditions were present in Li Ta-chao's view of the agrarian revolution. He saw the peasant movement as an independent revolutionary force that was to remain unencumbered by urban political considerations. He dispensed with the role of the proletariat of the cities, and although he did not disregard the need for Communist leadership in the agrarian revolution, he ignored the role of the Communist party as the representative of the proletariat. In 1926, as in 1919, Li Ta-chao looked to the forces of peasant revolt as the wellspring of the entire Chinese revolutionary movement and identified the liberation of China with the liberation of the peasantry.

In his writings on the agrarian revolution, Li departed not only from Leninist premises but also from the policies of the Comintern and the central committee of the Chinese Communist party. The central committee regarded the peasant secret societies, particularly the Red Spears, as "basically reactionary," whereas Li treated them as a genuine and spontaneous expression of the forces of peasant revolution. At the very time that Li was calling for an intensification of the armed struggle of the peasantry, the Comintern and the central committee were attempting to curb these very "excesses," fearing that too powerful a revolutionary upsurge in the countryside would upset the precarious alliance with the Kuomintang.

In view of the fact that Li Ta-chao had been one of the most ardent Communist advocates of the policy of collaboration with the Kuomintang, why was it that he apparently did not share this concern? Part of the explanation lies in the fact that it was inconsistent with Li's interpretation of the national revolution to accept the prospect that the aims of the alliance would be limited to "bourgeois-democratic" measures. Perhaps equally important was the *de facto* collapse of the alliance in the North. However, Li's growing lack of interest in the fate of the united front did not mean that he abandoned the concept of national revolution. The ideological basis of his interpretation of the national revolution was the belief that the entire Chinese nation, by virtue of its proletarian status in international society, was inherently allied to the forces of the world socialist revolution. When the united front began to break apart, and when the peasants began to rise in revolt, it was not difficult to find in the peasantry those revolutionary potentialities and that latent proletarian consciousness that he had previously attributed to the nation as a whole. The peasants not only constituted the great majority of the Chinese people, as Li often pointed out, but embodied China's national traditions as well. If Li's call for an agrarian class struggle between Chinese peasants and their Chinese oppressors was somewhat inconsistent with his theory that China was a "proletarian nation" exploited by international capitalism, the class struggle was, after all, to be undertaken by the overwhelming majority of the nation against those relatively few Chinese oppressors who could conveniently be seen as allied with, or dependent upon, foreign imperialism.

In 1926 the voluntaristic and nationalistic predispositions that had governed Li's interpretation of Marxist theory finally became firmly joined in a practical program for revolution. Since the economic preconditions for the realization of socialism were lacking in China, since the Chinese proletariat alone was too weak to bear the burden of revolution, and since the united front with the Kuomintang had proved too undependable a revolutionary instrument, the rising tide of agrarian revolution must be sufficient to overcome all these deficiencies. The revolutionary energies of the peasantry should be utilized immediately to realize the "national revolution" and consummate China's alliance with the forces of world revolution.

Yet Li Ta-chao's revolutionary voluntarism was in itself insufficient to explain his ability to appreciate the revolutionary potentialities of the peasantry; Chinese nationalism was also an essential ingredient. The national characteristics and traditions generally typical of rural environments, which had always repelled most European Marxists, were the very things that attracted Li. Trotsky, whose revolutionary voluntarism Li shared but whose internationalism he did not, once wrote that the Chinese peasants were incapable of sustained political action because the peasantry, "by virtue of its entire history and the condition of its existence, is the least international of all classes. What are commonly called national traits have their chief source precisely in the peasantry."[52] What for Trotsky was a major defect in the revolutionary qualifications of the peasantry was for Li a major virtue. The more internationalistic and Western-oriented Chinese Marxists, such as Ch'en Tu-hsiu, felt a need to be identified with the Chinese urban proletariat because, quite apart from Marxist ideological considerations, that social class (however embryonic) was forged in the image of the West. Li Ta-chao felt instead the need to be identified with the elemental forces of the Chinese nation. In the peasantry he found not only a great revolutionary force but also a class that seemed the embodiment of the vital energies of China and the carrier of her national traditions.

EPILOGUE

ON THE morning of April 6, 1927, a large force of troops and policemen were dispatched to the Legation Quarter in Peking by Chang Tso-lin, the Manchurian warlord who was then in control of the Peking government. Acting in accordance with prior arrangements made with members of the Western and Japanese diplomatic corps, Chang's troops and police were allowed through the gates of the Legation Quarter and proceeded to the Soviet embassy compound, which they surrounded and raided. Documents were seized and about one hundred Russians and Chinese were arrested. Among those arrested was Li Ta-chao.

The official justification later put forth by the Peking regime for this violation of diplomatic immunity was that the Soviet embassy had become a haven for Chinese Communists (notably Li Ta-chao) who were engaged in revolutionary activities. In support of this particular charge there was no lack of evidence. Although Chinese Communist accounts are understandably reluctant to acknowledge that Li had been forced to find sanctuary in the Soviet embassy, they do report that "under the most difficult circumstances" he continued to direct Communist activities in Peking during the year prior to his arrest. It is known that Communist activists frequently met with Li in his home in the Soviet embassy compound and that on some occasions he secretly ventured into the city to speak at meetings and attend to affairs of the underground Communist organization.

Li Ta-chao's eldest daughter, Hsing-hua, has described the events surrounding the arrest and execution of her father. She recalled that there had been forewarnings of the danger. Suspected agents of Chang Tso-lin appeared at the Li household in the weeks prior to the raid. At the beginning of April one of the Li family's two servants failed to return from a shopping expedition into the city. It was assumed that he had been arrested, and a sense of apprehension pervaded the family. "For several days father's friends continually came to warn him to leave Peking, but he disregarded their warnings. Mother also pleaded with him . . . but this had absolutely no effect on father."[1]

On the morning of April 6, Hsing-hua recalled, she was sitting on a bench outside their house reading a newspaper while her father was writing inside at his desk. Suddenly she heard the sound of gunfire and fled into the house. Li told her not to be frightened, but he proceeded to take out a pistol.

After a while I heard the sound of heavy leather shoes. My heart beat violently but I didn't make a sound, only my terrified eyes looked to father. "Don't let anyone escape," a gruff voice shouted from outside the window.

Suddenly military police in gray uniforms and black boots, detectives in plain clothes, and [civil] police in black uniforms swarmed into the small room. Like a horde of devils they surrounded us, each of them holding pistols which they coldly and cruelly pointed at father and me. Among the police and soldiers was the servant Yen Chen who had been arrested a few days before. His arms were bound with a thin white rope that was grasped tightly by a fat detective who held him like a dog. From behind his long hair there appeared a pale face. At a glance, we knew he had been tortured. They had brought him to identify us.

The fat detective of cruel features and evil eyes pointed to my father and asked Yen Chen: "Do you know him?" He simply shook his head, indicating that he did not. "You don't know him? Well I know him," replied the detective with a cunning, cold grin; he then ordered his men: "Take care of him. Don't let him commit suicide. Grab his pistol." They immediately took father's pistol and searched him. Father maintained his habitual serene attitude. He did not argue with them because he knew it would be useless . . .

Shouting cruel and violent curses, [they] tied up father. I saw them dragging him out. And I too was arrested by this mob."[2]

Later that same day Li Ta-chao's wife and a younger daughter were also arrested and imprisoned. Ten days later Hsing-hua, her mother, and a younger sister were taken to a courtroom, where she saw her father for the last time. Li Ta-chao was wearing the traditional gray scholar's gown in which he was almost always seen. In the course of the proceedings Li pleaded with the judge to release his wife and two daughters. His wife was a simple country girl and his daughters were very young, he argued; they had not in any way been involved in his political activities. The judge thereupon ordered Hsing-hua, her mother, and her younger sister removed from the courtroom and returned to prison.

For nearly two weeks Li Ta-chao's wife and two daughters languished in jail and heard nothing about his fate. Finally, on the evening of April 28, the three were released from prison. On the following day they read in a Peking newspaper that Li, along with nineteen other Communists and left-wing Kuomintang members, had been executed by strangulation the previous day.[3]

Li's execution aroused bitter nation-wide protests that were by no means confined to Communist circles. Newspaper opinion generally condemned Chang Tso-lin's act. The Peking authorities, fearing that a formal funeral for Li might become the occasion for an antigovernment demonstration, refused to release Li's body to his family. He was given a temporary resting place in a Buddhist temple in Peking. Not until four years later, when Chiang Meng-lin, the chancellor of Peking University, intervened with the Nationalist authorities on behalf of Li's widow, was he finally permitted a proper funeral and burial. At that time the political disturbances that Chang Tso-lin had feared in 1927 were partially realized. A Reuter agency dispatch from Peking on April 24, 1931, read as follows:

The funeral of the late Mr. Li Ta-chao, former professor of the Peking National University and well-known leader of the Chinese Communist Party, yesterday morning was the occasion for a radical demonstration, which resulted in forty students being arrested by police and gendarmes.

More than 700 persons, mostly students and workers, walked in the funeral procession, which started from a Buddhist temple outside Shunchihmen, where the remains had been kept since Mr. Li was executed by Marshal Chang Tso-lin in 1927. When the casket reached Hsitanpailou, one of the busiest sections of the city, the 32 professional pall bearers paused for a while in order to enable street sacrifices to be made before the coffin. Taking advantage of the congestion of traffic at this point as well as the presence of large crowds of spectators, some of the radical students in the procession started to sing the Internationale and distribute communist literature.

Police and gendarmes immediately intervened in an attempt to prevent the students from further distributing their handbills, but the latter refused to heed the warning. A clash ensued in which about forty

259

students were arrested. The rest escaped. Twenty students were taken to the Bureau of Public Safety and the others to the headquarters of the Gendarmerie. The funeral procession later resumed its journey to the Western Hills, where interment took place in the afternoon.

The funeral brought out a variety of scrolls of condolence sent by friends and admirers of the deceased leader. One from a Japanese named Yamada bore this inscription: "To Comrade Li Ta-chao, our beloved leader and teacher of the proletariat. Although your mortal remains will soon be buried, your spirit is still with us, and the blood which you shed, has become a source of strength to our movement. Comrade, may you rest in peace! We are determined to fight until we have freed ourselves from our fetters and become free." A Korean communist sent a scroll written in his native language.[4]

A sequel to the rather macabre events surrounding Li's death and its aftermath took place in Communist China in 1951. A Communist newspaper in Hong Kong, the *Ta-kung pao*, carried a dispatch from Mukden that told of the arrest of one Chao Yü-shu for counterrevolutionary activities. Following the arrest of Chao Yü-shu it was discovered that "the said culprit had concealed his past evil history . . . In 1927 he was aide-de-camp with rank of captain to Chang Tso-lin, and commanding some forty bodyguards of Marshal Chang, had arrested our revolutionary martyr Li Ta-chao and twenty others. The culprit was the first one to tie up Li, and upon Li's shouting for justice, he even tightened the ropes and struck him with his fists . . . He took away Li's clothing and money for his own use . . . He [Chao] was sentenced to death by the Municipal Peoples Court in accordance with law and executed by firing squad on February 22 [1951]."[5]

Li Ta-chao was still in his thirty-ninth year when Chang Tso-lin ordered that he be executed, but his fate was perhaps less tragic than the fate that befell his friend and colleague Ch'en Tu-hsiu, with whom he had shared responsibility for founding the Communist movement in China. Ch'en escaped the executioner's rope in 1927, but the years that followed were filled with the deepest disappointment and frustration. He was held entirely to blame for the defeats that virtually demolished the Chinese Communist party in 1927. Accused of the sin of "right-wing opportunism," he was dismissed from his post of secretary-general. Two years later he was expelled from the party altogether, this time for the alleged heresy of "Trotskyism." Half the years remaining to him were spent in a Kuomintang prison. He died of cancer in 1941, a tragic and disillusioned figure who had spent his last years vainly attempting to reconcile Marxism with his pre-Marxian democratic faith.[6]

Although Ch'en Tu-hsiu was the acknowledged leader of the New Culture movement, to which the Communists claim to be the rightful heirs, his role in that period has been mostly ignored in Communist historical accounts. When his name does appear, it is usually as the symbol of an arch-renegade.[7] Between the two types of extreme nationalism that have monopolized modern Chinese politics there has been no room for either a Social Democratic or a viable liberal movement that might have provided a political haven for Ch'en when he was alive, or an honest record of his very considerable role in modern Chinese history after he was dead.

No one knows what role Li Ta-chao might have played in the history of Chinese Communism had he lived after 1927. Nor can one be sure that his last words were to shout "Long live Communism" at his executioners, as later Communist accounts have claimed. But insofar as it is possible to know of such matters, it would seem that he went to his death with his Communist faith unshaken. During the turbulent early years of the Chinese Communist movement, as well as in the fateful year of 1927, he realized the aim he had set for himself in 1919 when he embarked upon his revolutionary career. "The life of superior attainment," he had then proclaimed, "always lies in ardent sacrifice."[8]

Today Li Ta-chao is honored in China as the most heroic of revolutionary martyrs. In Communist historical writings he is treated as the real leader of the May Fourth movement, the pioneer of Marxism in China, and the true founder of the Chinese Communist party. In such writings Li's role in modern Chinese history is magnified beyond its real proportions, although never so much as to dim the luster of Mao Tse-tung in the areas in which the latter was also involved. In the glorification of Li Ta-chao and the vilification of Ch'en Tu-hsiu, there is reflected more than the obvious political need to find heroes and heretics, for Li was the forerunner of those revolutionary voluntaristic tendencies and nationalistic impulses that have since governed the Maoist version of Marxism-Leninism, whereas Ch'en represented the internationalistic and Westernizing Marxist influences that were to perish in the Chinese environment.

There is no way to know for certain how much of the young

Mao Tse-tung's intellectual orientation was derived from the ideas and writings of Li Ta-chao, for those who claim to have made historic and universally valid innovations in theory are reluctant to acknowledge intellectual debts, even in the rare cases where they are fully conscious of such debts. Yet it seems highly likely, as Stuart Schram has argued in his excellent study of Mao's intellectual development, that Mao's ideas in his formative years were shaped in large measure by the ideas of Li. Li not only introduced Mao to Marxist theory in the winter of 1918–1919, when Mao served as assistant to the librarian of Peking National University, but he also communicated to Mao his own particular version of Marxism and his chiliastic feelings on the significance of the October Revolution. Nor is it likely that Mao was uninfluenced by the heretical Populist notions intermingled with Li's Marxist ideas, particularly Li's passionate appeals in 1919 for young intellectuals to leave the cities and devote their energies to the liberation of the peasantry in the countryside. Mao did not rediscover the peasantry until 1925, but as Schram has suggested, "Li Ta-chao in 1919 may well have started him on the road to that rediscovery." [9]

The earliest political writings of the young Mao Tse-tung, published in mid-1919, faithfully echoed the nationalist, Populist, and Bolshevik ideas of his teacher. A belief that the whole Chinese nation was essentially united against its external oppressors, a faith in the "intrinsic energy" of the Chinese people, an affirmation of the historic greatness and future glory of the Chinese nation, and a chiliastic feeling that the Bolshevik Revolution was a "great tide" about to sweep over the world — such were the notions that Mao derived from Li in 1919.[10] In the years thereafter Mao's treatment of Marxist theory followed closely the pattern set by Li. In the hands of both the deterministic laws of Marxism were to bend, and eventually break, before an inexhaustible faith in the power of the human will and consciousness to shape historical reality. Neither was willing to allow predetermined levels of social and economic development to restrict opportunities for immediate revolutionary action. In fact, the very absence of the objective prerequisites for socialism seemed to demand that the Chinese exert ever greater energies to achieve those prerequisites, and both treated this situation as an advantage that would enable China to move all the more rapidly to the socialist utopia of the future.

Both Li and Mao felt the need to find objective Marxist correlatives for what was basically a subjective system of revolutionary values, and both drew from the materialist conception of history the assurance of the inevitability of socialism. But their socialist faith was ultimately based not upon confidence in the workings of the objective laws of social development, but rather upon confidence in their abilities to bring forth the powerful subjective forces latent in the present — the great storehouses of "surplus energy" that Li argued had been accumulating in China over the centuries. The ideas, the wills, and the "self-consciousness" of men would really determine the course of Chinese history.

These activistic and voluntaristic impulses were inspired by and also reinforced even more deeply rooted nationalistic impulses. For Mao, as well as for Li, the salvation and rebirth of the Chinese nation was the major concern, but it was to be a socialist rebirth, China's precapitalist social and economic structure notwithstanding, for China was not to be allowed to fall behind in the progressive march of history. It was to achieve this rebirth that both undertook to transform Marxist doctrine. In the process of the transformation the internationalist and cosmopolitan content of the original doctrine gave way to a messianic nationalism, which saw China not only fully qualified to join the forces of international socialism but destined to play a special role in the world revolution.

The combination of revolutionary voluntarism and Chinese nationalism made for a curious dichotomy in both Li's and Mao's vision of the rebirth of China. Although their confidence in this rebirth was based upon their faith in the energies of the people, particularly the youth, who were to write a new Chinese history in accordance with the new Marxist ideals and values which had come from the West, this very real rejection of the values of old China was accompanied by a nationalistic attachment to Chinese traditions and a feeling of pride in the glories of the Chinese past.

The combination of voluntarism and nationalism was also reflected in their treatment of the concept of class struggle, the theoretical area most directly related to political practice. Both Li and Mao promoted class struggle in theory as well as in practice. However, they drew from Marx's theory more the notion of struggle than the need to analyze political situations upon the basis of objective social class criteria. "Proletarian consciousness" was more important than the proletariat itself. Li was quite explicit in attributing a latent proletarian consciousness to the entire Chinese nation by virtue of China's "proletarian" status in the international capitalist economy, and this idea was implicit in Mao's thesis that the major contest was not so much within China as between the Chinese nation and foreign imperialism. These notions reflected not only the voluntarist's impatience with the economic forces of history and his impulse to carry out the proletarian revolution, even without the actual proletariat if need be, but also the willingness of the Chinese nationalist to abandon the only progressive social class in Chinese society that had been formed in the image of the West and instead look to broader, "national" sources of revolution.

It perhaps matters little how much of his ideology Mao Tse-tung derived directly from Li Ta-chao. Without Li, Mao might have arrived at much the same ideas and followed the same ideological and political path. What is important, however, is that the immersion of Marxism in the Chinese environment gave rise to their particular intellectual and ideological orientations, and that those orientations were intimately related to the political strategies that brought the Chinese Communist party to power.

This close relationship between politics and ideology was apparent in the striking parallels between Li's and Mao's political positions in the years before 1927. Like Li, Mao was an enthusiastic, not a reluctant, supporter of the alliance with the Kuomintang, for he too looked to the revolutionary energies of the whole nation rather than of a single social class, and eventually both Li and Mao abandoned that particular united front to embrace the elemental forces of peasant revolt. In the mid-1920's Mao probably did not look to Li for political leadership as he had looked to him for intellectual guidance in 1919, but their advocacy of similar political strategies followed from similar intellectual and ideological assumptions.

On the basis of these two elements of revolutionary strategy that appeared before 1927 — the united front and, especially, peasant revolution — the Chinese Communist party was eventually to triumph. In the application of these very general strategies Mao developed a variety of particular innovations that were esssential to the Communist success. Although it may be true, as has often been noted, that Mao's real innovations lay in the realm of political strategy and tactics rather than in the realm of Marxist theory, what is frequently ignored are the intellectual and ideological elements that were the prerequisites for those innovations. It was not predetermined that Communism would come to power in China upon a wave of peasant revolt — or indeed that it would come to power at all. Even if it is assumed that the peasant risings that began in the mid-1920's were entirely spontaneous in character (an historically erroneous assumption), the ability fully to appreciate the forces of peasant revolt and the willingness to build Communist revolutionary strategy upon a purely peasant foundation required certain general but fundamental theoretical perspectives and intellectual orientations. Some Chinese Communists were able to entertain this possibility; others were not.

The reasons why Li Ta-chao was willing to abandon the Western-influenced cities and the proletariat for the Chinese countryside also applied to Mao Tse-tung. Mao was a better student of Leninist organizational techniques and methods of manipulating mass movements. He was also more concerned than Li had been with maintaining at least the appearance of doctrinal orthodoxy. However, essentially the same voluntaristic interpretation of Marxism, the same nationalistic impulses, and a similar Populist emphasis on the inherent unity of the people governed the thought of Mao Tse-tung as had governed Li Ta-chao's. These ideological factors were essential preconditions for the development of the Maoist strategy of peasant revolution.

There is, of course, that peculiarly deterministic variety of contemporary social science theory that tends to see the Chinese Communists as little more than playthings in the hands of vaster and deeper social forces. To the practitioners of this "science" the ideological tendencies that have been considered in this study will seem of little moment, for they are convinced that history can be analyzed without inquiring into the ideas and emotions of the men who made that history. For such practitioners, the nationalist aspect of Chinese Communism, for example, might appear as no more than the function of the Communist party's inevitable immersion in a rural environment. Yet the Chinese Communists who went to the countryside were profoundly nationalistic long before they left the cities. In fact, a particular kind of nationalistic predisposition drew them to the peasantry. The rural environment no doubt reinforced this nationalism, but no less important was the role played by the Communists in transforming the innate antiforeign feelings of the Chinese peasantry into genuine nationalist feelings. "Mass nationalism" was not something that welled up from the elemental forces of the countryside and eventually reached Mao Tse-tung and his associates. It is more historically accurate to say that nationalism was brought to the peasants from without by an ardently nationalistic elite intent upon shaping history in accordance with its ideals.

Li Ta-chao did not live to see the triumph of the Communist movement that he had founded, but he did much to mold the ideological orientations that guided his successors to that triumph. He could hardly have objected to the unorthodox strategy by which Mao Tse-tung reached power, for he had pioneered in promoting the general outlines of that strategy. He might not have found in Communist China the "truly human life" that he had thought a Marxist revolution would bring, but he would have been more than fully satisfied with the resurgence of the Chinese nation and the power of the Chinese Communist state, for the notion of the rebirth of a "young China" had always been at the emotional core of his entire world view.

NOTES   BIBLIOGRAPHY   GLOSSARY   INDEX

NOTES

HC   *Li Ta-chao hsüan-chi* (The selected writings of Li Ta-chao)
HCN *Hsin ch'ing-nien* (New youth)

CHAPTER I.   THE EARLY YEARS

1. Ch'ü Yüan (320–278 B.C.), a minister of the state of Ch'u, failed to win the support of the king for his proposals to save the state because of the intrigues of the corrupt court nobility. He eventually drowned himself out of both love and grief for his king and country. The traditional "Dragon Boat Festival" of the fifth of May symbolizes the attempt to recover his body from the waters.

2. For a brief account of Li's early years, see the article by the Communist historian Chia Chih, "Li Ta-chao t'ung-chih chan-tou ti i-sheng" (Comrade Li Ta-chao's life of struggle), *Kuang-hui ti wu-ssu* (The glorious May Fourth; Peking, 1959), p. 29. Chia Chih is said to be the husband of one of Li Ta-chao's three surviving daughters.

3. Li Ta-chao, "My Autobiography." This is a short composition Li wrote for an English language class taught by Mr. Arthur Robinson, a YMCA worker, at Waseda University in Tokyo in 1914. Mr. Robinson kindly made this composition available to me.

4. For an analysis of this phenomenon in a variety of societies, see Dorian Apple, "The Social Structure of Grandparenthood," *American Anthropologist,* 58:656–657 (August 1956).

5. Li Ta-chao's daughter, Li Hsing-hua, has written a number of articles about her father that include descriptions of his relationship with his children. In one article she recalls: "Father was always kind and never scolded or beat us." Li Hsing-hua, "Shih-liu-nien ch'ien ti hui-i" (Memories of sixteen years ago), in Hua Ying-shen, ed., *Chung-kuo Kung-ch'an-tang lieh-shih chuan* (Biographies of heroes of the Chinese Communist party; Hong Kong, 1949), pp. 10–16. See also Li Hsing-hua, "Hui-i wo-ti fu-ch'in Li Ta-chao" (Memories of my father Li Ta-chao), *Chung-kuo ch'ing-nien* (Chinese youth), No. 8:19–25 (1959).

6. Chia Chih, "Chan-tou ti i-sheng," p. 29.

7. Li Ta-chao, "My Autobiography."

8. Lü Chien, *Li Ta-chao ho Ch'ü Ch'iu-pai* (Li Ta-chao and Ch'ü Ch'iu-pai; Shanghai, 1951), p. 1.

9. Li was the father of four daughters and two sons. Chung-hua, the daughter who was said to have been his favorite, died of pneumonia in 1924. Li Hsing-hua, "I-nien," (Thoughts) *Chiao-shih-pao* (Apr. 23, 1957), p. 4. After Li's execution, his widow returned with the children to her village

home. A son later went to Japan and then returned to join the Communists in Yenan. He was recently said to have been a military garrison commander of the Peking region.

10. For Ch'en Tu-hsiu's views on the Boxers, see his essay "K'o-lin-te pei" (The Von Ketteler monument), HCN, 5.5:449–458 (Nov. 15, 1918).

11. Chia Chih, "Chan-tou ti i-sheng," p. 30.

12. Li Ta-chao, "Ch'ing-ch'un" (Spring), HCN, 2.1:1–12 (Sept. 1, 1916). For an excellent English translation of a portion of this essay by Yang Hsien-yi and Gladys Yang, see Chinese Literature (May 1959), pp. 11–18; unless otherwise noted, references are to this translation.

13. Ibid., p. 17.

14. "Hsi-sheng" (Sacrifice; Nov. 9, 1919), in HC, p. 247. All translations from the Chinese throughout the text are mine unless otherwise noted.

15. Yü I, "Sung Li Kuei-nien yü Jih-pen hsü (A farewell to Li Kuei-nien [Li Ta-chao] on his leaving for study in Japan), Yen-chih (Statesman), No. 4: 85–86 (Sept. 1, 1913).

16. Kao I, "T'an hsien-lieh Li Ta-chao t'ung-chih ti i-wen" (On the translations of the martyr, Comrade Li Ta-chao), Wen-hui-pao (Shanghai, Sept. 17, 1957), p. 3.

17. Li Ta-chao, "I-yüan-chih yü erh-yüan-chih" (Unicameralism and bicameralism), Yen-chih, No. 4:53–57 (Sept. 1, 1913).

18. Li Ta-chao, "Lun kuan-liao chu-i" (On bureaucracy), Yen-chih, No. 4:17–20 (Sept. 1, 1913).

19. "Ta-ai p'ien" (The great grief; Apr. 1, 1913), HC, pp. 2–3.

20. Ibid., pp. 1–2. It might be noted that Li's view of the Chinese past was not altogether a happy one. In a still very Confucian fashion he looked back to the golden age of the sages, especially the "Spring and Autumn" period (722–481 B.C.) and the Era of the Warring States (481–221 B.C.), as the zenith of Chinese civilization, and he characterized the following two thousand years of Chinese history as no more than a process of "evil replacing evil." His essay on "The Great Grief" begins with the following description of Chinese history: "Alas! How can the people be considered guilty? We have had a history of several thousand years and yet we are still not awakened. Since the evil Ch'in emperors [221 B.C.], local brigands have arisen everywhere and the fires of tyranny have expanded continuously to oppress the people, destroy scholarship, violate respectfulness, support evils, pollute the air men breathe, and destroy human rights. Who has dared to oppose it! Speaking slanders, the evil foreigners were established . . . [The pattern of] evil replacing evil has continued up to now. How tragic it is! It is the leaders who are to blame."

21. Ibid., p. 2.

22. Ibid.

23. Ibid.

24. This point is emphasized in Satoi Hikoshichiro, "Ri Taisho no shuppatsu, Genji ki no seiron o chūshin ni" (The departure of Li Ta-chao, with emphasis on the political writings of the Statesman period), Shirin (History), 40.3:1–39 (May 1957).

25. "Yao tzu-yu chi-ho ti kuo-min ta-hui" (There ought to be a freely convened national assembly; Aug. 17, 1920), HC, p. 330.

26. The statement that Li was a member of the T'ung-meng hui, the predecessor of the Kuomintang, during the period of the 1911 Revolution

appeared in one of the earliest Communist accounts of his life. See Hua Ying-shen, p. 2.

27. Li Ta-chao, "An-sha yü ch'ün-te" (Assassination and social morality), *Yen-chih*, No. 2:98 (May 1, 1913).

28. *Ibid.*, pp. 97–99.

29. Li Ta-chao, "Shih-fei p'ien" (Essay on right and wrong), *Yen-chih*, No. 4:71–73 (Sept. 1, 1913).

30. The proposition that anarchism was the prelude to the spread of Marxism in China is argued by Robert Scalapino and George Yu in *Chinese Anarchism* (Berkeley, 1961), p. 60.

31. In his "autobiography" Mao recalls this aspect of his life in Peking in 1918: "I read some pamphlets on anarchy, and was very much influenced by them. With a student named Chu Hsun-pei, who used to visit me, I often discussed anarchism and its possibilities in China. At that time I favored many of its proposals." Edgar Snow, *Red Star Over China* (New York, 1938), p. 135.

32. Lü Chien, p. 3. Li was introduced to T'ang Hua-lung by Sun Hung-i, a member of the Chihli provincial assembly during the last years of the Ch'ing dynasty and later a leading figure in the Chinputang.

33. "Ta-ai p'ien," *HC*, pp. 1–2.

34. Li Ta-chao, "My Autobiography."

35. Yü I, p. 86.

36. According to Mr. Robinson, Li also attended a Bible class for a short period, although he seemed to be more interested in learning the English language than the Christian Bible. Interview with Mr. Arthur Robinson in Wellesley, Massachusetts, 1963.

37. Li Ta-chao, "Feng-su" (Customs), *Chia-yin tsa-chih* (Tiger magazine), Vol. I, No. 3 (Summer 1914).

38. Chia Chih, "Chan-tou ti i-sheng," p. 31. The Chung-hua ko-ming-tang was created in 1914 as a secret society very much in the image of the earlier T'ung-meng hui. The T'ung-meng hui had been succeeded after the Revolution of 1911 by the Kuomintang, which was organized as an "open party" to participate in the elections to the republican parliament. After Yüan Shih-k'ai's usurpation of power and the assassination of Sung Chiao-jen (who had been the main advocate of an "open party"), Sun returned to his original secret party organization.

39. "Kuo-ch'ing" (The national condition, Nov. 10, 1914), *HC*, p. 4. Ariga Nagao was then serving as political adviser to Yüan Shih-k'ai.

40. *Ibid.*, pp. 4 and 6.

41. *Ibid.*, p. 5. Li characterized the traditional Chinese attitude toward political power by quoting the proverb: "I till the fields and eat, dig wells and drink, for what relation does the emperor have to me?"

42. *Ibid.*

43. Chow Tse-tsung, *The May Fourth Movement* (Cambridge, Mass., 1960), p. 33.

44. "Kuo-min chih hsin-tan" (To rouse the courage of the citizens; June 1915), *HC*, pp. 17–18.

45. "Ching-kao ch'uan-kuo fu-lao shu" (A letter of admonition to the elders of the nation; 1915), *HC*, pp. 19–27.

46. *Ibid.*, p. 26.

47. The problem of the transition from culturalism to nationalism is

analyzed by Joseph Levenson in *Liang Ch'i-ch'ao and the Mind of Modern China* (Cambridge, Mass., 1959). See esp. pp. 109–122.

48. While in Japan, Li Ta-chao became a close friend of Chang Shih-chao (b. 1881), who published several of Li's essays in *Chia-yin tsa-chih*. Late in 1915 *Chia-yin tsa-chih* was suppressed by the Japanese government at the request of Yüan Shih-k'ai. Chang's constitutionalism soon gave way to a strongly traditionalist viewpoint. After 1949 he supported the Communist government and in 1954 became a delegate from Hunan to the National People's Congress.

49. Ch'en Tu-hsiu, "Ai-kuo-hsin yü tzu-chüeh-hsin" (Patriotism and self-consciousness), *Chia-yin tsa-chih*, 1.4:1 (Apr. 1915).

50. *Ibid.*, pp. 1 and 4.

51. "Yen-shih-hsin yü tzu-chüeh-hsin" (Pessimism and self-consciousness; Aug. 10, 1915), *HC*, pp. 28–29.

52. *Ibid.*, p. 30. The Chinese term for patriotism, *ai-kuo*, literally means "to love the country." Thus, when Li wrote of "making a country lovable and loving it," the phrase carried a particularly strong connotation of patriotic feeling.

53. *Ibid.*, p. 31. Li specifically referred to Bergson's *Creative Evolution* in discussing the "theory of free will."

54. *Ibid.*, p. 28.

55. *Ibid.*, p. 32.

56. Li Ta-chao, "Spring," p. 13.

57. *Ibid.*, p. 14.

58. *Ibid.*, pp. 14–15.

59. *Ibid.*, pp. 16–17.

60. Chia Chih, "Li Ta-chao t'ung-chih ti ku-shih" (The story of Comrade Li Ta-chao), *Chung-kuo ch'ing-nien* (Apr. 16, 1957), p. 10.

CHAPTER II. PRELUDE TO REVOLUTION

1. Li's close personal and political relationship with T'ang Hua-lung is reluctantly acknowledged in Communist accounts. See, for example, Chia Chih, "Li Ta-chao t'ung-chih ti ku-shih," pp. 9–10.

2. *Ch'en-chung pao* was the predecessor of the famous *Ch'en pao* (Morning post), which played so important a role in the May Fourth movement. Li resigned from *Ch'en-chung pao* in October 1917; eleven months later the newspaper was suppressed by the Peking government. Li became associated with the more radical *Ch'en pao* in February 1919 as editor of its "page seven" supplement. For a history of *Ch'en pao* and particularly Li's relationship with it, see *Wu-ssu shih-ch'i ch'i-k'an chieh-shao* (An introduction to the publications of the May Fourth period; Peking, 1959), I, 98–143.

3. "Min-i yü cheng-chih" (The rules of the people and politics; May 15, 1916), *HC*, pp. 36–40. This essay appeared in the short-lived periodical *Min-i* (The rules of the people), which Li Ta-chao edited in Japan shortly before returning to China. In a later essay Li explicitly identified *min-i* with the notion of popular sovereignty. See "K'ung-tzu yü hsien-fa" (Confucius and the constitution; Jan. 30, 1917), *HC*, p. 77.

4. "Min-i yü cheng-chih, *HC*, p. 40.

5. *Ibid.*

6. "Kuo-ch'ing," *HC*, p. 7.

7. "Min-i yü cheng-chih," *HC*, pp. 42–46.

8. *Ibid.*, pp. 48–50.

9. Li Ta-chao, "Lun kuan-liao chu-i," p. 20.

10. Chia Chih, "Li Ta-chao t'ung-chih ti ku-shih," pp. 10–11.

11. Between January 28, 1917, and the end of May, Li contributed a total of 57 articles to *Chia-yin jih-k'an*. Files of the newspaper are unavailable except in mainland China. However, several of Li's articles that originally appeared in *Chia-yin jih-k'an* have been reprinted in *HC*.

12. Chia Chih, "Chan-tou ti i-sheng," p. 33.

13. "K'ung-tzu yü hsien-fa" (Jan. 30, 1917), and "Tzu-jan ti lun-li-kuan yü K'ung-tzu" (The ethical view of nature and Confucius; Feb. 4, 1917), *HC*, pp. 77–80. The immediate occasion for Li's attack upon the Confucian tradition was the movement of late 1916 and early 1917 to establish Confucianism as a state religion.

14. Li Ta-chao, "Pao-li yü cheng-chih" (Violence and politics), *T'ai-p'ing yang* (Pacific ocean), 1.7:9–11 (Oct. 15, 1917).

15. Besides Ch'en and Li the editorial board consisted of Hu Shih, Ch'ien Hsüan-t'ung, Liu Fu, and Shen Yin-mo.

16. Benjamin Schwartz, "The Intelligentsia in Communist China. A Tentative Comparison," *Daedalus* (Summer 1960), pp. 612–614.

17. Needless to say, contemporary political issues were in fact discussed in many articles appearing in *HCN* despite Ch'en Tu-hsiu's stated desire to shun them.

18. "Chen-li chih ch'üan-wei" (The authority of truth; Apr. 17, 1917), *HC*, pp. 86–87.

19. Ch'en Tu-hsiu, "Reply to the Letter of Wang Shu-ch'ien," in *Tu-hsiu wen-ts'un* (The collected works of Ch'en Tu-hsiu; Shanghai, 1922), IV, 11–12.

20. Ch'en Tu-hsiu, "Reply to the Letter of Ku K'e-kang," *ibid.*, p. 126.

21. "Chan-cheng yü jen-k'ou wen-t'i" (War and the population question; Mar. 30, 1917), *HC*, pp. 83–85.

22. Benjamin Schwartz, *In Search of Wealth and Power: Yen Fu and the West* (Cambridge, Mass., 1964), pp. 45–46.

23. "Chan-cheng yü jen-k'ou wen-t'i," *HC*, p. 85.

24. Li Ta-chao, "Ch'ing-nien yü lao-jen" (Youth and old people), *HCN*, 3.2:1 (Apr. 1, 1917).

25. *Ibid.*, pp. 1–2.

26. *Ibid.*, p. 3.

27. *Ibid.*, p. 4. The "Christiansen" mentioned here is the Danish political scientist Arthur Christensen. In his essay Li referred to Christensen's book *Politics and Crowd Morality* (London, 1915).

28. *HCN*, 4.5:446 (May 15, 1918).

29. *Ibid.*, p. 449.

30. Ch'en Tu-hsiu, "Tung-hsi min-tsu ken-pen ssu-hsiang chih ch'a-i," *Tu-hsiu wen-ts'un*, I, 35–40.

31. Ch'en Tu-hsiu, "Chin-jih Chung-kuo chih cheng-chih wen-t'i" (The political problems of China today; July 15, 1918), *ibid.*, I, 224.

32. *Selected Works of Lu Hsün* (Peking, 1956), I, 8–21.

33. Li Ta-chao, "Tung-hsi wen-ming ken-pen chih i-tien," *Shou-ch'ang wen-chi* (The collected works of [Li] Shou-ch'ang; Shanghai, 1951), pp.

37–48. The date of the essay is incorrectly given in *Shou-ch'ang wen-chi* as 1920. Actually Li's essay appeared in *Yen-chih chi-k'an* (Statesman quarterly) in July 1918. Wen Ts'ao, "Shih-p'ien Li Ta-chao (Shou-ch'ang) i-chu hsi-nien mu-lu" (A preliminary chronological index to the writings of Li Ta-chao), pt. 3, *Hsüeh-shu yüeh-k'an* (Scholarship monthly), No. 3:61 (1957). Although not published until after the October Revolution, this essay was written well before Li's acceptance of Marxism, and in view of the similarity of its content to his earlier attitudes toward the Chinese tradition, it may be taken as an accurate expression of his pre-Marxian views on this subject.

34. Li Ta-chao, "Tung-hsi wen-ming ken-pen chih i-tien," *Shou-ch'ang wen-chi*, p. 40.

35. *Ibid.*

36. *Ibid.*

37. Levenson, *Liang-Ch'i-ch'ao*, esp. pp. 109–122.

38. For an excellent brief analysis of Li's pre-Marxian world view, see Benjamin Schwartz, *Chinese Communism and the Rise of Mao* (Cambridge, Mass., 1952), pp. 10–11.

39. Li Ta-chao, "Chin" (Now), HCN, 4.4:309 (Apr. 15, 1918).

40. Li Ta-chao, "Spring," p. 13.

41. H. Stuart Hughes, *Consciousness and Society* (New York, 1958), p. 341.

42. Li Ta-chao, "Spring," p. 13.

43. Li Ta-chao, "Chin," p. 310. Chinese Communist historians have interpreted the dialectical element in Li's thought as evidence of his "dialectical materialism." In Marxist terms Li can more properly be classified as a "dialectial idealist" at this time for he quite clearly regarded "spiritual forces" as the motivating factor in history.

44. Li Ta-chao, "Chin," p. 310.

45. *Ibid.*, pp. 307–308.

46. *Ibid.*, pp. 303, 308–309.

47. *Ibid.*, p. 310.

CHAPTER III. THE RUSSIAN REVOLUTION AND THE INTRODUCTION OF MARXISM

1. Chu Chih-hsin, "Te-i-chih she-hui ko-ming-chia hsiao-chuan" (Short biographies of German social revolutionaries), *Min-pao* (People's paper), No. 2 (January 1906) and No. 3 (June 1906).

2. Liang described the doctrine of Marx as holding that the majority of weak people are oppressed by a minority of strong people and stated that Marx and Nietzsche represented the two main schools of German thought. He criticized both Marx and Nietzsche for looking only to the present and failing to look to the future. He also frowned upon Marx's opposition to religion and the theory of evolution. Liang Ch'i-ch'ao, "Chin-hua-lun ko-ming-che Chieh-te chih hsüeh-shuo" (The theory of Kidd, a revolution in the discussion of evolution), *Ying-ping-shih ch'üan-chi* (Collected works of the Ice-Drinkers' Studio; Shanghai, 1925), XXV, 27, 33.

3. Jung Meng-yüan, "Hsin-hai ko-ming ch'ien Chung-kuo shu-k'an shang tui Ma-k'o-ssu chu-i ti chieh-shao" (The introduction of Marxism in Chinese

publications before the Revolution of 1911), *Hsin chien-she* (New reconstruction), No. 3:6 (1953).

4. Chang Ching-lu, *Chung-kuo ch'u pan shih-liao pu-pien* (Supplement to materials on the history of Chinese publications) (Peking, 1957), 442.

5. The writings of Russian Marxists were not available in Chinese translation until after the October Revolution. One of the first to appear was Lenin's "Report on Party Principles to the Eighth Congress of the Russian Communist Party (Bolshevik)," translated under the title "National Self-determination" (Min-tsu tzu-chüeh) and published in *HCN*, Vol. 8, No. 3 (Nov. 1920). See Chang Ching-lu, *Supplement*, 452.

6. Ch'en Tu-hsiu, "Fa-lan-hsi jen yü chin-shih wen-ming" (The French and modern civilization), *Tu-hsiu wen-ts'un*, I, 11–15.

7. Ch'en Tu-hsiu, "T'ung-hsin" (Correspondence), *HCN*, 2.5:4–5 (Jan. 1, 1917).

8. Li Lung-mu, "Li Ta-chao t'ung-chih ho wu-ssu shih-ch'i Ma-k'o-ssu chu-i ssu-hsiang ti hsüan-ch'uan" (Comrade Li Ta-chao and the propagation of Marxism during the May Fourth period), *Li-shih yen-chiu* (Historical research), No. 5:4 (1957).

9. The Japanese *atarashiki mura* (new village) movement, like similar utopian socialist experiments in Europe and the U. S., promoted the establishment of ideal village communities whose members agreed to practice communist principles. The movement drew its main intellectual inspiration from Kropotkin's theory of "mutual aid" and its particular rural orientation from Tolstoy. In China the best-known advocate of the New Village movement was the younger brother of Lu Hsün, Chou Tso-jen, who had been educated in Japan.

10. Kao I-han, "Ho Ta-chao t'ung-chih hsiang-ch'u ti shih-hou" (The time I met Comrade [Li] Ta-chao), *Kung-jen jih-pao* (Daily worker; Apr. 27, 1957), p. 3.

11. Teng Ssu-yü and John K. Fairbank, *China's Response to the West: A Documentary Survey* (Cambridge, Mass., 1954), p. 238.

12. Li apparently took his duties as librarian quite seriously. In 1921 he wrote an article on the techniques of librarianship entitled "Mei-kuo t'u-shu-kuan yüan chih hsün-lien" (The training of American librarians). For a brief discussion of Li's contribution to the development of modern library techniques in China, see Ku T'ing-chuan, "Hsüeh-hsi Li Ta-chao t'ung-chih chien-k'u fen-tou ti ching-shen chien-t'an hsin Chung-kuo t'u-shu-kuan shih-yeh ti fa-chan" (Study Comrade Li Ta-chao's spirit of bitter struggle and also the development of the modern Chinese library profession), *Wen-hui-pao* (Shanghai, Aug. 24, 1957), p. 5.

13. Kuo Shen-po gives 1920 as the year that Li joined the history faculty at Peking University. *Chin wu-shih-nien Chung-kuo ssu-hsiang shih* (A history of Chinese thought for the past fifty years; Peking, 1936), p. 141.

14. "O-kuo ta ko-ming chih ying-hsiang" (The influence of the great Russian revolution), *HC*, p. 82.

15. Ch'en Tu-hsiu, "O-lo-ssu ko-ming yü wo kuo-min chih chüeh-wu" (The Russian revolution and our nation's awakening; Apr. 1, 1917), *Tu-hsiu wen-ts'un*, I, 143–144.

16. "O-kuo ta ko-ming chih ying-hsiang," *HC*, p. 81.

17. Li Ta-chao, "Ch'ing-ch'un," p. 6.

18. "O-kuo ta ko-ming chih ying-hsiang," *HC*, pp. 81–82.

19. Li Ta-chao, "Pao-li yü cheng-chih," p. 1.

20. P'eng Ming, "Wu-ssu shih-ch'i ti Li Ta-chao ho Ch'en Tu-hsiu" (Li Ta-chao and Ch'en Tu-hsiu in the May Fourth period), *Li-shih yen-chiu*, No. 6:52 (1962).

21. *Ibid.*

22. "Fa O ko-ming chih pi-chiao-kuan" (A comparison of the French and Russian revolutions). Li's article originally appeared in *Yen-chih chi-k'an*, No. 3 (July 1, 1918). The references here are to the reprint of the article in Shih Tsün, ed., *Chung-kuo chin-tai ssu-hsiang shih ts'an-k'ao tzu-liao chien-pien*, (Source materials for the study of the history of modern Chinese thought; Peking, 1957), pp. 1201–1204.

23. *Ibid.*, p. 1202.

24. *Ibid.*, pp. 1203–1204. Li apparently derived the notion of Russia as mediator between East and West from Paul Reinsch, whose *World Politics* (New York, 1900) he quoted in this essay.

25. *Ibid.*, p. 1204.

26. *Ibid.*, pp. 1202–1203.

27. Leon Trotsky, *Our Revolution* (New York, 1918), p. 84. For a discussion of this aspect of Trotsky's thought, see Isaac Deutscher, *The Prophet Armed* (London, 1954), p. 154.

28. Li Ta-chao, "Fa O ko-ming chih pi-chiao-kuan," in Shih Tsün, pp. 1202–1204.

29. Li Ta-chao, "Bolshevism ti sheng-li" (The victory of Bolshevism), *HCN*, 5.5:444 (Nov. 15, 1918). The date of publication in this issue of *HCN* is misprinted "October 15"; the actual date of publication was a month later.

30. *Ibid.*, pp. 442–443.

31. *Ibid.*, pp. 447–448.

32. *Ibid.*

33. Karl Mannheim, *Ideology and Utopia* (New York and London, 1952), p. 193.

34. Trotsky's *The Bolsheviki and World Peace*, which was written shortly after the outbreak of the First World War, predicted that the war was completing the conditions for "the final victory of socialism." The book was translated into English and published in New York early in 1918 by Boni and Liveright, Inc., with an introduction by Lincoln Steffens. This was apparently the edition that Li Ta-chao read.

35. Li Ta-chao, "Bolshevism ti sheng-li," pp. 446–447.

36. *Ibid.*, p. 447.

37. Li's speech, entitled "Shu-min ti sheng-li" (The victory of the masses), was printed in the issue of *HCN* that carried "The Victory of Bolshevism." The two are very similar in content. See *HCN*, 5.5:436–438 (Nov. 15, 1918).

CHAPTER IV.   THE POPULIST STRAIN

1. Lo Chia-lun, "Chin-jih chih shih-chieh hsin-ch'ao" (The new tide of today's world), *Hsin ch'ao* (New tide), Vol. 1, No. 1 (January 1919). Lo Chia-lun closely followed the image of the French Revolution as the "tide" of the nineteenth century world and the Russian Revolution as the "new

tide" of twentieth century humanity, which had been originally presented by Li Ta-chao in his article of July 1918, "Fa O ko-ming chih pi-chiao-kuan."

2. Li Ta-chao, "Wo ti Ma-k'o-ssu chu-i kuan" (My Marxist views), HCN, 6.5:521 (May 1, 1919).

3. An earlier group with anarchist inclinations, called the Society for the Study of Socialism, had been established by Chinese students in Tokyo in 1907. Tien-i-pao, the journal associated with this society, translated parts of the Communist Manifesto and Engels' Origins of the Family, Private Property, and the State. On the founding of this society, see Scalapino and Yu, pp. 29ff.

4. Hatano Kenichi, Saikin Shina nenkan (New China yearbook; Tokyo, 1935), p. 1597.

5. Chia Chih, "Chan-tou ti i-sheng," pp. 36–37.

6. Li Jui, Mao Tse-tung t'ung-chih ti ch'u-ch'i ko-ming huo-tung (The early revolutionary activities of Comrade Mao Tse-tung; Peking, 1957), p. 88. The room in the Peking University Library where Mao had his desk as Li's assistant was established as a "memorial room" to both Li and Mao in 1950. See Hsia Chia, "Pei-ching ta-hsüeh ti Mao chu-hsi ho Li Ta-chao t'ung-chih chi-nien-shih" (The Peking University memorial room for Chairman Mao and Comrade Li Ta-chao), Ch'ang-chiang jih-pao (The Yangtze daily) (June 29, 1951), p. 4.

7. Snow, p. 140. Although recent Communist accounts emphasize the close relations between Li and Mao during these months, another writer has suggested that Mao felt slighted because Li failed to pay sufficient attention to him. Hsiao Yü (Siao Yü), Mao Tse-tung and I Were Beggars (Syracuse, 1959), p. 173. Mao himself has indicated that he was none too happy with his position as Li's assistant: "My office was so low that people avoided me. One of my tasks was to register the names of people who came to read newspapers, but to most of them I didn't exist as a human being. Among those who came to read I recognized the names of famous leaders of the renaissance movement, men like Fu Ssu-nien, Lo Chai-lung [Lo Chia-lun] and others, in whom I was intensely interested. I tried to begin conversations with them on political and cultural subjects, but they were very busy men. They had no time to listen to an assistant librarian speaking southern dialect." Snow, pp. 134–135.

8. Teng Chung-hsia was arrested by Kuomintang authorities in Shanghai in 1933 and executed. Chang Kuo-t'ao was expelled from the Chinese Communist party in 1938 after a bitter dispute with Mao Tse-tung on the question of the relationship of the party to the urban proletariat.

9. "Hsin chi-yüan" (The new era; Jan. 5, 1919), HC, p. 121.

10. "Kuo-chi hu? Kuo-to hu?" (Extremism or extreme inertia?), HC, p. 124.

11. "Chan-hou chih shih-chieh ch'ao-liu" (The postwar world tide; Feb. 7 and 8, 1919), HC, p. 137.

12. "Tsai-chu-ch'ang shih ti cheng-chih" (The slaughterhouse form of politics; Apr. 20, 1919), HC, p. 167.

13. "Hsin-chiu ssu-ch'ao chih chi-chan" (The struggle between new and old tides of thought; Mar. 9, 1919), HC, p. 156.

14. "Ch'ing-nien yü nung-ts'un" (Youth and the villages; Feb. 20–23, 1919), HC, pp. 146–150.

15. For a comprehensive account of the history and ideology of the early Russian Populist movement, see Franco Venturi, *Roots of Revolution* (London, 1960).

16. For an analysis of the influence of Chernyshevskii on Lenin, see Leopold H. Haimson, *The Russian Marxists and the Origins of Bolshevism* (Cambridge, Mass., 1955), pp. 97–103.

17. Marx's views on the possibility of a socialist revolution in Russia varied considerably. Some of his letters on Russia are included in Karl Marx and Frederick Engels, The *Russian Menace to Europe*, ed. Paul Blackstock and Bert Hoselitz (Glencoe, Ill., 1952), pp. 203–226.

18. G. Plekhanov, *Our Differences* in his *Selected Philosophical Works* (Moscow, n.d.), I, 319.

19. Lenin's lengthy and tedious treatise was written between 1896 and 1899. Through the presentation of a mass of economic statistics, Lenin emphasized the extent of capitalist growth in Russia and argued that its further development was both inevitable and desirable.

20. Plekhanov, *Our Differences*, in *Selected Philosophical Works*, I, 326.

21. In Chinese Communist historical writings it is argued that in China, as in Russia, the Marxist phase of the revolutionary movement was preceded by a Populist phase. This interpretation, originally inspired by Lenin's article of 1912, "Democracy and Narodism in China," is based largely upon the interest of such anti-Manchu Chinese revolutionaries as Yang Tu-sheng and Wu Yüeh in the Russian Socialist Revolutionary movement. See T'an Pi-an, "O-kuo min-ts'ui chu-i tui T'ung-meng hui ti ying-hsiang (The influence of Russian populism on the T'ung-meng hui), *Li-shih yen-chiu*, No. 1 (1959), esp. pp. 39–41. Although there are certain ideological affinities between some Chinese revolutionaries of the T'ung-meng hui era and the Russian Socialist Revolutionaries, there is little evidence to suggest that the Chinese revolutionaries were influenced by Russian Populist ideology. Their lack of a basic emotional tie to the peasantry, and their failure to turn to the peasantry for support, make it difficult to speak of the emergence of a genuine Populist strain in the Chinese revolutionary movement during this period.

22. "Ch'ing-nien yü nung-ts'un," *HC*, p. 146. In an article discussing the problem of suicide among Chinese youth written late in 1919, Li extended the parallel between Russia and China back two decades: "Today's new Russia has been created by the youth who were soaked in the suicides of the 1850's. The new China that will necessarily be created in the future will come from the youth who are soaked in the blood of today's suicides." "Ch'ing-nien yen-shih tzu-sha wen-t'i" (The problem of pessimism and suicide among youth), *Hsin ch'ao* (New tide), 2.2:356 (Dec. 1, 1919).

23. "Ch'ing-nien yü nung-ts'un," *HC*, pp. 146–148.

24. *Ibid.*, pp. 148–149.

25. *Ibid.*, p. 149.

26. "Wu-i chi-nien jih yü hsien-tsai Chung-kuo lao-tung-chieh ti i-i" (The significance of May Day for the contemporary Chinese labor world; May 1, 1922), *HC*, p. 384.

27. "Ch'ing-nien yü nung-ts'un," *HC*, pp. 149–150.

28. In 1923 Ch'ü Ch'iu-pai attacked Chang Shih-chao's concept of "traditional agrarian socialism." See his "Hsien-tai Chung-kuo ti kuo-hui-chih

yü chün-fa" (The parliamentary system of contemporary China and the warlords), in *Chung-kuo ko-ming wen-t'i lun-wen chi* (A collection of articles on problems of the Chinese Revolution; Shanghai, 1927), esp. pp. 458–467. For a discussion of Liao Chung-k'ai's use of the "well-field" concept, a highly idealized version of ancient Chinese communal organization, see Joseph Levenson, "Ill Wind in the Well-Field," in Arthur Wright, ed., *The Confucian Persuasion* (Stanford, 1960). Li Ta-chao, in an article written in 1925 entitled "T'u-ti yü nung-min" (Land and the peasants), *HC*, pp. 523–536, described the well-field as "a kind of ideal land system spoken of by politicians since the times of Chou and Ch'in." Although he stated that communally held land was "a common phenomenon of human life under primitive economic conditions," the well-field concept played no part in his approach to contemporary agrarian problems.

29. Stuart R. Schram, *The Political Thought of Mao Tse-tung* (New York, 1963), p. 33.

30. "Ch'ing-nien yü nung-ts'un," *HC*, p. 147.

31. " 'Shao-nien Chung-kuo' ti shao-nien yün-tung" (The youth movement of "Young China"; Sept. 15, 1919), *HC*, p. 237.

32. Ts'ai Yüan-p'ei was among the first to employ this slogan in a speech delivered in the autumn of 1918 and later published under the title "Lao-kung shen-sheng" (The dignity of labor), *HCN*, Vol. 5, No. 5 (Nov. 15, 1918), the same issue that carried Li's "The Victory of Bolshevism."

33. "Hsien-tai ch'ing-nien huo-tung ti fang-hsiang" (The direction of the activity of the present generation of youth; Mar. 14–16, 1919), *HC*, pp. 160–161.

34. " 'Shao-nien Chung-kuo' ti shao-nien yün-tung," *HC*, pp. 236–237. This article was written after Li had defended his Bolshevik and Marxist beliefs in the "problems and isms" controversy.

35. Ting Shou-ho, Yin Hsü-i, and Chang Po-ch'ao, *Shih-yüeh-ko-ming tui Chung-kuo ko-ming ti ying-hsiang* (The influence of the October Revolution on the Chinese Revolution; Peking, 1957), pp. 137–138.

36. *Che-chiang hsin-ch'ao* (The Chekiang new tide), No. 1 (November 1919), as quoted in Ting Shou-ho et al., p. 141.

37. Ting Shou-ho et al., p. 142.

38. Conrad Brandt, *Stalin's Failure in China* (Cambridge, Mass., 1958), pp. 48–49.

CHAPTER V. MARXISM AND THE MAY FOURTH MOVEMENT

1. Among the contributors to *HCN*'s special issue on Marxism (Vol. 6, No. 5), the best-known were Ku Meng-yü (Ku Chao-hsiung), who wrote the article entitled "Ma-k'o-ssu hsüeh-shuo" (Marxist theory), and Ch'en Ch'i-hsiu (Ch'en Pao-yin), who wrote "Ma-k'o-ssu ti wei-wu shih-kuan yü chen-ts'ao wen-t'i" (Marx's materialist conception of history and the chastity question). Ku Meng-yü, who was Li Ta-chao's colleague on the history faculty at Peking University, was a leading member of the Kuomintang and for many years a follower of Wang Ching-wei. Ch'en Ch'i-hsiu, although the first to translate a portion of *Capital* into Chinese, apparently did not regard himself as a Marxist and was never a Communist. It is curious that the special issue

included biographical sketches both of Marx and of his archrival, the anarchist Bakunin. The former was written by Liu Ping-lin, a student of economics and a member of the New Tide Society.

2. These four works were specifically referred to by Li, and short passages from them were translated. Li's article, "Wo ti Ma-k'o-ssu chu-i kuan" (My Marxist views), appeared in *HCN* in two parts. Part 1, dealing with Marx's general historical theory, was published in Vol. 6, No. 5, pp. 521–537. Part 2, concerned with the economic theories of Marx, appeared in Vol. 6, No. 6 (Nov. 1, 1919), pp. 612–624.

3. Although Hu Han-min rejected the practical political implications of Marxist theory, he accepted the materialist conception of history in its orthodox form and attempted, in an impressively sophisticated fashion, to apply it to the study of traditional Chinese history. See his "Chung-kuo che-hsüeh shih chih wei-wu ti yen-chiu" (A materialist study of the history of Chinese philosophy), *Chien-she* (Reconstruction), Vol. 1, Nos. 3 and 4 (October and November 1919).

4. Li Ta-chao, "Wo ti Ma-k'o-ssu chu-i kuan," Pt. 1, p. 521.

5. *Ibid.*, Pt. 1, pp. 531–533.

6. *Ibid.*, Pt. 2, pp. 622–624.

7. *Ibid.*, Pt. 1, pp. 525–526; 533–534.

8. *Ibid.*, p. 535.

9. *Ibid.*, p. 536. For a discussion of the influences of neo-Kantian philosophy in European Marxist circles, see George Lichtheim, *Marxism, an Historical and Critical Study* (New York, 1961), pp. 290–300.

10. Li Ta-chao, "Wo ti Ma-k'o-ssu chu-i kuan," Pt. 2, p. 619.

11. *Ibid.*, Pt. 1, p. 537.

12. "Kuo-chi-p'ai ti yin-hsien" (The fuse of Bolshevism; Mar. 2, 1919), *HC*, p. 152.

13. For an excellent detailed survey of the events of May 4 and after, see Chow Tse-tsung.

14. "Mi-mi wai-chiao yü ch'iang-tao shih-chieh" (Secret diplomacy and the robber world; May 18, 1919), *HC*, p. 212.

15. "Kuo-ch'ing," *HC*, p. 6.

16. Although Bolshevik appeals to Asian nationalism were largely directed to the "Muslims of the East" before 1920, the Bolshevik expression "European imperialist robbers" had already gained currency among Chinese nationalists in 1919 and was undoubtedly the inspiration for Li's frequent references to "the big robber states." For an excellent account of early Soviet policy with respect to Asian nationalism, see Demetrio Boersner, *The Bolsheviks and the National and Colonial Question* (Paris and Geneva, 1957).

17. "Hsin chi-yüan" (The new era; Jan. 1, 1918), *HC*, p. 121.

18. "Ta Ya-hsi-ya chu-i yü hsin Ya-hsi-ya chu-i" (Pan-Asianism and new Asianism; Feb. 1, 1919), *HC*, p. 128.

19. "Mi-mi wai-chiao," *HC*, p. 213.

20. Chow Tse-tsung, p. 171.

21. Bertrand Russell, *The Problem of China* (London, 1922), p. 235.

22. "Hsien-tai ch'ing-nien huo-tung ti fang-hsiang" (The direction of activities of the present generation of youth), *HC*, pp. 161–162.

23. " 'Wu-i-chieh' (May Day) tsa-kan" (Thoughts on May Day; May 1, 1919), *HC*, p. 171.

24. Chia Chih, "Chan-tou ti i-sheng," p. 38.

25. See Ts'ai Yüan-p'ei. "Lao-kung shen-sheng" (The dignity of labor), *HCN*, 5.5:438–439.

26. "Lao-tung chiao-yü wen-t'i" (The labor education question; Feb. 14–15, 1919), *HC*, pp. 138–139.

27. "T'ang-shan mei-kuang ti kung-jen sheng-huo" (The life of the workers of the T'ang-shan coal mines; Mar. 9, 1919), *HC*, pp. 153–154.

28. "Chung-kuo hsüeh-sheng chieh ti 'May Day'" (The "May Day" of the Chinese student world; May 4, 1921), *HC*, p. 358.

29. "Chi-nien wu-yüeh ssu-jih" (Commemorating May Fourth), from a lecture to the Peking Students Union on May 4, 1923, *HC*, p. 463.

30. Thirty-seven issues of *Mei-chou p'ing-lun* appeared between December 1918 and August 1919. It was suppressed by the Peking government early in September 1919, at the time that Ch'en Tu-hsiu was released from prison and forced to flee to Shanghai. For a history of the periodical, see *Wu-ssu shih-ch'i ch'i-k'an chieh-shao*, I, 41–62.

31. "Tsai-lun wen-t'i yü chu-i" (Again on problems and isms; Aug. 17, 1919), in Shih Tsün, p. 1260.

32. "Huan-ying Tu-hsiu ch'u-yü" (Welcoming [Ch'en] Tu-hsiu on his release from prison), *HCN*, 6.6:588–589 (Nov. 1, 1919).

33. As a result of political pressure Ch'en had been forced to resign his position as Dean of the School of Letters of Peking University in March 1919 but retained his professorship until September.

34. Hu Shih, "To yen-chiu hsieh wen-t'i, shao t'an hsieh chu-i" (More study of problems, less talk about "isms"; July 20, 1919), *Hu Shih wen-ts'un* (Collected essays of Hu Shih; Shanghai, 1926), II, 147–153.

35. "Tsai-lun wen-t'i yü chu-i," in Shih Tsün, p. 1256.

36. *Ibid.*, p. 1258.

37. Hu Shih, "To yen-chiu hsieh wen-t'i" in *Hu Shih wen-ts'un*, II, 151.

38. Hu Shih, "The Significance of the New Thought" (Nov. 1, 1919), in Teng and Fairbank, p. 255.

39. "Tsai-lun wen-t'i yü chu-i," in Shih Tsün, p. 1261.

40. Karl Mannheim, *Ideology and Utopia* (New York, 1952), p. 228.

41. Chow Tse-tsung, p. 221.

42. Max Weber, "Politics as a Vocation," in H. H. Gerth and C. Wright Mills, eds., *From Max Weber: Essays in Sociology* (New York, 1958), pp. 77–128.

43. Schwartz, "Intelligentsia," p. 611.

44. Lan Kung-wu's article "Wen-t'i yü chu-i" (Problems and isms), written under the name Lan Chih-hsien, is in *Hu Shih wen-ts'un*, I, 153–167. For a Communist interpretation of the "problems and isms" debate, see Ai Ssu-ch'i, "Chieh-shao wu-ssu wen-hua yün-tung chung ti i-ko chung-yao cheng-lun" (Introduction to an important controversy in the May Fourth cultural movement), *Yu-ti fang-shih chi ch'i-t'a* (Some arrows and others; Shanghai, 1951), pp. 17–33.

45. Hu Shih's other essays in this debate were: "San-lun wen-t'i yü chu-i" (Third discussion on problems and isms), *Hu Shih wen-ts'un*, I, 177–190; "Ssu-lun wen-t'i yü chu-i" (Fourth discussion on problems and isms), *ibid.*, pp. 190–198; and "Hsin-ssu-ch'ao ti i-i" (The significance of the new tide of thought), *HCN*, Vol. 7, No. 1 (Dec. 1919). In addition to "Again on Problems and Isms," many of the questions relevant to this debate were discussed by Li Ta-chao in the following essays: "Wu-chih pien-tung yü

tao-te pien-tung" (Material change and ethical change), *Hsin ch'ao*, Vol. 2, No. 2 (Dec., 1919); and "Yu ching-chi shang chieh-shih Chung-kuo chin-tai ssu-hsiang pien-tung ti yüan-yin" (An economic explanation of the causes of the changes in modern Chinese thought), *HCN*, Vol. 7, No. 2 (Jan. 1, 1920).

46. "Tsai-lun wen-t'i yü chu-i," in Shih Tsün, pp. 1261–1262.

47. "Wu-chih pien-tung yü tao-te pien-tung." This essay is reprinted in *HC*, pp. 256–273.

48. Li Ta-chao, "Yu ching-chi shang chieh-shih Chung-kuo chin-tai ssu-hsiang pien-tung ti yüan-yin," *HCN*, 7.2:53 (Jan. 1, 1920).

49. "Wei-wu shih-kuan tsai hsien-tai shih-hsüeh shang ti chia-chih" (The value of the materialist conception of history in contemporary historical studies), *HC*, pp. 334–340.

50. In "Again on Problems and Isms" Li stated: "My colleagues on the *New Youth* and the *Weekly Critic* rarely speak about Russian Bolshevism. According to the views of the Japanese *Daily News*, the thought and literary movement of Chung-fu [Ch'en Tu-hsiu] and yourself [Hu Shih] is said to be the orthodox thought of Chinese democracy. On the one hand, you struggle against the old forms of stupid and superstitious thought, and yet on the other hand, you want to repress the tide of Russian Bolshevism. As for myself, I can say that I enjoy and welcome discussing Bolshevism." Tsai-lun wen-t'i yü chu-i, in Shih Tsün, pp. 1259–1260.

51. Ch'en Tu-hsiu, "Ehr-shih shih-chi O-lo-ssu ti ko-ming" (The twentieth century Russian Revolution), *Tu-hsiu wen-ts'un*, II, 29. See also Ch'en's reference to the Russian Revolution in a "Random Thoughts" column of February 1919 (*ibid.*, pp. 12–13).

52. Ch'en Tu-hsiu, "Kuo-chi-p'ai yü shih-chieh ho-p'ing" (The Bolsheviks and world peace), *HCN*, 7.1:115–116.

53. Ch'en Tu-hsiu, "Shih-hsing min-chih ti chi-ch'u" (The basis for the realization of democracy), *HCN*, 7.1:13–21 (Dec. 1, 1919).

54. For the evolution of Ch'en's Marxist views between May and December 1920, see Ch'en Tu-hsiu, *Tu-hsiu wen-ts'un*, IV, 215–266.

55. *Ibid.*, IV, 259.

56. Schwartz, *Chinese Communism*, p. 22.

57. Ch'en Tu-hsiu, "Letter to Cheng Hsien-tsung," *Tu-hsiu wen-ts'un*, IV, 250–266.

58. Karl Marx, "Theses on Feuerbach," Karl Marx and Frederick Engels, *Selected Works* (Moscow, 1958), II, 405.

59. Ch'en set forth the reasons for his political commitment in "T'an cheng-chih" (On politics), *HCN*, Vol. 8, No. 1 (September 1920).

60. For an account of these activities, see Ting Shou-ho et al., esp. pp. 59–82, 134–164.

61. A. A. Muller, *V plameni revoliutsii (1917–1920 gg.). Vospominaniia komandira internatsional 'nogo otriada Krasnoi gvardii* (In the flames of the Revolution, 1917–1920: Reminiscences of the commander of the international detachment of the Red Guards; Irkutsk, 1957), as quoted by Iu. M. Garushiants, "Bor'ba Kitaiskikh Marksistov za sozdanie Kommunisticheskoi Partii Kitaia" (The struggle of the Chinese Marxists for the foundation of the Chinese Communist party), *Narody Azii i Afriki*, No. 3:85 (1961). N. Bortman is described as a young Russian who joined the Russian Communist party in 1919 and "met a tragic death" in Siberia in

1920. I am indebted to Dr. Ellis Joffe for calling my attention to this source and for translating the passage quoted here.

62. The role of the *Ch'en-pao fu-k'an* in the popularization of Marxism is discussed in *Wu-ssu shih-ch'i ch'i-k'an chieh-shao*, I, 98–143.

63. Ting Shou-ho et al., pp. 81–82. For a bibliography of the publications of Chinese translations of the writings of Marx and Engels, see Chang Ching-lu, III, 442–451.

64. Chang Ching-lu, III, 452.

65. Chu Wu-shan, "Hui-i Shou-ch'ang t'ung-chih" (Memories of Comrade Shou-ch'ang), *Jen-min jih-pao* (Apr. 29, 1957), p. 2. After the establishment of the Chinese Communist party the Society for the Study of Marxist Theory continued as a discussion group. It included Communists, non-Communist Marxists, and even such non-Marxists as Ku Meng-yü and Kao I-han.

66. According to Russian sources there was a third member of the Voitinsky mission, identified only as I. K. Manaev. Garushiants, pp. 86–87.

67. The Russian professor was Sergei A. Polevoy, who although not a Communist, is said to have been "sympathetic to the Russian Revolution." Garushiants, p. 86.

68. Chia Chih, "Chan-tou ti i-sheng," p. 40.

69. "A Brief History of the Chinese Communist Party," C. Martin Wilbur and Julie Lien-ying How, *Documents on Communism, Nationalism and Soviet Advisers in China, 1918–1927* (New York, 1956), p. 48. See also Ting Shou-ho et al., p. 148.

70. Ting Shou-ho et al., p. 148.

71. Wilbur and How, pp. 50–51.

72. *Ibid.*, pp. 49–50.

73. Li Jui, p. 120; Ting Shou-ho et al., p. 80.

74. In addition to Chou and Li Li-san, the Paris group included such present-day notables as Li Fu-ch'un, the Chinese Communist economic planner, and the Chinese Foreign Minister Ch'en Yi. Shortly after the organization of the Paris group, Communist groups were formed among Chinese students in Germany (by Chu Teh), in Moscow (by Ch'ü Ch'iu-pai), and in Tokyo.

75. Kao I-han, p. 3.

76. Chang Ching-ju, "Chih-shih fen-tzu pi-hsü yü kung-nung ch'ün-chung hsiang chieh-ho" (The intelligentsia must unite with the worker and peasant masses), *Kuang-ming jih-pao* (May 1, 1957), p. 3.

77. According to a hostile source, Mao is said to have favored Li rather than Ch'en to head the party. Hsiao Yü, p. 202.

78. According to an early Chinese Communist source, the membership of the party as late as the beginning of 1925 was only 994, and the membership of the Youth Corps was only 2,365. Wilbur and How, p. 90.

CHAPTER VI. DETERMINISM AND ACTIVISM

1. Li Ta-chao, "Spring," pp. 16–17.

2. See the discussion of Li's essay "Wo ti Ma-k'o-ssu chu-i kuan" (My Marxist Views) in Chapter V.

3. Li Ta-chao, "Wo ti Ma-k'o-ssu chu-i kuan," Pt. 1, pp. 534, 535.

4. Karl Marx, "Economic and Philosophic Manuscripts," tr. T. B.

Bottomore, in Erich Fromm, *Marx's Concept of Man* (New York, 1961), p. 96.

5. *Ibid.*, p. 107.

6. Karl Marx, "Theses on Feuerbach," in Karl Marx and Frederick Engels, *The German Ideology* (New York, 1947), p. 199.

7. Karl Marx, "Preface to a Contribution to the Critique of Political Economy," in Marx and Engels, *Selected Works*, I, 363.

8. In one of the most important statements of the materialist conception of history Marx wrote: "The first premise of all human history is, of course, the existence of living human individuals." Marx and Engels, *The German Ideology*, p. 7.

9. George Lukacs, "What Is Orthodox Marxism?" *New International* (Summer 1957), p. 193.

10. Herbert Marcuse, *Reason and Revolution* (New York, 1954), pp. 318–319.

11. Karl Lowith, "Man's Self-Alienation in the Early Writings of Marx," *Social Research* (Summer 1954), p. 230.

12. Probably the best argument for the "two Marx" theory is presented in an article by Leonard Krieger, "Marx and Engels as Historians," *Journal of the History of Ideas*, 14.3:381–403 (June 1953). For interpretations that emphasize the continuity between Marx's early philosophical ideas and those of the "mature Marx," see the Introduction to Erich Fromm, *Marx's Concept of Man*; Raya Dunayevskaya, *Marxism and Freedom* (New York, 1958); and Robert Tucker, *Philosophy and Myth in Karl Marx* (Cambridge, 1961). The best analysis of the philosophy of Marx is still that of Herbert Marcuse in *Reason and Revolution*, particularly pp. 273–322.

13. The attraction of the Paris Commune as the model for the "dictatorship of the proletariat" is one particularly strong element of continuity in the Marxist, Leninist, and Maoist traditions. See Li Ta-chao, "I-pa-ch'i-i nien ti Pa-li 'k'ang-miao-ssu'" (The Paris Commune of 1871), written in February 1923 for the fiftieth anniversary of the Shanghai *Shen-pao, HC*, pp. 447–456; see also the symposium on the Paris Commune in *Li-shih yen-chiu* (Historical research), No. 2 (1961).

14. For an interesting discussion of the philosophic basis of *Capital*, see Dunayevskaya.

15. Letter of Engels to J. Bloch (Sept. 21 and 22, 1890), in Karl Marx and Frederick Engels, *Selected Correspondence* (Moscow, 1953), p. 498.

16. George Plekhanov, *Fundamental Problems of Marxism* (New York, 1930), p. 54.

17. In analyzing the period from the 16th century (which Marx identified as the century of the genesis of capitalism) until the bourgeoisie actually acquired state power (the 17th century in the case of England and the late 19th century in the case of France), Marx and Engels were confronted with the problem of identifying "the ruling class" at a time when neither the disintegrating feudal class nor the emerging bourgeoisie were actually in control of political power. This led to the notion that under certain historical conditions the state itself could govern, ruling *over* the contending classes, as it were. This idea was stated explicitly by Marx in *The Eighteenth Brumaire of Louis Bonaparte* and somewhat more timidly by Engels in *The Origin of the Family, Private Property and the State.*

Engels' statement read: "periods occur in which the warring classes balance each other so nearly that the state power, as ostensible mediator, acquires, for the moment, a certain degree of independence of both. Such was the absolute monarchy of the seventeenth and eighteenth centuries, which held the balance between the nobility and the class of burghers; such was the Bonapartism of the First, and still more of the Second French Empire, which played off the proletariat against the bourgeoisie and the bourgeoisie against the proletariat." Marx and Engels, *Selected Works*, II, 320–321. The notion that state power can exist independently has been consistently rejected in Stalinist ideology since it provides ideological grounds to oppose the claim that the Soviet state must necessarily be the agency of proletarian class rule.

18. See esp. Karl Marx, *The Eighteenth Brumaire of Louis Bonaparte* (Chicago, 1919).

19. The concept of "Oriental despotism" was most clearly outlined in the article "The British Rule in India," which Marx wrote in 1853 for the *New York Tribune*. See Marx and Engels, *Selected Works*, I, 345–351. The significance of this concept for the present discussion lies in the notion that the political power of the state dominates the economic power of society. Although this concept is highly deterministic, it is a form of geographic-political determinism, rather than strict economic determinism.

20. See, e.g., Karl Marx, *Capital* (Chicago, 1912), I, 823–824.

21. Karl Marx, "Zur Kritik der Hegelschen Rechtphilosophie," in Marx and Engels, *Werke* (Berlin, 1957), I, 389–391.

22. Several of Marx's letters on Russia have been translated into English and appear in the volume of writings of Marx and Engels edited by Paul Blackstock and Bert Hoselitz, published under the rather misleading title *The Russian Menace to Europe*. See pp. 203–226.

23. Karl Marx, "Revolution in China and Europe," *New York Tribune*, (June 14, 1853), p. 4. In 1926 Li Ta-chao translated and interpreted Marx's article. Li's interpretation is discussed in Chapter X.

24. For a discussion of the differences between the theory of Marx himself and orthodox, pre-Leninist Marxism, see Lichtheim, pp. 234–277.

25. For a perceptive discussion of Plekhanov's confidence in the objective forces of history and Lenin's lack of faith in them, see Haimson, pp. 44–48, 110–114.

26. This notion was developed by Lenin in his work of 1902, "What Is to Be Done?" See V. I. Lenin, *Selected Works* (Moscow, 1952), Vol. 1, Pt. 1, pp. 203–409.

27. Even in "What Is to Be Done?," the most explicit expression of the premises of Leninist strategy, Lenin did not discuss the theoretical implications of the centralized party organization that he advocated in this work.

28. Russian voluntarists like Lenin drew from Hegel the belief that consciousness was not merely a reflection of nature but a phenomenon external to it. Haimson, p. 100.

29. Li Ta-chao, "O-lo-ssu ko-ming ti kuo-ch'ü chi hsien-tsai" (The past and present of the Russian Revolution) HCN, 9.3:12–13 (July 1, 1921).

30. Li Ta-chao, "Wo ti Ma-k'o-ssu chu-i kuan," Pt. 1, p. 534.

31. "Tsai-lun wen-t'i yü chu-i," in Shih Tsün, p. 1262.

32. Marx, *The German Ideology*, p. 40.

33. Li's antipathy to Social Darwinism did not extend to Darwinism itself. He admired Darwin and compared his contributions to the study of biological evolution to Marx's contributions to the understanding of social evolution in the essay "Wu-chih pien-tung yü tao-te pien-tung" (Material change and ethical change), Shih Tsün, pp. 1218ff.

34. "Hsin chi-yüan" (The new era; Jan. 5, 1919), HC, p. 120.

35. "Chieh-chi ching-cheng yü hu-chu" (Class struggle and mutual aid; July 6, 1919), HC, p. 222.

36. Ibid., pp. 223–224.

37. Ibid., p. 224.

38. "Wu-chih pien-tung yü tao-te pien-tung," in Shih Tsün, p. 1221.

39. Li Ta-chao, "Yu ching-chi shang chieh-shih," pp. 50–51.

40. Ibid., pp. 52–53.

41. Tai Chi-t'ao, best known as an ideological adviser to Chiang K'ai-shek, actually participated in the founding of the Chinese Communist party. Although he left the party shortly after the First Congress of 1921, he was an advocate of the materialist conception of history, a promoter of the Leninist theory of imperialism, and a practitioner of Leninist methods of party organization. For a discussion of Tai's "Marxism-Leninism," see Brandt, p. 57.

42. "Wu-chih pien-tung yü tao-te pien-tung," in Shih Tsün, p. 1222.

43. Li Ta-chao, "Yu ching-chi shang chieh-shih," HC, pp. 47–53.

44. "Wu-chih pien-tung yü tao-te pien-tung," in Shih Tsün, pp. 1218–1219.

45. Ibid., p. 1220.

46. Li Ta-chao, "Wei-wu shih-kuan tsai hsien-tai shih-hsüeh shang ti chia-chih" (The value of the materialist conception of history in contemporary historical study) (Dec. 1, 1920), in Shih Tsün, pp. 1245–1248.

47. Ibid., pp. 1248–1249.

48. Ibid., p. 1249.

49. "P'ing-min cheng-chih yü kung-jen cheng-chih (Democracy and ergotocracy; July 1, 1922), HC, pp. 399–400.

50. Seven of Chang Tung-sun's articles on the question of industrialization were reprinted in 1922 in the symposium "Kuan-yü she-hui chu-i ti t'ao-lun" (Discussions concerning socialism). See She-hui chu-i ti t'ao-lun-chi (A collection of discussions on socialism; Canton, 1922), pp. 32–33, 43–58, 60–62.

51. Chow Tse-tsung, p. 230.

52. In The Problem of China Russell stated: "So far, in China proper, it [Bolshevism] has affected hardly anyone except the younger students, to whom Bolshevism appeals as a method of developing industry without passing through the stage of private capitalism. This appeal will doubtless diminish as the Bolsheviks are more and more forced to revert to capitalism. Moreover, Bolshevism, as it has developed in Russia, is quite peculiarly inapplicable to China." (p. 185).

53. For Ch'en Tu-hsiu's contributions to this debate, see She-hui chu-i ti t'ao-lun-chi, pp. 44–45, 62–97.

54. "Chung-kuo ti she-hui chu-i yü shih-chieh ti tzu-pen chu-i" (Chinese socialism and world capitalism; Mar. 20, 1921), HC, pp. 356–357.

55. Leon Trotsky, Problems of the Chinese Revolution (New York, 1932), pp. 207, 208.

CHAPTER VII. PHILOSOPHY OF HISTORY

1. "Shih-kuan" (Historical interpretation), *HC*, p. 287.
2. "Fa O ko-ming chih pi-chiao kuan," in Shih Tsün, p. 1204.
3. "Yen-shih-hsin yü tzu-chüeh-hsin" (Pessimism and self-consciousness), *HC*, pp. 28–35.
4. Li Ta-chao, *Shih-hsüeh yao-lun* (The essentials of historical study; Shanghai, 1924).
5. See, e.g., Li Ta-chao, *Shih-hsüeh yao-lun*, p. 5.
6. Robert Michel, *First Lectures in Political Sociology* (Minneapolis, 1949), p. 21.
7. Karl Marx, *Selected Writings in Sociology and Social Philosophy*, ed. T. B. Bottomore and Maxmilian Rubel (London, 1956), p. 63.
8. Li Ta-chao, "Wo ti Ma-k'o-ssu chu-i kuan," Pt. 1, p. 534.
9. "Shih-kuan" (The interpretation of history), *HC*, p. 287.
10. *Ibid.*, pp. 288–291.
11. "Shih" (Time), *HC*, pp. 488–489.
12. Li Ta-chao, *Shih-hsüeh yao-lun*, pp. 1–2.
13. "Yen-chiu li-shih ti jen-wu" (The responsibilities of studying history; November 1923), *HC*, pp. 480, 483.
14. Li Ta-chao, *Shih-hsüeh yao-lun*, pp. 8–9.
15. "Shih-kuan," *HC*, p. 287.
16. "Ma-k'o-ssu ti li-shih che-hsüeh" (The historical philosophy of Marx; 1920), *HC*, p. 294.
17. Li Ta-chao, "K'ung-tao-hsi ti li-shih kuan" (The historical view of Condorcet), *She-hui k'o-hsüeh chi-k'an* (Social science quarterly), 2.1:60–62 (November 1923).
18. *Ibid.*, pp. 61–63.
19. "Sang-hsi-men ti li-shih kuan" (The historical view of Saint-Simon; August 1923), *HC*, pp. 469–471.
20. See the comments on Condorcet, Saint-Simon, Comte and Vico in Li Ta-chao, *Shih-hsüeh yao-lun*, pp. 54–58.
21. Li Ta-chao, "K'ung-tao-hsi ti li-shih kuan," p. 63.
22. Marx and Engels, *The German Ideology*, pp. 197–198.
23. "Sang-hsi-men ti li-shih kuan," *HC*, p. 465.
24. Max Weber, *The Protestant Ethic and the Spirit of Capitalism* (New York, 1958), pp. 111–112.
25. For a discussion of the influence of the "Realists" on Lenin, see Haimson, pp. 9–11, 98–100.
26. Li Ta-chao, "Wo ti Ma-k'o-ssu chu-i kuan," p. 534.
27. "She-hui chu-i ti ching-chi tsu-chih" (The economic organization under socialism; January 1923), *HC*, p. 428.
28. " 'Chin' yü 'ku' " ("Now" and "antiquity"; February 1923), *HC*, pp. 433–444.
29. *Ibid.*, p. 446.
30. "Shih" (Time), *HC*, p. 485. This essay appeared in the Peking *Ch'en-pao* on Dec. 1, 1923, and was written for the fifth anniversary of that newspaper, with which Li Ta-chao had been associated since its founding.
31. *Ibid.*, pp. 485–486.
32. *Ibid.*, pp. 487–488.

33. Letter of Karl Marx to P. V. Annekov, Dec. 28, 1846, Marx and Engels, *Selected Correspondence*, p. 40.

34. Mannheim, p. 219.

35. "Yüan-jen she-hui yü wen-tzu shu-ch'i shang chih wei-wu ti fan-ying" (The material reflection of primitive society in literary documents), *HC*, pp. 341–355.

36. Letter of Karl Marx to the editors of *Otechestvenniye Zapiski*, November 1877, Marx and Engels, *Selected Correspondence*, pp. 354–355.

37. Kuo Mo-jo, *Chung-kuo ku-tai she-hui yen-chiu* (A study of ancient Chinese society; Shanghai, 1930). Kuo began his book with the premise, "on the whole, the history of mankind has everywhere been the same."

38. Opposition to the unilinear view was forcefully expressed in the Communist debates on the question of the "Asiatic mode of production," which continued into the 1930's. For an account of those debates by a participant, see Karl Wittfogel, *Oriental Despotism* (New Haven, 1957), pp. 401–408.

39. Li Ta-chao, "Yu ching-chi shang chieh-shih," pp. 48–49.

40. "T'u-ti yü nung-min" (Land and the peasants), *HC*, p. 523.

41. Li Ta-chao, *Shih-hsüeh yao-lun*, pp. 37–39.

42. Li Ta-chao, "Yu ching-chi shang chieh-shih," pp. 47–48.

43. Marx and Engels, *The German Ideology* (1939), p. 7.

44. Marx, *Capital*, II, 176.

45. Plekhanov, *Fundamental Problems of Marxism*, p. 34.

46. Marx's most complete statement of the theory of the "Asiatic mode of production" appeared in his essay "The British Rule in India," which was published originally in *The New York Tribune*, June 25, 1853.

47. For some of the reasons why Marx failed to apply the concept to China, see my article "The Despotism of Concepts: Wittfogel and Marx on China," *The China Quarterly*, No. 16:99–111 (October–December 1963).

48. Marx and Engels, *Selected Works*, I, 363.

49. Li Ta-chao, "Wo ti Ma-k'o-ssu chu-i kuan," Pt. 1, p. 532.

50. Li Ta-chao, "Yu ching-chi shang chieh-shih," pp. 48–51.

51. The following statement, e.g., appeared in a booklet by Li published in January 1923: "Democracy originated in Europe and spread to America, and recently, by means of the power of the machine gun, the steamship, the newspaper, and the telegraph, it has brought a thunderous sound to awaken Asia, which has slumbered deep in despotism for several thousand years." Li Ta-chao, *P'ing-min chu-i* (Democracy) (Shanghai, 1923), p. 1.

52. See, e.g., "Sun Chung-shan hsien-sheng tsai Chung-kuo min-tsu ko-ming shih shang chih wei-chih" (Mr. Sun Yat-sen's place in the history of the Chinese national revolution), *HC*, pp. 537–538.

53. "Chung-shan chu-i ti kuo-min ko-ming yü shih-chieh ko-ming" (The Sun Yat-senist national revolution and the world revolution) *HC*, p. 561.

54. *Ibid.*, p. 562.

55. Li's use of Marx's articles on China will be examined in Chap. X.

CHAPTER VIII. NATIONALISM AND INTERNATIONALISM

1. Marx's critique of the nation-state system was based, in the first instance, on the view of human nature outlined in his early "Economic and Philosophic Manuscripts." There he spoke of a latent "human essence" which was universal and existed beneath all the differences and diversities that had developed among men in the course of history — which in Marx's view had been a history of man's self-alienation. Communism was defined as the "positive abolition" of human self-alienation and man's "return to himself"; thus, it was the abolition of all differences between men, including national differences.

2. Whereas Marx viewed the nation as a manifestation of human self-alienation, he interpreted the rise of the modern nation-state and modern nationalism as historically progressive phenomena since they were associated with the early development of capitalism and the overcoming of feudal decentralization. Although he seriously underestimated the power of nationalist feelings, he was very much concerned with the practical existence of nations, the concrete social and economic differences between them, and even the peculiarities in the traits and characteristics of different nationalities. He always insisted that political programs should be based on analyses of concrete conditions of particular nations. Moreover, under certain circumstances he felt that nationalist movements could still contribute to historical progress. The German revolutions of 1848, the Irish opposition to English colonialism, and even the T'ai-p'ing rebellion in China (which Marx interpreted as a "national war" against foreign intruders) were contemporary nationalist movements that Marx supported.

3. On the cosmopolitan nature of the capitalist commodity Marx wrote: "Just as money develops into world-money, so the commodity owner develops into a cosmopolitan. The cosmopolitan relation of man is originally only the relation of commodity owners. The commodity as such rises above all religious, political, national and language barriers. Price is its universal language and money its common form. But with the development of world-money as distinguished from national coin, there develops the cosmopolitanism of the commodity owner as the faith of practical reason opposed to traditional religious, national and other prejudices which hinder the interchange of matter among mankind." *The Critique of Political Economy*, p. 207.

4. "The Communist Manifesto" in Marx and Engels, *Werke*, IV, 479.

5. "Tung-hsi wen-ming ken-pen chih i-tien," in *Shou-ch'ang wen-chi*, p. 40.

6. *Ibid.*, p. 48.

7. "Tsai-lun hsin Ya-hsi-ya chu-i" (Again on New Asianism; Dec. 12, 1919), *HC*, p. 281.

8. Li Ta-chao, "Fa O ko-ming chih pi-chiao-kuan," in Shih Tsün, p. 1202.

9. Li Ta-chao, "Bolshevism ti sheng-li," p. 444.

10. "Hsin chi-yüan," *HC*, pp. 119, 121.

11. "Mi-mi wai-chiao," *HC*, p. 213.

12. "Tsai 'Kuo-min tsa-chih' chou-nien shang ti chiang-shuo" (Speech

at the anniversary celebration of the Citizens Magazine; November 1919),
HC, p. 255. On the second anniversary of the May Fourth Incident, Li
repeated this theme. The significance of May Fourth, he wrote, was that it
inspired Chinese students with "the spirit of human freedom." It "should
not be seen as only the commemoration of a patriotic movement." "Chung-
kuo hsüeh-sheng ti May Day" (The May Day of Chinese students), *HC*,
p. 358.

13. "Ya-hsi-ya ch'ing-nien ti kuang-ming yün-tung" (The bright movement of Asian youth), *HC*, p. 328.

14. Li Ta-chao, "Wu-i yün-tung shih" (The history of May Day),
HCN, 7.6:3 (May 1, 1920).

15. Li Ta-chao took part in the founding of the Young China Society
in Peking on June 18, 1918. The group eventually split into left and right
wing factions. Li, Mao Tse-tung, Yün Tai-ying, Chou Fu-hai, and two of
Li's most prominent students at Peking University, Teng Chung-hsia and
Liu Jen-ching, were the leading members of the left wing. For a discussion
of the split, see Chow Tse-tsung, pp. 251–253.

16. "Shao-nien Chung-kuo ti shao-nien yün-tung," *HC*, pp. 237–238.

17. See Li's articles of early 1917, "K'ung-tzu yü hsien-fa" (Confucius
and the constitution) and "Tzu-jan ti lun-li-kuan yü K'ung-tzu" (The
ethical view of nature and Confucius), *HC*, pp. 77–80.

18. "Hsin chi-yüan," *HC*, p. 119.

19. "Mi-mi wai-chiao," *HC*, p. 213.

20. "Hsiang-yüan yü ta-tao" (Hypocrites and big robbers; Jan. 26,
1919), *HC*, p. 125.

21. Li Ta-chao, "Yu ching-chi shang chieh-shih," p. 48.

22. "Ch'u-mai kuan-shih:jou-lin jen-ke" (Officials for sale: the human
personality trampled underfoot; Nov. 9, 1919), *HC*, p. 249.

23. Li Ta-chao, "Wu-chih pien-tung yü tao-te pien-tung," pp. 1225
and 1235. Li counterposed Chinese family ethics and the ethics of
Western nationalism because he held that traditional China "was only the
organization of a group of clans" and not really a nation. See Li Ta-chao,
"Yu ching-chi shang chieh-shih," pp. 51–52.

24. Li Ta-chao, "Bolshevism ti sheng-li," pp. 447–448.

25. Leon Trotsky, *The Bolsheviki and World Peace* (New York, 1918),
p. 28.

26. For a brief discussion of this controversy, see Isaac Deutscher, *The
Prophet Armed* (London, 1954), pp. 236–238.

27. "Lien-chih chu-i yü shih-chieh tzu-chih," *HC*, p. 134. Support for
federalist principles of organization can be found in Marx's work on the
Paris Commune, *The Civil War in France*.

28. "Ta Ya-hsi-ya chu-i yü hsin Ya-hsi-ya chu-i" (Pan-Asianism and
New Asianism; Feb. 1, 1919), *HC*, pp. 127–129.

29. "Ya-hsi-ya ch'ing-nien ti kuang-ming yün-tung," *HC*, p. 327.

30. "Tsai-lun hsin Ya-hsi-ya chu-i" (Again on New Asianism), *HC*,
p. 278; "Ya-hsi-ya ch'ing-nien ti kuang-ming yün-tung," *HC*, p. 327.

31. "Tsai-lun hsin Ya-hsi-ya chu-i," *HC*, pp. 279–280.

32. "Ya-hsi-ya ch'ing-nien ti kuang-ming yün-tung," *HC*, p. 327.

33. "Tsai-lun hsin Ya-hsi-ya chu-i," *HC*, p. 280.

34. Schram, p. 26.

35. Li Ta-chao, *Shih-hsüeh yao-lun*, pp. 37–40. By 1926 Li had

concluded that continuity with the Chinese tradition was an outstanding characteristic of the "Chinese national revolutionary movement." See "Sun Chung-shan hsien-sheng tsai Chung-kuo min-tsu kuo-ming shih-shang chih wei-chih" (Mr. Sun Yat-sen's place in the history of the Chinese National Revolution), *HC*, pp. 543–544.

36. Li's lecture was recorded by a member of the audience, Liu Pai-ching, and later published under the title "Jen-chung wen-t'i" (The race question), *Hsin min-kuo tsa-chih* (New republic magazine), Vol. I, No. 6 (June 1924). Although the published version was apparently based upon the notes of Liu Pai-ching, there is no reason to believe that it was not an accurate account of Li's lecture. There is no evidence to suggest that Li objected to its publication, nor did he ever repudiate its contents. Moreover, its major themes followed logically from Li's "proletarian nation" theory and were consistent with other ultranationalist elements that emerged in his writings at this time. "Jen-chung wen-t'i" is listed in an accurate and virtually complete bibliography of Li's writings published in China in 1957. Wen Ts'ao, "Shih-pien Li Ta-chao (Shou-ch'ang) i-chu hsi-nien mu-lu," (A preliminary chronological index to the writings of Li Ta-chao), *Hsüeh-shu yüeh-kan* (Scholarship monthly), Nos. 1–5 and 9 (1957).

37. Li Ta-chao, "Jen-chung wen-t'i," pp. 1–5.
38. *Ibid.*, pp. 6–8.
39. *Ibid.*, p. 5.
40. *Ibid.*, p. 9.
41. *Ibid.*, p. 6.
42. Quoted in Deutscher, p. 238.
43. See, e.g., Mao Tse-tung's statement of Aug. 8, 1963, on race relations in the U. S. *Survey of the China Mainland Press*, No. 3038 (Aug. 13, 1963).
44. Trotsky, *Problems of the Chinese Revolution*, p. 69.

CHAPTER IX. LENINISM AND POPULISM

1. Marx, *Economic and Philosophic Manuscripts*, p. 135.
2. For a stimulating discussion of the Marxist view of the relationship between theory and practice, see Mannheim, pp. 112 ff.
3. Perhaps the most notable example of a Marxist political movement in which theory was far removed from historical realities and political practice occurred in pre-World War One Germany. As has often been noted, the practice of the German Social Democratic party corresponded less to its official Marxist theory as outlined by Kautsky than to the supposedly heretical "revisionist" theory of Bernstein.
4. Li Ta-chao, "Tsai-lun wen-t'i yü chu-i," pp. 1256–1258.
5. Lenin, "What Is to Be Done?," *Selected Works* (Moscow, 1952), Vol. 1, Pt. 1, pp. 233, 244.
6. *Ibid.*, pp. 233–234.
7. Haimson, p. 100.
8. Lenin, "What Is to Be Done?," *Selected Works*, Vol. 1, Pt. 1, p. 348.
9. *Ibid.*, p. 390.
10. "Ch'ing-nien yü nung-ts'un," *HC*, pp. 147–148.
11. "Hsien-tai ch'ing-nien huo-tung ti fang-hsiang" (The direction of

the activity of the present generation of youth; Mar. 14–16, 1919), HC, p. 161.

12. "Chih-shih chieh-chi ti sheng-li" (The victory of the intelligentsia), HC, p. 308.

13. Li Ta-chao, "O-lo-ssu ko-ming ti kuo-ch'ü chi hsien-tsai," pp. 8–10.

14. Ibid., pp. 11–13.

15. "Chui-tao Lieh-ning ping chi-nien 'erh-ch'i' " (In memory of Lenin and in commemoration of "February Seventh"; Feb. 7, 1924), HC, p. 499.

16. "Lieh-ning pu ssu" (Lenin is not dead; Mar. 30, 1964), HC, p. 501.

17. For an excellent discussion of the influence of Populist ideas on Lenin, see Haimson, pp. 97 ff.

18. Ibid., pp. 138–139.

19. See, e.g., Li's essay of 1915, "Ching-kao ch'üan-kuo fu-lao shu," HC, p. 27.

20. "Ch'ing-nien yü nung-ts'un," HC, p. 147.

21. "Hsien-tai ch'ing-nien huo-tung ti fang-hsiang," HC, p. 162.

22. "P'ing-min cheng-chih yü kung-jen cheng-chih" (Democratic politics and workers' politics; July 1, 1922), HC, p. 395.

23. Li Ta-chao, P'ing-min chu-i, pp. 2–4, 10–11.

24. "P'ing-min cheng-chih yü kung-jen cheng-chih," HC, p. 400.

25. Ibid., p. 396. Although this definition undoubtedly was drawn from Lenin's State and Revolution, Li followed it with a statement that struck a most non-Leninist note: "If one wants to put contemporary democracy into practice, it is not necessary to study how to obtain power but only necessary to study the techniques of how to manage things." Nevertheless, Li also supported the need for a "dictatorship of the proletariat" in order to "repress the dead ashes of the reactionaries." Ibid., pp. 397–398.

26. Li Ta-chao, P'ing-min chu-i, p. 7. The appeal of the utopian strain in Marxism also drew Li's attention to the Paris Commune and Marx's Civil War in France. See his essay "I-pa-ch'i-i nien ti Pa-li 'k'ang-miao-en' " (The Paris Commune of 1871; Feb. 1923), HC, pp. 447–456.

CHAPTER X.   NATIONAL REVOLUTION

1. "Chung-kuo ti she-hui chu-i yü shih-chieh ti tzu-pen chu-i" (Chinese socialism and world capitalism), HC, p. 356.

2. "The First Decision as to the Objects of the Communist Party of China 1921," Appendix 2 of Ch'en Kung-po, The Communist Movement in China (Columbia University East Asian Series, No. 7; New York, 1960), p. 108.

3. Chang Ching-ju, Li Ta-chao t'ung-chih ko-ming ssu-hsiang ti fa-chan (The development of Comrade Li Ta-chao's revolutionary thought; Wuhan, 1957), p. 11.

4. Lü Chien, Li Ta-chao ho Ch'ü Ch'iu-pai (Li Ta-chao and Ch'ü Ch'iu-pai; (Shanghai, 1951), pp. 9 and 10; Chia Chih, "Li Ta-chao t'ung-chih ti ku-shih," p. 11.

5. For an account of the relations between Wu P'ei-fu and the Communists, see Brandt, pp. 24–26.

6. Liu Li-k'ai and Wang Chen, *1919–1927-nien ti Chung-kuo kung-jen yün-tung* (The Chinese workers' movement from 1919 to 1927; Peking, 1957), pp. 27–28.

7. Lü Chien, pp. 9–10; Chu Wu-shan, "Hui-i Shou-ch'ang t'ung-chih" (Memories of Comrade Shou-chang), *Jen-min jih-pao* (Apr. 29, 1957), p. 2.

8. "Chui-tao Lieh-ning ping chi-nien 'erh-ch'i'," HC, pp. 499–500.

9. Ting Shou-ho et al., p. 169.

10. This was the general import of Lenin's work of 1917, "Imperialism, the Highest Stage of Capitalism," *Selected Works*, Vol. 1, Pt. 2, pp. 433–568.

11. This notion was by no means an original creation of Lenin's. Marx himself suggested it in his writings on China.

12. Lenin believed that the Asian bourgeoisie, in contrast to the Russian bourgeoisie, would play a progressive historical role because of its opposition to foreign imperialism.

13. This strategy is outlined by Lenin in "Two Tactics of Social Democracy in the Democratic Revolution," *Selected Works*, Vol. 1, Pt. 2, pp. 11–151.

14. "Preliminary Draft of Theses on the National and Colonial Questions," June 5, 1920, in V. I. Lenin, *The National-Liberation Movement in the East* (Moscow, 1957), p. 254.

15. "Report of the Commission on the National and Colonial Questions to the Second Congress of the Communist International," July 26, 1920, *ibid.*, pp. 266–269.

16. Wilbur and How, pp. 66–67. On the formation of the alliance with the Kuomintang, see Schwartz, *Chinese Communism*, Chap. 3; Brandt, Chaps. 1 and 2.

17. Ch'en Tu-hsiu, *Kao ch'üan-tang t'ung-chih shu* (A letter to all party comrades; Shanghai, 1929), p. 2.

18. Wilbur and How, p. 62.

19. According to the account of Wang Ching-wei, Li went to Shanghai for discussions with Sun Yat-sen after the meeting of the special plenum of the CCP central committee at Hangchow in August 1922. It was then that Sun agreed to allow Communists to join the Kuomintang as individuals while retaining their CCP membership. Lang Hsing-shih, ed. *Ko-ming yü fan ko-ming* (Revolution and counterrevolution; Shanghai, 1928), p. 595.

20. Fang Lu, "Ch'ing-suan Ch'en Tu-hsiu" (Liquidating Ch'en Tu-hsiu), *Ch'en Tu-hsiu p'ing-lun* (Critical discussions of Ch'en Tu-hsiu; Peking, 1933), pp. 68–70.

21. Chu Wu-shan, p. 2.

22. According to the account of one participant, Li called a meeting of the Peking district committee in February 1923 (apparently after the "February Seventh" incident) to discuss preparations for the united front with the Kuomintang. The meeting, which was attended by a Comintern representative, found a majority at first opposed to the Comintern position. But Li finally overcame most objections by agreeing that the Communist party would retain its class identity and by promising that the united front would be put into operation only after Sun Yat-sen reorganized the Kuomintang into a more suitable instrument for the realization of Communist objectives. Li's main argument was that the Communist party was still too

weak to bear alone the burden of the national revolution. Hsi-wu lao-jen, "Hui-i Li Ta-chao t'ung-chih" (Memories of Comrade Li Ta-chao), *Chung-kuo kung-jen* (The Chinese worker), No. 9:23 (May 1957).

23. Fang Lu, pp. 69–70.

24. Brandt, p. 43.

25. Yü Shu-te and T'an P'ing-shan were the other Communists elected to the Kuomintang Central Executive Committee in 1924.

26. Interview with Mr. Tso Shun-sheng (Hong Kong, 1961). See also Schwartz, *Chinese Communism*, pp. 44–45. It is ironic that by 1924 Chang Chi was calling for the termination of Communist membership in the Kuomintang; in November 1925 he participated in the organization of the right-wing "Western Hills" faction. (See Wilbur and How, pp. 89–90, 151, and 209–210.)

27. This phrase is frequently used to describe Li Ta-chao by non-Communist intellectuals who knew him. Interviews with Mr. Mao I-heng and Mr. Tso Shun-sheng, Hong Kong, 1961.

28. See, e.g., Tso Shun-sheng, "*Chin san-shih nien chien-wen tsa-chi* (Recollections of the past thirty years; Hong Kong, 1952), p. 19.

29. Chow Tse-tsung, p. 250. Before they could be moved back to Peking, the offices were raided by the police of the French concession of Shanghai and *HCN* was suppressed. Ch'en Tu-hsiu thereupon moved the magazine to Canton, where it was published until July 1922. It was revived in Canton in 1923 by Ch'ü Ch'iu-pai and appeared sporadically until 1926. *Wu-ssu shih-ch'i ch'i-k'an chieh-shao*, I, 1–40.

30. "Cheng tzu-yu ti hsüan-yen" (Manifesto of the struggle for freedom), *Tung-fang tsa-chih* (Eastern miscellany), Vol. 17, No. 16 (Aug. 25, 1920); "Wo-men ti cheng-chih chu-chang" (Our political proposals), *ibid.*, Vol. 19, No. 8 (Apr. 25, 1922).

31. The "third collection" of Hu Shih's writings, published in 1930, was dedicated to "four recently departed friends: Li Ta-chao, Wang Kuo-wei, Liang Ch'i-ch'ao, and Tan Pu-an." *Hu Shih wen-ts'un san-chi* (Shanghai, 1930).

32. "Kung-tu" (Workers' education, Dec. 21, 1919), *HC*, pp. 284–285.

33. "Lao-tung wen-t'i ti huo-yüan" (The sources of the labor question; Dec. 4, 1923), *HC*, p. 495.

34. "Ma-k'o-ssu ti ching-chi hsüeh-shuo" (The economic theory of Marx), *HC*, pp. 376–377.

35. Speech delivered on April 5, 1927, and quoted in Harold Isaacs, *The Tragedy of the Chinese Revolution* (Stanford, 1951), p. 162.

36. "Shih-yüeh ko-ming yü Chung-kuo jen-min" (The October Revolution and the Chinese people), *HC*, p. 401.

37. "Chung-shan chu-i ti kuo-min ko-ming yü shih-chieh ko-ming" (The Sun Yatsenist national revolution and the world revolution; 1926), *HC*, p. 562.

38. "Sun Chung-shan hsien-sheng tsai Chung-kuo min-tsu ko-ming shih shang chih wei-chih," *HC*, p. 538.

39. "Chung-shan chu-i ti kuo-min ko-ming yü shih-chieh ko-ming," *HC*, p. 563.

40. Karl Marx, "The British Rule in India," *The New York Tribune* (June 25, 1853).

41. Karl Marx, "Revolution in China and Europe," *The New York Tribune* (June 14, 1853).

42. *Ibid.*

43. Marx, *The New York Tribune* (Apr. 10, 1857), p. 4; and (Oct. 1, 1859), p. 6.

44. Marx, *The New York Tribune* (June 5, 1857), p. 6.

45. Letter of Marx to Engels, Dec. 10, 1869, *Selected Correspondence,* pp. 280–281.

46. Marx, "Letter on the Russian Village Commune," 1881, Marx and Engels, *The Russian Menace*, p. 219.

47. "Ma-k'o-ssu ti Chung-kuo min-tsu ko-ming kuan" (Marx's views on the Chinese national revolution), *HC*, pp. 545–555.

48. *Ibid.*, pp. 553–555. In addition to the article "Revolution in China and Europe," which he translated, Li was apparently familiar with some of Marx's other articles on China for he referred to an article dealing with the T'ai-p'ing Rebellion that Marx wrote in 1862. All the articles on China written by Marx and Engels have since been translated into Chinese. See Marx and Engels, *Ma-k'o-ssu En-ke-ssu lun Chung-kuo* (Marx and Engels on China; Peking, 1957).

49. "Report of the Commission on the National and Colonial Questions" in Lenin, *The National-Liberation Movement in the East*, p. 266.

50. "Chui-tao Lieh-ning ping chi-nien 'erh-ch'i'," *HC*, p. 500.

51. "Chung-shan chu-i ti kuo-min ko-ming yü shih-chieh ko-ming," *HC*, p. 562.

52. For an analysis of Ch'en's views of the alliance with the Kuomintang, see Schwartz, *Chinese Communism*, Chap. 4.

53. Ch'en Tu-hsiu, "Chung-kuo kuo-min ko-ming yü she-hui ko-chieh-chi" (The Chinese national revolution and the various social classes), *Chung-kuo ko-ming wen-t'i lun-wen chi* (A collection of articles on problems of the Chinese revolution; Shanghai, 1927), pp. 33–38. The essay was written in late 1923 and appeared originally in *Ch'ien-feng* (Vanguard), No. 2.

54. *Ibid.*, pp. 34, 38.

55. *Ibid.*, pp. 43, 45–48.

56. "P'u-pien ch'üan-kuo ti Kuo-min-tang" (A universal, national Kuomintang), *Hsiang-tao chou-pao* (Guide weekly), No. 21 (Apr. 18, 1923).

CHAPTER XI. PEASANT REVOLUTION

1. Chia Chih, "Li Ta-chao t'ung-chih ti ku-shih," pp. 11–12. When Li went to Chang-li-wu-feng his wife took their five younger children to her family home in the country.

2. Chia Chih, "Chan-tou ti i-sheng," p. 41.

3. "Su-O min-chung kuan-yü Chung-kuo ko-ming ti t'ung-ch'ing" (The sympathy of the Soviet masses for the Chinese Revolution), *HC*, pp. 511–515.

4. For a discussion of the complex relations between Feng Yü-hsiang, the Communists, and the Kuomintang, see Wilbur and How, pp. 318–335.

5. For the Communist position on Sun's efforts, see Wilbur and How, pp. 319–320. Ch'en Tu-hsiu favored Sun's proposal for a national assembly, but he opposed Sun's trip to Peking and his negotiations with the Tuan Ch'i-

jui government in January 1925. Li Ta-chao, on the other hand, according to Communist accounts, played an important role in the preparations for the negotiations. See, e.g., Chang Ching-ju, pp. 12–13. Since Li was the principal Communist link to Feng Yü-hsiang, who was then the real power behind the Tuan government, it seems likely that Li approved of, and was involved in, Sun's talks with the Peking regime.

6. Confirmation for Li's role in the relations between Feng Yü-hsiang and Karakhan was provided by Mr. Mao I-heng, who had been an aide to Feng in the 1920's, during a conversation with me in Hong Kong in 1961. According to Mao I-heng, Li had particularly warm relations with Karakhan, who was then considered to be a follower of Trotsky.

7. In November 1925 a mass demonstration jointly sponsored by the Communist party and the left wing of the Kuomintang against the Tuan Ch'i-jui government was held in Peking. At this time Feng clearly indicated his support for the government and not for its opponents. This was perhaps partly because Feng's own position in Peking was being undermined as a result of defeats suffered by his armies at the hands of a new warlord coalition led by Chang Tso-lin and Wu P'ei-fu. Feng personally retired from Peking in January 1926, and his armies were forced to withdraw from the capital several months later. The Peking government then came under the control of the new, more reactionary warlord group dominated by Chang Tso-lin.

8. Ku Kuan-chiao, *San-shih-nien lai ti Chung-kung* (Thirty years of Chinese Communism; Hong Kong, 1955), pp. 28–29. Ku gives December 23, 1925, as the date for Li's "expulsion" from the Kuomintang central executive committee. In all probability, it was November 23, 1925, the date of the organization of the Western Hills faction.

9. Peking Local Committee (CCP), "Our Immediate Attitude Toward the Kuomintang in the North," Nov. 25, 1925, Wilbur and How, p. 238.

10. "T'u-ti yü nung-min" (Land and the peasants) was later reprinted in issue No. 5 of *Chung-kuo nung-min* (The Chinese peasant) (May 1926). Although an official Kuomintang organ, *Chung-kuo nung-min* published many articles by Communists such as Mao Tse-tung and P'eng P'ai. The references are from *HC*, pp. 523–536.

11. Li Ta-chao, "O-lo-ssu ko-ming ti kuo-ch'ü chi hsien-tsai," p. 5.

12. "She-hui chu-i hsia ti ching-chi tsu-chih" (Economic organization under socialism; Jan. 16, 1923), *HC*, p. 429.

13. "T'u-ti yü nung-min," *HC*, pp. 525, 532.

14. *Ibid.*, pp. 525, 535.

15. *Ibid.*, p. 534.

16. *Ibid.*, pp. 534–535.

17. *Ibid.*, p. 535.

18. For an account of the Kwangtung peasant movement, see Shinkichi Eto, "Hai-lu-feng — The First Chinese Soviet Government," *The China Quarterly*, No. 8 (October–December 1961) and No. 9 (January–March 1962).

19. For an analysis of the controversy between the Ch'en and Ch'ü factions, see Schwartz, *Chinese Communism*, esp. Chaps. 4 and 5.

20. Ch'en Tu-hsiu, "Chung-kuo nung-min wen-t'i" (The Chinese peasant question), *Ch'ien-feng* (Vanguard), 1:51 (July 1, 1923).

21. Ch'en Tu-hsiu, "Chung-kuo kuo-min ko-ming yü she-hui ko-chieh-chi," pp. 39, 42–43.

22. *Ibid.*, p. 34. "After the completion of the national revolution," Ch'en wrote, "the bourgeoisie, under ordinary conditions, would, of course, hold political power." However, Ch'en raised the possibility that "under special circumstances" there might be "a new transformation in which the working class would be able to seize a certain amount of political power . . . (This) to a certain degree would be determined by world conditions. The 1917 Russian Revolution is a good example." *Ibid.*, p. 50.

23. *Ibid.*, pp. 42–43.

24. Ch'ü Ch'iu-pai, "Hsien-tai Chung-kuo ti kuo-hui-chih yü chün-fa," pp. 461–467.

25. See Schwartz, *Chinese Communism*, Chap. 4.

26. Wilbur and How, p. 67.

27. "Political Report of the Central Committee (of the C.C.P.)," Second Enlarged Plenum, Shanghai, July 12–18, 1926, Wilbur and How, p. 277.

28. "Resolutions on the Peasant Movement," Second Enlarged Plenum, *ibid.*, pp. 298–300.

29. *Ibid.*, pp. 304–305.

30. *Ibid.*, p. 302.

31. N. Nassonov, N. Fokine, and A. Albrecht, "Letter from Shanghai," appendix in Trotsky, *Problems of the Chinese Revolution*, p. 417.

32. This is the explicit assumption underlying Ch'ü's arguments in his book *Chung-kuo ko-ming chung chih cheng-lun wen-t'i* (Controversial problems of the Chinese Revolution; Shanghai, 1927).

33. Ch'ü Ch'iu-pai, "Chung-kuo ko-ming ho nung-min yün-tung ti ts'e-lüeh (The Chinese Revolution and the strategy of the peasant movement), *Pu-erh-sai-wei-k'e* (The Bolshevik), 3.4–5: 114, 141 (May 12, 1930).

34. For an account of political developments in Peking during these months, see Wilbur and How, pp. 318–35.

35. This was the so-called "Taku Ultimatum." According to the Boxer Protocol of 1901, the foreign powers were guaranteed access from Peking to the sea and were to exercise police powers along that route.

36. Hua Ying-shen, ed., *Chung-kuo Kung-ch'an-tang lieh-shih chuan*, p. 3.

37. According to Communist accounts, Li decided to remain in Peking out of a sense of party responsibility. A hostile account claims that he was simply too well-known to escape from the capital. Kuo Hua, "Tsai O ta-shih-kuan chih Li Ta-chao" (Li Ta-chao in the Russian embassy), *Hsien-tai shih-liao* (Contemporary historical materials; Shanghai, 1935), IV, 248.

38. *Ibid.*, pp. 240–249. Chia Chih, "Chan-tou ti i-sheng," p. 44.

39. Chu Wu-shan, p. 2.

40. "Lu, Yü, Shan teng-sheng ti Hung-ch'iang-hui" (The Red Spear Societies of Shantung, Honan, and Shensi) was originally published in the Peking Communist organ *Cheng-chih sheng-huo*. The issue in which Li's article appeared has been lost, and therefore the exact date of publication cannot be determined. Both in *Li Ta-chao hsüan-chi* and in the earlier *Shou-ch'ang wen-chi*, as well as in bibliographies of Li's writings, only the year 1926 is given as the date of publication. The article appeared sometime after the March 18th incident, according to internal evidence, and before the end of the summer, when *Cheng-chih sheng-huo* seems to have ceased publication. The references are from *HC*, pp. 564–570.

41. One Communist who later achieved extraordinary success in mobil-

izing the resources of the secret societies and organizing peasant armies was Ho Lung, a leader of the Nanchang uprising of August 1927. In *Red Star Over China*, Edgar Snow reported: "Ho Lung's fame in the 'Elder Brother Society' extends over all China. The Reds say that he can go unarmed into any village of the country, announce himself to the Ke Lao Hui, and form an army. The society's special ritual and language are quite difficult to master, but Ho Lung has the highest degrees and is said to have more than once enlisted an entire Ke Lao Hui branch in the Red Army." (p. 54). Mao Tse-tung, of course, was another who came to appreciate the value of the secret societies. See, e.g., Mao's "Appeal to the Ke Lao Hui" in Schram, pp. 189–190.

42. "Lu, Yü, Shan teng-sheng ti Hung-ch'iang-hui," *HC*, pp. 564, 565, 568. Liu Chen-hua, the warlord of Shensi, was then engaged in a struggle with the forces of Feng Yü-hsiang for control of Sian. The Second National Army was a warlord force nominally under the control of Feng.

43. *Ibid.*, p. 566.

44. *Ibid.*

45. *Ibid.*, p. 565.

46. *Ibid.*, p. 566.

47. *Ibid.*

48. *Ibid.*, p. 568.

49. *Ibid.*, pp. 569–570.

50. "T'u-ti yü nung-min," *HC*, p. 532.

51. *Mao Tse-tung hsüan-chi* (Selected works of Mao Tse-tung; Peking, 1960), I, 5–7.

52. Leon Trotsky, "Summary and Perspectives of the Chinese Revolution," *The Third International after Lenin* (New York, 1936), p. 224.

EPILOGUE

1. Li Hsing-hua, "Shih-liu nien ch'ien ti hui-i," p. 11. Hsing-hua's account was written in 1943.

2. *Ibid.*, pp. 12–13.

3. *Ibid.*, pp. 13–16. Li was sentenced to death by a military court at 10 A.M. on April 28 and executed at 2 P.M. Chia Chih, "Chan-tou ti i-sheng," p. 46.

4. *North China Star* (Tientsin, Apr. 25, 1931).

5. *Survey of the China Mainland Press*, No. 82:5 (Mar. 11 and 12, 1951).

6. Ch'en's last articles and letters were collected and published in Hong Kong in 1949 with a preface by Hu Shih. See *Ch'en Tu-hsiu tsui-hou tui-yü min-chu cheng-chih ti chien-chieh* (Ch'en Tu-hsiu's last views on democracy; Hong Kong, 1949).

7. A much less hostile view of Ch'en's role in the period before 1921 appeared in 1962 in *Li-shih yen-chiu*, the major Chinese Communist historical journal. See P'eng Ming.

8. "Hsi-sheng" (Sacrifice), *HC*, p. 247.

9. Schram, pp. 14–19.

10. See the extracts from Mao's essay "The Great Union of the Popular Masses" that appeared in July 1919 in *Hsiang-chiang p'ing-lun*, a journal of which Li was an editor. Schram, pp. 105–106.

Ai Ssu-ch'i 艾思奇. Yu-ti fang-shih chi ch'i-t'a 有的方矢及其 他 (Some arrows and others). Shanghai: Hsin-wen, 1951.

Apple, Dorian. "The Social Structure of Grandparenthood," American Anthropologist, 58.4:656-663 (August 1956).

Boersner, Demetrio. The Bolsheviks and the National and Colonial Question. Paris and Geneva: Minard, 1957.

Brandt, Conrad. Stalin's Failure in China. Cambridge, Mass.: Harvard University Press, 1958.

Chang Ching-ju 張靜如. Li Ta-chao t'ung-chih ko-ming ssu-hsiang ti fa-chan 李大釗同志革命思想的發展 (The development of Comrade Li Ta-chao's revolutionary thought). Wuhan: Hupei jen-min ch'u-pan she, 1957.

Chang Ching-lu 張靜廬. Chung-kuo hsien-tai ch'u-pan shih-liao 中國現代出版史料 (Materials on the history of modern Chinese publications). 3 vols.; Shanghai and Peking: Chung-hua, 1954-1956.

Chang P'ing 張平. "Li Ta-chao ho ch'ing-nien" 李大釗和青年 (Li Ta-chao and youth); Chung-kuo ch'ing-nien-pao 中國青年 报 (Chinese youth newspaper; Apr. 29, 1957), p. 3.

Chang Tsün-yen 張俊彥. "Li Ta-chao yü hsin-wen-hua yün-tung" 李大釗与新文化运动 (Li Ta-chao and the New Culture Movement); Li-shih yen-chiu 歷史研究 (Historical research), No. 8:1-19 (1959).

Ch'en Kung-po 陳公博. The Communist Movement in China (Columbia University East Asian Series, No. 7). New York, 1960.

Ch'en Tu-hsiu 陳獨秀. "Kuo-chi-p'ai yü shih-chieh ho-p'ing" 過激派与世界和平 (The Bolsheviks and world peace); Hsin ch'ing-nien 新青年 (New youth), 7.1:115-116.

-----"Ai-kuo-hsin yü tzu-chüeh-hsin" 愛國心与自覚心 (Patriotism and self-consciousness); Chia-yin tsa-chih 甲寅雜志 (The tiger magazine), 1.4:1-6 (1915).

-----"K'o-lin-te pei" 克林德碑 (The Von Ketteler monument); Hsin ch'ing-nien, 5.5:449-458 (Nov. 15, 1918).

-----"Shih-hsing min-chih ti chi-ch'u" 實行民治的基礎 (The basis for the realization of democracy); Hsin ch'ing-nien, 7.1:13-21 (Dec. 1, 1919).

-----"Kuan-yü she-hui chu-i ti t'ao-lun" 关於社会主义的討論 (Discussions concerning socialism); She-hui chu-i t'ao lun chi 社会主义討論集 (A collection of discussions on socialism), pp. 32-73. Canton: Hsin-ch'ing-nien she, 1922.

----- Tu-hsiu wen-ts'un 獨秀文存 (The collected works of Ch'en Tu-hsiu). 4 vols.; Shanghai: Ya-tung t'u-shu-kuan, 1922.

-----"Chung-kuo nung-min wen-t'i" 中國農民問題 (The Chinese peasant question); Ch'ien-feng 前鋒 (Vanguard), No. 1:51-57 (1923).

-----"Chung-kuo kuo-min ko-ming yü she-hui ko-chieh-chi" 中國國民革命与社会各階級 (The Chinese national revolution and the various social classes); Chung-kuo ko-ming wen-t'i lun-wen chi 中國革命問題論文集 (A collection of articles on problems of the Chinese revolution), pp. 33-50. Shanghai: Hsin-ching-nien she, 1927.

-----Kao ch'üan-tang t'ung-chih shu 告全党同志書 (A letter to all party comrades). Shanghai, 1929.

-----Ch'en Tu-hsiu tsui-hou tui-yü min-chu cheng-chih ti chien-chieh 陳獨秀最後对于民主政治的見解 (Ch'en

Tu-hsiu's last views on democracy). Hong Kong: Tzu-yu Chung-kuo she, 1949.

Chia Chih 賈芝. "Li Ta-chao t'ung-chih erh-san-shih" 李大釗 同志二三事 (A few things about Comrade Li Ta-chao); Hsin kuan-ch'a 新观察 (New observer; July 1, 1956), pp. 36-37.

-----"Li Ta-chao t'ung-chih ti ku-shih" 李大釗同志的故事 (The story of Comrade Li Ta-chao); Chung-kuo ch'ing-nien 中 國青年 (Chinese youth), No. 8:9-12 (1957).

-----"Li Ta-chao t'ung-chih chan-tou ti i-sheng" 李大釗同志 战斗的一生 (Comrade Li Ta-chao's life of struggle); Kuang-hui ti wu-ssu 光輝的五四 (The glorious May Fourth), pp. 29-46. Peking: Chung-kuo ch'ing-nien ch'u-pan she, 1959.

Chih-shen 蟄伸 (Chu Chih-hsin 朱執信). "Te-i-chih she-hui ko-ming-chia hsiao-chuan" 德意志社會革命家小 傳 (Short biographies of German social revolutionaries); Min-pao 民報 (People's paper), No. 2:1-17 (January 1906) and No. 3:1-20 (June 1906).

Ch'in Te-chün 秦德君. "Hui-i Li Ta-chao, Teng Chung-hsia, Yün Tai-ying san t'ung-chih" 回憶李大釗, 邓中夏,惲代英 三同志 (Memories of Comrades Li Ta-chao, Teng Chung-hsia, and Yün Tai-ying); Hsin kuan-ch'a (Sept. 15, 1956), pp. 9-11.

Chow Tse-tsung. The May Fourth Movement. Cambridge, Mass.: Harvard University Press, 1960.

Chu Chih-hsin, see Chih-shen.

Chu Wu-shan 朱务善. "Hui-i Shou-ch'ang t'ung-chih" 回忆守常 同志 (Memories of Comrade Shou-ch'ang); Jen-min jih-pao 人民日报 (People's daily; Apr. 29, 1957), p. 2.

Ch'ü Ch'iu-pai 瞿秋白. Chung-kuo ko-ming chung chih cheng-lun wen-t'i 中國革命之爭論問題 (Controversial problems of the Chinese revolution). Shanghai, 1927.

-----"Hsien-tai Chung-kuo ti kuo-hui-chih yü chün-fa" 現代中國 的國会制与軍閥 (The parliamentary system of contemporary China and the warlords); Chung-kuo ko-ming wen-t'i lun-wen chi 中國革命問題論文集 (A collection of articles on problems of the Chinese revolution), pp. 439-467. Shanghai: Hsin ch'ing-nien she, 1927.

----- "Chung-kuo ko-ming ho nung-min yün-tung ti ts'e-lüeh" 中國 革命和农民运动的策略 (The Chinese revolution and the strategy of the peasant movement); Pu-erh-sai-wei-k'e 布尔塞維克 (The Bolshevik), 3.4-5:111-149 (May 15, 1930).

Deutscher, Isaac. The Prophet Armed. London: Oxford University Press, 1954.

Dunayevskaya, Raya. Marxism and Freedom. New York, 1958.

Eto Shinkichi. "Hai-lu-feng: The First Chinese Soviet Government," The China Quarterly, No. 8:160-183 (October-December 1961); and No. 9:149-181 (January-March 1962).

Fang Lu 坊鲁. "Ch'ing-suan Ch'en Tu-hsiu" 清算陳獨秀 (Liquidating Ch'en Tu-hsiu); Ch'en Tu-hsiu p'ing-lun 陳獨秀 評論 (Critical discussions of Ch'en Tu-hsiu), pp. 67-71. Peking, 1933.

Garushiants, Iu. M. "Bor'ba Kitaiskikh Marksistov za sozdanie Kommunisticheskoi Partii Kitaia" (The struggle of the Chinese Marxists for the foundation of the Chinese Communist party); Narody Azii i Afriki (Peoples of Asia and Africa), No. 3:81-96 (1961).

Haimson, Leopold H. The Russian Marxists and the Origins of Bolshevism. Cambridge, Mass.: Harvard University Press, 1955.

Ho Hui 何惠 . "Kuang-jung ti i-sheng: Li Ta-chao t'ung-chih ko-ming shih-chi chien-chieh" 光荣的一生 —— 李大釗同志革命事迹簡介 (A glorious life: A brief introduction to the revolutionary work of Comrade Li Ta-chao); Kung-jen jih-pao 工人日报 (Workers' daily; Apr. 27, 1957), p. 3.

Hsi-wu lao-jen 棲梧老人 . "Hui-i Li Ta-chao t'ung-chih" 回忆李大釗同志 (Memories of Comrade Li Ta-chao); Chung-kuo kung-jen 中國工人 (The Chinese worker), No. 9:21-23 (May 1957).

Hsia Chia 夏伽 . "Pei-ching-ta-hsüeh ti Mao chu-hsi ho Li Ta-chao t'ung chih chi-nien-shih" 北京大学的毛主席和李大釗同志紀念室 (The Peking University memorial room for Chairman Mao and Comrade Li Ta-chao); Ch'ang-chiang jih-pao 長江日报 (June 29, 1951), p. 4.

Hsiao Yü (Siao Yü). Mao Tse-tung and I Were Beggars. Syracuse, 1959.

Hu Shih 胡適 . Hu Shih wen-ts'un 胡適文存 (Collected essays of Hu Shih). 4 vols.; Shanghai: Ya-tung t'u-shu-kuan, 1926.

----- Hu Shih wen-ts'un san-chi 胡適文存三集 (The third collection of the essays of Hu Shih). 4 vols.; Shanghai: Ya-tung t'u-shu-kuan, 1930.

Hua Kang 華崗 . Wu-ssu yün-tung shih 五四运动史 (History of the May Fourth Movement). Shanghai, 1951.

Hua Ying-shen 華應申 , ed. Chung-kuo Kung-ch'an-tang lieh-shih chuan 中國共產党烈士傳 (Biographies of heroes of the Chinese Communist party). Hong Kong, 1949.

Huang Ho 黃河 . Chung-kuo Kung-ch'an-tang san-shih-wu-nien chien-shih 中國共產党三十五年簡史 (A brief history of thirty-five years of the Chinese Communist party). Peking, 1957.

303

Hughes, H. Stuart. Consciousness and Society. New York, 1958.

Isaacs, Harold R. The Tragedy of the Chinese Revolution. Stanford: Stanford University Press, 1951.

Jung Meng-yüan 榮孟源. "Hsin-hai ko-ming ch'ien Chung-kuo shu-k'an shang tui Ma-k'o-ssu chu-i ti chieh-shao" 辛亥革命前中國書刊上對馬克思主義的介紹 (The introduction of Marxism in Chinese publications before the revolution of 1911); Hsin chien-she 新建設 (New reconstruction), No. 3 (1953).

Kao Chüan-p'u 高全朴 and Chang Ch'i-chih 張豈之. "Wu-ssu shih-ch'i Li Ta-chao t'ung-chih fan-tui tzu-ch'an chieh-chi kai-leng chu-i ti tou-cheng" 五四時期李大釗同志反对資産階級改良主义的斗争 (Comrade Li Ta-chao's struggle against bourgeois reformism in the May Fourth period); Li-shih yen-chiu, No. 6:19-32 (1959).

-----"Wu-ssu yün-tung ch'i-chien Li Ta-chao ti Ma-k'o-ssu chu-i hsüan-ch'uan yün-tung" 五四运动期間李大釗的馬克思主义宣傳运动 (Li Ta-chao's propagation of Marxism during the period of the May Fourth Movement); Li-shih chiao-hsüeh 歷史教学 (Historical education; May 1959), pp. 5-10.

Kao I 高鎰. "T'an hsien-lieh Li Ta-chao t'ung-chih ti i-wen" 談先烈李大釗同志的譯文 (On the translations of the martyr, Comrade Li Ta-chao); Wen-hui-pao 文匯报 (Sept. 17, 1957), p. 3.

Kao I-han 高一涵. "Ho Ta-chao t'ung-chih hsiang-ch'u ti shih-hou" 和大釗同志相处的时候 (The time I met Comrade [Li] Ta-chao); Kung-jen jih-pao (Apr. 27, 1957), p. 3.

Krieger, Leonard. "Marx and Engels as Historians," Journal of the History of Ideas, 14.3:381-403 (June 1953).

Ku Kuan-chiao 古貫郊. San-shih-nien lai ti Chung-kung
三十年來的中共 (Thirty years of Chinese communism).
Hong Kong: Ya-chou ch'u-pan she, 1955.

Kuo Chan-po 郭湛波. Chin wu-shih-nien Chung-kuo ssu-hsiang
shih 近五十年中國思想史 (A history of Chinese
thought for the past fifty years). Peking: Jen-wen, 1936.

Kuo Hua 國華. "Tsai O ta-shih-kuan chih Li Ta-chao" 在俄
大使館之李大釗 (Li Ta-chao in the Russian embassy);
Hsien-tai shih-liao 現代史料 (Contemporary historical
materials), IV, 240-249. Shanghai, 1935.

Kuo Mo-jo 郭沫若. Chung-kuo ku-tai she-hui yen-chiu 中國
古代社會研究 (A study of ancient Chinese society).
Shanghai, 1930.

Lang Hsing-shih 郎醒石, ed. Ko-ming yü fan ko-ming 革命与
反革命 (Revolution and counterrevolution). Shanghai, 1928.

Lao Jung 勞榮. "Wu-ssu yün-tung ti ling-tao-che Li Ta-chao"
五四运动的領导者李大釗 (Li Ta-chao, the leader
of the May Fourth Movement); Wu-ssu sa-chou-nien chi-nien
chuan-chi 五四卅周年紀念專輯 (A symposium for the
thirtieth anniversary of May Fourth), pp. 139-149. Shanghai, 1949.

Lenin, V.I. Selected Works. 2 vols.; Moscow, 1952.

-----The National-Liberation Movement in the East. Moscow: Foreign
Languages Publishing House, 1957.

-----"The Development of Capitalism in Russia," in his Collected Works,
III, 23-607. Moscow, 1960.

Levenson, Joseph. Confucian China and Its Modern Fate, Vol. 1.
Berkeley: University of California Press, 1958.

-----Liang Ch'i-ch'ao and the Mind of Modern China. Cambridge,
Mass.: Harvard University Press, 1959.

Li Hsing-hua 李星華 . "Shih-liu-nien ch'ien ti hui-i" 十六年
前的回憶 (Memories of sixteen years ago); in Hua Ying-shen
華應申 , ed., Chung-kuo Kung-ch'an-tang lieh-shih chuan
中國共產黨烈士傳 (Biographies of heroes of the
Chinese Communist party), pp. 10-16. Hong Kong, 1949.

-----"I-nien" 意念 (Thoughts); Chiao-shih-pao 教師報 (Teachers'
news; Apr. 23, 1957), p. 4.

-----"Hui-i wo-ti fu-chin Li Ta-chao 回忆我的父亲李大钊
(Memories of my father, Li Ta-chao); Chung-kuo ch'ing-nien,
No. 8:19-25 (1959).

Li Jui 李銳. Mao Tse-tung t'ung-chih ti chu-ch'i ko-ming huo-tung
毛澤东同志的初期革命活动 (The early revolu-
tionary activities of Comrade Mao Tse-tung). Peking: Chung-
kuo ch'ing-nien ch'u-pan she, 1957.

Li Lung-mu 李龍牧. "Li Ta-chao t'ung-chih ho wu-ssu shih-ch'i
Ma-k'o-ssu chu-i ssu-hsiang ti hsüan-ch'uan" 李大釗同志
和五四時期馬克思主义思想的宣傳
(Comrade Li Ta-chao and the propagation of Marxism during
the May Fourth period); Li-shih yen-chiu, No. 5:1-18 (1957).

Li Ta-chao 李大釗. "Hsin-te chiu-te" 新的旧的 (The new
and the old); Hsin ch'ing-nien, 4.5:446-449.

-----"Jen-chung wen-t'i" 人種問題 (The race question); Hsin min-kuo
tsa-chih 新國民杂誌 (New republic magazine), 1.6:1-8.

-----"An-sha yü chün-te" 暗殺与群德 (Assassination and social
morality); Yen-chih 言治 (Statesman), No. 2:97-99 (May 1, 1913).

-----"I-yüan-chih yü erh-yüan-chih" 一院制与二院制
(Unicameralism and bicameralism); Yen-chih, No. 4:53-57
(Sept. 1, 1913).

-----"Lun kuan-liao chu-i 論官僚主义 (On bureaucracy); Yen-chih,
No. 4:17-20(Sept. 1, 1913).

-----"Shih-fei-p'ien" 是非篇 (Essay on right and wrong); Yen-chih, No. 4:71-73 (Sept. 1, 1913).

-----"Yüan-sha: an-sha yü tzu-sha" 原殺——暗殺与自殺 (Death: Assassination and suicide), Yen-chih, No. 4:11-16 (Sept. 1, 1913).

-----"Feng-su" 風俗 (Customs); Chia-yin tsa-chih, Vol. 1, No. 3 (Summer 1914).

-----"Ch'ing-ch'un" 青春 (Spring); Hsin ch'ing-nien, 2.1:1-12 (Sept. 1. 1916). English tr. by Yang Hsien-yi and Gladys Yang, in Chinese Literature (May 1959), pp. 11-18.

-----"Ch'ing-nien yü lao-jen" 青年与老人 (Youth and old people); Hsin ch'ing-nien, 3.2:1-4 (Apr. 1, 1917).

-----"Pao-li yü cheng-chih" 暴力与政治 (Violence and politics); T'ai-p'ing yang 太平洋 (Pacific ocean), 1.7:1-12 (Oct. 15, 1917).

-----"Chin" 今 (Now); Hsin ch'ing-nien, 4.4:307-310 (Apr. 15, 1918).

-----"Bolshevism ti sheng-li" 的胜利 (The victory of Bolshevism); Hsin ch'ing-nien, 5.5:442-448 (Oct. 15, 1918).

-----"Shu-min ti sheng-li" 庶民的胜利 (Victory of the masses); Hsin ch'ing-nien, 5.5:436-438 (Oct. 15, 1918).

-----"Huan-ying Tu-hsiu ch'u-yü" 歡迎獨秀出獄 (Welcoming Ch'en Tu-hsiu on his release from prison); Hsin ch'ing-nien, 6.6:588 (Nov. 1, 1919).

-----"Wo ti Ma-k'o-ssu chu-i kuan" 我的馬克思主义观 (My Marxist views), Pt. 1; Hsin ch'ing nien, 6.5:521-537 (May 1919); Pt. 2, ibid., 6.6:612-624 (November 1919).

-----"Ch'ing-nien yen-shih tzu-sha wen-t'i" 青年厭世自殺問題 (The problem of pessimism and suicide among youth); Hsin ch'ao 新潮 (New tide), 2.2:351-356 (Dec. 1, 1919).

-----"Yu ching-chi shang chieh-shih Chung-kuo chin-tai ssu-hsiang pien-tung ti yüan-yin" 由經濟上解釋中國近代思想变动的原因 (An economic explanation of the changes in modern Chinese thought); Hsin ch'ing-nien, 7.2:47-53 (Jan. 1, 1920).

-----"Wu-i yün-tung shih" 五一运动史 (The history of May Day); Hsin ch'ing-nien, 7.6:1-13 (May 1, 1920).

-----"O-lo-ssu ko-ming ti kuo-ch'ü ho hsien-tsai" 俄罗斯革命的过去和现在 (The past and present of the Russian revolution); Hsin ch'ing-nien, Vol. 9, No. 3 (July 1, 1921); photo-reproduction copy, 9.3:375-394.

-----"Lun tzu-sha" 論自殺 (On suicide); Hsüeh-i tsa-chih 学艺杂志 (Scholarship and art magazine), 3.8:1-20 (February 1922).

-----P'ing-min chu-i 平民主义 (Democracy). Shanghai: Shang-wu yin-shu kuan, 1923.

-----"P'u-pien ch'üan-kuo ti Kuo-min-tang" 普遍全國的國民党 (The Kuomintang which spread throughout the country); Hsiang-tao chou-pao 响导周报 (Guide weekly), No. 21:154-155 (Apr. 18, 1923).

-----"K'ung-tao-hsi ti li-shih kuan" 孔道西的歷史观 (The historical view of Condorcet); She-hui k'o-hsüeh yüeh-k'an 社会科学月刊 (Social science quarterly), 2.1:59-66 (November 1923).

-----Shih-hsüeh yao-lun 史学要論 (The essentials of historical study). Shanghai: Shang-wu yin-shu kuan, 1924.

-----Shou-ch'ang wen-chi 守常文集 (Collected writings of Shou-ch'ang). Shanghai, 1950.

-----Li Ta-chao hsüan-chi 李大釗选集 (Selected writings of Li Ta-chao). Peking: Jen-min ch'u-pan she, 1959.

Lichtheim, George. Marxism: An Historical and Critical Study. New York, 1961.

Liu Ching-chün 劉靜君. "Chi-i-li ti Li Shou-ch'ang hsien-sheng"
記忆里的李守常先生 (In memory of Mr. Li Shou-ch'ang);
Jen-min jih-pao (May 7, 1957), p. 8.

Liu Li-k'ai 劉立凱 and Wang Chen 王真. 1919-1927-nien ti Chung-
kuo kung-jen yün-tung 1919-1927年的中國工人运动 (The
Chinese Workers' Movement from 1919-1927). Peking: Kung-jen
ch'u-pan she, 1957.

Liu Yeh 劉埜. "Li Ta-chao i-wen 'Tzu-jih' k'ao" 李大釗軼文
"此日"考 (Notes on the article "This Day" by Li Ta-chao);
Li-shih yen-chiu, No. 1:98 (1957).

Lo Chia-lun 羅家倫. "Chin-jih chih shih-chieh hsin-ch'ao"
今日之世界新潮 (The new tide of today's world); Hsin-ch'ao,
Vol. 1, No. 1 (January 1919).

Lowith, Karl. "Man's Self-Alienation in the Early Writings of Marx,"
Social Research, 21.2:204-230 (Summer 1954).

Lu Hsün. Selected Works of Lu Hsün. 4 vols.; Peking: Foreign
Languages Press, 1956.

Lü Chien 呂健. Li Ta-chao ho Ch'ü Ch'iu-pai 李大釗和瞿秋白
(Li Ta-chao and Ch'ü Ch'iu-pai). Shanghai, 1951.

Mannheim, Karl. Ideology and Utopia. New York: Harcourt, Brace
and Co., and London: Routledge and Kegan Paul, Ltd., 1952.

Mao Tse-tung 毛澤東. Mao Tse-tung hsüan-chi 毛澤東选集
(Selected works of Mao Tse-tung). 4 vols.; Peking: Jen-min ch'u-
pan she, 1960.

Marcuse, Herbert. Reason and Revolution. New York, 1954.

Marx, Karl. "Revolution in China and Europe," New York Tribune
(June 14, 1853), p. 4.

-----Capital. 3 vols.; Chicago: Kerr, 1912.

----- The Eighteenth Brumaire of Louis Bonaparte. Chicago, 1919.

-----Selected Writings in Sociology and Social Philosophy, ed. T.B.
Bottomore and Maximilian Rubel. London: Watts, 1956.

-----"Economic and Philosophic Manuscripts, " tr. T.B. Bottomore,
in Erich Fromm, Marx's Concept of Man. New York, 1961.

Marx, Karl and Frederick Engels. The German Ideology. New York:
International Publishers, 1939 and 1947.

------The Russian Menace to Europe, ed. Paul Blackstock and Bert
Hoselitz. Glencoe, Illinois: Free Press, 1952.

-----Selected Correspondence. Moscow: Foreign Languages Publishing
House, 1953.

-----Ma-k'o-ssu En-ke-ssu lun Chung-kuo 馬 克 思 恩 格 斯 論
中 國 (Marx and Engels on China). Peking: Jen-min ch'u-pan
she, 1957.

-----Werke, Vols. 1 and 4. Berlin: Dietz, 1957.

-----Selected Works. 2 vols.; Moscow: Foreign Languages Publishing
House, 1958.

Michel, Robert. First Lectures in Political Sociology. Minneapolis,
1949.

North China Star. Tientsin, Apr. 25, 1931.

P'eng Ming 彭明. "Wu-ssu shih-ch'i ti Li Ta-chao ho Ch'en Tu-hsiu"
五 四 时 期 的 李 大 剑 和 陳 獨 秀 (Li Ta-chao and
Ch'en Tu-hsiu in the May Fourth period); Li-shih yen-chiu,
No. 6:47-68 (1962).

P'ing Hsin 平 心. "Lun Wu-ssu yün-tung ch'ien-hou Li Ta-chao
ssu-hsiang ti fa-chan" 論 五 四 运 动 前 后 李 大 剑 思 想
的 发 展 (On the development of Li Ta-chao's thought before
and after the May Fourth Movement); Li-shih chiao-hsüeh wen t'i

歴史教学問題 (Problems of historical education),
No. 4:13-17 and No. 5:10-16 (1959).

Plekhanov, George.　Fundamental Problems of Marxism.　New York:
International Publishers, 1930.

-----Selected Philosophical Works.　2 vols.; Moscow, n.d.

Russell, Bertrand.　The Problem of China.　London:　George Allen
and Unwin, 1922.

Satoi Hikoshichiro 里井彦七郎.　"Ri Taisho no shuppatsu,
Genji ki no seiron o chūshin ni" 李大釗の出発——
'言治' 期の政論を中心に (The departure of Li
Ta-chao, with emphasis on the political writings of the
Statesman period); Shirin 史林 (History), 40.3:1-39 (May 1957).

Scalapino, Robert and George Yu.　Chinese Anarchism.　Berkeley:
Center for Chinese Studies of the University of California, 1961.

Schram, Stuart R.　The Political Thought of Mao Tse-tung.　New York,
1963.

Schwartz, Benjamin I.　"Ch'en Tu-hsiu and the Acceptance of the
Modern West, " Journal of the History of Ideas, 12.1:61-74
(January 1951).

-----Chinese Communism and the Rise of Mao.　Cambridge, Mass.:
Harvard University Press, 1952.

-----"The Intelligentsia in Communist China, a Tentative Comparison, "
Daedalus (Summer 1960), pp. 604-621.

-----In Search of Wealth and Power: Yen Fu and the West.
Cambridge, Mass.: Harvard University Press, 1964.

She-hui chu-i t'ao-lun chi 社會主義討論集 (A collection
of discussions on socialism).　Hsin ch'ing-nien she 新青年社
(New youth society), ed. Canton: Hsin ch'ing-nien she, 1922.

Shen Yün-lung 沈雲龍. Chung-kuo Kung-ch'an-tang chih lai-yüan 中國共產党之來源 (The origin of the Chinese Communist party). Taipei: Min-chu ch'ao she, 1959.

Shih Tsün 石峻, ed. Chung-kuo chin-tai ssu-hsiang-shih ts'an-k'ao tzu-liao chien-pien 中國近代思想史參考資料簡編 (Source materials for the study of the history of modern Chinese thought). Peking: San-lien, 1957.

Snow, Edgar. Red Star Over China. New York: Random House, 1938.

T'an Pi-an 譚彼岸 . "O-kuo min-ts'ui chu-i tui T'ung-meng-hui ti ying-hsiang" 俄國民粹主义对同盟会的影响 (The influence of Russian populism on the T'ung-meng-hui); Li-shih yen-chiu, No. 1:35-44 (1959).

Teng Hua 邓樺. "Li Ta-chao t'ung-chih tui Chung-kuo che-hsüeh ssu-hsiang fa-chan ti kung-hsien" 李大剑同志对中國哲学思想发展的貢献 (Comrade Li Ta-chao's contribution to the development of Chinese philosophic thought); Pei-ching jih-pao 北京日报 (Apr. 26, 1957), p. 3.

Teng Ssu-yü and John K. Fairbank. China's Response to the West: A Documentary Survey. Cambridge, Mass.: Harvard University Press, 1954.

Ting Shou-ho 丁守和 and Yin Hsü-i 殷叙彝 . "Wu-ssu hsin-wen-hua yün-tung" 五四新文化运动 (The May Fourth New Culture Movement); Li-shih yen-chiu, No. 4:1-35 (1959).

Ting Shou-ho, Yin Hsü-i and Chang Po-chao 張伯昭 . Shih-yüeh ko-ming tui Chung-kuo ko-ming ti ying-hsiang 十月革命对中國革命的影响 (The influence of the October revolution on the Chinese revolution). Peking: Jen-min ch'u-pan she, 1957.

Trotsky, Leon. Our Revolution. New York, 1918.

-----The Bolsheviki and World Peace. New York, 1918.

-----Problems of the Chinese Revolution. New York: Pioneer Publishers, 1932.

-----The Third International After Lenin. New York: Pioneer Publishers, 1936.

Ts'ai Yüan-p'ei 蔡元培. "Lao-kung shen-sheng" 勞工神聖 (The dignity of labor); Hsin ch'ing-nien, 5.5:438-439 (Nov. 15, 1918).

Tso Shun-sheng 左舜生. Chin san-shih nien chien-wen tsa-chi 近三十年見聞雜記 (Recollections of the past thirty years). Hong Kong: Tzu-yu ch'u-pan she 自由出版社 (Free press), 1952.

Tung-fang tsa-chih 東方雜誌 (Eastern miscellany). 17.16:133-134 (Aug. 25, 1920); and 19.8:138-140 (Apr. 25, 1922).

United States Hong Kong Consul General. Survey of the Current Mainland Press, Nos. 82 (Mar. 11-12, 1951) and 3038 (Aug. 13, 1963).

Venturi, Franco. Roots of Revolution. London, 1960.

Wang Shen-jan 王森然. Chin-tai erh-shih-chia p'ing-chuan 近代二十家評傳 (Critical biographies of twenty contemporary scholars). Peking: Hsing-yen, 1934.

Weber, Max. From Max Weber: Essays in Sociology, tr. and ed. H. H. Gerth and C. Wright Mills. New York: Oxford University Press, 1958.

-----The Protestant Ethic and the Spirit of Capitalism. New York: Charles Scribner's Sons, 1958.

Wen Ts'ao 文操. "Shih-pien Li Ta-chao (Shou-ch'ang) i-chu hsi-nien mu-lu" 試編李大釗(守常)遺著繫年目錄 (A preliminary chronological index to the writings of Li Ta-chao); Hsüeh-shu yüeh-k'an 学术月刊 (Scholarship monthly), Nos. 1-5 and 9 (1957). No. 1, pp. 48-49; No. 2, pp. 64-66; No. 3, pp. 61-62; No. 4, pp. 66-68; No. 5, p. 58; No. 9, pp. 76-77.

Wilbur, C. Martin and Julie Lien-ying How. Documents on Communism, Nationalism and Soviet Advisers in China, 1918-1927. New York: Columbia University Press, 1956.

Wittfogel, Karl A. Oriental Despotism. New Haven, 1957.

Wu-ssu shih-ch'i ch'i-k'an chieh-shao 五四时期期刊介绍 (An introduction to the publications of the May Fourth period). 3 vols.; Peking: Jen-min ch'u-pan she, 1958-1959.

Yü I 郁嶷. "Sung Li Kuei-nien yu-hsüeh Jih-pen hsü" 送李龟年遊学日本序 (A farewell to Li Kuei-nien [Li Ta-chao] on his leaving for study in Japan); Yen-chih, No. 4:85-86 (Sept. 1, 1913).

GLOSSARY

ai kuo 愛國

Ariga Nagao 有賀長雄

Chang Chi 張繼

Chang Hsün 張勳

Chang Kuo-t'ao 張國燾

Chang Shih-chao 章士釗

Chang Tso-lin 張作霖

Chang Tung-sun 張東蓀

Ch'ang-hsin-tien 長辛店

Ch'ang-li-wu-feng 昌黎五峰

Chao Chi-lan 趙級蘭

Chao Yü-shu 趙玉書

chen chu 真主

Ch'en Ch'i-hsiu 陳啟修

  (Ch'en Pao-yin 陳豹隱)

Ch'en Chiung-ming 陳炯明

Ch'en-chung pao 晨鐘報

Ch'en-pao fu-k'an 晨報副刊

Ch'en Pao-yin, see Ch'en

  Ch'i-hsiu

Ch'en Wang-tao 陳望道

Ch'en Yi 陳毅

Cheng-chih sheng-huo

  政治生活

Chia-yin jih-k'an 甲寅日刊

Chiang K'ang-hu 江亢虎

Chiang Meng-lin 蔣夢麟

Ch'ien-feng 前鋒

Ch'ien Hsüan-t'ung 錢玄同

chih-chieh hsing-tung 直接行動

Chin-pu tang 進步黨

Chiu-kuo hui 救國會

Chou Fu-hai 周佛海

Chou Tso-jen 周作人

Chu Teh 朱德

Chung-hua ko-ming tang

  中華革命黨

Chung-kuo nung-min 中國農民

Ch'ü Yüan 屈原

Chüeh-wu she 覺悟社

Fa-yen pao 法言報

Fei Chüeh-t'ien 費覺天

Feng-t'ien 奉天

Feng Yü-hsiang 馮玉祥

Feng Yü-tung 馮毓東

fu-ch'iang 富強

Fu Ssu-nien 傅斯年

Ho Lung 賀龍

Ho Meng-hsiung 何孟雄

Hsiang-chiang p'ing-lun

  湘江評論

315

hsiang-yüan 鄉愿

Hsien-fa t'ao-lun hui
憲法討論會

Hsin-ch'ao she 新潮社

Hsin-min hsüeh-hui
新民學會

Hsin shih-chieh 新世界

Hsin wen-hua yün-tung
新文化運動

hsin Ya-hsi-ya chu-i
新亞細亞主義

Hu Han-min 胡漢民

Hung-ch'iang hui 紅槍會

hung lou 紅樓

jen-chung 人種

K'ang Yu-wei 康有為
Kao I-han 高一涵
Kawakami Hajime 河上肇
Ko-lao hui 哥老會
Ku Chao-hsiung, see Ku Meng-yü
Ku Meng-yü 顧孟餘 (Ku Chao-
hsiung 顧兆熊)
Kung-ch'an tang 共產黨
Kung-jen chü-le-pu
工人俱樂部
Kuo-min-chün 國民軍
Kuo-min jih-pao 國民日報

Lan Chih-hsien, see Lan Kung-wu

Lan Kung-wu 藍公武 (Lan Chih-
hsien 藍志先)
lao-kung chieh-chi 勞工階級
Lao-tung chieh 勞動界
Lao-tung yin 勞動音
Li Fu-ch'un 李富春
Li Hsing-hua 李星華
Li Li-san 李立三
Li Sao 離騷
Liang Ch'i-ch'ao 梁啟超
Liu Chen-hua 劉鎮華
Liu Fu 劉復
Liu Jen-ching 劉仁靜
Liu Jih hsüeh-sheng tsung-hui
留日學生總會
Liu Pai-ching 劉伯青
Liu Ping-lin 劉秉麟
Lo Chang-lung 羅章龍
Lo Chia-lun 羅家倫
Lo-ting hsien 樂亭縣
Lu Hsün 魯迅

Ma-k'e-shih chu-i yen-chiu hui
馬客士主義研究會
Ma-k'o-ssu hsüeh-shuo yen-chiu hui
馬克思學說研究會
Mao I-heng 毛以亨
Mei-chou p'ing-lun 每週評論
min-chih chu-i 民治主義
min-i 民彝

316

Min pao 民報
min-sheng 民生
min-tsu 民族
min-t'uan 民團

"Nan-Ch'en, Pei-Li" 南陳北李
Ning Yang 寧陽

Pai Chien-wu 白堅武
Pei-ta cheng-chih hsüeh-hui
　北大政治學會
Pei-yang fa-cheng chuan-men hsüeh-
　hsiao 北洋法政專門學校
Pei-yang fa-cheng hsüeh-hui
　北洋法政學會
P'eng P'ai 彭湃
P'ing-min chiao-yü chiang-yen t'uan
　平民教育講演團
p'ing-min chu-i 平民主義
p'u-pien ch'üan-kuo 普遍全國

Shao-nien Chung-kuo hsüeh-hui
　少年中國學會
She-hui chu-i yen-chiu hui
　社會主義研究會
She-hui fu-li hui 社會福利會
Shen-chou hsüeh-hui 神州學會
Shen pao 申報
Shen Yin-mo 沈尹默
Shou-ch'ang 守常 (Li Ta-chao)

Sun Hung-i 孫洪伊
Sung Chiao-jen 宋教仁

Ta-hei-t'o 大黑坨
Ta-kung pao 大公報
ta tao 大盜
ta Ya-hsi-ya chu-i
　大亞細亞主義
Tai Chi-t'ao 戴季陶
Tan Pu-an 單不庵
T'an P'ing-shan 譚平山
T'ang Hua-lung 湯化龍
T'ang-shan 唐山
Teng Chung-hsia 鄧中夏
T'ien-an men 天安門
t'ien-chih tzu-yu 天秩自由
T'ien-i pao 天義報
T'ien-ti hui 天地會
Ts'ai Ao 蔡鍔
Ts'ai Ho-shen 蔡和森
Ts'ai Yüan-p'ei 蔡元培
Ts'ao K'un 曹錕
tsung-i 宗彝
Tuan Ch'i-jui 段祺瑞
t'ung-chih 統治
T'ung-meng hui 同盟會

wan-jen 完人
Wang Ching-wei 汪精衛
wang-kuo 亡國

317

Wang Kuo-wei 王國維
wei-min chu-i 唯民主義
Wen Shang 汶上
wen-t'i yü chu-i 問題与主义
Wu P'ei-fu 吳佩孚
Wu Yüeh 吳樾

Yang Ch'ang-chi 楊昌濟
Yang Ming-chai 楊明齋

Yang Tu-sheng 楊篤生
Yen Chen 閻振
Yen-chiu hsi 研究系
Yü I 郁嶷
Yü Shu-te 于樹德
Yüan Shih-k'ai 袁世凱
Yün Tai-ying 惲代英
Yung-p'ing-fu 永平府

INDEX

Activism (political): and Li's pre-Marxian world view, 7, 23-28 *passim*, 38-40, 48-51, 155, 161, 166; and Chinese reception of Marxism, 56-57; and Li's interpretation of Marxism, 91-95, 140-154 *passim*, 156, 158-170, 198; and May Fourth era, 99-104 *passim*, 106, 109; and "ethic of responsibility," 109-111; in Marxist theory, 113-114, 128-139 *passim*; and doctrines of inevitability, 163-165; and unity of theory and practice, 197-198. *See also* Voluntarism

Alienation, Marxist concept of, 128-131, 133-134, 289n1; influence on Li, 148, 184; and nationalism, 176-177; and proletariat, 176-177

Anarchism: Li on, 11-14, 35; in China, 30, 53, 54, 100, 117; and Populism, 77; and Society for Study of Socialism, 116, 277n3

Antiforeignism: of Li, 15-20, 36, 181, 190-193; of peasantry, 250-251, 266. *See also* Nationalism

Antiurbanism, 81-84, 87-88, 222, 237, 253-254, 265. *See also* Populism

Ariga Nagao, 16, 271n39

"Asiatic mode of production," 173, 225-226, 288n38, 288n46. *See also* Oriental despotism

Backwardness, Advantages of: Li on, 65-67, 151-154; Trotsky on, 66-67, 77, 126, 153; Populists on, 76. *See also* Rebirth of China

Bacon, Francis, 167

Bakunin, M., 54, 100, 280n1

Bergson, Henri, 21, 23, 25, 28, 49, 272n53

Bernstein, Eduard, 90, 198, 214, 293n1

Blanqui, A., 78

Bodin, Jean, 167

Bolshevism. *See* Russian October Revolution

Bortman, N., 115, 282n61

Boxer Protocol, 287n61

Boxer Rebellion, 2, 4-6, 174

Buddhism, 14, 28

Calvinism, 163-164

Capital, 72, 134, 173, 279n1

CCP. *See* Chinese Communist Party

Chang Chi, 220, 294n26

Chang Kuo-t'ao, 73, 88, 277n8; and labor movement, 114-115, 211; and organization of CCP, 117, 119; and CCP-KMT alliance, 219

Chang Shih-chao, 21, 84, 159, 243, 272n48; and *Tiger Daily*, 33; and agrarian socialism, 278n28

Chang Tso-lin, xii, 257-260, 296n7

Chang Tung-sun, 150-151

Chao Ch'i-lan, 3-4, 6, 118, 258-259, 269n9

Chao Yü-shu, 260

Ch'en Ch'iung-ming, 117

Ch'en-chung pao, 30, 33, 272n2

Ch'en-pao, 75, 101-102, 115, 272n2, 287n30

Ch'en-pao fu-k'an, 115, 283n62

Cheng-chih sheng-huo, 228, 237, 297n40

Ch'en Tu-hsiu, 6, 39, 110, 126, 279n1; and CCP, xi, 117-120, 260-

INDEX

Kautsky, Karl, 115, 137–138, 291n3
Kawakami Hajime, 56
Kepler, J., 159
KMT. *See* Kuomintang
Ko-lao-hui (Society of Elder Brothers), 240, 298n41
Kropotkin, Michael, 54, 90, 100; influence on Li, 13–14; theory of mutual aid, 141–144, 206, 275n9
Ku Meng-yü, 279n1, 283n65
Kung-ch'an tang, 119
Kung-jen chu-le-pu (Workers' Association), 118
Kuo-min jih-pao, 62, 235
Kuomintang (KMT), 9–10, 30, 100–101, 296n10; Li on, 11, 14, 233; and Ch'ien Hsüan-t'ung, 41; and Chu Chih-hsin, 53; First National Congress of, 220, 235; left-wing of, 234, 236, 247, 259; Western Hills faction, 234–236, 296n8. *See also* Chinese Communist alliance with Kuomintang
Kuo Mo-jo, 171

Lan Kung-wu, 111
Lao-tung chieh, 118
Lao-tung yin (The Sound of Labor), 118, 211
Lao Tzu, 21, 24
Lassalle, Ferdinand, 52, 55
Lenin, V. I.: on World War I, 60; on Russia's backwardness, 65; influence on Li, 69, 94, 139–140, 204, 292n25; and Populism, 77; on capitalism, 78, 214, 278n19; on anti-imperialism, 97; Chinese translation of, 116, 275n5; on subjective factors in history, 164; on historical periodization, 171; on "world revolution," 178–179, 185–186; concept of spontaneity, 199–201, 205–206; on Asia, 204, 213, 216–217, 293n12; on "national revolution," 229; on China, 278n21; influence of Hegel on, 285n28. *See also* Leninism
Leninism: and Li, 69, 94, 138–140, 201–209, 295n25; appeals of in May Fourth period, 100; on imperialism, 126, 199, 213–214; on determinism, 137–139, 205; nature of, 138–140, 198–201; on economic prerequisites for socialism, 150; on unity of theory and practice, 198; on party organization, 199–201, 208–209; on peasantry, 199, 253–

254; Li on, 201–209 *passim*; strategy for Asia, 213–217; theory of democratic dictatorship, 215; on revolutionary stages, 232–233
Levenson, Joseph, 47
Liang Ch'i-ch'ao, 52; and Chinputang, 14; and Research Clique, 30; and Tuan Ch'i-jui alliance, 33; Li's criticism of, 34–35, 159; and Marxism, 274n2; and Hu Shih, 294n31
Liao Chung-k'ai, 84
Liberalism in China, 108–111, 120, 261
Li Chung-hua, 269n9
Li Fu-ch'un, 283n74
Li Hsing-hua, 257–259, 269n5
Li Li-san, 283n74
Li Ta-chao: youth, 1–6; at Peiyang College, 6–8; early political orientations, 8–15, 29–35; student in Japan, 15–21, 56; pre-Marxian world view, 26–28, 46–51, 166–167; role in founding CCP, 114–121; role in CCP-KMT alliance, 218–221, 234–236; arrest and execution, 257–260. *See also specific topics*
Liu Chen-hua, 249, 298n42
Liu Fu, 273n15
Liu Jen-ching, 117, 290n15
Liu-Jih hsüeh-sheng tsung-hui (Association of Chinese Students in Japan), 18
Liu Pai-ching, 291n36
Liu Ping-lin, 280n1
Lo Chang-lung, 117, 219
Lo Chia-lun, 71, 88, 276n1, 277n7
Lowith, Karl, 133
Lu Hsün, 44–45
Lukacs, George, 132

Ma-k'e-shih chu-i yen-chiu hui (Marxist Research Society), 71–73, 102, 116
Ma-k'o-ssu hsüeh-shuo yen-chiu hui (Society for the Study of Marxist Theory), 72, 116, 283n65
Malthusian theory, 39
Manaev, I. K., 283n66
Mannheim, Karl, 106, 169
Mao I-heng, 296n6
Mao Tse-tung, xii, 3, 277n7, 296n10; influence of Li on, xii–xiii, xv, 72, 261–262, 264; and anarchism, 13, 271n1; nationalism of, 48, 189, 193, 194; on peasantry, 80, 239, 240, 253; and Leninism, 85; views of, compared to Li's, 95, 145, 193–

322

Atheneum Paperbacks

HISTORY

HISTORY—ASIA

Atheneum Paperbacks

THE NEW YORK TIMES BYLINE BOOKS

THE ADAMS PAPERS

ECONOMICS AND BUSINESS

PHYSICAL SCIENCES AND MATHEMATICS

Atheneum Paperbacks

POLITICAL SCIENCE

Atheneum Paperbacks

HISTORY—AMERICAN—1900 TO THE PRESENT

Atheneum Paperbacks

STUDIES IN AMERICAN NEGRO LIFE

Atheneum Paperbacks